THE OPTIONS ADJUSTMENT PLAYBOOK

MASTER THE MOVES.
CONTROL THE BOARD.
WIN THE GAME.

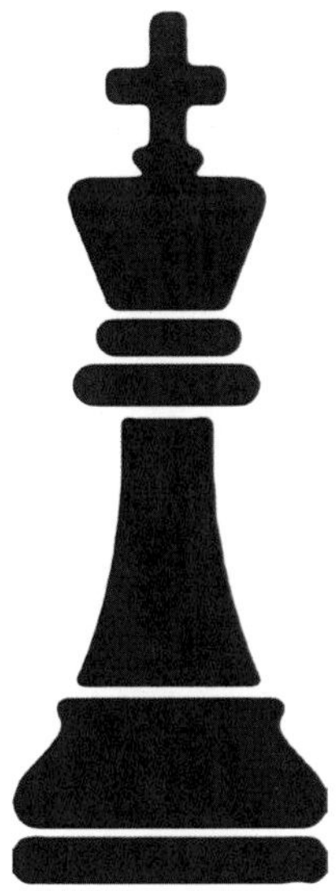

MIKE WADE

Case ID: 1-15022329372

ISBN: 979-8-9933389-0-3 (Paperback)
979-8-9933389-1-0 (Ebook)
979-8-9933389-2-7 (Hardcover)

DEDICATION

I owe a deep debt of gratitude to two extraordinary individuals who shaped the very foundation of my journey as a trader, teacher, and coach: ***George Fontanills and Tom Gentile.***

It was George and Tom who welcomed me into the Optionetics fold, first as a passionate and dedicated student. They saw something in me—potential I hadn't yet fully seen in myself—and gave me the opportunity to teach alongside them. Under their mentorship, I not only grew as a trader but learned the true art of instruction, watching firsthand how master educators teach with clarity, rigor, and heart.

Tom Gentile, in particular, has been more than a mentor—he's become a trusted friend and collaborator. Over the past decade, we've worked side-by-side to develop some of the most innovative options education in the industry. His belief in me and his commitment to our shared vision made it possible to launch and grow ***Michael Wade Trade Coaching*** *(www.mwtradecoach.com).*

Without their wisdom, generosity, and belief in me, this book—and the entire body of work it represents—would not exist. I am forever grateful to these remarkable men.

ACKNOWLEDGEMENT

I want to extend my deepest gratitude to Joe Contes.

Joe and I have been trading and teaching stock options around the world together for nearly two decades. He is a seasoned trader, has a sharp mind, and most importantly—is someone who tells the whole truth about what it really takes to trade successfully.

Many of the insights, tools, and strategies in this book were shaped by Joe's expertise and generous contributions. His fingerprints are all over these pages.

Beyond being a trusted colleague, Joe is a dear friend. We share a deep commitment to empowering others, and that spirit of contribution runs through everything we've created—individually and together.

This book would not be what it is without him.

I also want to extend my heartfelt thanks to **Gerardo Rojas**, who has been absolutely instrumental in bringing **Michael Wade Trade Coaching** (www.mwtradecoach.com) to life. Together, we built this company from the ground up with a shared vision: To create a nurturing, high-integrity environment where traders could grow, thrive, and succeed.

MWTC would not exist without Gerardo's dedication, brilliance, and heart. His relentless commitment to our mission has shaped not only the business but the community we've built around it.

With Gerardo's partnership and the contribution of **Joe Contes**, we were able to create a truly unique and transformative program called **The Adjustment Club**—an 8-week course that brought clarity, strategy, and confidence to the often-confusing world of trade adjustments. The content of that course became the foundation for this book.

Welcome To

Options Adjustment Playbook

Master the Moves. Control the Board. Win the Game.

THE MWTC COMMUNITY

Trading can feel like a solitary pursuit, but it doesn't have to be. At MWTC, we have created a community where traders come together daily to share ideas, learn from experience, and support one another through every stage of the journey.

In this arena, veteran traders lead the way—offering not only technical guidance, but also honesty, encouragement, and accountability. It is a place where truth is valued, where challenges are faced together, and where traders are nurtured as players in a bigger game, not just as individuals studying charts in isolation.

The strategies we practice range from foundational setups to advanced adjustments. At the very center lies the adjustment game—the essential skill that transforms trading from chance into strategy. Like any game, mastery comes only through play. You cannot simply read about adjustments; you must engage with them, test them, and refine them in real time.

This playbook reflects that spirit. It is both a guide and a set of pieces on the board, waiting to be put into motion. The MWTC Trade Club is where these moves are practiced daily, side by side, until they become second nature.

To take the first step, Mike and Joe invite you to **play three live adjustment hands with them**—three real positions taught in our **8-week Adjustment Club** course, walked through move by move. It is the most direct way to lift the pieces in this playbook off the page and put them into play.

Scan the QR code below to play the three hands with Mike and Joe.

Mike Wade & Joe Contes
mwtradecoach.com

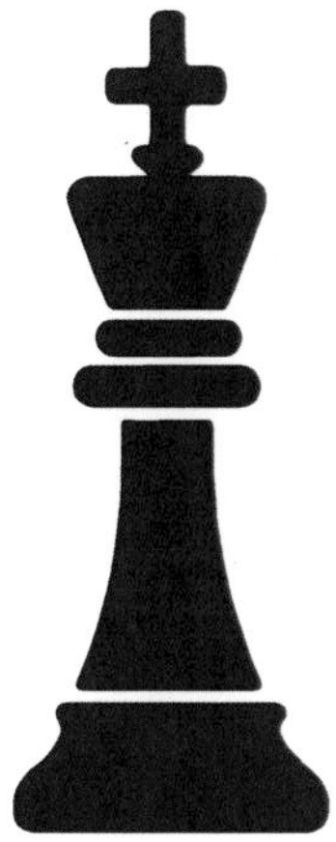

"The only way to learn the adjustment game is to play the adjustment game"

MWTC PLAYBOOK

Mike Wade
mwtradecoach.com

THE OPTIONS ADJUSTMENT PLAYBOOK

Master the Moves. Control the Board. Win the Game.

TABLE OF CONTENTS

PART III

READING THE MARKET — THE GREEKS & VOLATILITY

Turning the Greeks and IV into a forward-looking prognosis.

PART IV

VERTICAL SPREADS & RISK-SHAPING PLAYS

Protect the position and reshape the risk graph in your favor.

PART V

BUTTERFLY PLAYS

Building, defending, and stretching the butterfly.

PART VI

CALENDARS & ADVANCED STRUCTURES

Adding time as a dimension and repositioning on the fly.

PART VII

DIRECTIONAL & STOCK STRATEGIES

Playing direction with high probability and hedging stock.

PART VIII

ADVANCED & HYBRID PLAYS — MASTERING THE BOARD

Multi-fly structures, the hybrid FlyCal, and bringing it all together.

INTRODUCTION

INTRODUCTION

Welcome to a whole new world of options trading. I have been trading for over 25 years and have been living in the world of adjustments for a long time. I am a trader and know what's real and what's not. Our mission at Michael Wade Trade Coaching is to turn trading dreams into reality for novice and advanced traders. You are in good hands, and we feel this playbook will make a profound difference in your trading life, bringing consistency and a healthy psychology.

What is an Adjustment?

Great question—and the first step in learning to play the game like a pro.

Trading options can be successful using a wide variety of strategies—from simple calls and puts to complex multi-leg spreads. With the proper rules and probabilities, you can stack the odds in your favor.

But what is the peak of the probability-of-profit mountainn? That's where adjustments live.

Adjustments are what separate good trades from great ones. They're what transform near-losses into wins. And most importantly, they give you the power to protect yourself when the market surprises you.

Why Most Traders Fail—And How You Won't

Most traders focus on profits first and risk second—if at all. They fall into the trap of emotions:

- Hope that a losing trade will recover.
- Faith that tomorrow will turn things around.

Here's the truth:

- Hope and faith are not strategies. They are emotional defaults that wreck trades and destroy confidence.
- Winning traders flip the switch. They put the risk first, and let the profits take care of themselves.

MANAGE THE RISK AND LET THE WINNERS TAKE CARE OF THEMSELVES!

This mantra will transform your results—and your mindset. When you lead with risk management, everything changes:

- Your psychology calms.
- Your consistency improves.
- Your trades become calculated, not chaotic.

So... What Is an Adjustment, Really?

At its core, an adjustment is any change made to a trade after it has been opened. And the goal is simple:

- Reduce or eliminate risk
- Turn uncertainty into control
- (Sometimes) Lock in a guaranteed profit

Think of it like repositioning your pieces in a chess game. You're not starting over—you're playing smarter with what's already on the board.

The Game You're About to Learn

This manual is your Adjustment Playbook. Inside, you'll find powerful techniques—not just to protect your capital, but to play like a strategist.

You're not here to memorize theory. You are here to practice, adjust, and win—again and again.

Just like chess, you will learn:

- What each move does
- When to make it
- And how to think several steps ahead

The Power of Context

Options adjustments can seem intimidating at first glance. There are so many moving parts, so many choices—and the stakes can feel high. It's easy to fall into the trap of thinking it's all just too complicated or that only experts can master it.

But here's the truth: **How you see the game determines how well you play it.**

That's why this book is written with one powerful context in mind: **We're playing a game**—a fun, challenging, and gratifying game.

Just like chess, options trading involves a set of tools (or pieces), each with its strengths, limitations, and movement. And just like in chess, success doesn't come from memorizing every possible move. It comes from *playing*. From getting your hands on the board and from testing, adjusting, losing a few pawns, and learning through each match.

To help you engage with this learning in a playful spirit, we've added cartoon figures and friendly visuals throughout. These aren't just decorations—they're anchors to remind you of the **context** we're operating in: **This is a fun game to play!**

Yes, there's complexity. Yes, there are risks. But learning to trade and adjust options doesn't have to be heavy or stressful. With the proper context, it becomes a puzzle to solve, a strategy to refine, a craft to master.

You're not just reading a book. You're entering a game. And the more you play, the better you'll get.

Let's begin.

CHAPTER 1

WHAT IS ADJUSTMENT?

CHAPTER 1
What Is an Adjustment?

An adjustment is any transaction made to an existing position, most often to reduce or eliminate risk, and/or to lock in profits. You can think of an adjustment as a strategic move during the life of a trade—not the beginning or end, but a thoughtful decision made once you're already in the game.

Closing the trade entirely? That's what we call the Ultimate Trade Adjustment.

Adjustments aim to shift the balance from risk to profits—often by making timely, strategic moves during the trade.

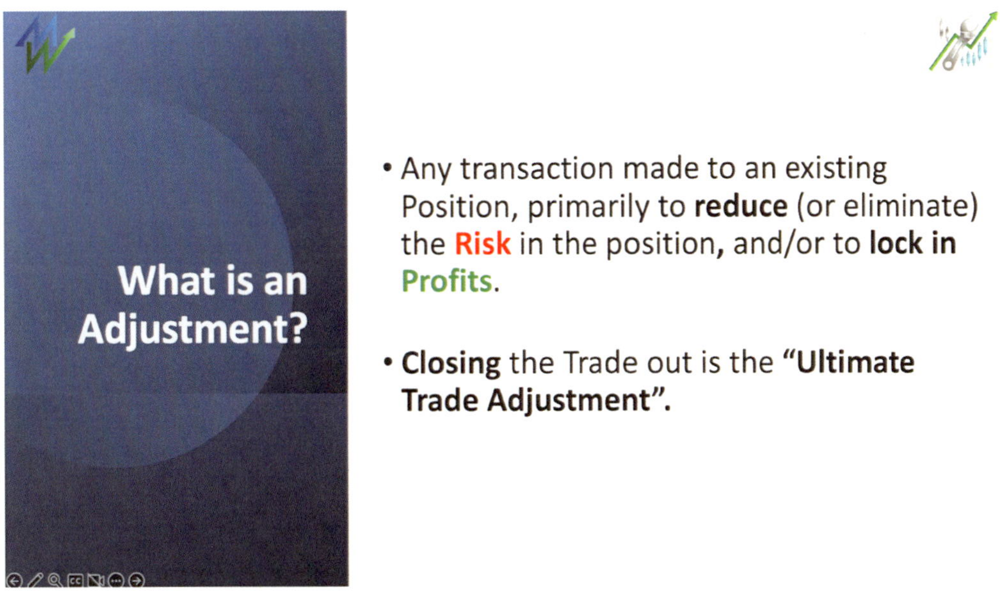

The Outcomes of Trade Adjustments

Every adjustment you make serves one or more of these strategic purposes:

1. Reduce or eliminate risk
2. Lock in profits
3. Stay in the trade and position for more upside.

Adjustment Summary

At its core, adjustments reframe trading completely. You're no longer entering a trade and hoping it works. You're **actively managing it like a game in progress.**

The chess analogy is key:

You're not starting over. You're repositioning your pieces based on what the market is doing.

This is also where the mindset shift begins:

- Bad traders rely on hope and emotion
- Skilled traders rely on adjustments and control

The biggest takeaway:

A trade is not a single decision. It's a series of decisions.

Now that you understand what an adjustment is, the next step is learning how to actually see your trade clearly, through the lens of risk graphs.

CHAPTER 2

YOUR GAME BOARD - "RISK GRAPHS"

CHAPTER 2
Your Game Board- "Risk Graphs"

Playing the Game with Risk Graphs

When you step into the options arena, the risk graph is your scoreboard. It takes all the moving parts—stock price, time, volatility—and translates them into the one thing that really matters: Your profit or loss prediction. Without it, you're essentially playing blindfolded. With it, you're playing with X-ray vision.

The NVDA $185 Call Example

Take a simple trade: buying a long $185 call on NVDA.

The first graph shows what happens at expiration:

- The red zone is Loss.
- The green zone is Profit.
- The black line is your outcome if you hold until the very end.

If NVDA closes at $199 on expiration day, this trade makes about $730 profit.

Leg Date	Position	Num	Option Symbol	Expire	Type	Entry	Bid/ Ask	Leg Profit	IV %	Vol	OI	Days	Delta %	Gamma %	Vega %IV	Theta $/day
2025-08-25	Bought	1	NVDA250926C185	2025 Sep 26	185 Call	7.15	7.10 7.20	$0.00	42.98	1681	3390	32	44.77	1.73	21.1	-15.0

That's the score at the final buzzer.

But the second graph adds a whole new dimension - **TIME**:

- **Red line (T-0):** Today
- **Blue line:** One-third of the way to expiration
- **Green line:** Two-thirds of the way
- **Black line:** Expiration

Here's the kicker: If NVDA hit $199 today, the red line shows about $1,200 profit. That's nearly double the expiration result. Why? Because options are time machines—the earlier the move, the bigger the payoff. Wait too long, and the profit shrinks.

Leg Date	Position	Num	Option Symbol	Expire	Type	Entry	Bid/Ask	Leg Profit	IV %	Vol	OI	Days	Delta %	Gamma %	Vega %IV	Theta $/day
2025-08-25	Bought	1	NVDA250926C185	2025 Sep 26	185 Call	7.15	7.10 7.20	$0.00	42.98	1681	3390	32	44.77	1.73	21.1	-15.0

How to Read a Risk Graph

Think of a risk graph like the playbook of the game. Every curve and angle tells you something about your trade:

1. **The X-Axis (Stock Price):** This is the playing field, showing where the stock could be at expiration.
2. **The Y-Axis (Profit & Loss):** This is the scoreboard—your wins and losses measured in dollars.
3. **The Expiration Line (Black):** This shows the final outcome if you hold to the end. It's the game result with or without adjustments.

4. **The T-0 Line (Red):** This is what your trade looks like today. It's your current live score as the underlying stock moves around.
5. **The Time Slices (Blue, Green):** These are time checkpoints at 1/3 and 2/3's through the life of the trade that show how your score changes as the clock runs. They remind you that time is both an ally and an enemy.
6. **Breakeven Points:** Where the line crosses zero. That's where your trade stops losing and starts winning.
7. **Slope of the Line (Delta):** The angle of the curve tells you how sensitive your trade is to price moves. Steeper = bigger moves in your P&L.

Risk Graphs: The Foundation of Adjustments

Here's the secret: Adjustments don't start with the stock—they start with the risk graph.

When you look at the black expiration line and compare it to the red T-0 line, you're really asking:

- If the stock moves now, what's my score?
- If it waits until later, how does my score change?

That difference is the heartbeat of every adjustment.

Example: In our NVDA call, the T-0 line shows $1,200 profit if it pops to $199 today. But the expiration line only pays $730 if it waits until the end. That gap is your opportunity.

- If the stock moves early, you can take profits, roll, or spread off risk before time decay chews away at your winnings.
- If the move is slower, you can adjust—buy time, add protection, or shift strikes—so you stay in the game.

Think of it this way:

- The stock moves.
- The graph tells the truth.
- You make the adjustment.

This is why pros live by risk graphs. They aren't just pictures. They're maps of the battlefield. They show you where the landmines are, where the safe zones lie, and how the terrain changes as time passes.

So, when you hear me talk about the "adjustment game," remember: The game board isn't the stock chart. It's the risk graph. Master reading it, and every adjustment you make will feel less like a guess and more like a winning move.Summary – Seeing the Game Clearly

Now you're given your scoreboard.

Risk graphs translate everything—price, time, volatility—into one clear picture: **your potential profit and loss.**

Without them, you're guessing. With them, you're operating with clarity.

You learned how to read the key components:

One of the biggest insights: **Time changes everything.**

- **X-axis →** Stock price (the playing field)
- **Y-axis →** Profit/loss (the score)
- **Expiration line →** Final outcome
- **T+0 line →** Where you stand today

The same price move can produce very different results depending on when it happens.

This is where traders start to "see" trades instead of just placing them.

Because once you understand the graph, you can:

- Spot risk early
- Identify opportunity
- Plan adjustments before problems grow

Now that you can see your trade clearly, the next step is understanding what kinds of adjustments you can bring to bear on your trades. A whole new world emerges with your **Adjustment Game Pieces** coming up next.

CHAPTER 3

YOUR ADJUSTMENT GAME PIECES

CHAPTER 3
Your Adjustment Game Pieces

Like any great strategy game, mastering trade adjustments involves knowing your moves and having the right tools in place.

Inside the Adjustment Club, we treat each of these tools like chess pieces. You'll learn to play with precision, creativity, and confidence. We've identified 17 high-impact adjustment pieces—proven strategies that can be used individually or in powerful combinations to:

- Reduce or eliminate risk
- Lock in profits
- Stay in the trade and go for more

These pieces make up your Adjustment Arsenal. Just as a chess master learns how and when to move each piece, you'll do the same with these.

There are more than 17 techniques available, but this collection provides everything you need to adjust like a pro.

These are your 17 Adjustment Chess Pieces. Get to know them. They'll be your strongest allies in this game.

These **17 adjustment pieces** are the trader's core arsenal—tools that can be used individually or combined to reduce risk, lock in profits, and stay in the trade for more upside.

That matters because adjustments stop feeling abstract at this point. They become tangible. They become movable pieces on the board.

The big shift in this chapter is identity:
you are no longer just someone placing trades. You are a player with an expanding toolkit.

And just like in chess, the advantage does not come from owning the pieces. It comes from knowing:

- What Each One Does
- When To Use It
- How To Combine Them Intelligently

There is a complete system here—not random tricks, but a coordinated set of adjustment moves designed to help traders respond with precision and confidence.

Now that the pieces are on the board, the next step is to understand the hidden forces that make those pieces powerful: **Understanding the Greeks.**

CHAPTER 4

UNDERSTANDING THE GREEKS

CHAPTER 4
Understanding the Greeks

Before you can master the adjustment game, you need to understand the tools that help you read the board—and nothing is more important than the Greeks.

While they may seem complicated, the Greeks are actually quite simple once you understand what they're doing: They measure how sensitive your option position is to changes in the various factors that affect its value. Literally, the Greeks measure your position's sensitivities to direction, acceleration, implied volatility shifts, and the passage of time.

Here's what each Greek measures:

- **Delta** – Sensitivity to stock price movement explains how much the option's price will change with a $1 move in the underlying. More importantly, the sign of Delta indicates your stock directional bias—whether you benefit from the stock going up, down, or sideways.
- **Gamma** – Sensitivity to acceleration in Delta (think of this as the gas pedal). It measures how quickly Delta is changing. Gamma helps you understand whether your position is becoming more or less directional. Another way to think of Gamma is that if it's negative, the position will lose money with a stock price change (NO GO), and if it's positive, you want the stock price to change (GO).
- **Vega** – Sensitivity to implied volatility (IV) fluctuations. Vega indicates how much the option's price changes with a 1% move in IV. The key point: The sign of Vega shows whether you want IV to go up or down for your position to increase in value.
- **Theta** – Sensitivity to time decay. This indicates how much value an option loses each day as it approaches expiration. Positive Theta means you gain from time decay; negative Theta means time decay works against you.
- **Rho** – Sensitivity to interest rate changes. While this is less significant daily, it becomes more crucial in long-term options or during changing rate environments.

You'll see the Greeks used throughout this manual because they help you decide how to adjust, when to adjust, and how to manage risk.

We'll explore them in more detail later, but for now, remember:

- Greeks measure sensitivity to price, implied volatility, time, acceleration and interest rates
- The sign of Delta = stock directional bias
- The sign of Vega = implied volatility directional bias

Option Greeks Overview

What are they and what are they telling you?

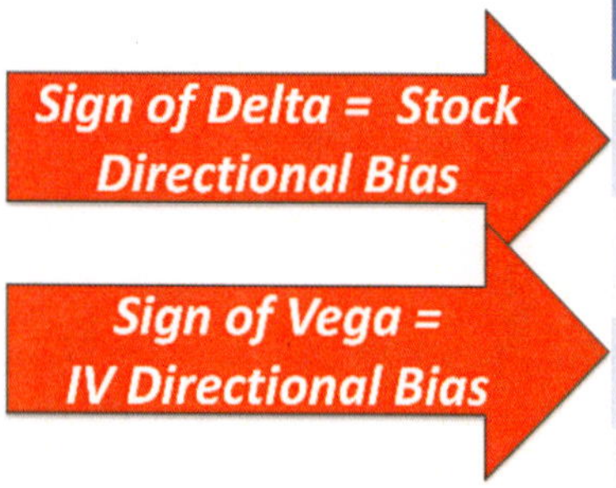

Name	Sensitivity to:
Delta	Price Direction
Gamma	Go or Don't Go (Gas Pedal)
Vega	Implied Volatility
Theta	Time Decay
Rho	Interest Rates

Summary – Learning the Forces Behind the Moves

This is where the game starts to gain depth.

In this chapter, the Greeks are introduced as the sensitivities that explain how an option position responds to price, acceleration, implied volatility, time, and interest rates. Delta, Gamma, Vega, Theta, and Rho are not presented as intimidating math concepts, but as practical signals that help traders read the board and manage risk.

The essential takeaway is simple:
The Greeks tell you what your position wants, what hurts it, and what helps it.

You learn that:

- **Delta** reveals directional bias
- **Gamma** shows how fast that directional exposure changes
- **Vega** tracks volatility impact
- **Theta** measures the effect of time passing

- **Rho** rounds out the picture with rate sensitivity

This chapter matters because it gives meaning to adjustments. Without the Greeks, an adjustment is just movement. With the Greeks, it becomes a calculated decision.

The reader now begins to see that every trade has a living structure underneath it—and those structures can be read, anticipated, and managed.

Now that you understand the major forces affecting a trade, it's time to see one of the simplest and most powerful ways to remove risk from a winning position: **The "House Money" Adjustment.**

CHAPTER 5

THE “HOUSE MONEY” ADJUSTMENT

CHAPTER 5
The "House Money" Adjustment

Let's discuss one of the simplest, smartest, and most powerful strategies in the entire playbook—the "House Money" adjustment. This move is a must-have tool for every serious trader, especially when you have a winning position and want to play with zero risk.

The "House Money" Adjustment

Produce a **$0 risk** or **guaranteed profit** trade by **selling ½ the position** at a **double** or more. This strategy can be applied to:

- Any option position with at least 2 contracts

Objective: Create a Risk-Free or Guaranteed-Profit Trade

The "House Money" adjustment allows you to turn a winning position into a risk-free play (or even lock in guaranteed profit) by selling half (or more) of your stake once it doubles in value. In casino terms, you are pulling your chips off the table, keeping your original investment, and letting the rest ride on the house's dime. You're literally trading with house money.

How It Works

- Start with at least two contracts on any option trade.
- When the trade doubles in value (e.g., from $1.00 to $2.00), sell one contract to recoup your full initial investment.
- Now you hold the second contract with $0 risk—no matter what happens, you can't lose.
- If the second leg continues to run, you enjoy unlimited upside using only profits.

Why It's Brilliant

- Psychological freedom—removes fear and hesitation.
- Built-in risk management—automatically eliminates risk.
- Perfect for scaling—works in multi-contract setups.
- Encourages patience. You stay in the game longer with no stress.

Gameboard Tip

If trading is like chess, then this move is your castle wall. It ensures a no-lose situation while you send your remaining forces out to battle the next move. Don't skip it. Use it often. Win repeatedly with it.

The "House Money" Adjustment

Description: *The simplest adjustment to eliminate risk or even guarantee a profit in a trade. Start the trade with at least 2 contracts and when the position doubles, sell half your contracts to eliminate risk in the position. If your position has more than doubled, doing the house money adjustment will guarantee a profit. Alternatively, sell more than ½ your contracts at a double to guarantee a profit.*

Strategies: *Any option position with at least 2 contracts.*

Outcome: *The adjustment will result in a $0 risk or guaranteed profit position.*

Timing: *Easy. When you position has doubled or has more than a double, this adjustment will result in Job #1 in trading: Managing Risk and letting the profits take care of themselves.*

Summary – Pulling Your Chips Off the Table

This chapter delivers one of the cleanest adjustment concepts in the entire playbook.

The "House Money" adjustment shows how a trader can turn a winning multi-contract position into a **zero-risk trade or guaranteed-profit trade** by selling half, or more than half, once the position has doubled.

That is the brilliance of this move:
It transforms success into safety without removing opportunity.

Instead of riding a winner while exposing both principal and profits to reversal, the trader recovers the original investment and lets the remaining contracts continue on "house money." The emotional benefit is just as important as the financial one. Fear drops. Clarity improves. Patience becomes easier.

This chapter reinforces a major principle of the playbook:
Risk management comes first, and profits can take care of themselves.

It is simple, elegant, and powerful because it solves one of the trader's biggest problems—what to do with a strong winner before it turns into stress.

Now that you know how to take risk off the table in a winning trade, the next move is to take risk off the table in by selling an extended long option and redeploying into a fresh position to maximize continued upside using **The "Pony Express" Adjustment.**

CHAPTER 6

THE "PONY EXPRESS" ADJUSTMENT

CHAPTER 6
The "Pony Express" Adjustment

The "Pony Express" adjustment is one of the simplest—and most powerful—adjustment strategies in your playbook.

Just like the riders of the old Pony Express in the Wild West, who swapped tired horses for fresh ones to keep up their speed and stamina, you'll learn to swap your options at the perfect moment to maintain power and maximize your edge.

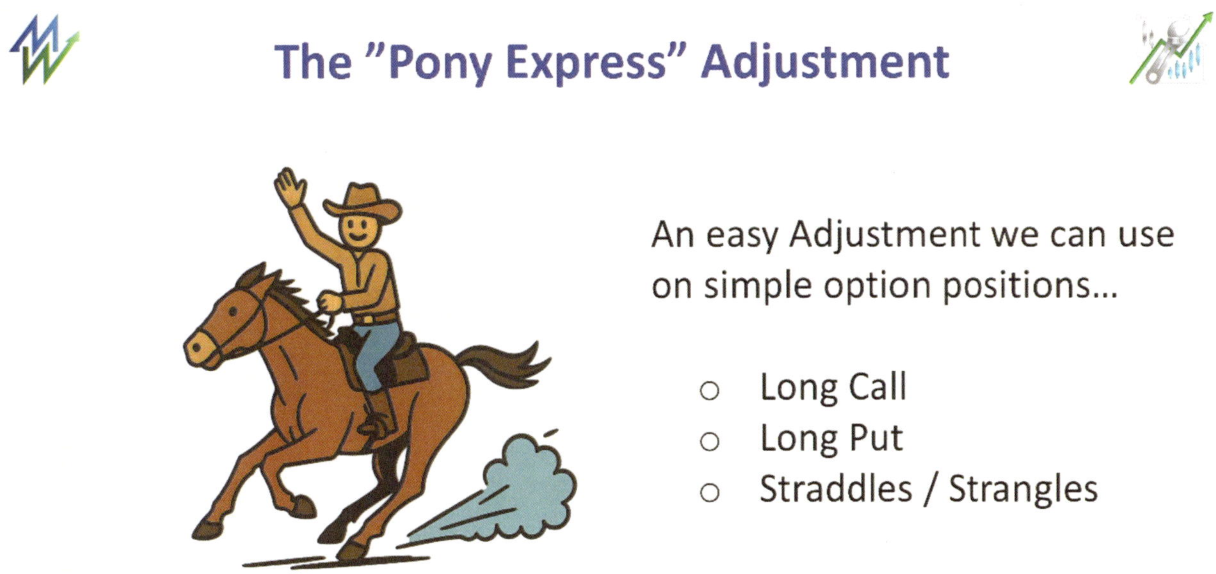

The "Pony Express" adjustment can keep your position strong and fast, mile after mile.

The "Pony Express" adjustment takes advantage of the Gamma/Delta sweet spot—specifically the area where a 30 Delta gives you greater ROI when the stock moves in your favor.

Here's how it works:

1. Start with a Long Call or Long Put with approximately 30 Delta.
2. As the trade moves in your favor and Delta crosses 50 (or the position doubles in value)
3. You sell the current position—the tired horse.
4. Then, you buy a new Long Call or Put with ~30 Delta—your fresh horse.

This keeps you in the ideal zone where risk is relatively low and reward is high—and it allows you to stay in the game with momentum on your side. Even better, this adjustment often results in lower risk and can generate a guaranteed profit while still leaving room to pursue more.

This adjustment is ideal for:

- Long Calls
- Long Puts
- Straddles and Strangles (adjusting one side at a time)

Using the "Pony Express" adjustment reduces the risk of a big winner reversing on you and helps you maintain longer distances with controlled risk and fresh energy.

Practice it to learn the rhythm. You'll soon find this technique becomes a go-to move in your adjustment toolbox.

"Pony Express" Adjustment – Quick Reference Summary

The "Pony Express" Adjustment

Description: *Selling a profitable call or put to finance a cheaper further OTM call or put. This adjustment focuses on dropping position delta to 30 taking advantage of the delta/gamma sweet-spot and maximizing potential ROI. The adjustment results in a credit to the position.*

Strategies: *Long Calls, Long Puts, Straddles / Strangles*

Outcome: *The roll will result in taking profits off the table and providing the opportunity to make more profit. This roll can also result in a risk free or guaranteed profit trade. Additionally, the resulting option will offer a higher ROI potential than the original.*

Timing: *Typically applied on a profitable trade when the delta of the long approaches or surpasses +/- 50. This adjustment should only be applied with a directional prognosis. It can also be used in conjunction with other adjustment moves.*

"Pony Express" Adjustment – Real Trade Example: SHAK

To illustrate the "Pony Express" adjustment, let's walk through a real example using Shake Shack (SHAK).

This trade was executed on February 12, 2025, employing a Long Call strategy. The position involved purchasing four call contracts, each with an individual risk of $229. This results in a total position risk of $916.

The chart and risk graph below show the starting point of the trade, illustrating the setup before any adjustments were made.

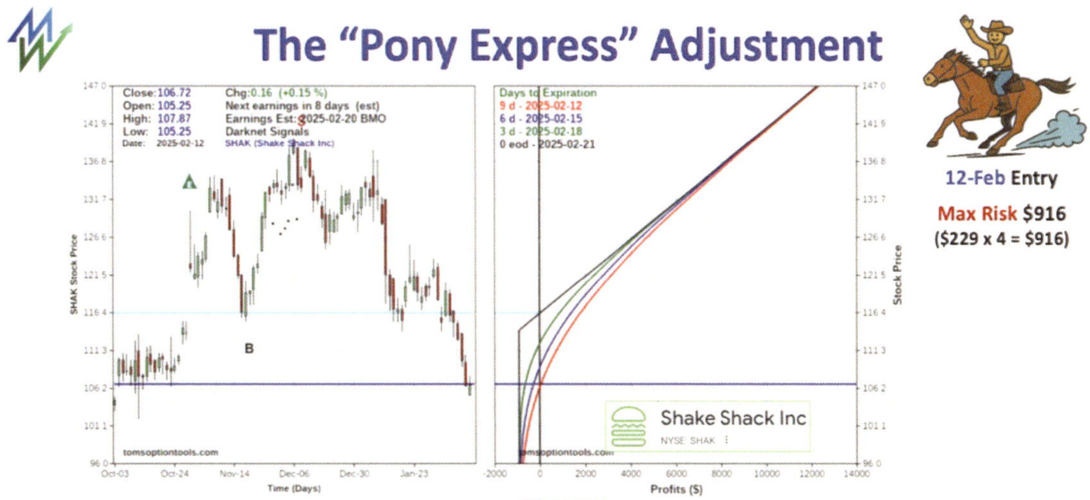

Quote Type	Entry Debit	Profit	Rate of Return	Max Profit	Max Risk	Delta (Shares)	Gamma	Vega	Theta
Mid Quote	$916.00	$44.00	4.8%	$Unlimited	$-916.00	125.12	11.186	$23.73	$-101.19
Mid Quote/4	$229.00	$11.00	4.8%	$Unlimited	$-229.00	31.28	2.80	$5.93	$-25.30

SHAK Long Call Position – February 12, 2025 Entry - Total Risk: $916 ($229 x 4 contracts)

Fast forward six days to February 18, 2025—and the trade has shifted significantly in our favor.

The result? A 170.7% profit—$1,564 gained on a $916 entry debit. But here's the key insight: Although the initial risk was $916, we now have $1,564 in unrealized profit on the table. Our real risk is now $916 + $1,564 = $2,480.

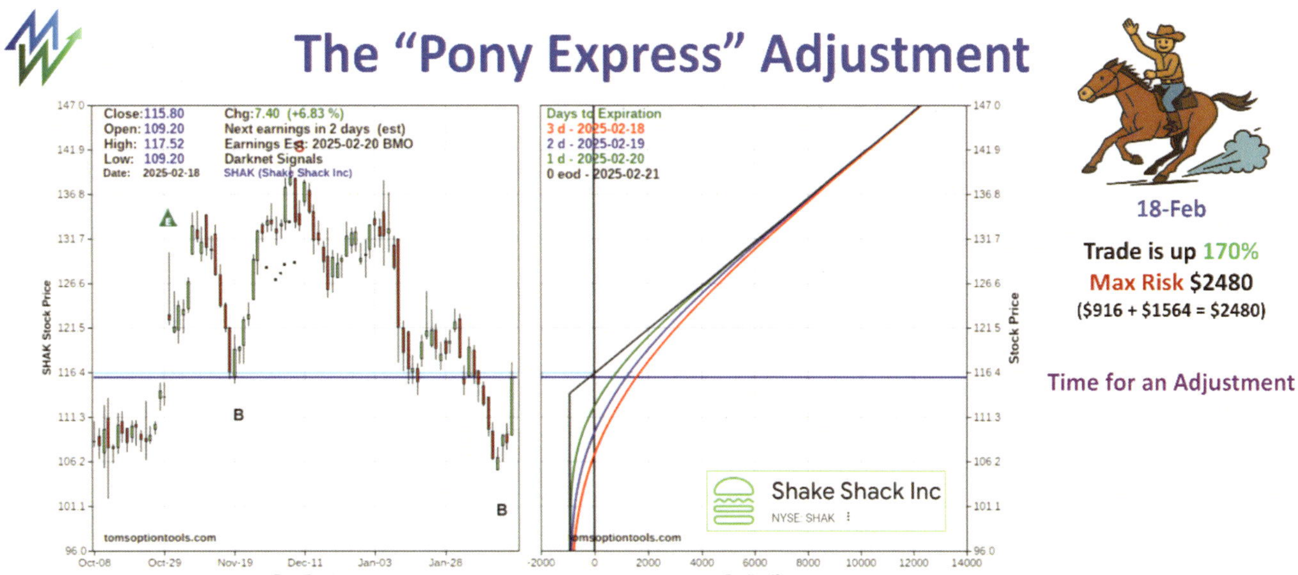

Quote Type	Entry Debit	Profit	Rate of Return	Max Profit	Max Risk	Delta (Shares)	Gamma	Vega	Theta
Mid Quote	$916.00	$1564.00	170.7%	$Unlimited	$-916.00	231.29	11.839	$16.42	$-347.84
Mid Quote/4	$229.00	$391.00	170.7%	$Unlimited	$-229.00	57.82	2.96	$4.11	$-86.96

This is the perfect moment to apply the "Pony Express" adjustment:

- We have crossed a Delta of 50.
- Our trade is deep in profit territory.
- And our main job now? Protect that win.

Time to sell the tired horse and bring in a fresh one.

SHAK – February 18, 2025. A profitable setup, but risk has grown. Time to adjust.

"Pony Express" Adjustment – SHAK Example: The Move

Here's where we put the "Pony Express" adjustment into action.

On February 18, with the trade displaying a significant unrealized profit, we locked in gains and reset the trade by doing the following:

- Sold to close (STC) the original 114 Calls for $6.45
- Bought to open (BTO) the 123 Calls for $2.75

This generated a credit of $3.70 per contract, or $1,480 total (4 contracts x $3.70).

Minimum Profit Locked In: **$564**

That's a **62% GUARANTEED** return in just six days—and we still have room to grow if the trade stays in our favor.

The "Pony Express" Adjustment

Shake Shack Inc
NYSE: SHAK

Stock: SHAK Stock News
Name: Shake Shack Inc
Sector: Eating And Drinking Places
Dividend: 0 %
100 Day SV: 36.60%
Trade: SHAK 25Feb21 114 Call - Pony

Quote Type	Entry Credit	Profit	Rate of Return	Max Profit	Min Profit	Delta (Shares)	Gamma	Vega	Theta
Mid Quote	$564.00	$1744.00	n/a	$Unlimited	$564.00	133.90	10.242	$15.29	$-347.28
Mid Quote/4	$141.00	$436.00	n/a	$Unlimited	$141.00	33.48	2.56	$3.82	$-86.82

Downside Breakeven	Upside Breakeven	Max Profit/Max Risk	Max Profit/Cost
unknown	unknown	0%	Unlimited%

Leg Date	Position	Num	Option Symbol	Expire	Type	Entry	Bid/ Ask	Leg Profit	IV %	Vol	OI	Days	Delta %	Gamma %	Vega %IV	Theta $/day
2025-02-12	Bought	4	SHAK250221C114	2025 Feb 21	114 Call	2.29	5.70 6.70	$1564.00	125.96	45	53	3	57.82	2.96	4.1	-87.0
2025-02-18	Bought	4	SHAK250221C123	2025 Feb 21	123 Call	2.75	2.00 3.90	$80.00	135.54	9	12	3	33.48	2.56	3.8	-86.8
2025-02-18	Sold	4	SHAK250221C114	2025 Feb 21	114 Call	6.45	5.70 6.70	$100.00	125.96	45	53	3	-57.82	-2.96	-4.1	87.0

18-Feb

Exchange a Tired Horse for a Fresh Horse

STC the 114 Call & BTO the 123 Call for a CREDIT of $1480
(3.70 x 4 = $1480)

Min Profit $564 LOCKED IN
(+62% in 6 Days)

This is the true power of adjustments:

- Take profit off the table
- Reduce risk
- Maintain upside potential

The Adjustment – Locking in profit, reducing risk, and resetting for more.

Final Adjustment Setup: Risk Graph View

Now that we've finished the "Pony Express" adjustment, let's review the risk/reward profile of the new trade setup. The risk graph below shows the updated risk profile of the position after the adjustment.

- The entire risk graph now lives to the right of the breakeven line, meaning we've secured a $564 guaranteed profit regardless of the outcome.

With the profit secured, we are in a strong position. We can stick to our planned exit on February 19, 2025, and may even profit more if the stock moves in our favor.

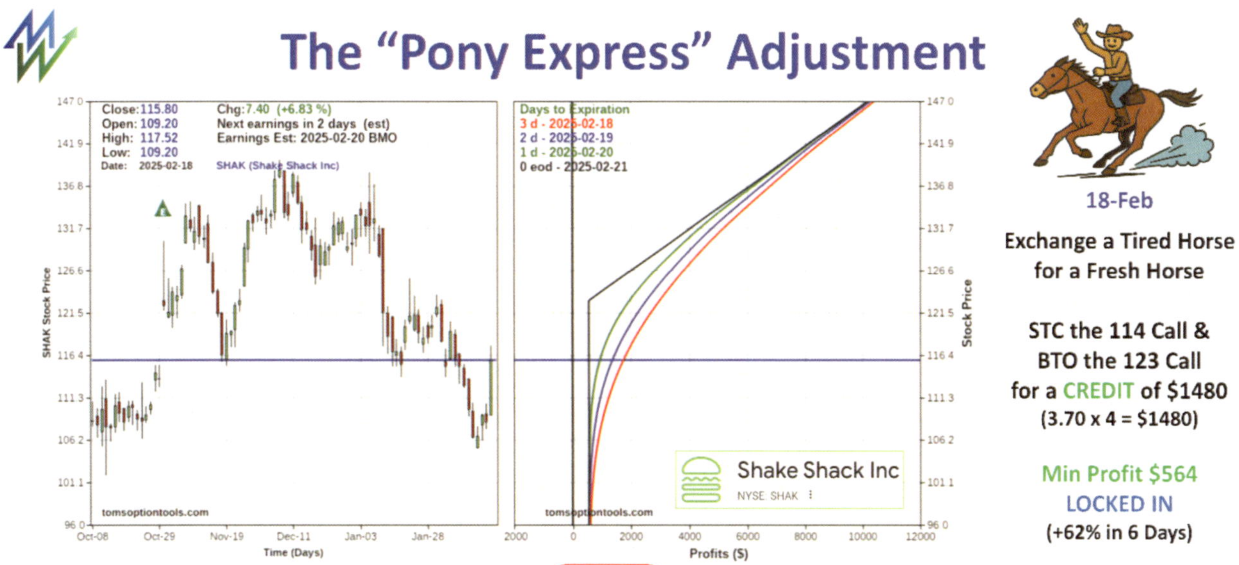

Quote Type	Entry Credit	Profit	Rate of Return	Max Profit	Min Profit	Delta (Shares)	Gamma	Vega	Theta
Mid Quote	$564.00	$1744.00	n/a	$Unlimited	$564.00	133.90	10.242	$15.29	$-347.28
Mid Quote/4	$141.00	$436.00	n/a	$Unlimited	$141.00	33.48	2.56	$3.82	$-86.82

The "Pony Express" Adjustment – Closing the Adjusted Trade

On February 19, one day before earnings, we reached our planned exit date.

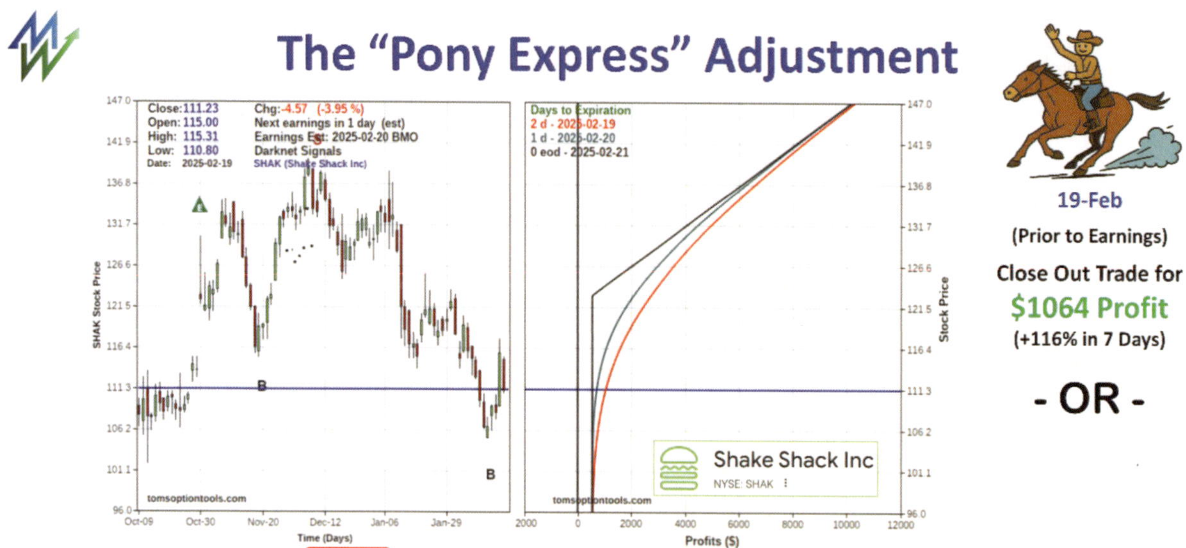

Quote Type	Entry Credit	Profit	Rate of Return	Max Profit	Min Profit	Delta (Shares)	Gamma	Vega	Theta
Mid Quote	$564.00	$1064.00	n/a	$Unlimited	$564.00	77.88	9.037	$9.07	$-336.99
Mid Quote/4	$141.00	$266.00	n/a	$Unlimited	$141.00	19.47	2.26	$2.27	$-84.25

Despite the pullback in price, our risk-managed "Pony Express" adjustment allowed us to lock in:

- A guaranteed minimum profit of $564 (already secured the day prior)
- And a final closing profit of $1,064—a 116% ROI on the original $916 risk

While our position had higher gains the day before, we followed our forecast and stayed in, aiming for more upside. The market moved against us, yet we walked away with a confident win, demonstrating the strength of our adjustments.

Compare this to the unadjusted version of the trade, which only yielded $764 in profit and carried a higher risk the entire time.

This is what professional trade management looks like.

Unadjusted Trade – Feb 19 Without Adjustment

Had we not made any adjustments, the original position would have still been profitable—closing out with a gain of $764 or 83% in seven days. However, this trade carried a full risk of $916 the entire time, exposing us to unnecessary downside. The "Pony Express" adjustment significantly reduced our risk while boosting our final return.

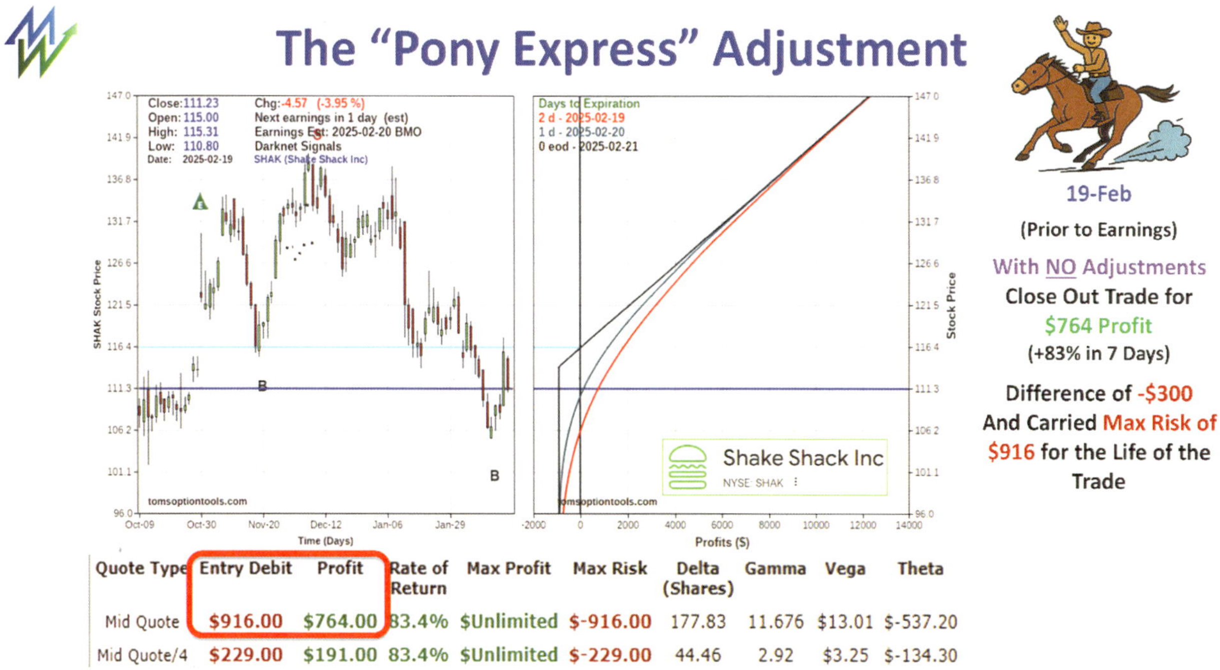

Final Comparison: Adjusted vs Unadjusted

Here's how the "Pony Express" adjustment impacted the SHAK trade compared to leaving it unadjusted:

	Adjusted Trade	Unadjusted Trade
Profit	$1,064	$764
ROI	116%	83%
Risk Carried	None (after lock-in)	$916 (full risk held)
Outcome Certainty	Guaranteed $564 minimum	Could lose entire position
Emotional Benefit	Stress-free + strategic	Hope-based risk exposure

Summary – Keep the Trade Moving Forward

This adjustment is all about **continuity**.

The "Pony Express" teaches you how to take a position that has already worked and **roll it forward to amplify profit potential**, giving the trade a fresh runway to continue producing gains. Instead of closing a winning trade and walking away, you pass the baton—extending duration while maintaining structure.

The key idea:
Incremental profits don't have to wane just because the trade is winning.

By rolling the option into a cheaper, further OTM option, you:

- Maintain directional or structural exposure
- Reduce risk
- Stay engaged in a high-probability setup

This move is especially powerful when the trade is behaving well, but incremental profits are starting to wane.

It reinforces a critical mindset:
Great trades aren't just managed. They're extended intelligently.

Now that you know how to keep a good trade alive, the next step is learning how to consistently pull income out of your positions while they're working with **The "Collect the Rent" Adjustment**.

CHAPTER 7

THE "COLLECT THE RENT" ADJUSTMENT

CHAPTER 7
The "Collect the Rent" Adjustment

Imagine owning a house. Every month, you can collect rent from your tenants. In the options world, we can do something very similar with our long calls or puts. These positions are assets—and the "Collect the Rent" adjustment is how we use those assets to generate income while lowering risk.

This strategy involves selling options against your long positions:

- Selling a call against a long call (creating a bullish vertical spread)
- Selling a put against a long put (creating a bearish vertical spread)

The result? You get a credit—which lowers your cost basis, helps offset risk, and can even lock in a profit.

This adjustment can be used on its own or combined with other chess piece moves to create even more control and reward potential.

The "Collect the Rent" Adjustment

Finance **(collect rent on)** a position to **reduce risk** and potentially **guaranteeing a profit** by:

- Selling a call
- Selling a put
- Selling a credit spread

The "Collect the Rent" Adjustment – Quick Summary

This adjustment involves monetizing profitable positions by selling a higher strike call or lower strike put against your long position—effectively turning it into a debit spread. This generates a credit, which reduces risk and lowers the breakeven point.

It's a smart way to:

- Reduce risk and lock in profits
- Reduce Vega exposure
- Cap the upside in exchange for improved risk/reward

Strategies

- Long Calls
- Long Puts
- Straddles / Strangles

Outcome

You'll take profits off the table, reduce your breakeven point (move risk further away), and might even establish a risk-free or guaranteed profit position. Just remember: Upside is limited to the new short strike.

Timing

Apply when your long leg is profitable and Delta has reached or exceeded +/- 50. This strategy works best with a clear directional prediction and can also be combined with other adjustments.

The "Collect the Rent" Adjustment

Description: *Selling a higher strike call or lower strike put against the one you own to bring in credit which lowers risk. This adjustment converts a long option position into a debit spread configuration lowering the breakeven. It also can be used to reduce Vega (Implied Volatility) exposure. The adjustment results in a credit to the position.*

Strategies: *Long Calls, Long Puts, Straddles / Strangles*

Outcome: *The adjustment will result in taking profits off the table and improving the breakeven of the position. It can also result in a risk free or guaranteed profit trade. Additionally, the profit potential does get "capped" at the new short strike.*

Timing: *Typically applied on a profitable trade when the delta of the long approaches or surpasses +/- 50. This adjustment should only be applied with a directional prognosis. It can also be used in conjunction with other adjustment moves.*

HSBC Example – Initial Trade Setup

On February 7, 2025, we initiated a bullish trade on HSBC Holdings (symbol: HSBC) by buying 20 February 21 $55 call options at $0.50 each, resulting in a total risk of $1,000. This trade has a clear bullish prognosis, and we plan to hold it until expiration. This setup offers us the chance to apply the "Collect the Rent" adjustment if the position becomes profitable before expiration.

The "Collect the Rent" Adjustment

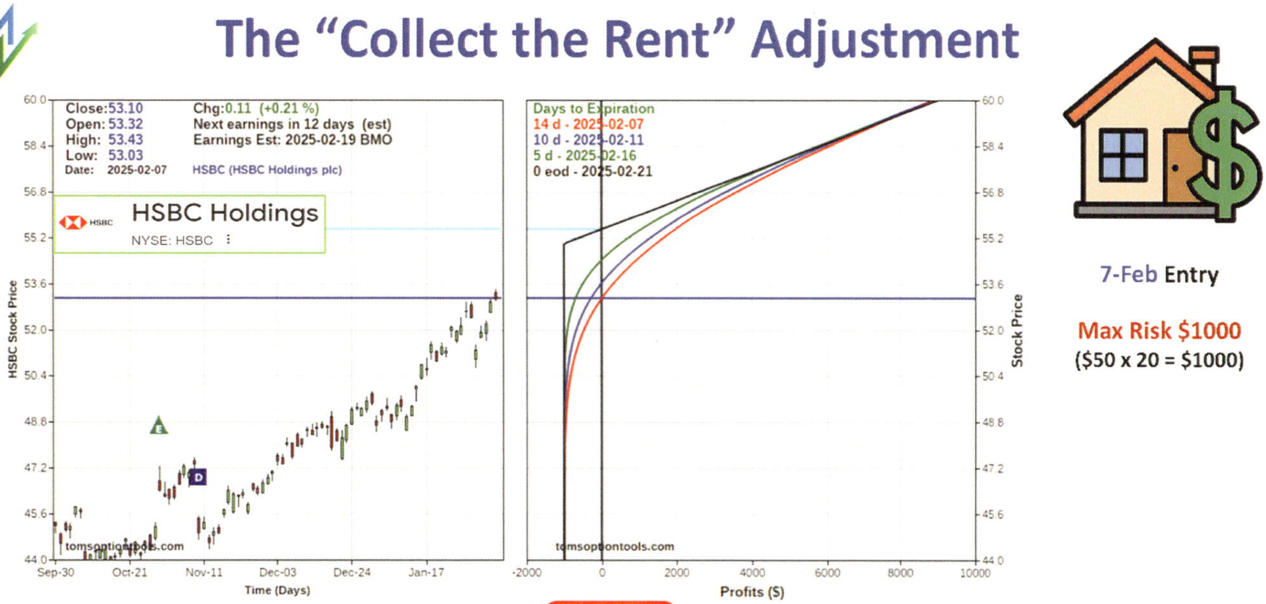

7-Feb Entry

Max Risk $1000
($50 x 20 = $1000)

Quote Type	Entry Debit	Profit	Rate of Return	Max Profit	Max Risk	Delta (Shares)	Gamma	Vega	Theta
Mid Quote	$1000.00	$0.00	0.0%	$Unlimited	$-1000.00	535.36	208.537	$68.29	$-67.45
Mid Quote/20	$50.00	$0.00	0.0%	$Unlimited	$-50.00	26.77	10.43	$3.41	$-3.37

The "Collect the Rent" Adjustment – Feb 11 Update

Just four days later, on February 11, 2025, our HSBC trade had more than doubled in value. The profit was $1,060, which, when added to our original $1,000 debit, increased our total risk exposure to $2,060. This rapid change emphasizes both the potential of directional trades and the greater risk if not adjusted.

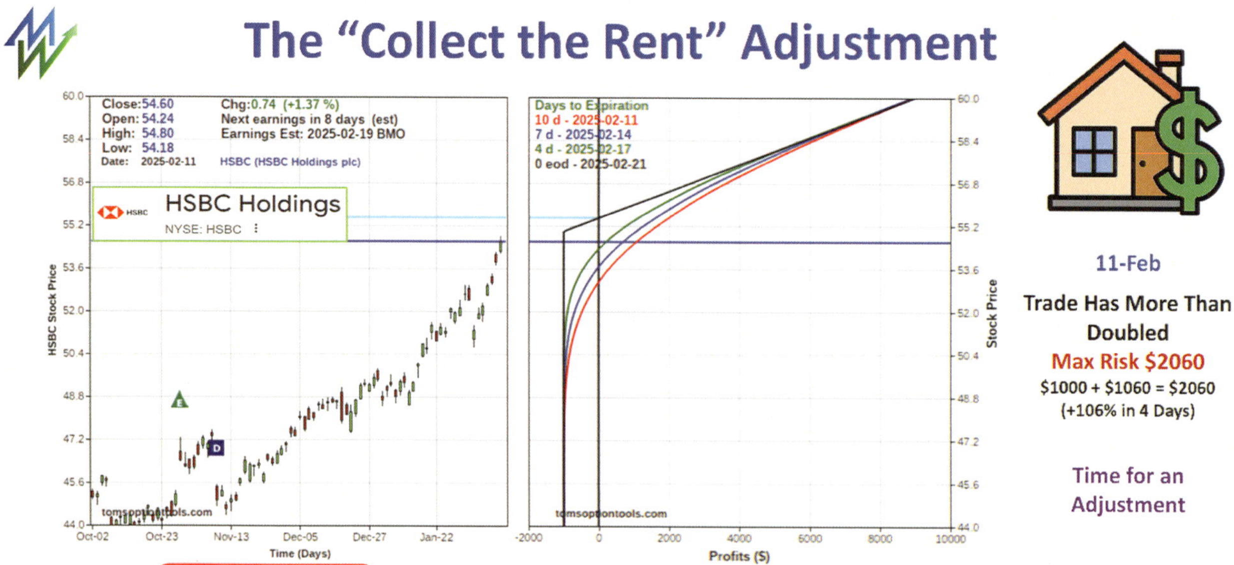

Quote Type	Entry Debit	Profit	Rate of Return	Max Profit	Max Risk	Delta (Shares)	Gamma	Vega	Theta
Mid Quote	$1000.00	$1060.00	106.0%	$Unlimited	$-1000.00	890.28	247.115	$71.20	$-114.61
Mid Quote/10	$100.00	$106.00	106.0%	$Unlimited	$-100.00	89.03	24.71	$7.12	$-11.46

Let's take a look at where we stand just before the adjustment.

With 20 contracts in play, we have an excellent opportunity to reduce our exposure with the "House Money" adjustment by selling 10 contracts to lock in a solid profit. This move effectively cuts our position size in half while realizing some gains—and sets us up to apply the "Collect the Rent" adjustment. Remember, up to this point, we haven't even collected any rent on this position yet!

Adjustment #1 – "House Money" Adjustment - Locking in Profit by Selling Half

On February 11, with the position showing a profit of $1,060, we executed our first adjustment: Selling half of the long call position (10 contracts out of 20) at $1.03 each. This generated a credit of $1,030, which more than covered the initial $1,000 entry debit.

This simple move of applying the "House Money" adjustment—selling half the position—effectively locked in a minimum profit of $25 while allowing the remaining 10 calls to continue riding the bullish move.

The "House Money" Adjustment

Leg Date	Position	Num	Option Symbol	Expire	Type	Entry	Bid/ Ask	Leg Profit	IV %	Vol	OI	Days	Delta %	Gamma %	Vega %IV	Theta $/day
2025-02-07	Bought	20	HSBC250221C55	2025 Feb 21	55 Call	0.50	0.95 1.10	$1060.00	35.30	13	189	10	44.51	12.36	3.6	-5.7
2025-02-11	Sold	10	HSBC250221C55	2025 Feb 21	55 Call	1.03	0.95 1.10	$-5.00	35.30	13	189	10	-44.51	-12.36	-3.6	5.7

Hover the mouse on a risk line to see the line data. Hover in stock chart to see stock data.

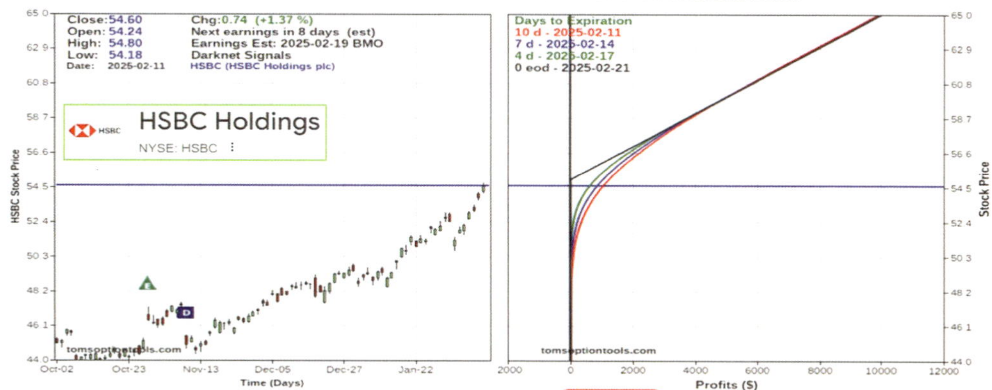

Quote Type	Entry Credit	Profit	Rate of Return	Max Profit	Min Profit	Delta (Shares)	Gamma	Vega	Theta
Mid Quote	$25.00	$1055.00	n/a	$Unlimited	$25.00	445.14	123.557	$35.60	$-57.31
Mid Quote/10	$2.50	$105.50	n/a	$Unlimited	$2.50	44.51	12.36	$3.56	$-5.73

11-Feb

Adjustment #1

Sell ½ of the Position

STC 10 at 1.03

Credit of $1030

($103 x 10 = $1030)

Min Profit

$25

LOCKED IN

By reducing exposure, we lowered our risk and secured a win—no matter what the market does next.

The "Collect the Rent" Adjustment – Adjustment #2

Now that we've secured a guaranteed profit from selling half the position, we move to further capitalize on our asset's value. With the 10 remaining long calls now worth over $1,000, we use a classic "Collect the Rent" adjustment. This involves selling a higher strike call against the remaining position, creating a vertical spread.

On February 11, we sold 10 Feb 21 $56 call options at a credit of $0.63 each. This brings in a total credit of $630 (10 contracts x $0.63), which adds to our locked-in profit.

This second adjustment converts our remaining long calls into a debit spread while securing a new guaranteed profit of $660. At this stage, our position has lower risk, guaranteed returns, and the potential to earn more if HSBC continues its bullish move into expiration.

The "Collect the Rent" Adjustment

Leg Date	Position	Num	Option Symbol	Expire	Type	Entry	Bid/ Ask	Leg Profit	IV %	Vol	OI	Days	Delta %	Gamma %	Vega %IV	Theta $/day
2025-02-07	Bought	20	HSBC250221C55	2025 Feb 21	55 Call	0.50	0.95 1.10	$1060.00	35.30	13	189	10	44.51	12.36	3.6	-5.7
2025-02-11	Sold	10	HSBC250221C56	2025 Feb 21	56 Call	0.63	0.55 0.70	$0.00	34.20	8	12	10	-32.21	-11.58	-3.2	5.1
2025-02-11	Sold	10	HSBC250221C55	2025 Feb 21	55 Call	1.03	0.95 1.10	$0.00	35.30	13	189	10	-44.51	-12.36	-3.6	5.7

2 Future Legs are not Displayed

Hover the mouse on a risk line to see the line data. Hover in stock chart to see stock data.

Quote Type	Entry Credit	Profit	Rate of Return	Max Profit	Min Profit	Delta (Shares)	Gamma	Vega	Theta
Mid Quote	$660.00	$1060.00	n/a	$1660.00	$660.00	123.01	7.724	$3.27	$-5.99
Mid Quote/10	$66.00	$106.00	n/a	$166.00	$66.00	12.30	0.77	$0.33	$-0.60

11-Feb
Adjustment #2
Convert to a Spread
STO Higher Strike Call
10 at 0.63
Credit of $630
($63 x 10 = $630)

Min Profit
$660
LOCKED IN

21-Feb – Trade Expiration and Outcome

On February 21 (expiration day) and time to close the trade. The stock fulfilled our bullish prediction and continued to rise. We held the trade until expiration and collected the full spread profit. This resulted in a final gain of $1,660—a 166% return on the original risk of $1,000. Even if the stock had not risen, the worst-case outcome after our adjustments was a guaranteed minimum profit of $660. This shows how adjusting not only allows for aiming for more but also protects the downside.

The "Collect the Rent" Adjustment

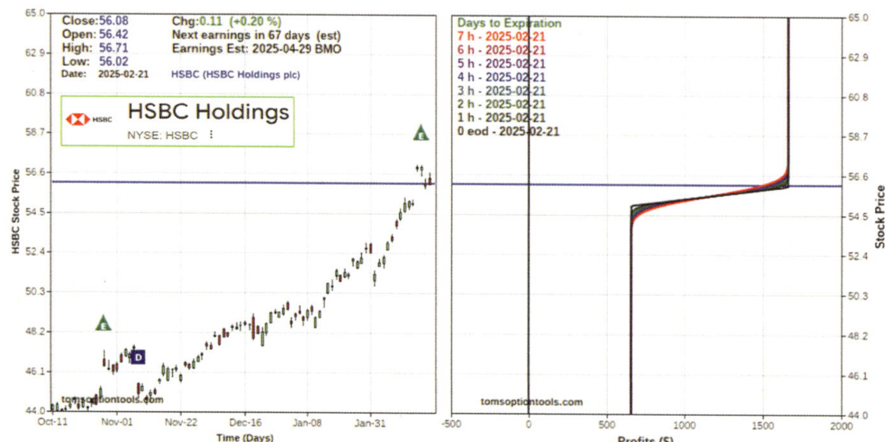

Quote Type	Entry Credit	Profit	Rate of Return	Max Profit	Min Profit	Delta (Shares)	Gamma	Vega	Theta
Mid Quote	$660.00	$1660.00	n/a	$1660.00	$660.00	420.98	-656.070	$-5.48	$321.65
Mid Quote/10	$66.00	$166.00	n/a	$166.00	$66.00	42.10	-65.61	$-0.55	$32.17

21-Feb
Option Expiration
Spread at Max Profit of
$1660
(+166% in 14 Days)

- OR -

Adjusted vs Unadjusted

So, how would we have done without these two adjustments? Here, you can see that without adjustments, the trade would have yielded a decent but smaller profit of $1,160. We would have had to accept the risk of losing $1,000 all the way to expiration. Once again, risk management and locking in profits are the key aspects of this game. There are times when you will make less with adjustments, but the psychological benefits and money management advantages are priceless.

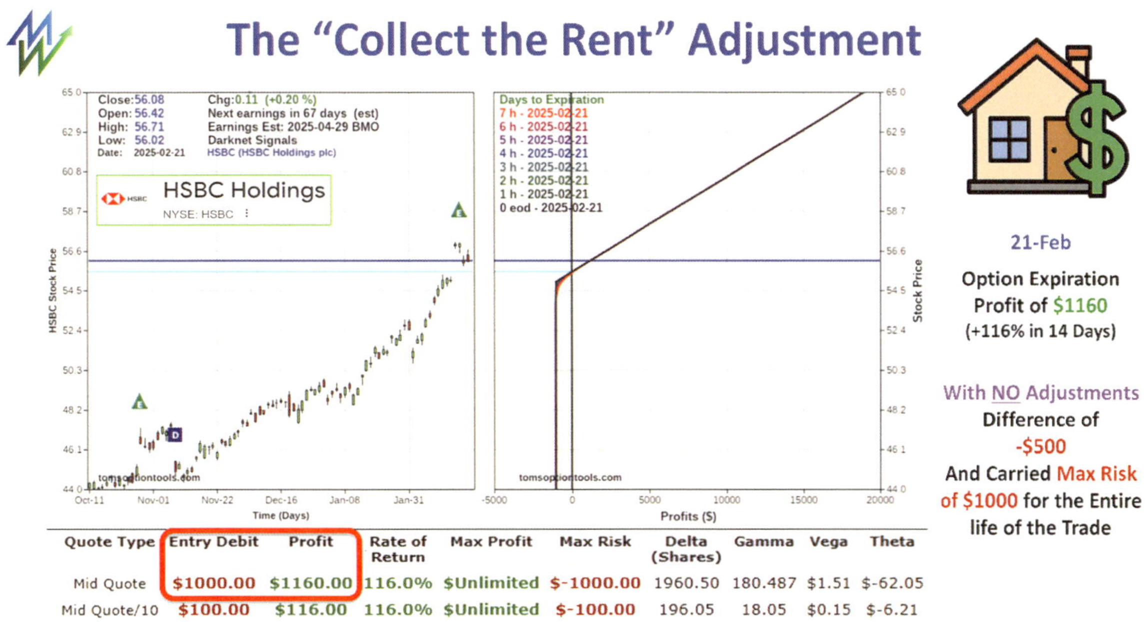

Final Comparison: Adjusted vs Unadjusted – HSBC Trade

Here's how the "House Money" and "Collect the Rent" adjustment impacted the HSBC trade compared to leaving it unadjusted:

	Adjusted Trade	Unadjusted Trade
Profit	$1,660	$1,160
ROI	166%	116%
Risk Carried	None (after lock-in)	$1,000 (full risk held)
Outcome Certainty	Guaranteed $660 minimum	Could lose entire position
Emotional Benefit	Stress-free + strategic	Hope-based risk exposure

Summary – Turn Time Into Income

This chapter introduces one of the most consistent income-producing concepts in the playbook.

"Collect the Rent" focuses on **selling premium against an existing position** to generate steady cash flow while the trade is in motion. Instead of waiting for a final outcome, you're actively getting paid along the way.

The principle is simple:
If your position allows it, **harvest time decay repeatedly**.

By layering in short premium, you:

- Create ongoing income
- Reduce overall cost basis
- Improve probability of profit

This turns your position into something that works for you daily—not just at expiration.

But it also introduces responsibility:
You must stay aware of added risk and manage new obligations created by the short premium.

The deeper lesson:
Time is not just something to endure. It's something you can monetize.

Now that you're generating income from your positions, the next step is learning how to neutralize directional risk and bring your trade back into balance with **The "DNA (Delta Neutral)" Adjustment**.

CHAPTER 8

THE "DNA (DELTA NEUTRAL)" ADJUSTMENT

CHAPTER 8
The "DNA (Delta Neutral)" Adjustment

The "DNA Adjustment" focuses on managing directional risk. Using Delta, we can tilt a position's bias to be bullish, bearish, or completely neutral—depending on our outlook. This is a crucial strategy for protecting profits and navigating uncertain markets.

Remember, Delta measures how much your position responds to stock price movement. Delta neutralization can be achieved by adding or reducing exposure—using long options, closing shorts, or changing spreads.

The "DNA" (Delta Neutral) Adjustment

Gain **dominion over directional risk** by adjusting the **Delta** in a position. Some ways to do so:

- Buying Calls or Puts
- Selling Calls or Puts
- Adding or Adjusting Spreads

Summary of the "DNA (Delta Neutral)" Adjustment

The "DNA" adjustment aims to neutralize the directional risk (Delta) in a position, especially after a profitable move. It is commonly used in Delta-neutral strategies like straddles and strangles when the stock makes a strong move that increases directional exposure. The main goal is to reduce or eliminate Delta risk while potentially locking in profits.

Applicable Strategies

- Calls and Puts
- Straddles / Strangles
- Butterflies
- Condors
- Calendar Spreads
- Other non-directional structures

Outcome

This adjustment:

- Adds to the cost of the trade
- Improves the neutrality of the position
- May convert the position into a risk-free or guaranteed profit trade
- Is most effective after the stock has made a significant move in one direction

Best Timing

Apply when your existing position has developed a higher positive (bullish) or negative (bearish) Delta, usually after a favorable price movement. It can also be layered with other adjustments to improve the overall trade structure.

The "DNA" (Delta Neutral) Adjustment

Description: *Used to neutralize the directional risk (delta) in a position. Commonly applied to "Delta Neutral" strategies such as Straddles and Strangles. Mainly applied when the underlying stock makes a move that creates a profit, but has directional risk. The idea is to re-neutralize the Delta of the position by reducing risk and/or locking in profit.*

Strategies: *Calls, Puts, Straddles / Strangles as well as Butterflies, Condors, Calendar spreads, etc.*

Outcome: *The adjustment will result in taking profits off the table and improving the non-directional bias of the position. It can also result in a risk free or guaranteed profit trade. The benefits are to reduce (or remove) the directional risk after the stock has made a significant price move.*

Timing: *Typically applied to a profitable trade when the Delta of the position has become either positive (bullish) or negative (bearish). It can also be used in conjunction with other adjustment moves.*

MARA Trade – Feb 21: Delta-Neutral Strangle

On February 21, 2025, we initiated a Delta-neutral strangle on Marathon Digital Holdings (MARA), purchasing 13 contracts of the Feb 28 $16 calls and $13.50 puts for a total debit of $962. This represented our maximum risk. The Delta of the position was neutral.

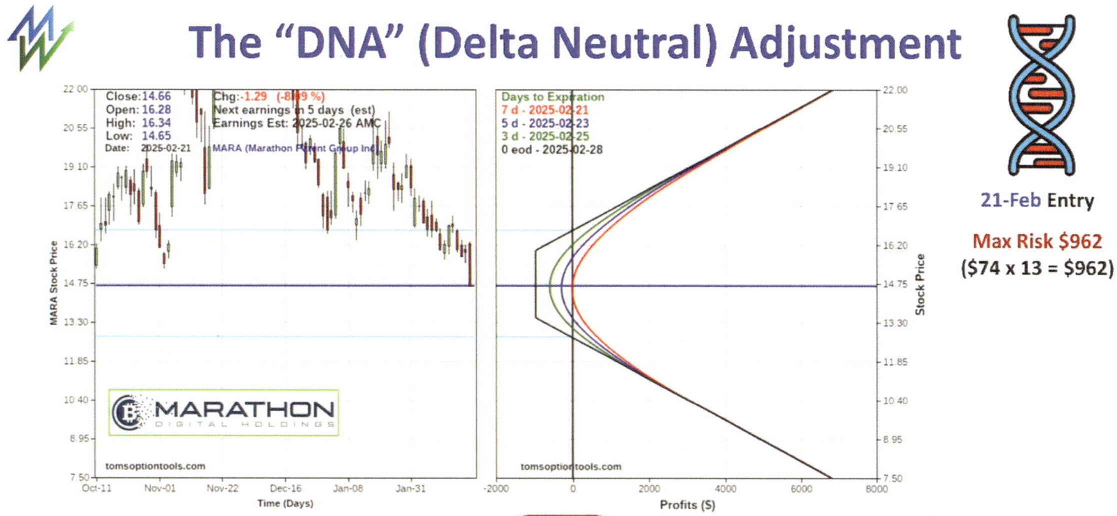

Quote Type	Entry Debit	Profit	Rate of Return	Max Profit	Max Risk	Delta (Shares)	Gamma	Vega	Theta
Mid Quote	$962.00	$0.00	0.0%	$Unlimited	$-962.00	47.27	409.234	$17.73	$-133.33
Mid Quote/13	$74.00	$0.00	0.0%	$Unlimited	$-74.00	3.64	31.48	$1.36	$-10.26

Feb 25: Profitable Move and Delta Imbalance

On February 25, just four days later, the stock moved sharply lower, producing a $923 profit. This increased our total risk to $1,885 (original risk + unrealized profit). But here's the catch—Delta had shifted to -817, exposing us to significant directional risk. If the stock reversed upward, we could lose over $800 on Delta.

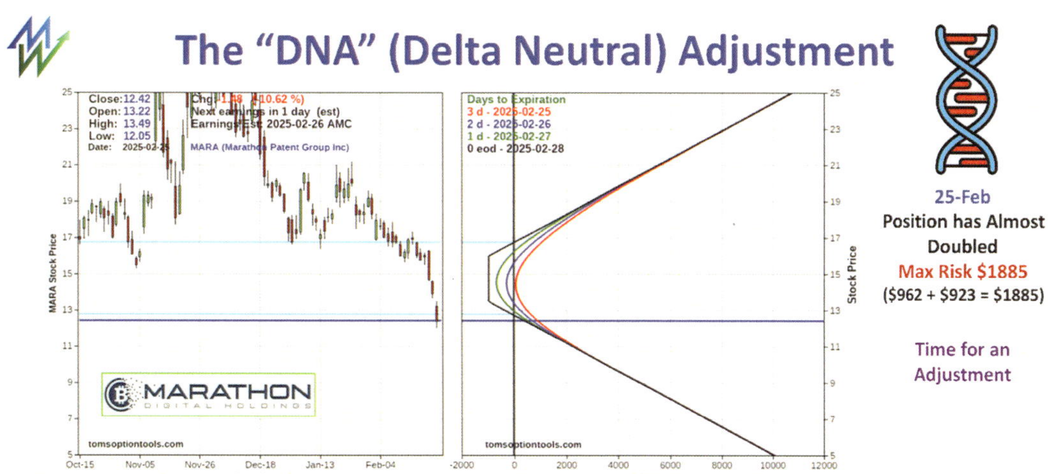

Quote Type	Entry Debit	Profit	Rate of Return	Max Profit	Max Risk	Delta (Shares)	Gamma	Vega	Theta
Mid Quote	$962.00	$923.00	95.9%	$Unlimited	$-962.00	-817.03	346.015	$7.08	$-190.07
Mid Quote/13	$74.00	$71.00	95.9%	$Unlimited	$-74.00	-62.85	26.62	$0.54	$-14.62

Large negative Delta signals a need to neutralize directional risk.

The "DNA" Adjustment in Action

To minimize risk and lock in gains, we performed a Delta Neutral adjustment by executing a "Pony Express" move on the put side. We sold profitable puts and bought cheaper puts further out of the money. This adjustment decreased Delta from -817 to -12.62 and secured a minimum profit of $741.

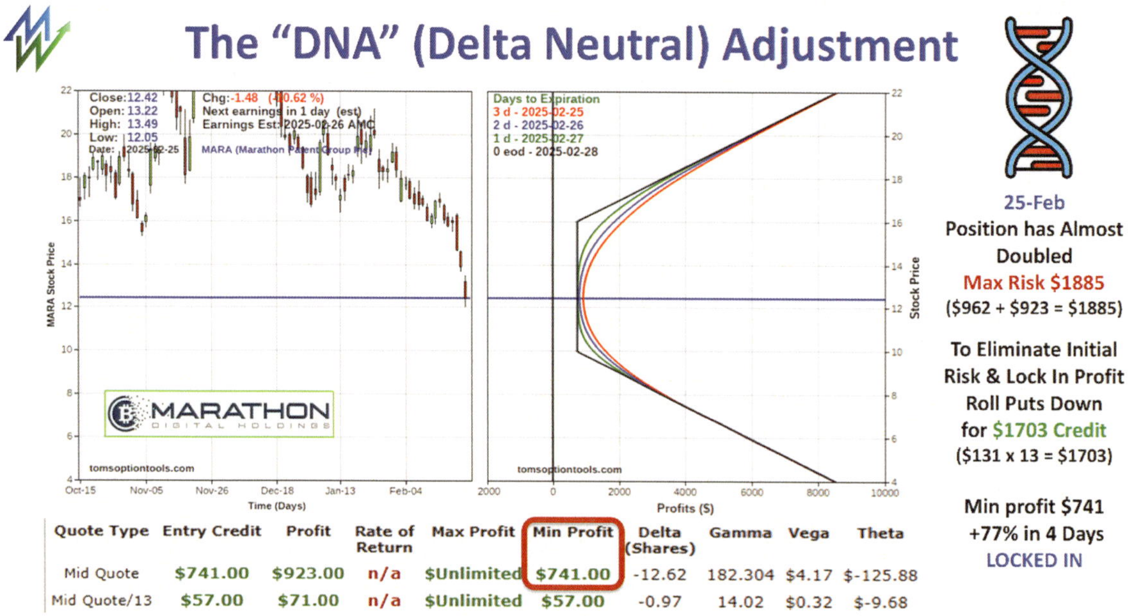

Delta reduced, profits locked. This is precision adjustment.

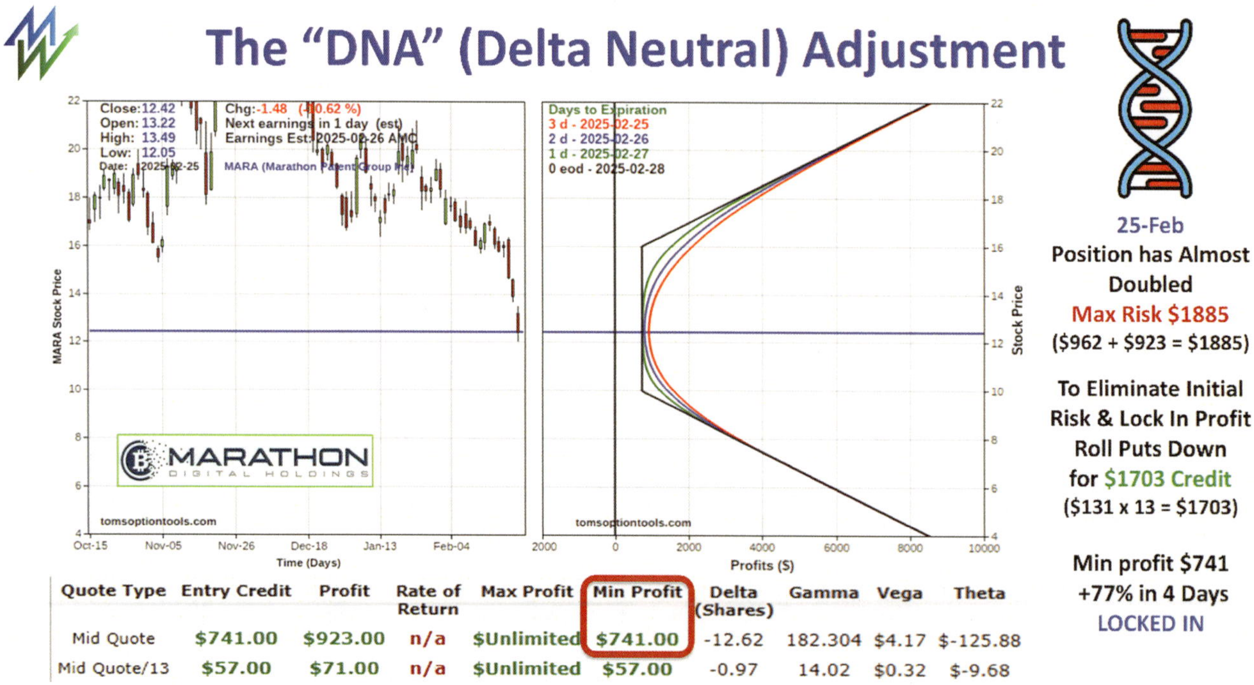

Post-adjustment risk graph confirms minimum $741 profit is locked in.

Feb 28 – Option Expiration (Adjusted Trade)

On expiration day, both options expired worthless. Thanks to the “DNA” adjustment, we walked away with a guaranteed profit of $741—a 77% return in seven days.

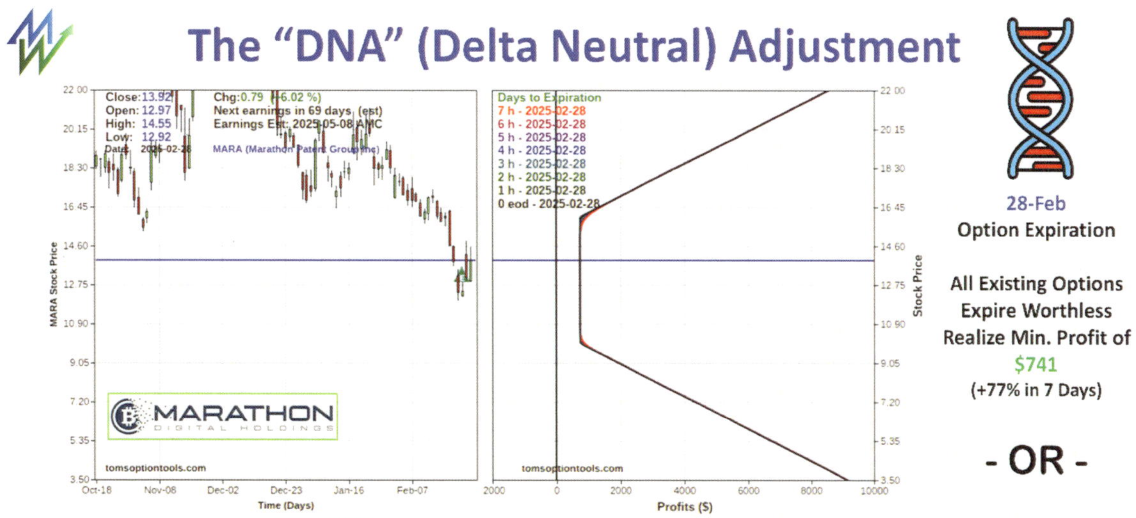

Quote Type	Entry Credit	Profit	Rate of Return	Max Profit	Min Profit	Delta (Shares)	Gamma	Vega	Theta
Mid Quote	$741.00	$741.00	n/a	$Unlimited	$741.00	0.00	0.002	$0.00	$0.00
Mid Quote/13	$57.00	$57.00	n/a	$Unlimited	$57.00	0.00	0.00	$0.00	$0.00

Adjusted trade expiration: safe, risk-free outcome.

Feb 28 – Option Expiration (Unadjusted Trade)

Had we not adjusted, the trade would have resulted in a full loss of the $962 debit. The trade expired worthless—a painful but preventable -100% result.

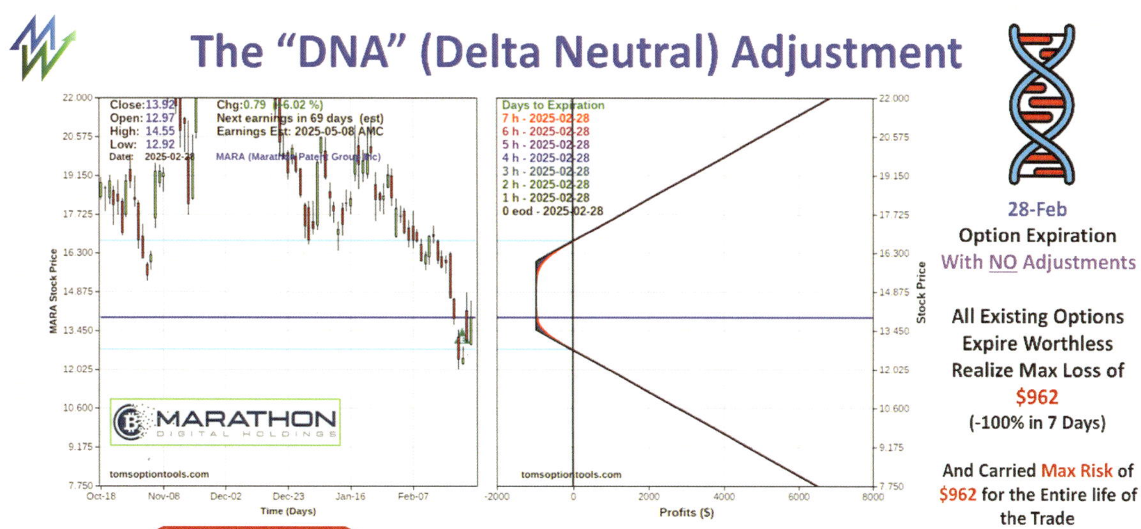

Quote Type	Entry Debit	Profit	Rate of Return	Max Profit	Max Risk	Delta (Shares)	Gamma	Vega	Theta
Mid Quote	$962.00	$-962.00	-100.0%	$Unlimited	$-962.00	-160.82	711.425	$1.04	$-170.92
Mid Quote/13	$74.00	$-74.00	-100.0%	$Unlimited	$-74.00	-12.37	54.73	$0.08	$-13.15

Without adjustment, the trade ended in a total loss.

Final Comparison: Adjusted vs Unadjusted

Here's how the adjustment impacted the MARA trade compared to leaving it unadjusted:

	Adjusted Trade	**Unadjusted Trade**
Profit	$741	-$962
ROI	77%	-100%
Risk Carried	None after lock-in	Full $962
Outcome Certainty	Guaranteed profit	Total loss
Emotional Benefit	Confidence + peace of mind	Stressful loss potential

Summary – Take Control of Risk and Lock in Opportunity

The "DNA" adjustment is about taking control of directional risk—whether the trade is winning or under pressure—and removing the market's ability to hurt you. As Delta expands, it creates exposure that can quickly work against you. By neutralizing that Delta, you reduce or eliminate that risk, protect profits when they're there, and stabilize the trade when they're not.

This is not about "restoring balance". It's about regaining control, improving your position, and, in many cases, converting the trade into a defined or even guaranteed outcome. Professional traders don't rely on being right. They manage risk, adapt quickly, and position themselves so the structure does the work.

Now that you understand how to control directional risk, the next step is to develop a deeper, working mastery of the **Greeks**—so you can see these opportunities before they happen and act with precision.

CHAPTER 9

DEEP DIVE INTO THE GREEKS

CHAPTER 9
Deep Dive into the Greeks

You've seen the Greeks before. We introduced them earlier as the key to reading your trades like a pro. But now it's time to go deeper. Because if you want to master the art of adjustments, you need more than just a surface understanding. You need to know how each Greek works—how it shifts, how it signals, and how to use it to play the game smarter.

Let me be clear:

- The Greeks aren't here to confuse you.
- They're here to empower you.
- They give you a dashboard—a way to read your position and predict what's likely to happen next.

Think of your trade like a position on the chessboard. Each Greek shows you how that position behaves under pressure.

Overview of the Greeks

- **Delta** shows your directional bias.
- **Gamma** reveals how that bias might accelerate.
- **Vega** tells you how sensitive your trade is to implied volatility.
- **Theta** tracks the silent pull of time.
- **Rho** (our quieter cousin) shows how interest rates might affect things.

Option Greeks Deep Dive

What are they and what are they telling you?

	Name	Sensitivity to:
Δ	**D**elta	Price **D**irection
Γ	**G**amma	**G**o or Don't **G**o (Gas Pedal)
ν	**V**ega	Implied **V**olatility
Θ	**T**heta	**T**ime Decay
Ρ	**R**ho	Interest **R**ates

Let's Go Deeper!

You don't have to be a math genius. You just need to understand what each number means and how to respond.

By the end of this section, you'll have real clarity on how to manage your positions like a Grandmaster. You'll see risk before it hits. You'll know when to adjust—and when to wait.

Let's break them down one at a time. Starting with the most essential Greek of them all: Delta.

Delta: Price Direction

Delta is your first and most important Greek. It plays several roles in your trade—and understanding them provides you with valuable insights.

Delta: Price Direction

Δ

Delta plays an Important Multifaceted Role!

1. **Delta** identifies the **Position** as being Bullish, Bearish or Neutral regarding stock price movement.
2. **Delta** identifies the rate an **Option** price changes relative to the price change of the underlying asset.
3. **Delta** identifies the odds that an **Option** will expire "In the Money" (ITM) OR "Out of the Money" (OTM).

Here's what Delta tells you:

1. **Directional Bias:** Delta identifies whether your position is bullish, bearish, or neutral.
    - A positive Delta means your trade benefits when the stock goes up.
    - A negative Delta means your trade benefits when the stock goes down.
    - A Delta near zero? That's a neutral position. You're not betting on direction.
2. **Rate of Change:** Delta tells you how much your position will gain or lose when the stock moves $1.
    - If your Delta is +30, and the stock rises $1, you'll gain about $30.
    - If your Delta is +30, and the stock drops $1, you'll lose about $30.
    - If your Delta is -30, and the stock rises $1, you'll lose about $30.
    - If your Delta is -30 and the stock drops $1, you'll gain about $30.
3. **Probability:** Delta also approximates the probability that an option will finish risk/reward (ITM).
    - A Delta of 50? About a 50/50 chance.
    - A Delta of 80? Roughly 80% chance the option will finish in the money.
    - A Delta of 20? Low odds—but maybe a high reward.

Delta forms the foundation of your position's risk and reward profile. When Delta changes, your position's core personality changes. Therefore, learning to read and adjust Delta is your first step toward mastery.

Now, let's look at a visual that brings this to life.

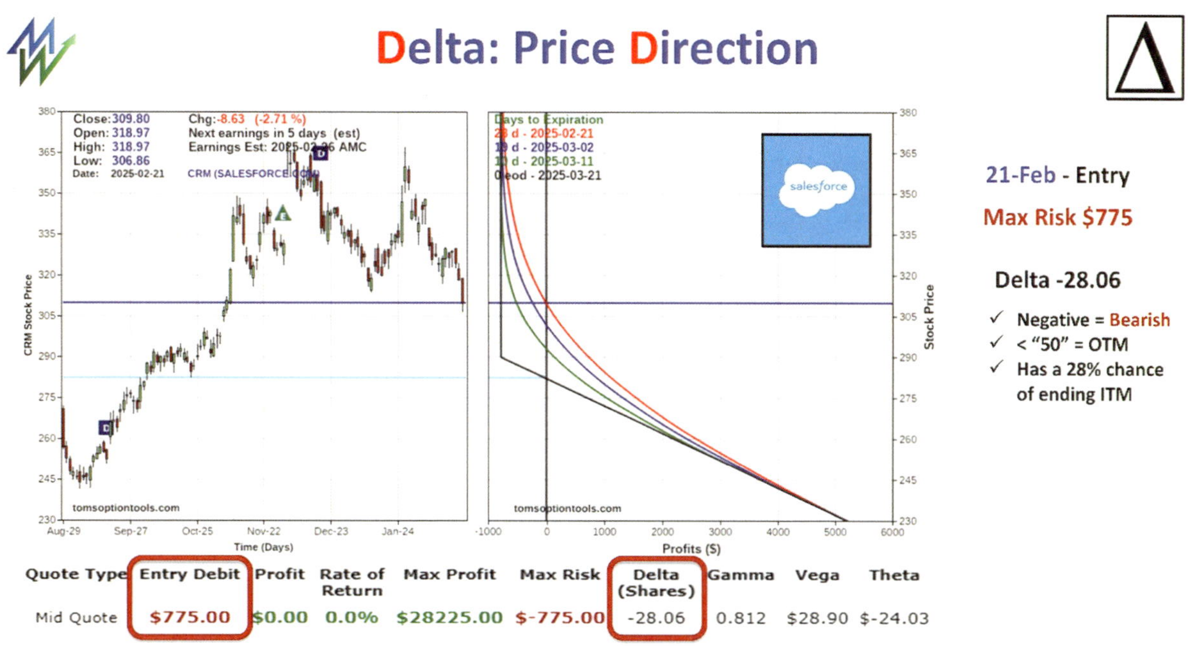

A Delta of -28.06 indicates that if SALESFORCE.COM (CRM) drops $1, the position will gain $28.06 from Delta.

Gamma: Acceleration and Sensitivity

If Delta shows the direction your trade wants to go, Gamma is the gas pedal.

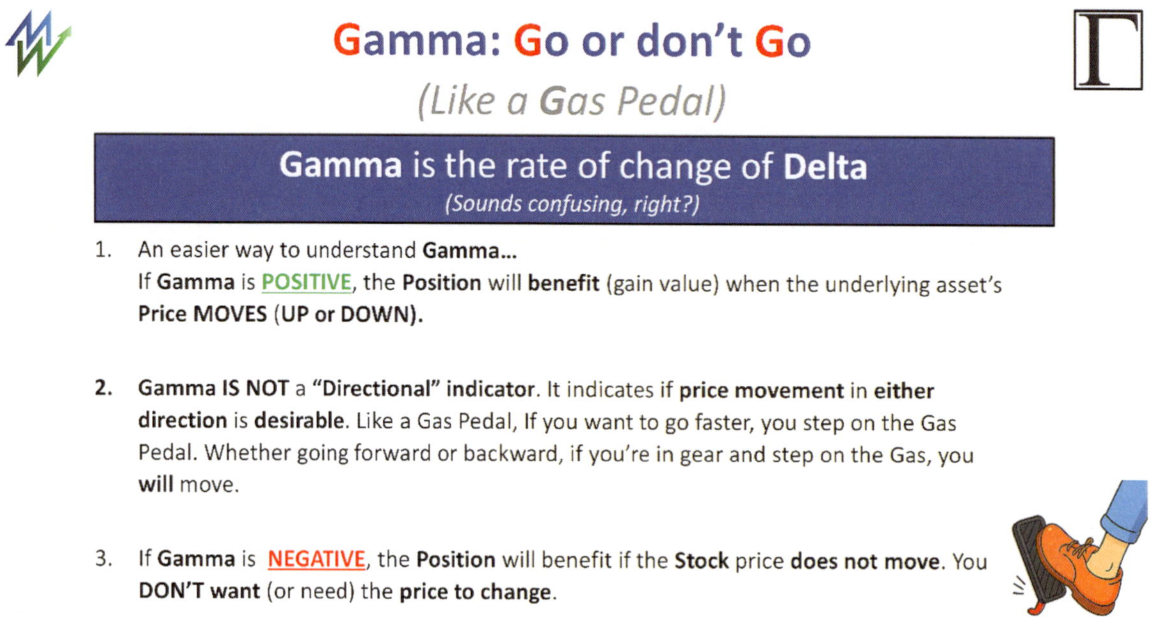

Gamma tells you how fast your Delta will change as the stock moves. It's not a directional Greek. It doesn't matter which way the stock is moving. It just tells you how quickly your position's directional sensitivity to price (Delta) will accelerate.

You can think of Gamma like this:

- **High Gamma?** You're pressing hard on the gas. Your Delta will change quickly.
- **Low Gamma?** You're coasting. Delta is fairly stable.

Gamma plays a critical role in fast-moving markets and near expiration—where small moves can lead to big Delta changes.

- Gamma measures how much your Delta changes when the stock price moves $1.
- A positive Gamma means your position will benefit from price movement—in either direction.
- A negative Gamma means your position prefers the stock to stay still.
- Gamma increases as expiration approaches—especially for At-the-Money(ATM) options.
- Here's a graphic that introduces Gamma using the gas pedal metaphor.

This real CRM trade shows Gamma of 0.812—meaning Delta will increase by about 0.81 if the stock drops $1. Another way to think about this is that as the stock drops, Gamma increases Delta and you make incrementally more the further the stock drops.

Vega: Implied Volatility

Alright, you've now seen how Delta gives your position its directional voice, and how Gamma acts like the gas pedal—speeding up that voice as the stock moves. But what happens when the market becomes unpredictable? Or when things go quiet and implied volatility drops?

That's where Vega steps in.

Vega measures how your trade is affected by implied volatility (IV). Basically, IV reflects how much movement the market anticipates going forward, but it can also be seen as demand.

Think of Vega like the wind in a sail. You can have the perfect boat (Delta), with your foot on the pedal (Gamma), but if the wind quiets (low Vega or decreasing IV), you'll end up moving slowly.

On the flip side, when IV increases, your option can gain value simply because the market expects more action or demand for your options is rising. Combine that with a good Delta and Gamma, and you'll reach your goal faster.

Vega: Implied Volatility

Vega measures the sensitivity to changes in Implied Volatility

1. The definition of **Volatility** is how much the price of a financial instrument fluctuates over time.
2. A way to think of **Implied Volatility (IV)** is the "Expected" price movement over time. In other words, how much expected (implied) volatility are we looking for in the future.
3. The **Greek Vega** is a way to measure our sensitivity to that future **Implied Volatility**.
4. If **Vega** is a **positive** value, the **Position** will benefit if **Implied Volatility (IV) increases** going forward.
5. If **Vega** is **negative**, then the opposite is true.
6. If **IV** is currently on the low side of its average and we expect it to increase, trading **Option Positions** with a **positive Vega** would be appropriate.
7. That said, if **IV** is high compared to its average and we expect it to decrease, having a **negative Vega** is best.

So, let's dive in and take a look at what Vega's really telling you.

Vega: Implied Volatility

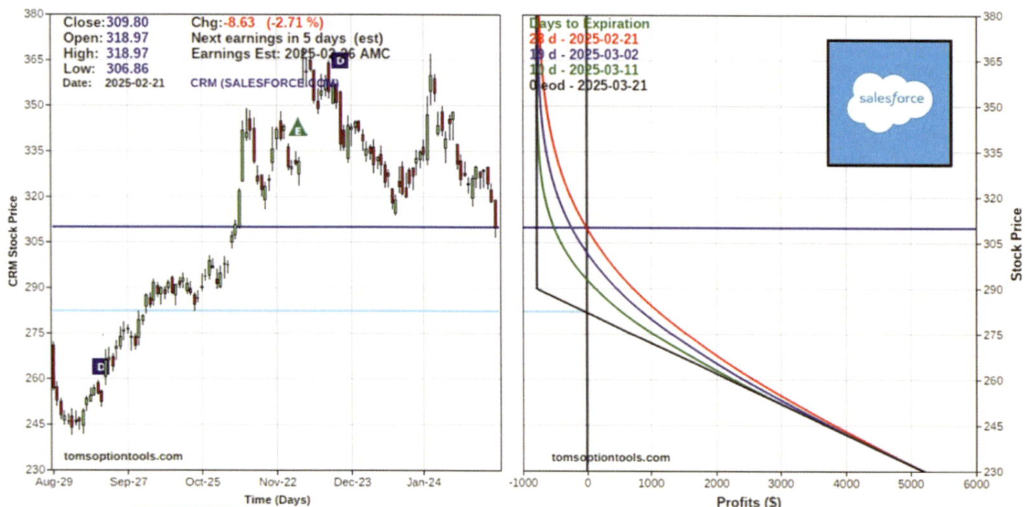

21-Feb - Entry

Max Risk $775

Vega +$28.90

- ✓ **Positive = Position will benefit if IV increases**
- ✓ **Position will lose if IV decreases**

Quote Type	Entry Debit	Profit	Rate of Return	Max Profit	Max Risk	Delta (Shares)	Gamma	Vega	Theta
Mid Quote	$775.00	$0.00	0.0%	$28225.00	$-775.00	-28.06	0.812	$28.90	$-24.03

To summarize, Vega measures how much your option's price will change as implied volatility shifts. If Vega is positive and IV increases, your position gains. If IV decreases, it loses.

Here's our CRM trade again. Take a look at the Vega reading: +28.90.

That means for every 1-point increase in implied volatility, our position gains $28.90 in value. But the reverse is also true: If IV drops by a point, we lose $28.90.

That's the hidden power (and risk) of Vega. It doesn't care about price direction. It cares about how jumpy the market expects the stock to be.

This is why when you enter a trade, you need to ask:

- Is implied volatility currently low or high?
- Do I expect it to rise or fall during the life of my trade?

That's how you align Vega to your strategy. Use it wisely. It's one of the stealthiest forces in the game.

Theta: Time Decay

Theta measures the impact of time passing—specifically, how much your option position gains or loses during a single day.

Theta is negative for long options and positive for short options. One way to think about negative Theta is: "How much will I lose or make if I hold this position for one more day?" On the flip side, a positive Theta shows how much you will gain if you hold the position for one more day.

Unlike the other Greeks, Theta is based on a certainty: Time will pass. That makes it the most predictable of the Greeks. It's a key metric, especially when planning the timing of your entries and exits.

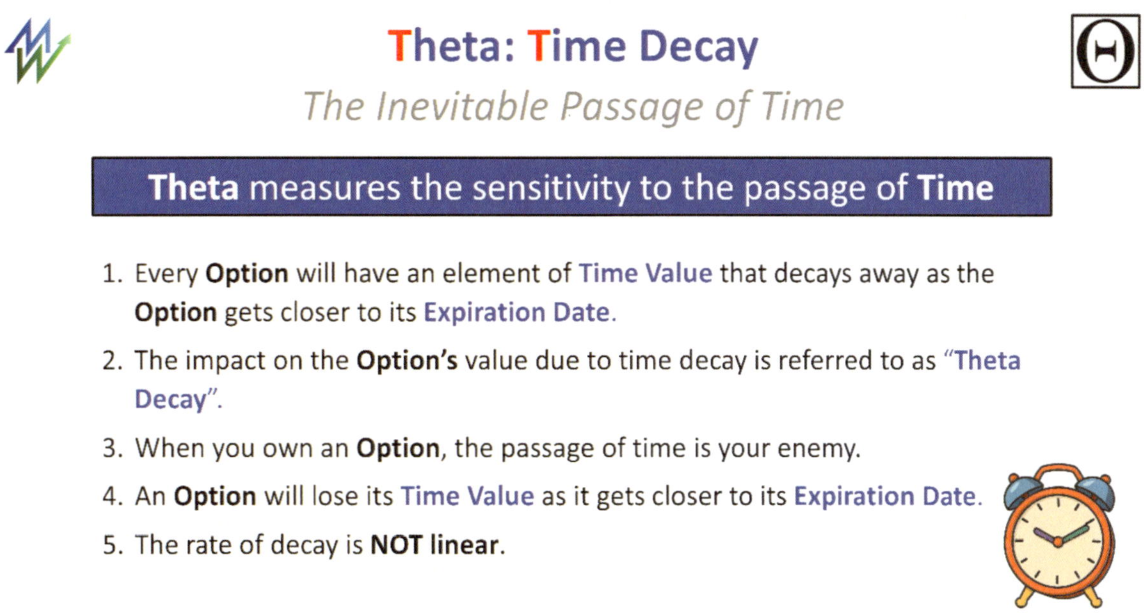

However, Theta decay is not linear; it accelerates as the trade approaches expiration. The most significant decay happens in the last 30 days before expiration, where the time value declines rapidly. That's why traders often prefer to short options during this time. They can benefit from this rapid decay.

Conversely, when purchasing options, it's typically wiser to choose a 60 to 90-day timeframe, where time decay is slower, and you give your trade more time to succeed.

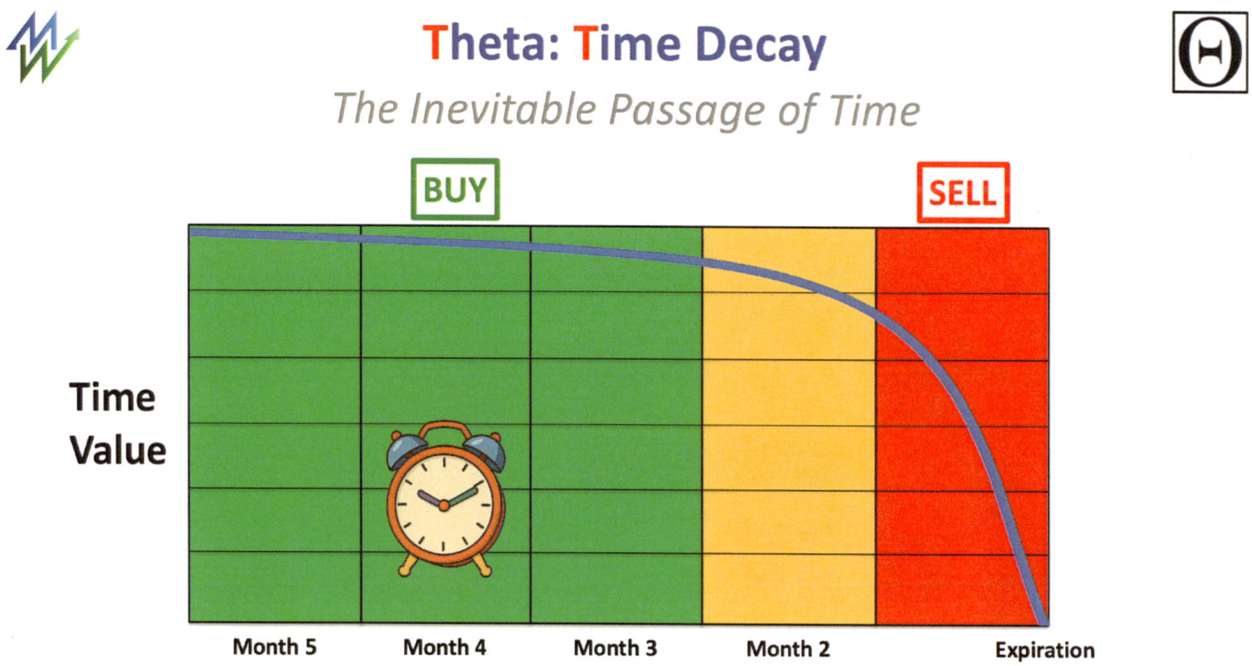

Let's look at this CRM long put example.

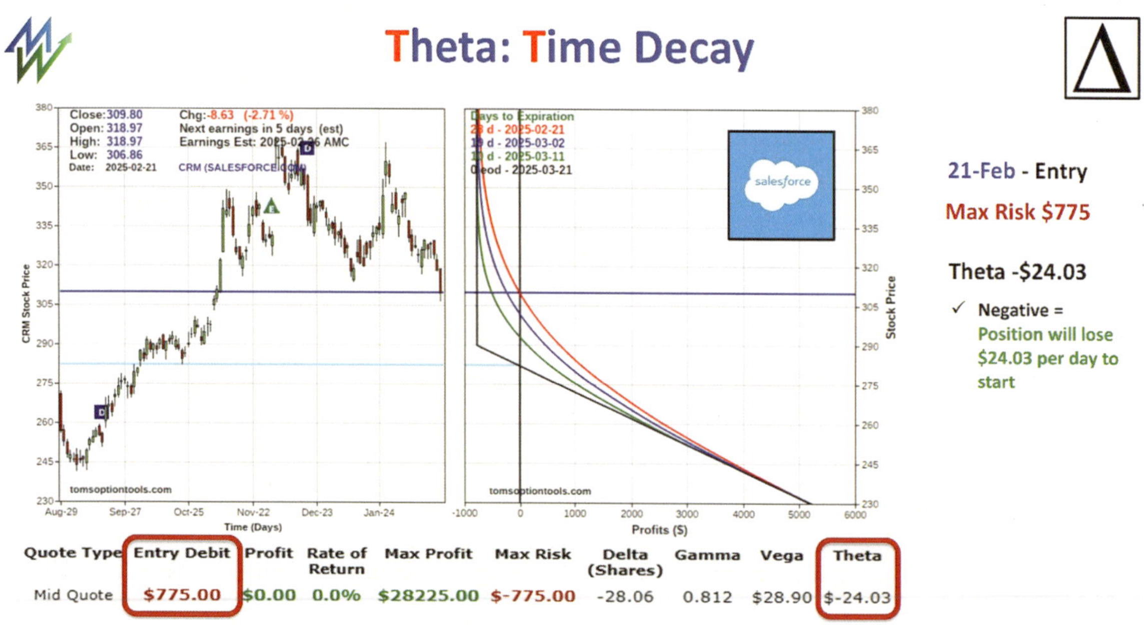

In this position, Theta is -$24.03. That means this trade will lose $24.03 in value each day due to the passage of time, assuming all other conditions remain unchanged. Since this is a long option, that Theta cost represents a real daily erosion of your premium.

Understanding this helps you recognize when time is working for or against you—and how quickly.

Rho: Interest Rates

Rho is the Greek that measures how sensitive your position is to changes in interest rates. While it doesn't receive as much attention as Delta, Gamma, Vega, or Theta, it still influences the overall pricing of an option—especially in long-dated options or during major shifts in interest rate policy.

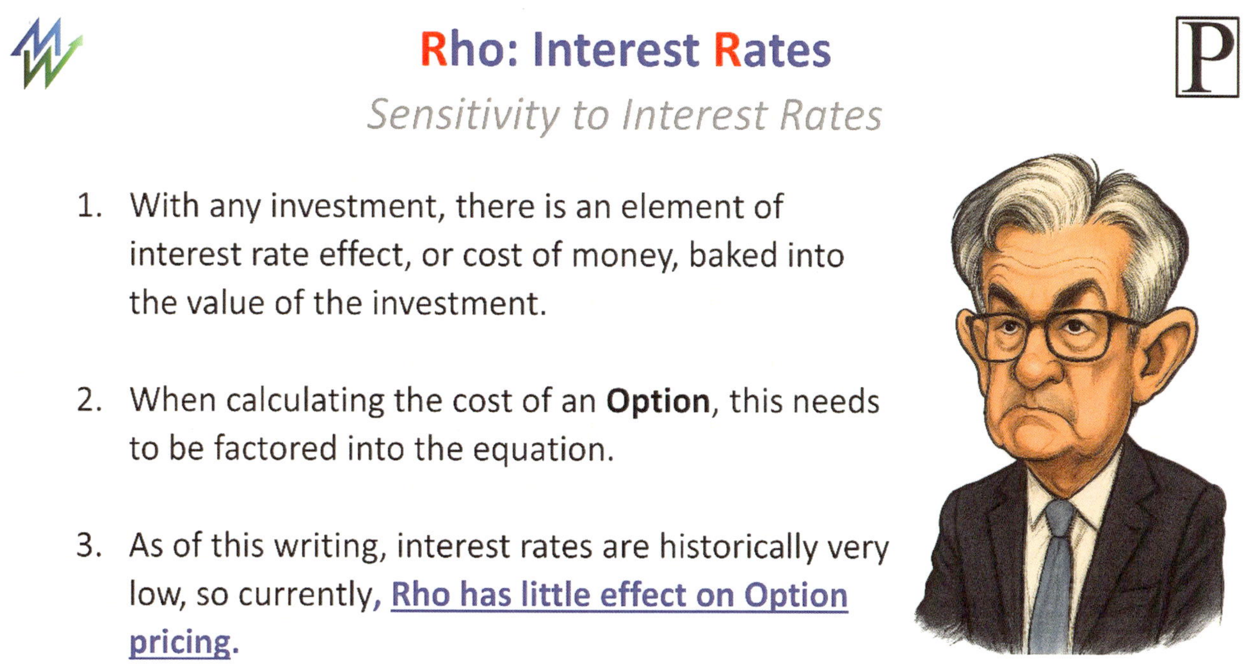

With any investment, there's an element of the cost of money—the opportunity cost—which is included in the option's premium. That's what Rho represents. If Rho is positive, your position benefits if interest rates rise.

If Rho is negative, it benefits when rates fall. But here's the thing: Interest rates don't change daily, and their movements tend to be gradual, meaning Rho's impact is often small unless you're trading LEAPS or holding positions for a long period.

As of this writing, interest rates are historically low, so Rho has little effect on short-term option trades and adjustments. Still, it's important to recognize that it's part of the overall picture.

Summary - Mastering the Engine Behind Every Trade

Now the playbook goes deeper.

This chapter builds on your earlier understanding and sharpens it—moving from basic awareness of the Greeks to **working mastery**. The focus here is not just what Delta, Gamma, Vega, and Theta are, but how they interact and evolve as the trade develops.

You begin to see that:

- **Delta** is not static. It shifts with price
- **Gamma** controls how fast that shift happens
- **Theta** is always working, but not always in your favor
- **Vega** can quietly become the biggest risk driver

This is where trades stop being simple shapes on a graph and start becoming **living, moving systems**.

The key takeaway:
Every adjustment you make is really a Greek decision.

Once you understand this, you stop reacting to P&L and start managing the underlying forces directly.

Now that you understand how these forces behave in detail, the next step is learning how to anticipate one of the biggest hidden drivers of option pricing—**Implied Volatility**.

CHAPTER 10

PREDICTING IV MOVEMENT

CHAPTER 10
Predicting IV Movement

Predicting IV Movement

Harnessing the Power of VEGA

Implied Volatility (IV) is the market's forecast of how much a stock is likely to move within a certain period. It is not based on past data. It's forward-looking, calculated from current option prices. When demand for options increases, IV rises. When demand decreases, IV falls.

Apart from the passage of time—which affects Theta with 100% certainty—IV is the second most predictable factor that influences option prices. Fortunately, there are reliable patterns and behaviors that enable us to forecast IV changes, giving you the power to harness Vega strategically.

The Typical IV and Stock Relationship

Typically, stock price and IV are negatively correlated. When stocks go up, IV usually falls. When stocks fall, IV tends to rise. Think of IV as a fear indicator—when the market drops, traders become fearful, demand for options increases, and IV spikes. When stocks go up, the market tends to be calm, and IV generally declines.

Take a look at this chart of SPY overlaid with IV (red line). You can clearly see this inverse relationship.

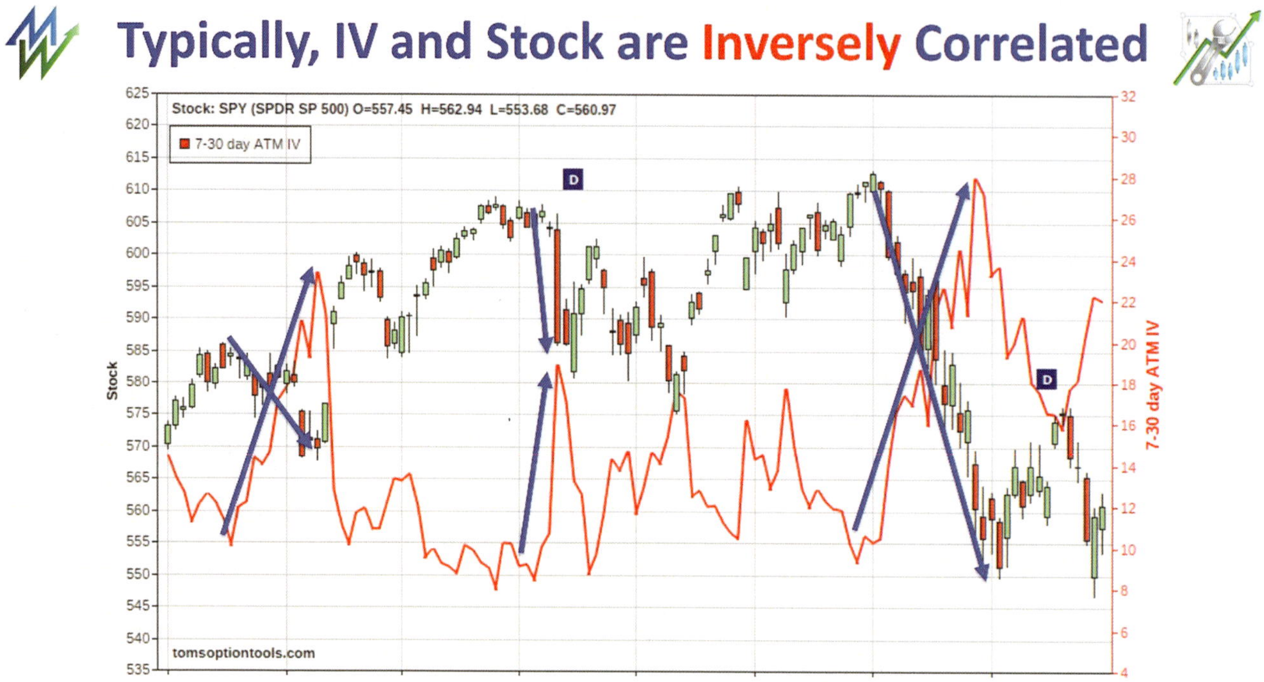

Exception: Short ETFs and VIX Instruments

There are exceptions where IV and stock prices are positively correlated. Short ETFs—like SQQQ—and volatility products—like VXX or UVXY—derive their value from market declines or implied volatility itself. In these instruments, when the underlying price rises, IV also tends to rise.

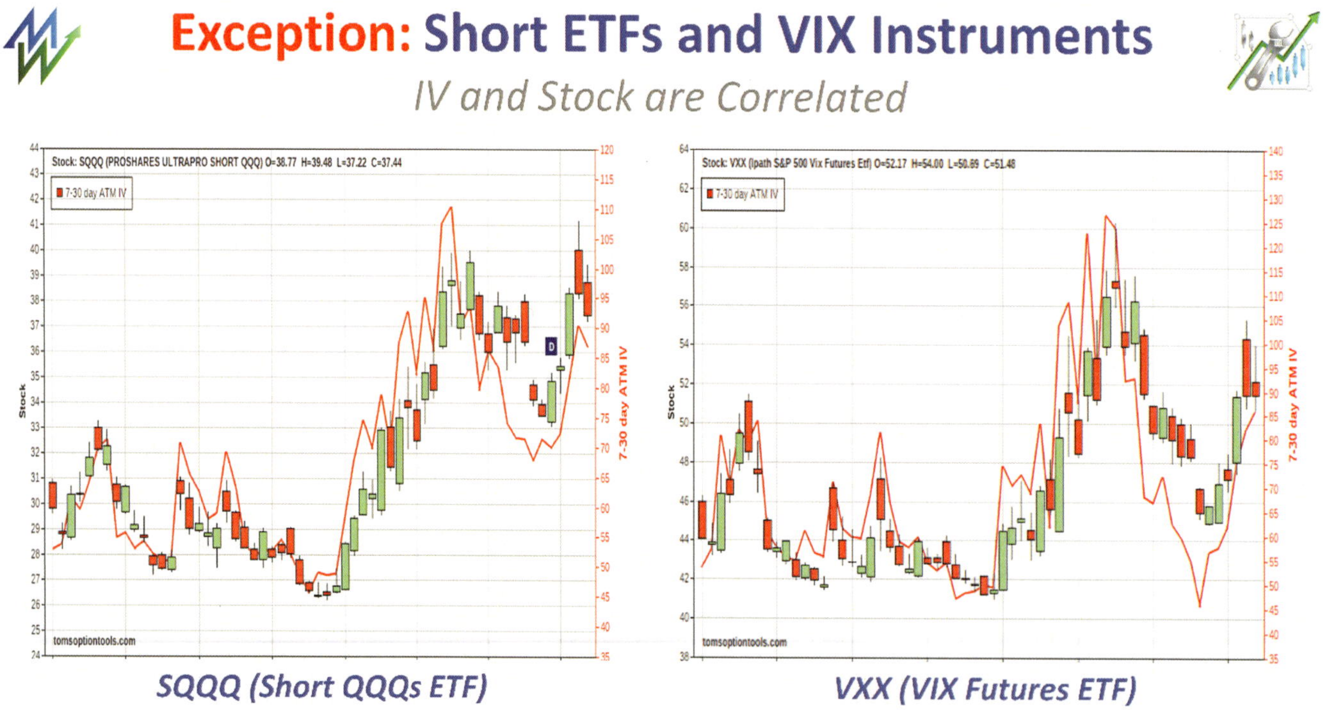

This makes sense. For example, when the QQQs fall, fear increases, IV rises—and the SQQQs (inverse QQQs) go up, carrying that IV increase with them. Similarly, VIX-based ETFs reflect the VIX index, which indicates the average IV of SPX options. If market fear grows, so does the VIX, and so does IV in these instruments.

Exception: IV Rush and Crush Around Earnings

Implied Volatility Rushes Up Before Earnings... and Crashes After

One of the most powerful and predictable movements in IV comes from earnings announcements.

IV Rush: Before Earnings

When a company is approaching its earnings date, traders start piling into options expecting a big move. And what happens when demand for options surges?

You got it—IV goes up. This is what we call the IV Rush.

This rush usually begins 7 to 14 days before earnings, when traders start positioning themselves for the announcement, aiming to catch the post-earnings move.

This means that if you're long options (like a long call or a long put) and you enter 7–14 days before earnings, your position will benefit from the Vega dollars resulting from IV rising—as long as you have positive Vega.

You don't even need the stock to move—Vega handles the heavy lifting as IV inflates with anticipation of the announcement.

Take a look at this chart of FedEx (FDX).

With 13 days to earnings, the IV is already starting to rise as it did the prior earnings

period (earnings dates are signified by green "E" triangles). This is a very reliable pattern for most stocks, allowing us to have a solid IV prognosis of up to 7-14 days before a scheduled earnings announcement.

IV Crush: After Earnings

But what goes up must come down.

Right after the earnings announcement, the demand that caused IV to rise disappears. The event is over. The mystery has been revealed. The news is out.

And with that—IV tanks. This is the infamous IV Crush.

If you're holding long options with positive Vega after earnings, you'll likely face Vega losses. It doesn't matter what the stock does—if IV drops sharply and you're not out of the trade, you'll give back a big chunk of the gains.

That's why you'll often hear me say: "You get in before earnings... and you get out before the announcement."

Look at what happened to FedEx right after their earnings were released.

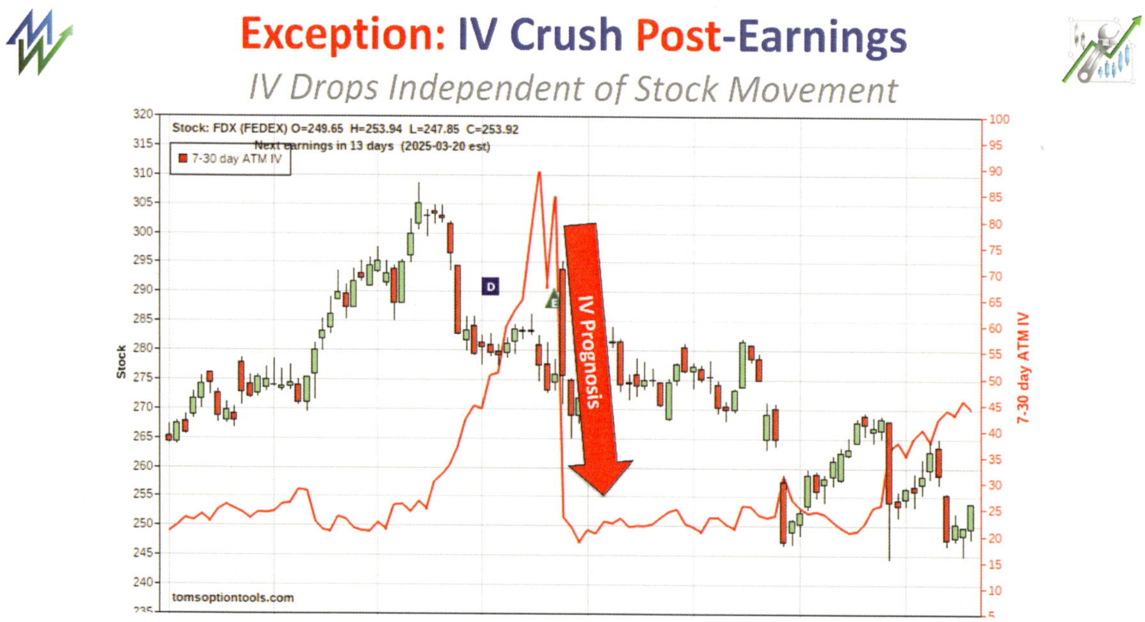

- **To harness IV Rush**, enter your long option trade about 7–14 days before earnings when IV is likely to rise.
- **To avoid IV Crush**, exit before earnings are announced—otherwise, even a good directional trade can lose money from a collapsing IV.

Aligning Vega with IV Prognosis Examples

Once you've made an IV prognosis, you want to align the sign of Vega with that forecast. If IV is likely to rise, you want a positive Vega. If IV is likely to fall, look for a negative Vega.

Example:1 Pre-Earnings Long Call on FedEx

On March 7, 2025, FedEx (FDX) has 13 days until earnings. Historically, its IV increases as earnings approach. With a bullish stock outlook and a positive IV forecast, buying a call that expires after earnings provides you with positive Delta and Vega.:

- **Delta:** +42.98
- **Vega:** +19.51

If the stock moves up $1 and IV rises by 1%, the trade gains roughly $62.49 ($42.98 from Delta and $19.51 from Vega).

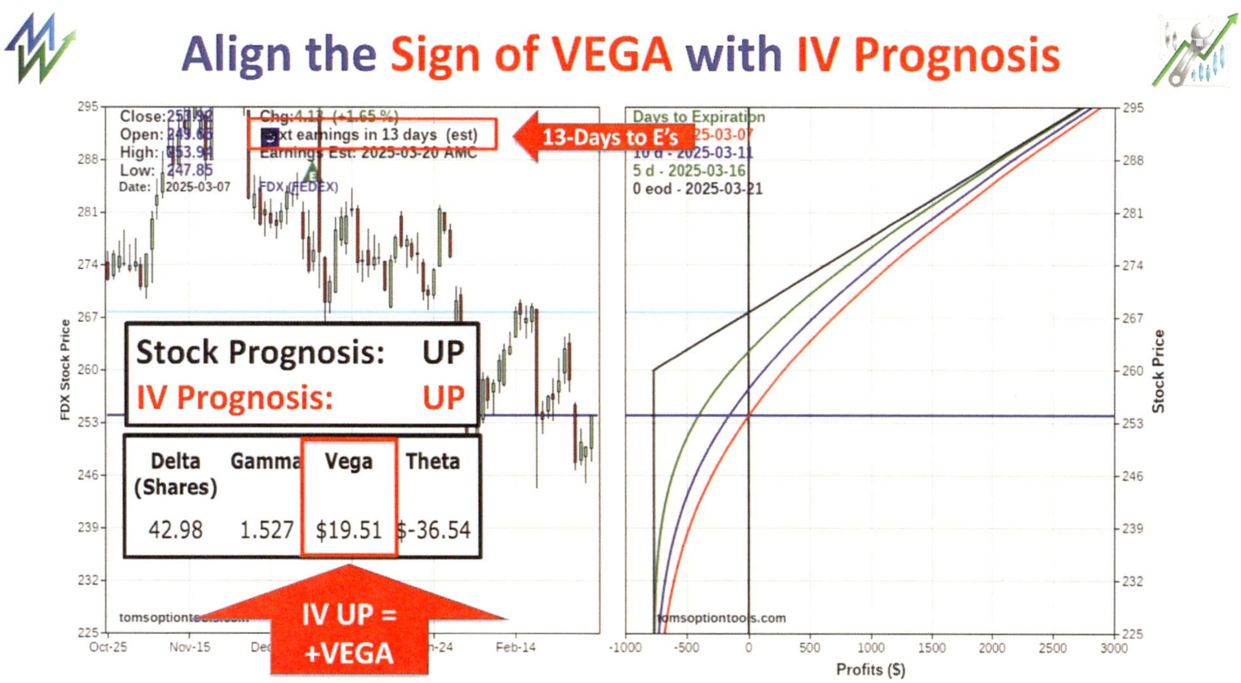

Example 2: Post-Earnings Broken Wing Butterfly

Now that you've seen classic pre-earnings IV rush trade, let's examine a very different type of play—a broken wing butterfly (BWB) setup on Wheaton Precious Metals (WPM).

This trade was entered on March 19, 2025, right after WPM delivered a strong earnings report. With positive momentum on the chart and fresh bullish sentiment, our stock outlook was clearly UP.

Here's where it gets interesting: BWBs are three-legged options strategies designed to profit from directional moves and time decay. Unlike the long call in the FedEx example, this WPM BWB had a positive Theta of +$3.60—meaning each day passing added value to our trade.

Now, let's look at implied volatility (IV). Usually, after a stock reports earnings, the IV drops, especially if the news was already priced in or if implied volatility was driven up in anticipation. That's the case here. IV was expected to decrease, so our IV outlook was DOWN.

And what do we want when IV is likely to fall? Negative Vega, and we have it. This BWB trade had a Vega of -$1.41. So, if IV dropped by 1 point, the trade would gain $1.41 from Vega alone—a nice edge.

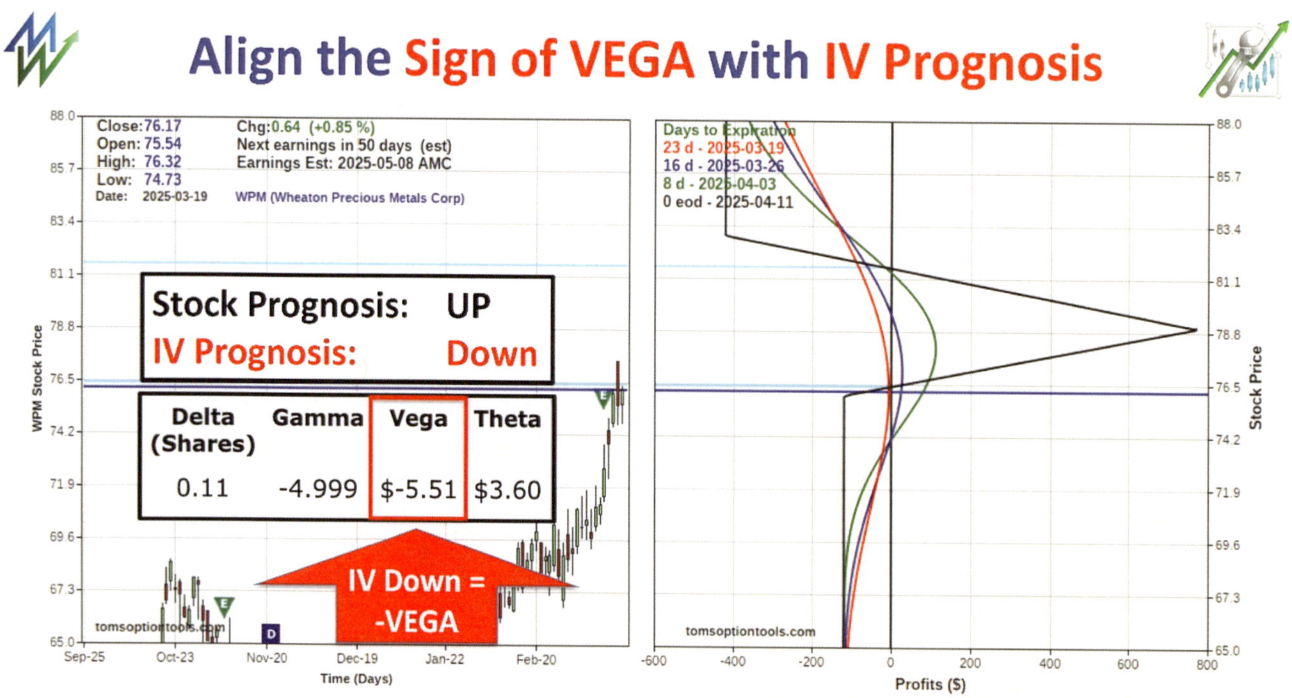

Bottom line: This was post-earnings, bullish setup with:

- A stock prognosis of UP (bullish setup)
- An IV prognosis of DOWN (IV tends to drop on a rising stock)
- A positive Theta of +$3.60 (time on our side)
- A negative Vega of -$1.41 (aligned with anticipated IV drop)

All three Greeks—Delta, Vega, and Theta—were aligned with our forecast, giving us a well-structured edge in the trade.

Summary – Anticipating the Invisible Force

This chapter introduces one of the most overlooked edges in options trading: **implied volatility movement.**

While price gets most of the attention, IV often determines whether a trade actually wins or loses. This chapter teaches you to think ahead—not just about where price might go, but how volatility is likely to behave.

You begin to recognize:

- IV expands during uncertainty and contracts after events
- Timing matters just as much as direction
- Entering trades at high or low IV changes the entire risk profile

This is where traders separate from gamblers.

Because instead of reacting to volatility shifts, you start planning for them:

- Positioning before expansion
- Protecting against contraction
- Aligning strategies with expected iv behavior

The deeper insight:
You're not just trading price. You're trading expectations.

And now, we're ready to take it one step further. In the next chapter, we'll discuss the most vital distinction that will guide your adjustment decisions: **Aligning Delta, Gamma, Vega and Theta with your stock, IV, and time forecast.**

CHAPTER 11

DERIVING A 3-PART PROGNOSIS

CHAPTER 11
Deriving a 3-Part Prognosis

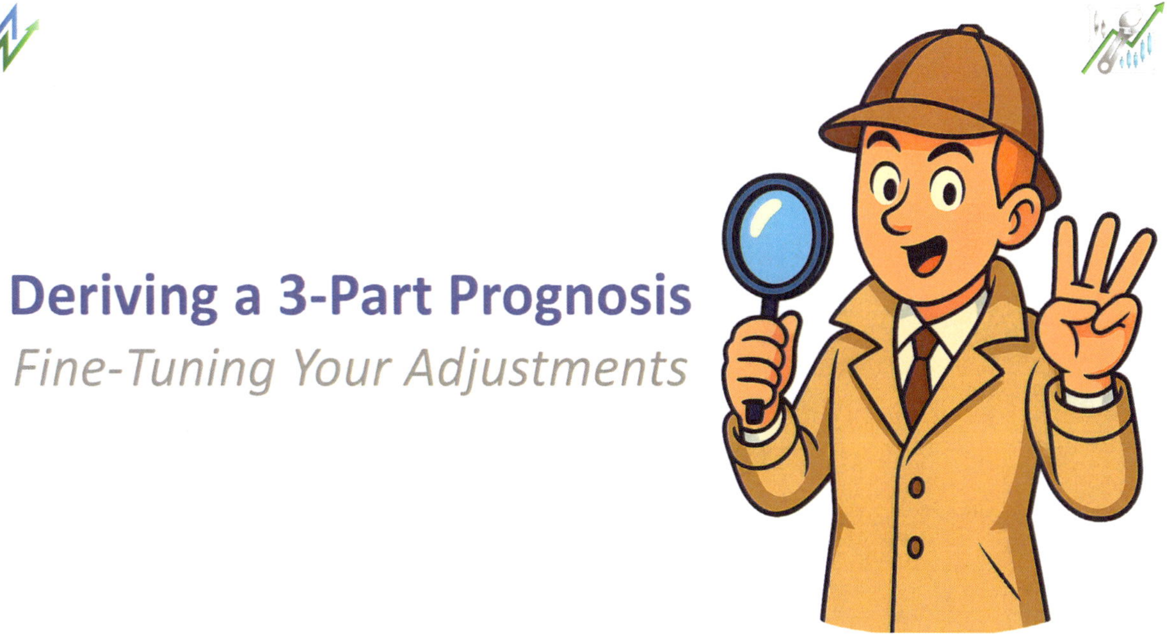

In order to have a place to stand with your trade and truly harness the power of the Greeks, it's vital that you derive a 3-part prognosis.

You do this both at the beginning of the trade and throughout the life of the trade—especially when you're evaluating whether to adjust or simply invoke the ultimate adjustment: Close and bail.

It's important to have an opinion about three things:

1. Where the stock is likely to move **(Direction)**
2. What the Implied Volatility **(IV)** will do
3. How long your outlook is valid **(Time)**

This chapter guides you through that three-part process—so you can confidently align your Delta, Vega, and Gamma with your evolving outlook.

Again, when starting or adjusting trades, estimate what might happen to the stock price, the IV, and how long you plan to stay in the trade.

Refer to the chart below for the common prognoses in each of the three areas.

Deriving a 3-Part Prognosis

Option positions are **sensitive to 3 primary things:**

1. **Stock Direction** *(DELTA)* — Up, Down, Flat, Volatile
2. **IV Fluctuations** *(VEGA)* — Up, Down, Flat, Volatile
3. **Passage of Time** *(THETA)* — 7, 14, 30, 60, 90+ Days

*When initiating or adjusting trades, **derive a prognosis** of what may happen to the **stock price**, the **IV**, and **how much time** you intend to be in the trade.*

Delta and Vega Alignment

Now that you know how to create a 3-part prognosis, it's time to refine your adjustments by aligning two key Greeks: Delta and Vega. This is one of the most valuable habits you can develop as a trader.

Here's your mantra: Match the sign of your Delta with your directional prognosis, and match the sign of your Vega with your IV prognosis.

The chart below summarizes what signs of Delta and Vega you want based on your market view. Let's walk through it:

- If your **directional prognosis is UP**, you want a **POSITIVE Delta**—because a $1 stock up move adds dollars to your trade.
- If your **IV prognosis is UP**, you want a **POSITIVE Vega**—because a 1% rise in IV will also add dollars to your position.
- If your **directional prognosis is DOWN**, then **Delta should be NEGATIVE**—so that you profit from price drops.
- Likewise, **if your IV prognosis is DOWN, Vega should be NEGATIVE**—because falling volatility will benefit your position.

Deriving a 3-Part Prognosis

Match Signs of Delta and Vega with Prognosis

Prognosis	Desired Delta	Desired Vega
Up	***Positive***	***Positive***
Down	***Negative***	***Negative***
Sideways	***Neutral***	****Neutral***
Volatile	***Neutral***	****Neutral***

**Note: There are exceptions for desired Vega with a sideways or volatile directional prognosis.*

TIP

Match the sign of delta with your directional prognosis + match the sign of Vega with your IV prognosis.

Now, if you're predicting that the stock will move SIDEWAYS or be VOLATILE (like a potential breakout), then you usually want a NEUTRAL Delta—close to zero. That way, you're not overly exposed to direction.

As for Vega, it depends. If IV is expected to stay flat, Vega's impact is minimal—so its sign doesn't matter as much.

However, if IV is expected to stay sideways but you expect a price GAP (up or down), some specific structures can use a positive or negative Vega strategically—more on that in advanced setups.

Again, when starting or modifying trades, forecast what might happen to the stock price, the IV, and how long you plan to stay in the trade. Then, align your Greeks accordingly.

Managing Time Prognosis and Theta

The first thing to note is that if you buy an option, Theta is always negative. This is true for calls, puts, and straddles. There's no getting around it—time is the enemy for long options.

The opposite is true for short options. They have positive Theta and UNLIMITED RISK. That's something to really watch out for. Unlimited risk isn't acceptable in a game that's all about managing risk. We're not gamblers. We're strategic.

Here's a mantra worth remembering:

"How much does it COST me (-Theta) or MAKE me (+Theta) to stay in the trade another day?"

That simple question gives you a solid foundation to evaluate whether holding the position makes sense.

Now, with that said, Theta doesn't operate alone. You need to consider the magnitude of Theta in relation to the other Greeks: Delta, Gamma, and Vega.

If the potential benefit from Delta, Gamma, and Vega outweighs the daily cost of Theta, then it's likely worth staying in the trade another day.

Let's say your Greeks look like this:

- **Delta:** +50
- **Gamma:** +2.00
- **Vega:** -2.00
- **Theta:** -10

If the stock rises by $1, Delta adds $50 to your position.

Gamma accelerates Delta to +52 (so your next $1 move would be even more profitable).

If implied volatility drops 1%, Vega adds $2.00 to the position.

So, net effect: +$52 ($50 for Delta + $2 for Vega).

Even after paying Theta's $10 toll, you're ahead by $42. That's a green light to stay in the trade.

Managing Theta

The main question Theta answers:

How much does it COST me (-Theta) or MAKE me (+Theta) to stay in the trade another day?

Actions to Take

Compare the magnitude of Theta with the magnitudes of Delta, Vega and Gamma to decide if waiting one more day is reasonable.

Adjust to reduce NEGATIVE Theta and possibly turn Theta POSITIVE.

Here's another key takeaway: With the adjustments you're learning in this guide, you'll eventually be able to reduce negative Theta—and even flip it positive.

When you trade with positive Theta, you get to harness the one guaranteed force in all of trading: The passage of time.

10 Basic Moves to Guide Your Adjustments

In this game of options, the goal is not just to survive but to thrive by practicing smart risk management. A key tool you can use is a thorough understanding of how each move impacts the Greeks—Delta, Vega, and Theta.

This section provides a summary of 10 essential adjustment moves—each one a lever you can use to realign your trade with your changing outlook. Whether you're adding or closing long or short calls, puts, or shares of stock, these moves alter your risk profile in very specific ways.

Take a look at the chart below. The left-hand column lists the adjustment move. The next three columns show the additive impact on Delta, Vega, and Theta. Think of each move as a precise instrument in your trading toolkit.

10 Basic Moves and Their Additive Impact on the Greeks

Adjustment Moves	Delta	Vega	Theta
Add Long Call *(Close Short Call)*	*Positive*	*Positive*	*Negative*
Add Long Put *(Close Short Put)*	*Negative*	*Positive*	*Negative*
Add Short Call *(Close Long Call)*	*Negative*	*Negative*	*Positive*
Add Short Put *(Close Long Put)*	*Positive*	*Negative*	*Positive*
Add Long Stock	*Positive*	*N/A*	*N/A*
Add Short Stock	*Negative*	*N/A*	*N/A*

Let's walk through an example. Suppose you've got a bearish position with a negative Delta. But now, based on your 3-part prognosis, you believe the stock is about to rise—and you expect Implied Volatility to climb too.

Your position already has positive Vega, so you should aim to strengthen both your Delta and Vega exposure. A good adjustment would be to add a long call. That provides you with positive Delta and positive Vega—precisely what you're looking for. Alternatively, if you're holding a credit spread, you might achieve the same goal by closing a short call leg.

Now consider the last two rows in the chart—long and short stock. These moves allow you to precisely neutralize Delta. One share of stock carries exactly a +1 Delta. 1 short share carries a -1 Delta. If your position's Delta is +100, shorting 100 shares of stock would reduce your Delta to exactly zero, neutralizing directional risk. This is a classic institutional strategy—powerful, but capital intensive.

Greeks Are Additive

One last example to reinforce this: Greeks are additive. The graphic below shows what happens when we add a short call to a long call, creating a bull call spread. Each row displays the Delta, Gamma, Vega, and Theta for the existing long call and the newly added short call. The resulting Greeks for the combined trade are simply the sum of each Greek. That's how it works—always. Position Greeks are a sum of the leg Greeks.

Here's the key point—every adjustment you make impacts all the Greeks. Delta doesn't move alone. When you change one, the others adjust too. That's why we need to be precise and mindful. In the upcoming chapters, we'll explore how to make these adjustments skillfully and intentionally, using each Greek as a lever to align your trade with your changing outlook.

Adding a Short Call to a Long Call

Greeks are Additive

	Delta (Shares)	Gamma	Vega	Theta
Current Long Call	42.98	1.527	$19.51	$-36.54
	+	+	+	+
Add Short Call	-29.22	-1.331	$-17.07	$32.00
	=	=	=	=
Resulting Greeks	13.76	0.196	$2.44	$-4.54

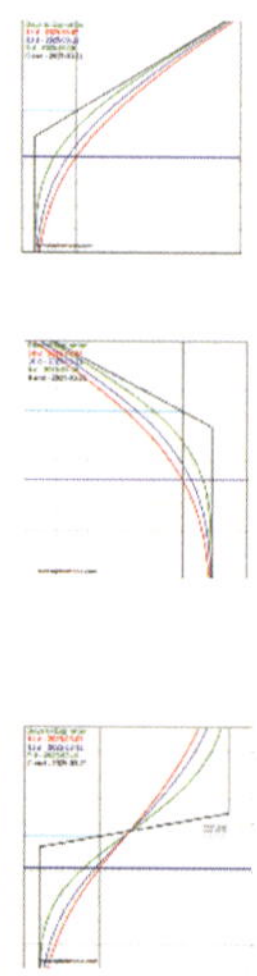

- You can derive a 3-part prognosis—stock direction, IV movement, and time horizon—giving you a foundation to confidently enter or adjust any trade.
- You know how to align the signs of Delta and Vega with your market outlook, ensuring your trades are positioned to win based on what you believe will happen.
- You understand how to manage Theta—the cost or benefit of staying in the trade another day—and compare it against Delta, Vega, and Gamma for smart decision-making.
- You've got the 10 basic adjustment moves memorized (or bookmarked!) and know exactly how they impact the Greeks.
- And finally, you learned that the Greeks are additive, and that every adjustment has a ripple effect across your position. This is how the pros think, plan, and play.

This isn't theory. This is applied skill. Strategic thinking. Chess, not checkers.

Summary - Building a Complete Trade Thesis

This chapter brings structure to your thinking.

The 3-part prognosis gives you a framework to define your outlook before entering or adjusting a trade. Instead of vague opinions, you now form a **clear, actionable thesis.**

The three components work together:

- Direction (where price may go)
- Volatility (how IV may behave)
- Time (how long the move may take)

This is where preparation replaces guesswork.

Every trade—and every adjustment—now has context. You're no longer reacting to movement; you're measuring reality against a defined expectation.

The power of this chapter is discipline:
When your prognosis changes, your trade should change.

This creates consistency, clarity, and confidence in decision-making.

Now that you can define a complete trade thesis, the next step is learning how to act on it—by choosing the right adjustment at the right time. In the next chapter, we'll introduce you to a new simple, powerful adjustment to limit downside risk while keeping your upside in play: **The "Insurance Policy" Adjustment.**

CHAPTER 12

THE "INSURANCE POLICY" ADJUSTMENT

CHAPTER 12
The "Insurance Policy" Adjustment

We insure our homes. We insure our cars. We even insure our lives. So, why do so many traders leave their trades totally exposed?

The Insurance Policy Adjustment

A simple approach to **adding a level of Insurance** to almost any position. Some ways to do so:

- Buying OTM Calls
- Buying OTM Puts

In this game of chess meets trading, your capital is your king—and you better believe the best players don't leave their king vulnerable.

The **"Insurance Policy"** adjustment is your safety net. It's the queen's gambit of defense—strategically spending a little to protect a lot. When things start to look unstable, this move allows you lock in peace of mind and dramatically lower risk without having to abandon the trade altogether.

Whether you're facing earnings volatility, a bad news cycle, or just an uncertain market, this strategy puts you in control. It's not a hedge just for the sake of hedging. It's a calculated play designed to keep you in the game longer—and ready to win.

What is the "Insurance Policy" Adjustment?

Used to protect or improve a position in case of a major directional move. This adjustment can be applied to a wide range of strategies, including long calls, long puts, straddles, strangles, butterflies, condors, calendar spreads, and even stock positions.

The outcome is lower directional risk and an explosion zone of potential profit. Most often this adjustment increases debit to the position and is most effective when a position has established a directional bias, whether positive or negative.

The Insurance Policy Adjustment

INSURANCE POLICY RISK

Description: *Used to protect or enhance a position in case of a significant directional move.*

Strategies: *Long Calls, Long Puts, Straddles / Strangles as well as Butterflies, Condors, Calendar spreads, even Stock positions, etc. Any trading strategy can be "insured" with this adjustment.*

Outcome: *The adjustment will result in reducing directional risk by creating an "explosion" position either to the upside, the downside, or both. In most cases this adjustment will add debit to the position.*

Timing: *Like the DNA (Delta Neutral Adjustment), this adjustment is typically applied to a profitable trade when the Delta of the position has become either positive (bullish) or negative (bearish), although it can be applied to a trade in a loss position. It can also be used in conjunction with other adjustment moves.*

Like the "DNA" adjustment, it can be added to both profitable and losing trades to reduce exposure and protect capital.

Case Study: Kimberly-Clark (KMB) Initial Entry – February 25

Insurance Policy Adjustment: CALL

INSURANCE POLICY RISK

Leg Date	Position	Num	Option Symbol	Expire	Type	Entry	Bid/ Ask	Leg Profit	IV %	Vol	OI	Days	Delta %	Gamma %	Vega %IV	Theta $/day
2025-02-25	Bought	12	KMB250321C145	2025 Mar 21	145 Call	0.80	0.40 1.20	$0.00	14.67	81	201	24	25.53	6.04	11.6	-3.6

Hover the mouse on a risk line to see the line data. Hover in stock chart to see stock data.

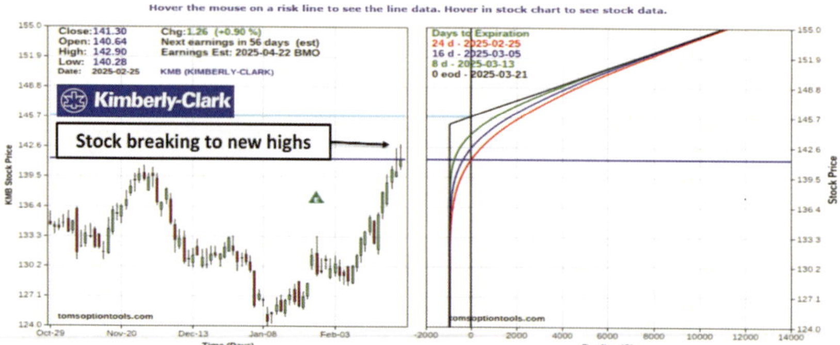

25-Feb - Entry

Max Risk $960

($80 x 12 = $960)

Quote Type	Entry Debit	Profit	Rate of Return	Max Profit	Max Risk	Delta (Shares)	Gamma	Vega	Theta
Mid Quote	$960.00	$0.00	0.0%	$Unlimited	$-960.00	306.31	72.483	$139.49	$-43.39
Mid Quote/12	$80.00	$0.00	0.0%	$Unlimited	$-80.00	25.53	6.04	$11.62	$-3.62

We opened a bullish position on Kimberly-Clark by buying 12 March 21 145 Calls at $0.80, risking a total of $960. The stock was reaching new highs, and our Delta-heavy setup provided strong upside exposure.

March 7 – Time to Adjust

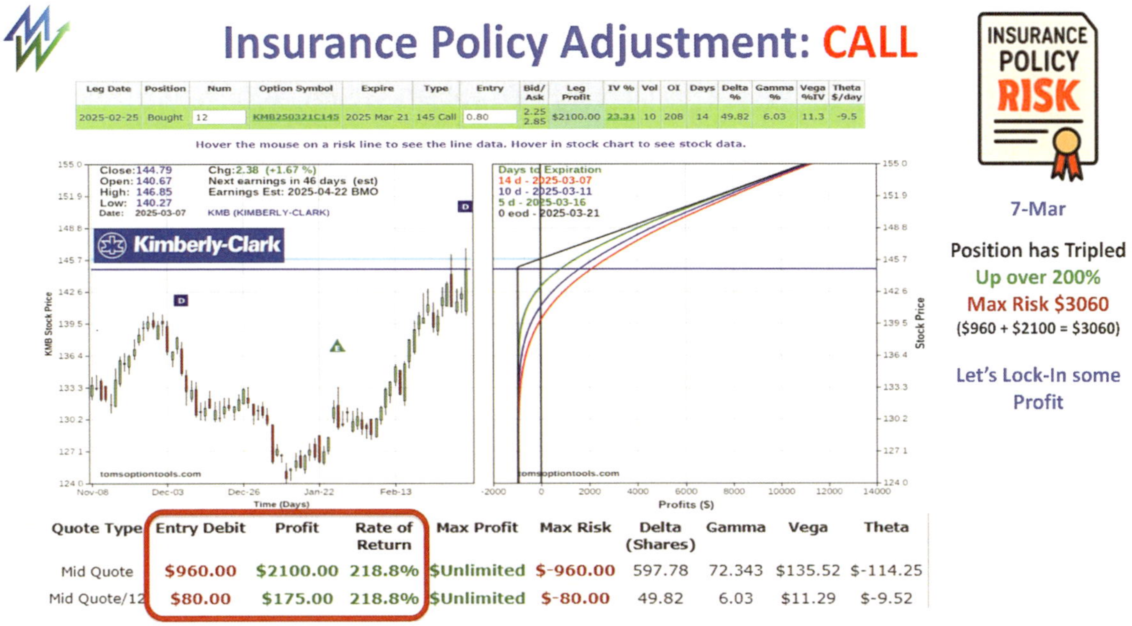

By March 7, the position had tripled. We gained $2,100 on a $960 investment—a 218.8% return. However, our Delta increased to +597.78, meaning a $1 drop in KMB would eliminate $597.78 in value. Our total exposure had risen to $3,060 (initial risk plus profit). It was time to take action.

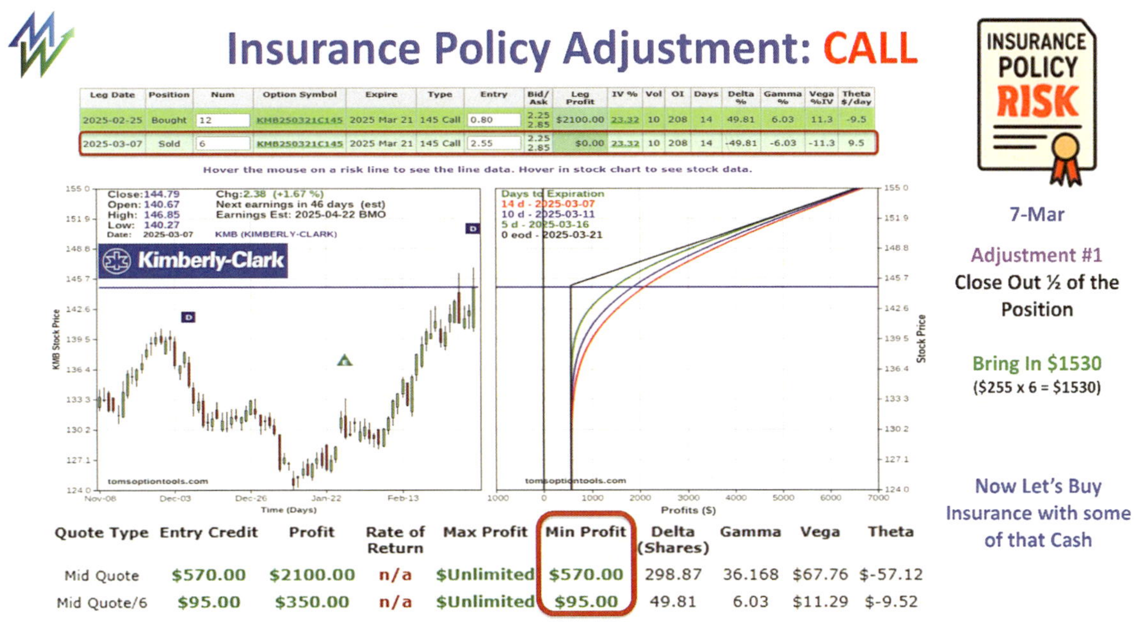

With a triple in hand, the first step is to apply the "House Money adjustment." To do that, we sold 6 of our 12 long calls at $2.55 each, bringing in $1,530 cash and locking in $570 of guaranteed profit.

Delta Still Too High – Let's Buy Insurance

Selling half helped, but a Delta of +298.87 was still too high. If the stock were to drop $1, we'd lose $298.87 of our position's value. To fix this, we added downside protection by buying 6 OTM puts at $0.75 each ($450 total). Each put had a Delta of -20.87, so they reduced our total Delta by 125.22, bringing us down to +173.65—much safer from a directional standpoint.

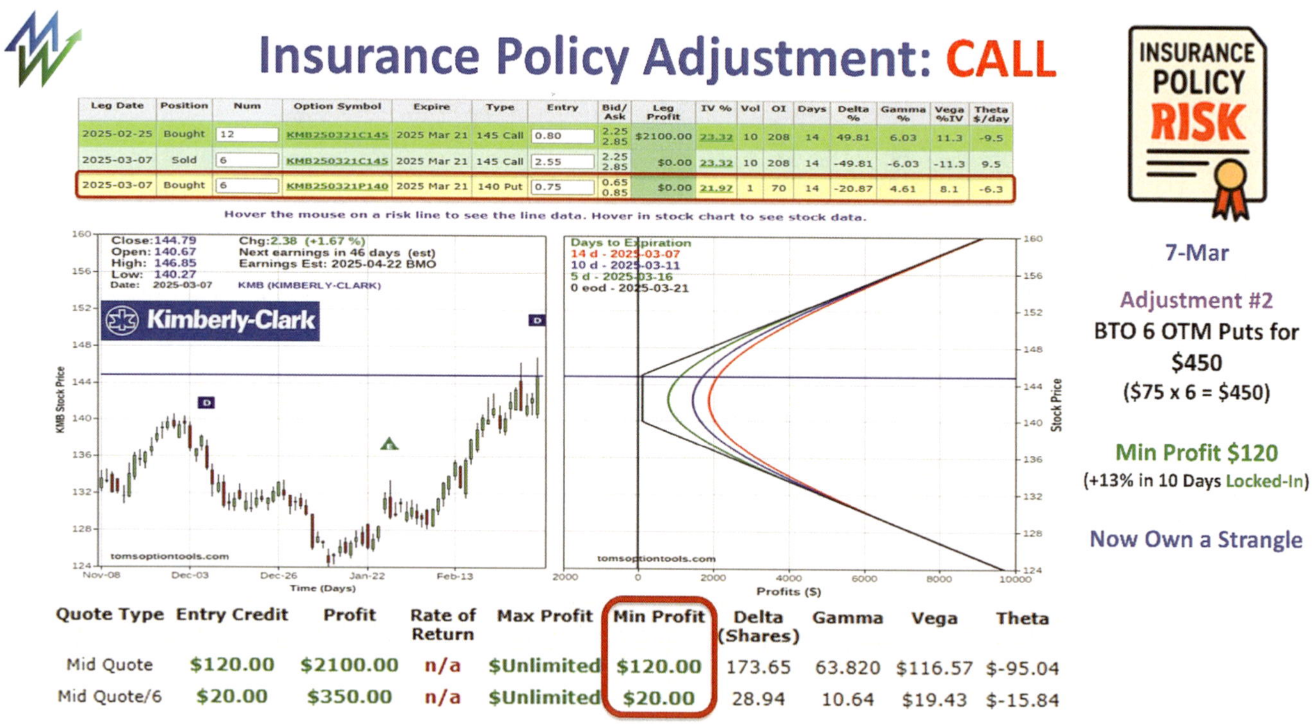

This action locked in $120 minimum profit and created a strangle. Theta, our new enemy, reached -$95 per day, so we needed to stay alert and ready for our next move.

March 21 – Close or Let Expire

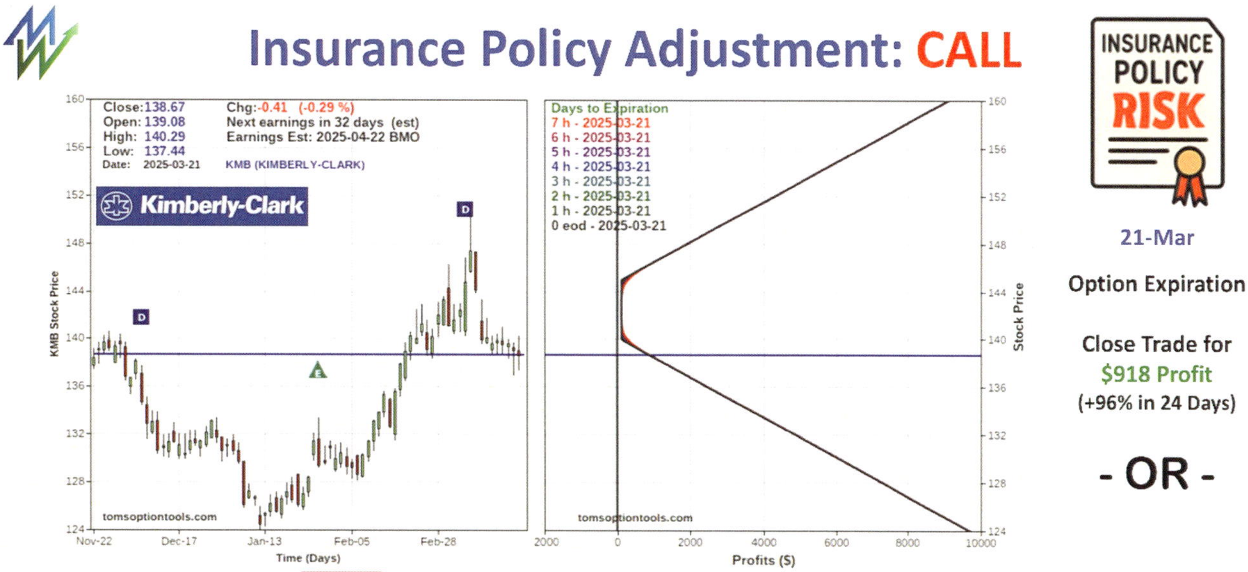

Quote Type	Entry Credit	Profit	Rate of Return	Max Profit	Min Profit	Delta (Shares)	Gamma	Vega	Theta
Mid Quote	$120.00	$918.00	n/a	$Unlimited	$120.00	-575.93	68.608	$2.02	$-65.88
Mid Quote/6	$20.00	$153.00	n/a	$Unlimited	$20.00	-95.99	11.43	$0.34	$-10.98

By expiration, the stock had pulled back sharply and closed at $138.67. Thanks to our earlier adjustments, we were able to close the trade for a $918 profit—96% in just 24 days.

What If We Did Nothing?

Compare this with what would have happened without any adjustment: All 12 calls would have expired worthless. We would have lost the entire $960.

Insurance Policy Adjustment: CALL

INSURANCE POLICY RISK

21-Mar

Option Expiration
With NO Adjustment

Calls Expires Worthless for
Max Loss of $960

Quote Type	Entry Debit	Profit	Rate of Return	Max Profit	Max Risk	Delta (Shares)	Gamma	Vega	Theta
Mid Quote	$960.00	$-960.00	-100.0%	$Unlimited	$-960.00	0.00	0.000	$0.00	$0.00
Mid Quote/6	$160.00	$-160.00	-100.0%	$Unlimited	$-160.00	0.00	0.00	$0.00	$0.00

No profit-locking. No insurance. Just hope.

On March 21, KMB closed at $138.67. Our 145 Calls would have expired worthless.

Result: -$960 loss

Stocks gap, markets reverse, volatility strikes. If you're not protected, it can wipe out weeks of gains. This is why we adjust. This is why we insure. This is how we stay in the game.

Key Takeaways

- Risk increases with profit—adjust before it's too late
- Lock in partial gains to protect the downside
- Use Out-of-the-Money puts or calls to reduce directional exposure
- Monitor Theta as the trade matures
- Play defense like a chess master—protect your board

The **"Insurance Policy"** adjustment won't win headlines—but it wins where it counts: In long-term consistency and risk-managed success.

Summary – Protect Before You're Forced To React

This chapter introduces proactive risk control at a higher level.

The "Insurance Policy" adjustment is about **adding protection before a trade gets into serious trouble**. Instead of reacting emotionally when risk spikes, you intentionally structure the trade to withstand adverse movement.

The key idea:
You don't wait for damage. You define the worst-case scenario in advance.

By layering in protection, you:

- Cap downside risk
- Stabilize the position
- Buy time for the trade to work

Yes, it may come at a cost—but that cost is strategic. It allows you to stay in trades that would otherwise need to be closed, preserving opportunity while controlling exposure.

This chapter reinforces a professional mindset:
Risk is not avoided. It's engineered.

Now that you understand how to protect a position, the next step is learning one of the most versatile structures that makes many of these adjustments possible: **The Magical World of Vertical Spreads**.

CHAPTER 13

THE MAGICAL WORLD OF VERTICAL SPREADS

CHAPTER 13
The Magical World of Vertical Spreads

Debit and Credit Spreads Overview

Welcome to the next level of the game: Vertical Spreads.

In the world of trading, vertical spreads are like your basic chess moves—simple, efficient, and essential to your mastery. They form the foundation of more advanced strategies. Any combination of long and short options with the same expiration falls under the "vertical" umbrella. Think of them as your tactical strikes—two to four coordinated legs, lined up in formation.

Let's start with the classic two-legged spread, the simplest structure. This setup is built by:

- Buying one option (a long position)
- And shorting another (a short position)
- Same type (calls or puts)
- Same expiration
- Different strike prices

This is the opening gambit of options strategy.

There are four basic ways to play this out—two from the debit camp and two from the credit camp:

Debit Spreads: You pay to enter the trade. That means your position starts with a debit in your account—just like buying a powerful piece for your strategy. The goal? Set up limited risk with favorable reward potential.

- Bull Call
- Bear Put

Credit Spreads: You collect premium upfront, but your broker holds a margin—think of it as collateral. This move adds some immediate weight to your side of the board, but you still have to play it smart to win.

- Bear Call
- Bull Put

Flipping the buy and sell sides creates the opposite spread—same structure, reversed directional bias. Another way to think about it is that the debit and corresponding credit spread are opposite sides of the same trade. Where one wins, the other loses, and vice versa.

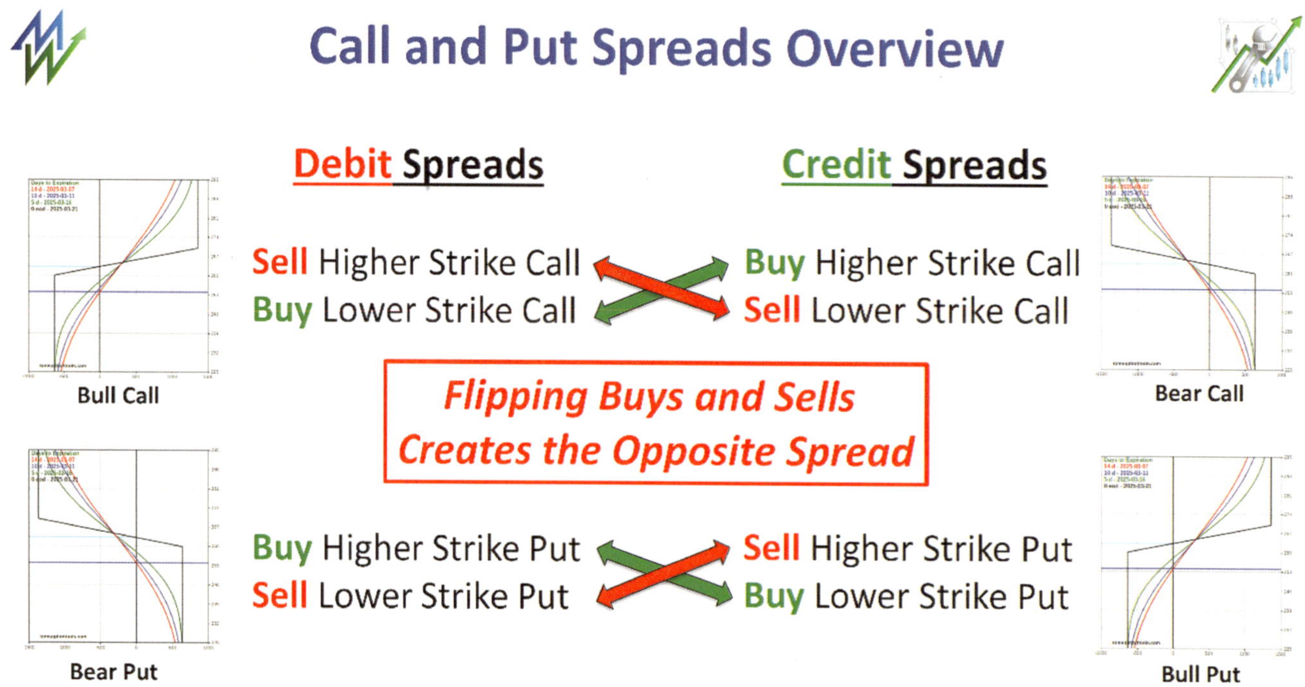

Now, it gets a bit more interesting.

Take a close look at the second graphic. Among these four combinations, you'll notice something surprising: There are only two different risk graphs. That's right—just two.

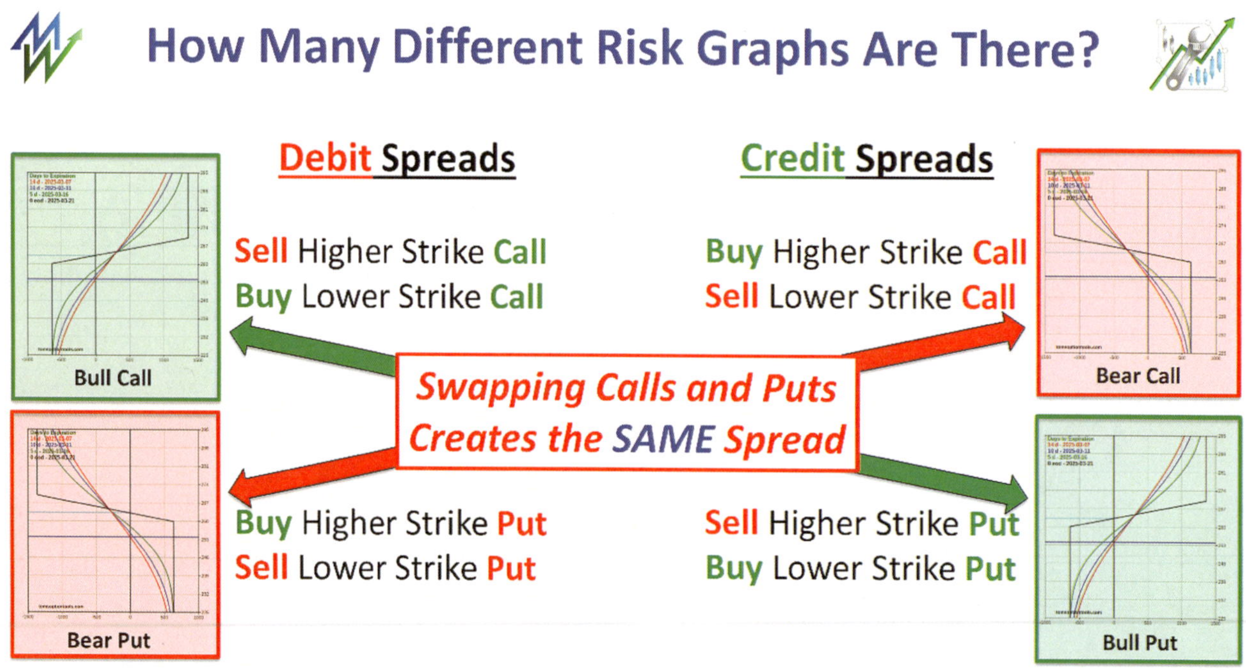

Most traders don't realize this. For example:

- Buying a higher strike put and selling a lower strike put gives you a bear put debit spread. If you flip those puts into calls—buy the higher strike call, sell the lower strike call—you now have a bear call credit spread, but guess what? The risk graph is exactly the same.
- The same logic applies on the bullish side. Buy a lower strike call and sell a higher strike call. That's a bull call debit spread. Flip those calls into puts and you have a bull put credit spread... Same risk profile.

In summary: Swapping calls for puts (or vice versa) in a vertical spread gives you the same risk graph.

Same moves, different names. But if you're playing the game right, it's the risk profile that matters—not the label.

Understanding the Greeks of a Vertical Spread

Let's step back from the big picture and zoom in on what really moves the pieces on the board: The Greeks.

This graphic illustrates the Greek profile of two individual options—a long call on the left and a short call on the right. Think of these like your individual chess pieces: each has its own strengths and weaknesses, but when combined properly, they support your overall strategy.

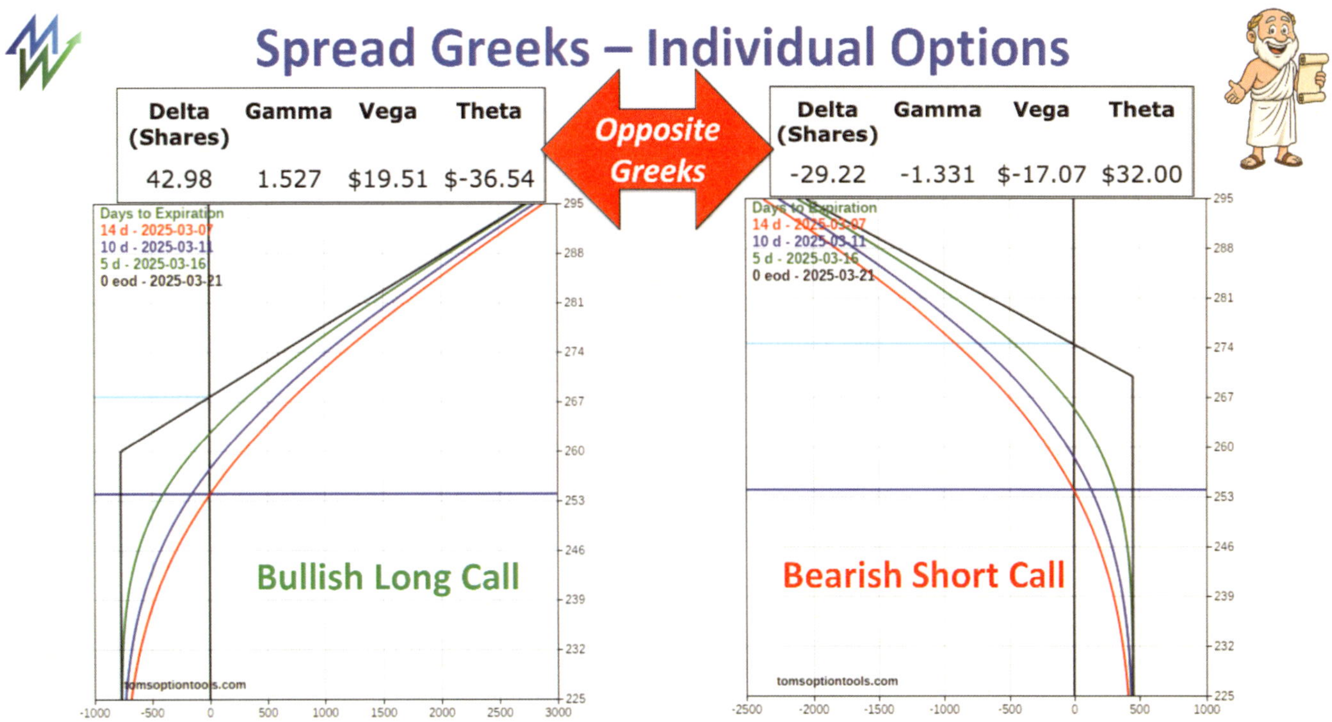

Long Call (Bullish Position)

A long call is your classic offensive piece. It wants the stock to rise and rewards you handsomely when it does.

- **Delta: +42.98**
  This is your directional weapon. A $1 rise in the stock adds $42.98 in profit to the position.
- **Gamma: +1.527**
  This is your momentum engine. Gamma increases Delta as the stock rises. Each dollar higher makes Delta more positive—a powerful compounding effect when you're on the right side of the trade.
- **Vega: +$19.51**
  Now here's the catch: Long calls benefit from rising implied volatility. But what typically happens when a stock rallies? Implied volatility contracts. So, positive Vega can become a liability.
- **Theta: -$36.54**
  The long call loses value with time decay. Every passing day subtracts $36.54—and it only gets worse as expiration nears.

Short Call (Bearish Position)

Now flip the piece—a short call is like your defensive counter. And its Greeks reflect that role.

- **Delta: -29.22**
  Opposite direction. This position gains if the stock drops.
- **Gamma: -1.331**
  As the stock rises, the short call's Delta becomes more negative (i.e., it starts losing faster). Gamma here is working against you.
- **Vega: -$17.07**
  A short call benefits from a drop in implied volatility. This aligns better with a typical stock rally.
- **Theta: +$32.00**
  Time is your ally. This position gains $32 a day from time decay.

Combining the Two: The Power of the Spread

When you combine the long call with the short call. You create a bull call debit spread. The magic here is in how the Greeks balance each other out:

- Delta remains positive (bullish).
- Gamma is reduced, but still positive.
- Vega is reduced and can be near neutral.
- Theta shifts toward neutral or even positive—time decay is no longer your enemy.

Basically, you transform an expensive, decaying, volatility-sensitive trade into a more controlled, probability-oriented position.

You've upgraded your piece. You're still playing to win, but now with more resilience on the board.

Combining the Greeks – Vertical Spreads in Action

Now that we've looked at the individual pieces—let's look at how they play together.

This slide reveals a key truth about vertical spreads that most traders never fully appreciate:

The Greeks are additive.

What does that mean?

It means that when you combine a long call with a short call to create a bull call spread, you're essentially adding their individual Greeks together to reveal the spread's position Greeks.

Let's break it down using the numbers:

Greek	Long Call	Short Call	Bull Call Spread
Delta	+42.98	-29.22	+13.76
Gamma	+1.53	-1.33	+0.196
Vega	+19.5	-17.1	+2.44
Theta	-36.5	+32.0	-4.54

Spread Greeks – Options Combined

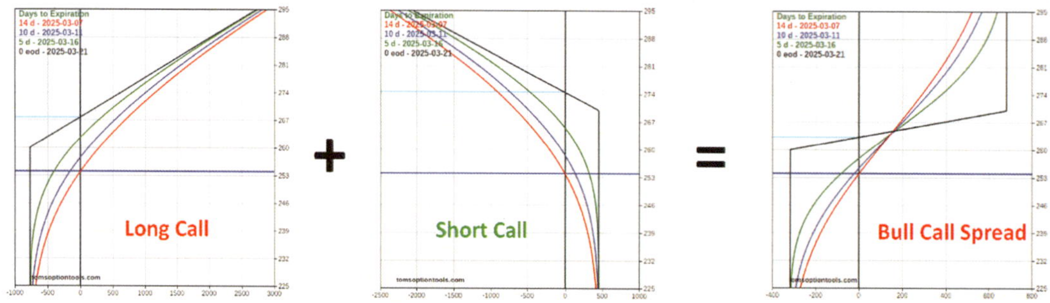

Entry Debit	Profit	Rate of Return	Max Profit	Max Risk	Delta (Shares)	Gamma	Vega	Theta
$318.00	$0.00	0.0%	$682.00	$-318.00	13.76	0.196	$2.44	$-4.54

Position	Num	Expire	Type	Entry	Delta %	Gamma %	Vega %IV	Theta $/day
Sold	1	2025 Mar 21	270 Call	4.50	-29.22	-1.33	-17.1	32.0
Bought	1	2025 Mar 21	260 Call	7.68	42.98	1.53	19.5	-36.5

Greeks are Additive

This is where the magic happens.

Individually, the long call is powerful—but volatile. Its Greeks are intense, making the trade more sensitive to changes in time and implied volatility fluctuations.

But when you add the short call? You mute the intensity. You reduce exposure. You balance the forces.

The bull call spread, with its tamed Theta and moderated Vega, becomes a smoother, more controlled position.

The game slows down slightly. You're still playing to win, but now with more careful, strategic moves. You've just shifted from speed chess to classical style—more time to think and fewer unforced mistakes.

This is the true strength of vertical spreads: They not only define risk and reward. They also influence how your trade behaves, giving you more consistency and control.

Theta Gravity – How Time Works For or Against You

In this part of the game, we're exploring something that's often overlooked—but incredibly powerful once you understand it: Theta behavior within a spread.

This graphic gives us a great visual of what's really going on.

When you build a bull call spread, you've got two moving pieces:

- A long call (lower strike) with **negative Theta**
- A short call (higher strike) with **positive Theta**

Now, Theta isn't static in a spread. It fluctuates depending on where the stock price is in relation to the long and short strikes.

Think of Theta like gravity.

Each leg has its own "gravity" that pulls on the net Theta of the position:

- **If the stock is closer to the long call**, Theta is negative.
- **If the stock is closer to the short call**, Theta becomes positive.
- **And right around the midpoint?** The Theta gravities cancel, leaving the position Theta-neutral.

This is illustrated beautifully in the curved P/L lines converging toward the black expiration line. These curves show how the position evolves over time. You can see:

- **In the lower left portion of the risk graph**, time is working against you (negative Theta).
- **In the upper right**, time is actually helping you (positive Theta).
- **And somewhere in the middle**, there's a sweet spot—Theta neutral—where time decay isn't affecting the position much at all.

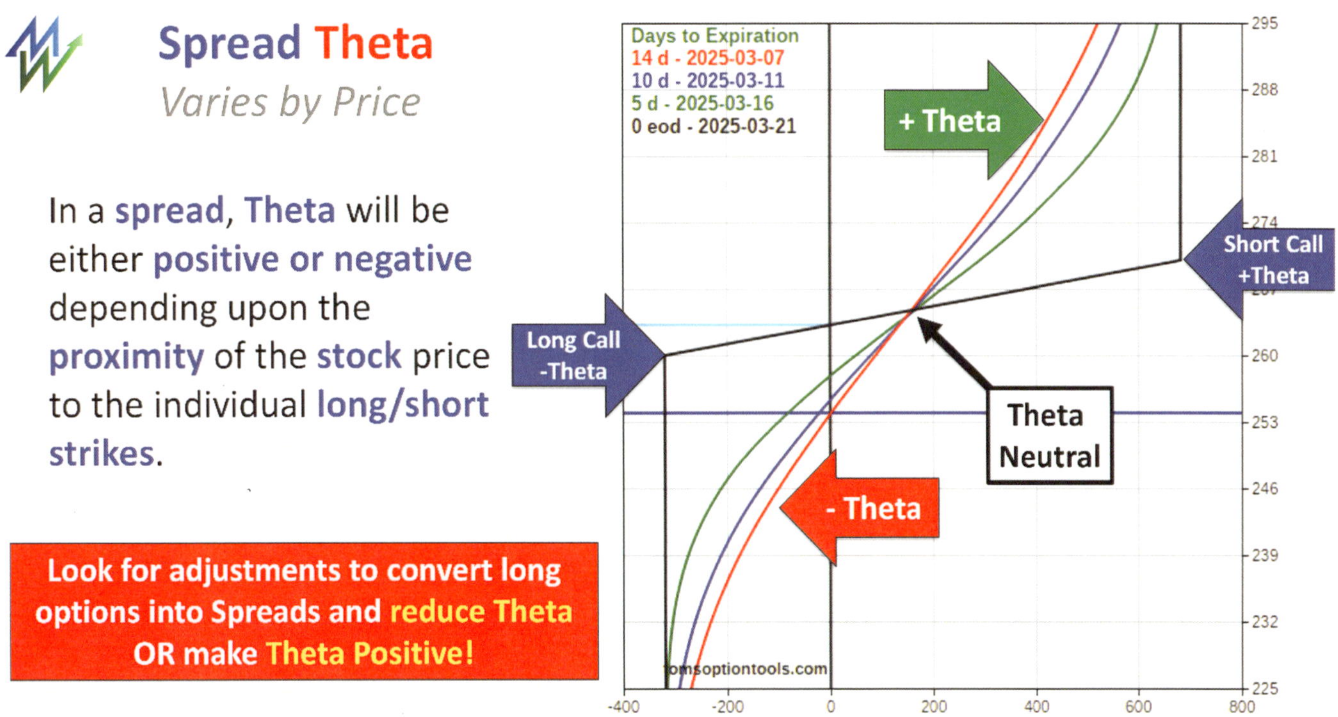

Why This Matters

This understanding gives you an edge when planning adjustments.

If your trade suffers from negative Theta, consider adjusting the structure so the stock is closer to your original setup. You can reshape Theta to positive or at least reduce the damage. Positive Theta is your ally. It means time is on your side.

So next time you're analyzing a spread, ask yourself: Which leg is the stock price closer to? Because that leg is defining your Theta experience.

Vega Gravity – Aligning with Implied Volatility

Time isn't the only invisible force affecting your spread—implied volatility also plays a key role. And like Theta, Vega isn't fixed; it varies depending on where the stock is within your vertical spread.

This graphic illustrates how Vega behaves in a bull call spread, and the lesson is just as powerful.

You've got two legs:

- **A long call (lower strike)** with positive Vega
- **A short call (higher strike)** with negative Vega

The net Vega of your position depends on which leg the stock is closer to.

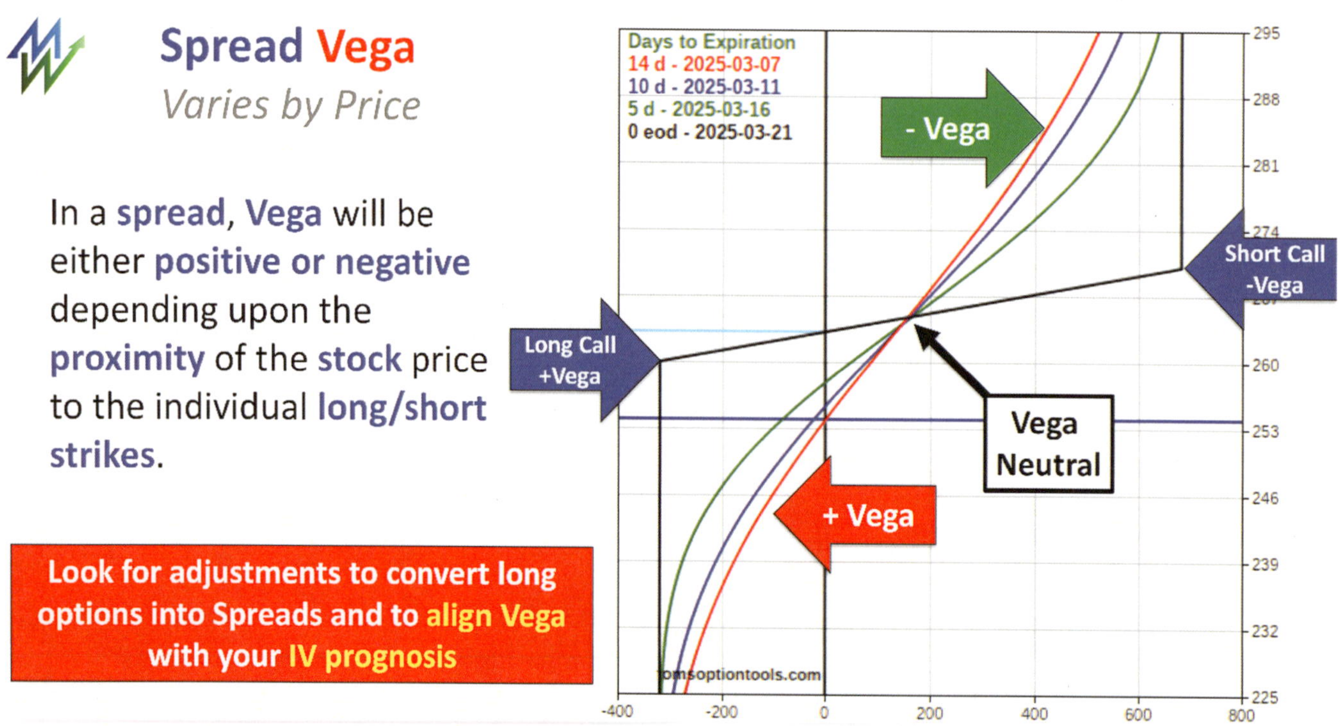

Each option leg has its own "Vega gravity":

- When the stock is closer to the long call, the spread behaves like a long option—Vega is positive.
- When the stock is closer to the short call, the spread behaves more like a short option—Vega is negative.
- Around the midpoint between the two strikes, the opposing Vega forces cancel each other, leaving your position Vega-neutral.As shown in the chart, if you're sitting in the lower part of the risk graph, you're in the +Vega zone. That means the trade benefits if implied volatility increases.

If you're in the upper right zone—closer to the short call—you've entered -Vega territory. Here, the trade actually benefits if implied volatility decreases.

Why This Matters for Adjustments

This distinction is critical for traders who rely on IV forecasts in their planning. If you expect implied volatility to increase, you'll want your trade to lean toward positive Vega. If you expect implied volatility to drop, then negative Vega becomes your ally.

So how do you influence that? The same way we did with Theta:

- Place your spread closer to the long leg to increase Vega
- Place it closer to the short leg to decrease or flip Vega negative

Once again, the lesson is clear: Vega, like Theta, responds to position. Use that gravity to your advantage.

Summary - Mastering the Power of Spreads

You've now seen how vertical spreads provide the first level of control in your trading strategy. By understanding how the Greeks change based on stock price proximity—especially Theta and Vega—you're learning to think strategically, not just tactically.

We've explored:

- The structure of debit and credit spreads
- The symmetry and equivalence of risk graphs
- How the Greeks are additive
- And how Theta and Vega "gravities" shift based on price

This is just the beginning.

Now that you know how vertical spreads behave, it's time to kick it up a notch.

In the next chapter, we'll explore amping up the power of adjustments—and specifically, how to layer on a second vertical spread. Yes, we're about to start spreading spreads.

You'll see how this unlocks a new level of flexibility and control—transforming your trades from static positions into dynamic plays.

With the power of vertical spreads in your trading arsenal, it's time to take a look at how spreads can be combined to amplify your risk management capabilities. **The "Spread the Spread" Adjustment** is next!

CHAPTER 14

THE "SPREAD THE SPREAD" ADJUSTMENT

CHAPTER 14
The "Spread the Spread" Adjustment

Welcome to the next evolution in your trading strategy—where we don't just stop at spreading a single long or short option. We now take it one level deeper: We spread the spread.

The Spread the Spread Adjustment

Take an existing Vertical Spread position and **morph it into a Butterfly or Condor** position by selling a credit spread.

Some ways to do so:

- Selling OTM Call Spreads
- Selling OTM Put Spreads

You've already learned how to collect "rent" by turning a single long call or put into a vertical spread. That move gave you better Theta, lower Vega, and a well-defined risk profile.

Now, we're going to do the same thing with a spread—by adding another spread to the mix. This move creates a more advanced structure like a Butterfly or Condor. Essentially, you're converting a basic vertical into a double vertical.

This is what we call the "Spread the Spread" adjustment.

Here's the core idea:

Take an existing spread (like a bull call or bear put) and morph it into a Butterfly or Condor by selling an Out-of-the-Money (OTM) credit spread.

Some common methods:

- **Selling OTM Call Spreads** (to form a Butterfly or Iron Condor)
- **Selling OTM Put Spreads** (same idea from the other side)

Think of it like adding the second slice of bread. You already have a tasty spread on one side. Now you're closing the sandwich—with another spread—to lock in structure, reduce risk, and refine your probability curve.

"Spread the Spread" Adjustment - Summary

Purpose: This adjustment is designed to reduce the debit or increase the credit of an existing options trade by selling a new spread against the original position.

Applicable To: Commonly used with debit spreads or credit spreads that need adjusting.

Effect: Selling an Out-of-the-Money (OTM) spread reduces the overall risk, brings in additional credit, and helps neutralize directional exposure (Delta).

When to Use: This is generally applied when the stock appears to have stalled in its directional move. Use technical analysis to help time this decision.

The Spread the Spread Adjustment

Description: *Used to reduce the debit or increase the credit of the original trade by selling a spread against the position.*

Strategies: *Debit spreads, credit spreads are typical candidates.*

Outcome: *This adjustment will result in a reduction in overall risk by selling a further OTM spread. This adjustment will bring in a credit to the position and reduce the overall risk in the position. Additionally, this adjustment applied to neutralize directional risk (Delta).*

Timing: *Generally, this adjustment can be applied whenever you feel that the stock has stalled its movement in your desired direction. Use technical analysis to determine when this is more likely the case.*

Trade Example: Microsoft (MSFT) – The "Spread the Spread" in Action

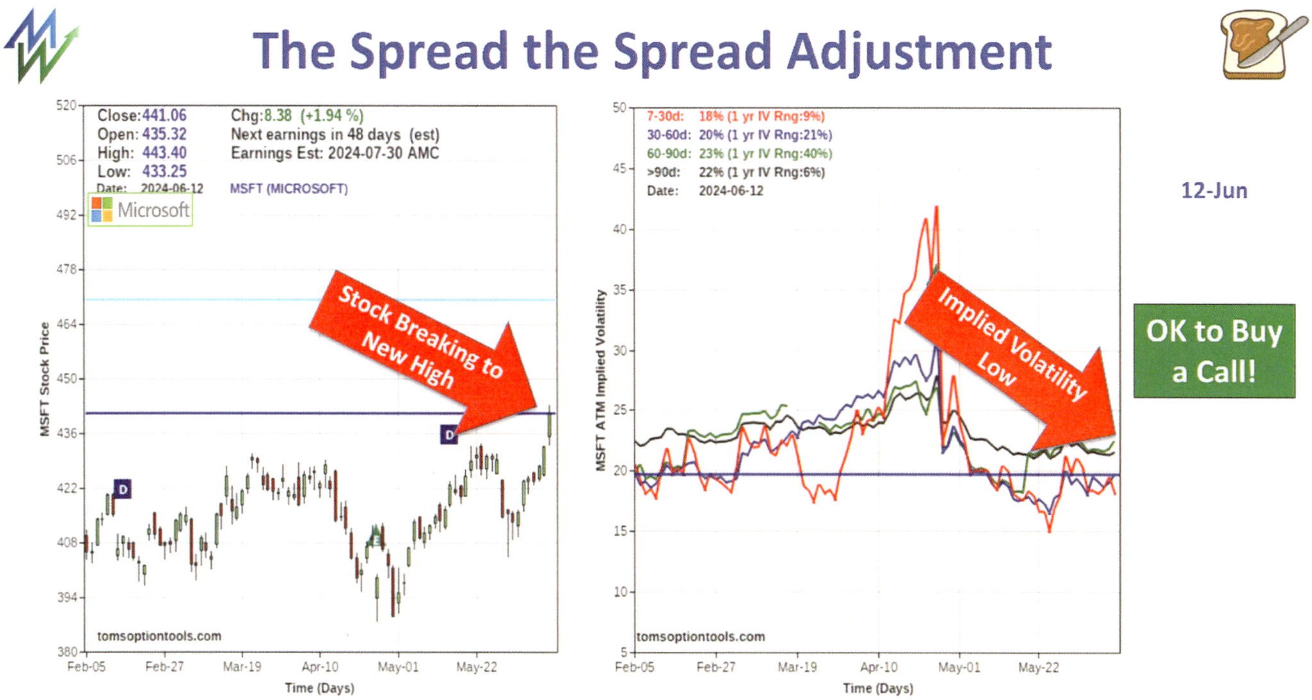

The best way to demonstrate the power of the "Spread the Spread" adjustment is by walking through a trade from start to finish, applying adjustments as conditions change. Here's our setup:

Microsoft (MSFT) has just broken above a key resistance level to make new highs. This technical breakout gives us a bullish prognosis on price movement.

Furthermore, we observe that implied volatility (IV) is low—a clear indication that buying a call or initiating a debit spread is appropriate at this time. We anticipate IV to decrease or stay steady, which benefits long call spreads or butterflies if adjustments are made later.

This is the perfect starting point to demonstrate how we can initiate with a basic bullish position and evolve it—step by step—into a strategic "Spread the Spread" adjustment.

Trade Entry – June 12, 2024

With our bullish prognosis in place, we initiated the trade on June 12, 2024. We purchased 2 contracts of the MSFT July 26th $465 calls at a premium of $5.18 each. This resulted in a total net debit of $1,036, which is also our maximum risk on the trade.

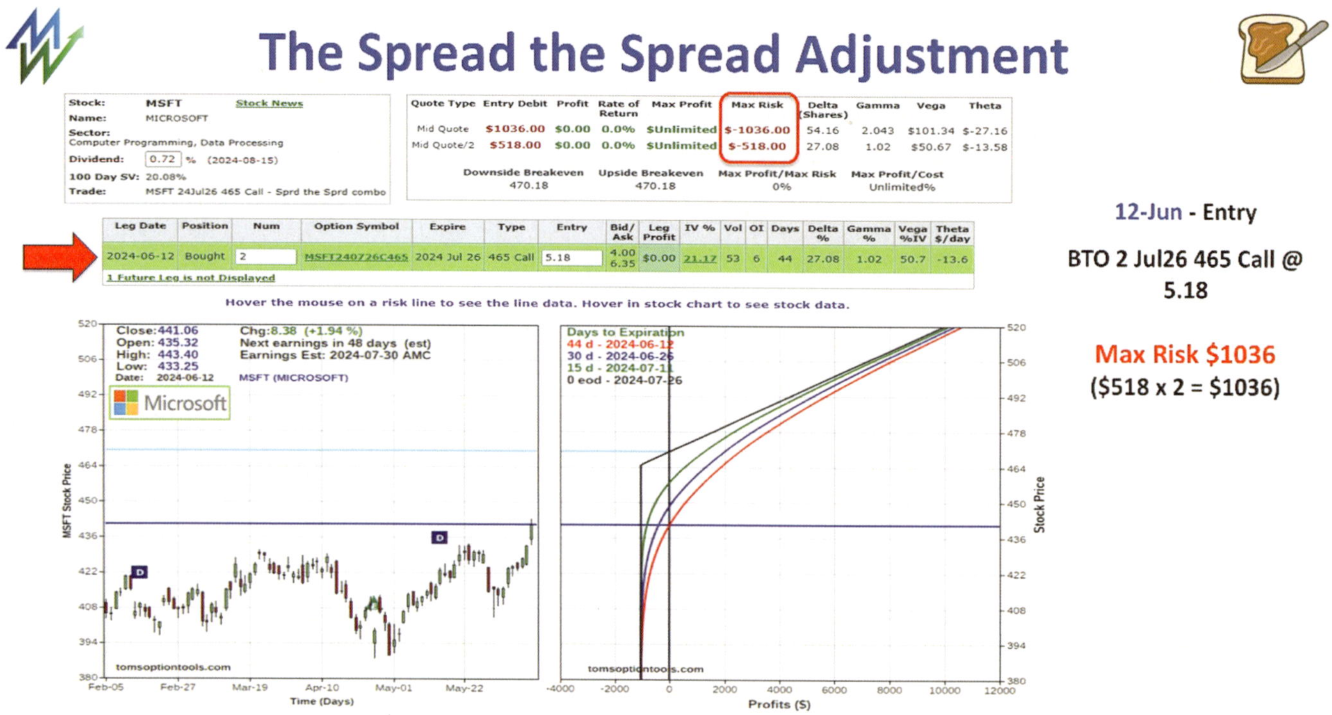

Trade Update – July 5, 2024

By July 5, 2024, Microsoft had risen significantly, and our position showed a strong unrealized gain of $1,510—a return of 145%. At this point, we've more than doubled the original position value.

However, with the stock continuing its bullish trend, we now face a new reality: The position is larger than ever. With a profit on the table and our original debit still at risk, we need to reassess the total exposure.

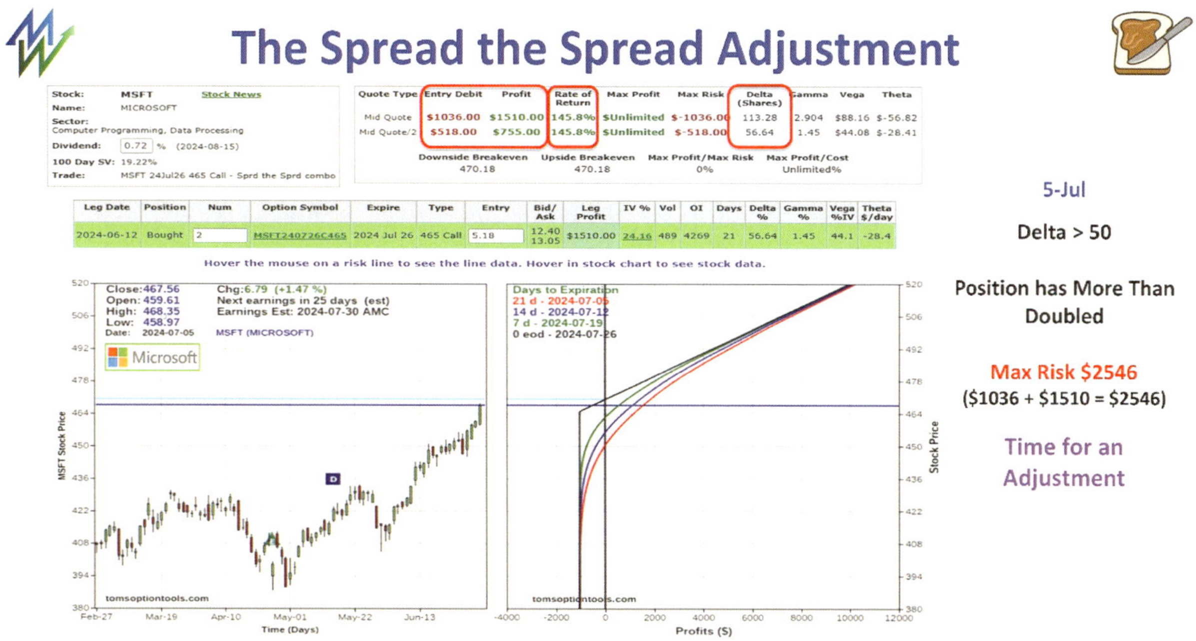

Max risk = $1,036 (initial debit) + $1,510 (unrealized profit) = $2,546 total exposure.
Delta is also above 50, signaling strong bullish exposure and directional risk. With all this in mind…
It's time for an adjustment.

Adjustment #1 – Lock-In Profit and Reduce Risk

The simplest way to control risk is to eliminate it altogether.

With two contracts in place and the position achieving a 145% gain, we decided to reduce risk by closing half of the position. On July 5, 2024, we applied the "House Money" adjustment and sold 1 of the 2 Jul26 $465 Calls at $12.73, generating $1,273 in credit.

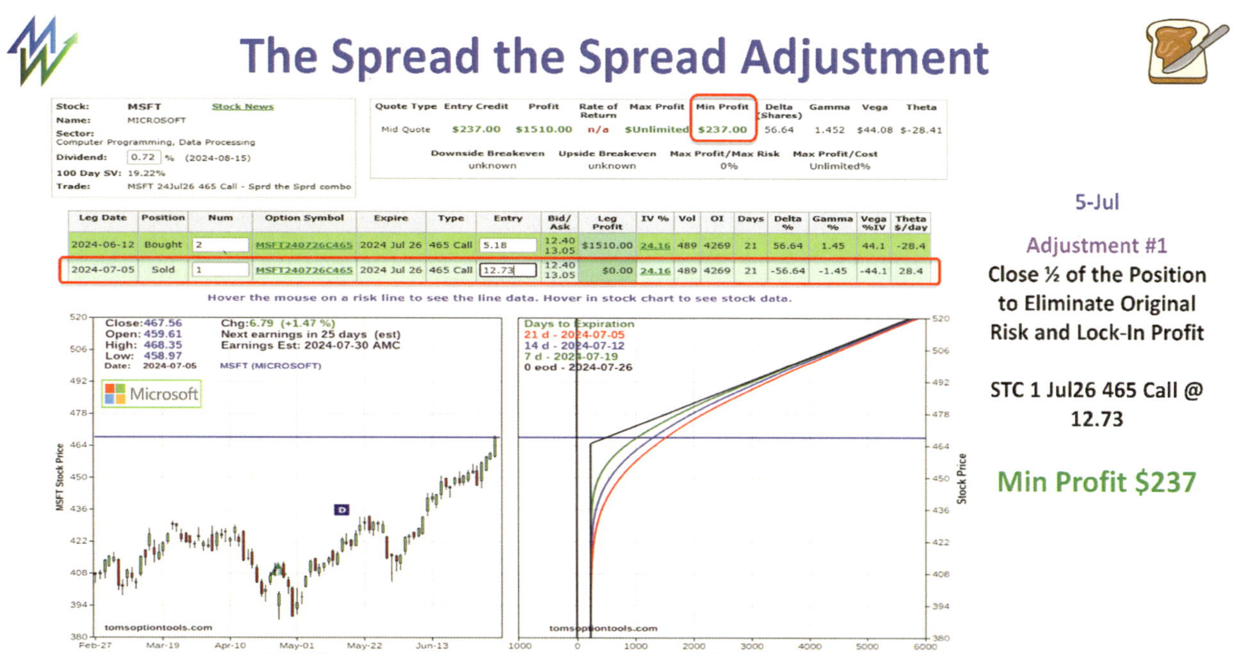

This adjustment achieves two things:

- Eliminates the original $1,036 of risk from the trade
- Locks in a minimum profit of $237 while still leaving one contract open for more upside

Now we're playing with house money.

Adjustment Signal – July 8, 2024

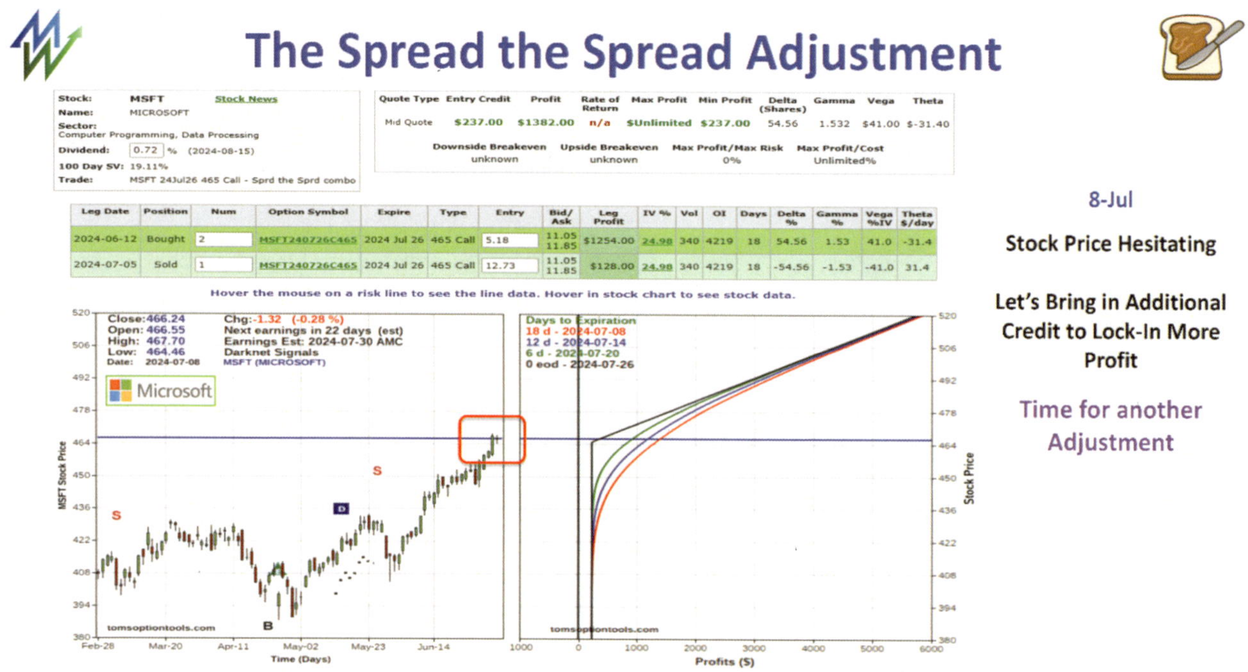

Just four days after locking in partial profit, Microsoft continued to rise but has now begun to stall.

With our bullish thesis taking a pause, it's time to reassess the risk profile. As of July 8, 2024, our position has a Delta of +56.64, meaning a $1 decrease in the stock price would lower our position's value by approximately $56.64.

That's too much directional exposure to leave unmanaged when momentum is hesitating.

This is the perfect moment to apply a "Spread the Spread" adjustment by selling a new Out-of-the-Money spread to:

- Bring in additional credit
- Lock in more of our profits
- Reduce directional risk (Delta)

Time for another adjustment.

Adjustment #2 – "Collect the Rent"

With the stock price hesitating, this is the perfect moment to bring in more credit and lock in additional profit.

On July 8, 2024, we sold 1 Jul26 $485 Call at $3.80, earning $380 in premium. This action transformed our remaining long call into a bull call spread, reduced our directional risk, and secured a guaranteed profit.

As of this adjustment, we've now locked in a total minimum profit of $617

Now that the position is secure… let's spread the spread and lock in even MORE profit!

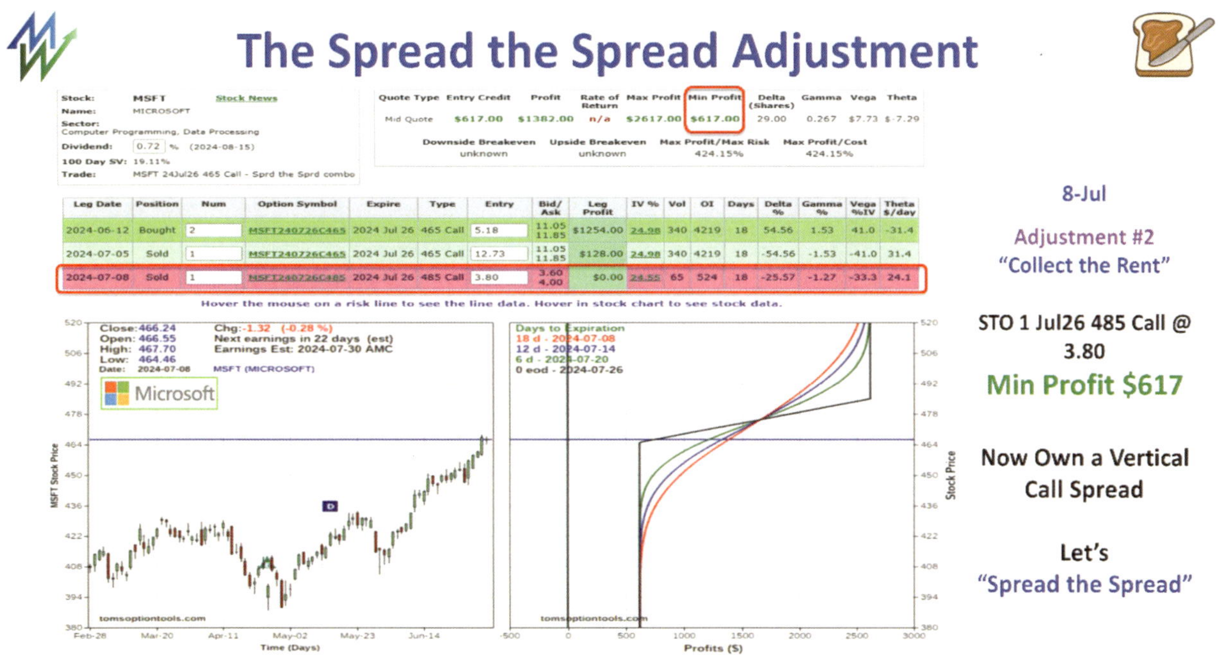

Adjustment #3 – "Spread the Spread"

This next adjustment illustrates the true power of vertical spreads.

With a profitable trade already secured and a solid minimum profit locked in, we advance to the next strategic step: Selling a bear call spread to create a condor.

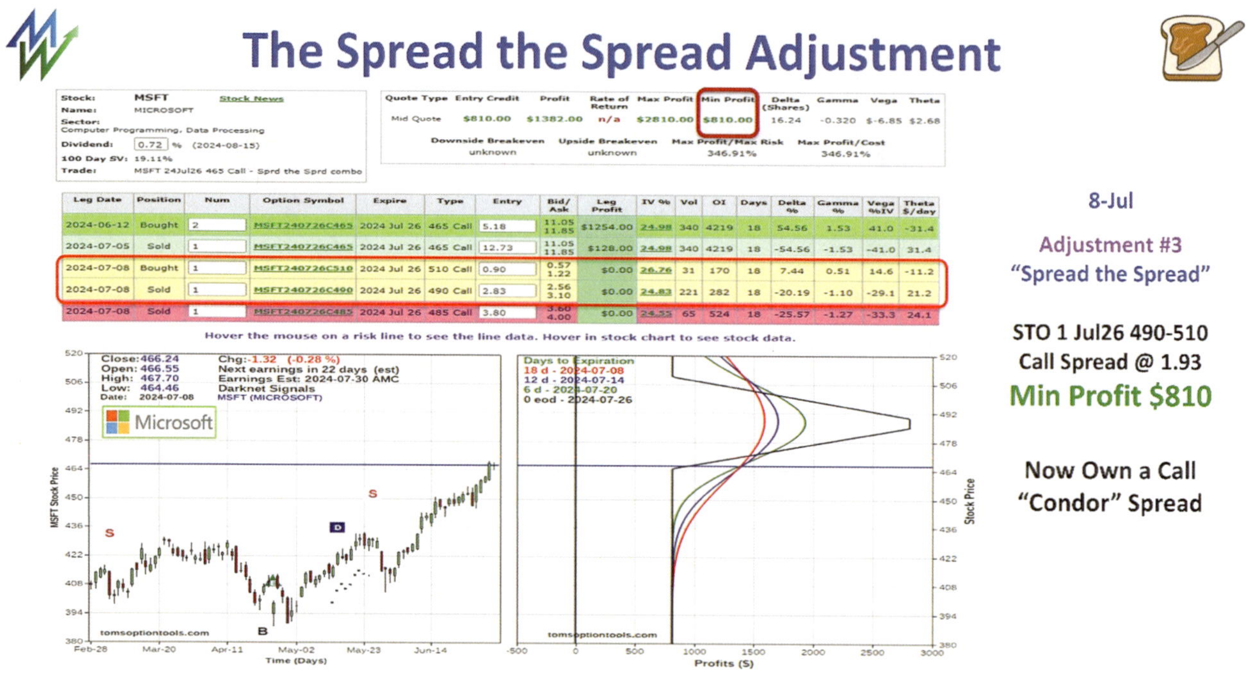

On July 8, 2024, we sold the Jul26 $490/$510 call spread for a credit of $1.93, earning an additional $193 and turning our long call spread into a condor.

With this move, we've now secured a guaranteed profit of $810—and we still have the potential to make up to $2,810 if the trade hits the sweet spot.

That's the magic of the "Spread the Spread" adjustment.

Adjustment Signal – July 9, 2024

Despite a successful position, the market has thrown us a new curve.

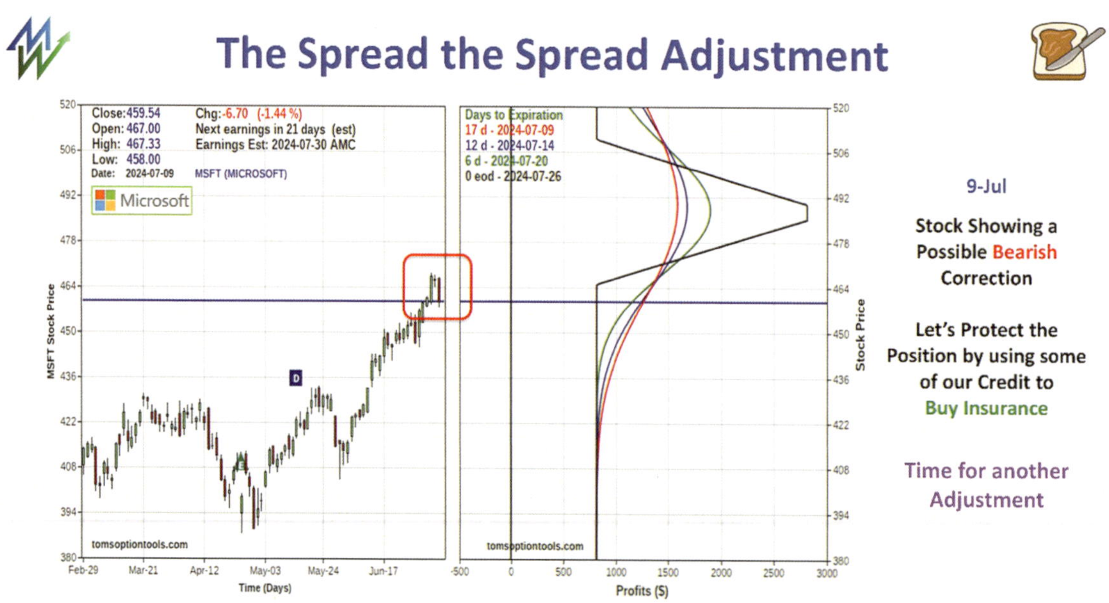

On July 9, 2024, Microsoft dropped sharply, signaling that a bearish correction may be beginning. While our position remains strong, a further decline in the stock could start to eat into our profit zone.

Rather than sit back and hope, we're going to take action.

We'll use part of the credit we've already locked in to buy protection on the downside—enter the Insurance Policy Adjustment.

This move will limit how much we can lose if the stock drops sharply, providing us peace of mind while keeping a strong position.

Time for another adjustment… this time, defensive.

Adjustment #4 – "Insurance Policy"

To protect against a potential downside move, we implemented the 'Insurance Policy' adjustment.

On July 9, 2024, we bought 1 MSFT Jul26 $440 put at $3.14, spending $314 of our previously locked-in profits to secure downside protection.

This provides us with a safety net if the market reverses sharply—while still maintaining a minimum profit.

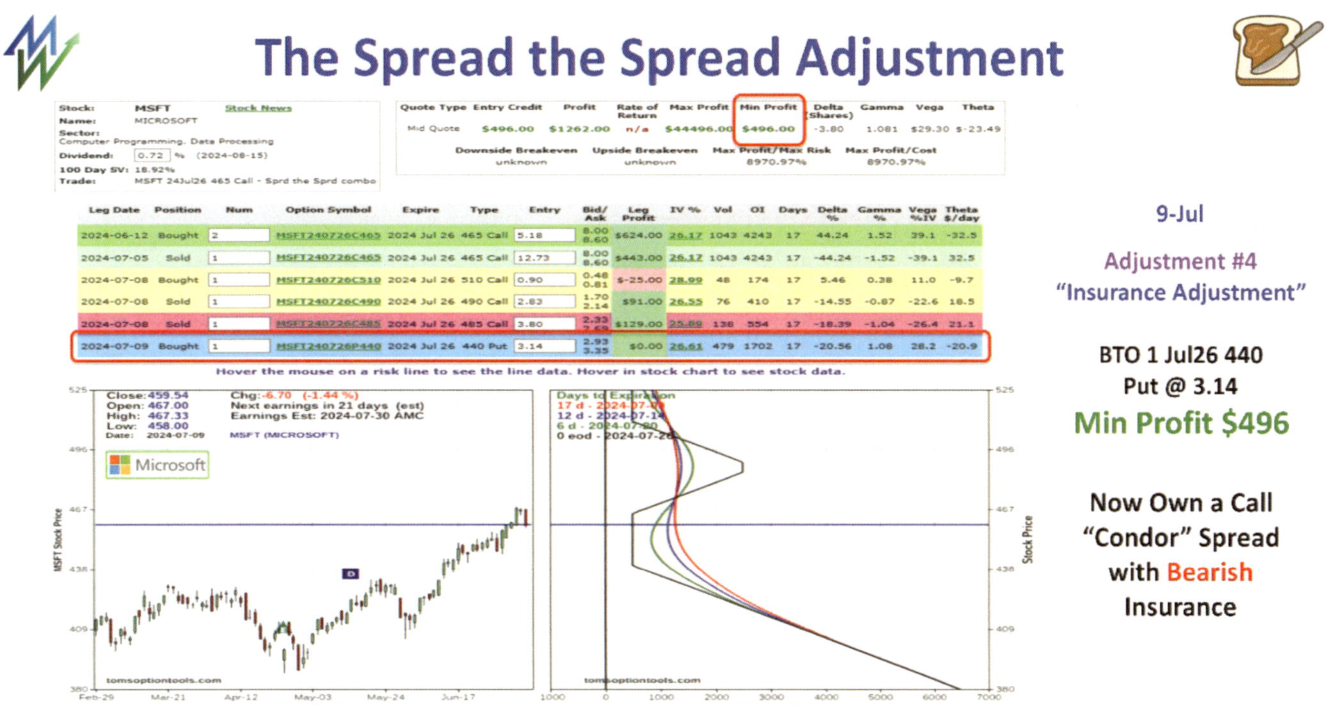

We now own a call condor with a bearish insurance leg—protecting the trade while keeping significant upside potential.

With this move, our guaranteed profit is now $496.

Final Outcome – July 25, 2024

As the trade approached expiration, the final move validated all the adjustments we made.

By July 25, 2024, Microsoft had rolled over hard—closing at $418.50. Thanks to our careful planning and layered adjustments, our position remained strong and protected.

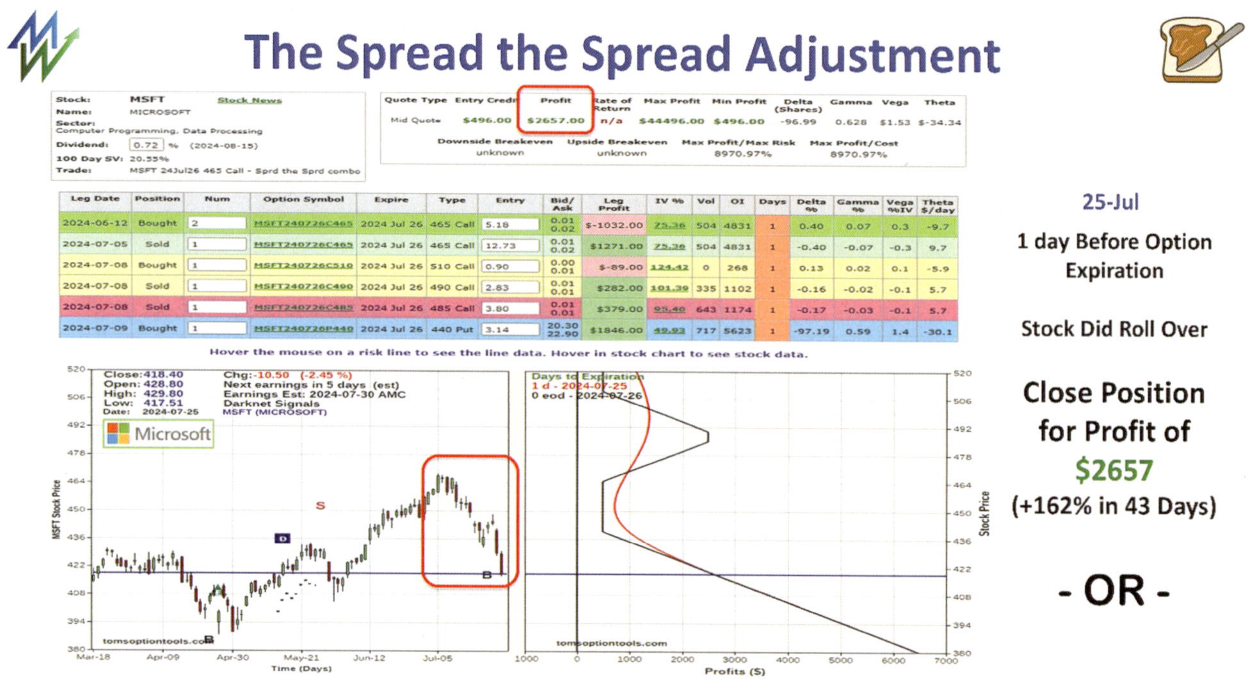

The result: a total profit of $2,657 —a 162% return over just 43 days!

This case study shows how vertical spreads can develop into powerful multi-leg strategies through timely adjustments. By securing profits, controlling directional risk, and purchasing protection, we turned a simple call trade into a winning, high-probability structure.

This is the full power of the "Spread the Spread" adjustment.

What If We Didn't Adjust? – The Unadjusted Outcome

Let's take a moment to compare what would have happened had we made no adjustments at all…

By July 25, 2024, the same date we closed our adjusted position for a strong profit, an unadjusted position would have suffered a maximum loss of $1,032—a full 100% loss over 43 days.

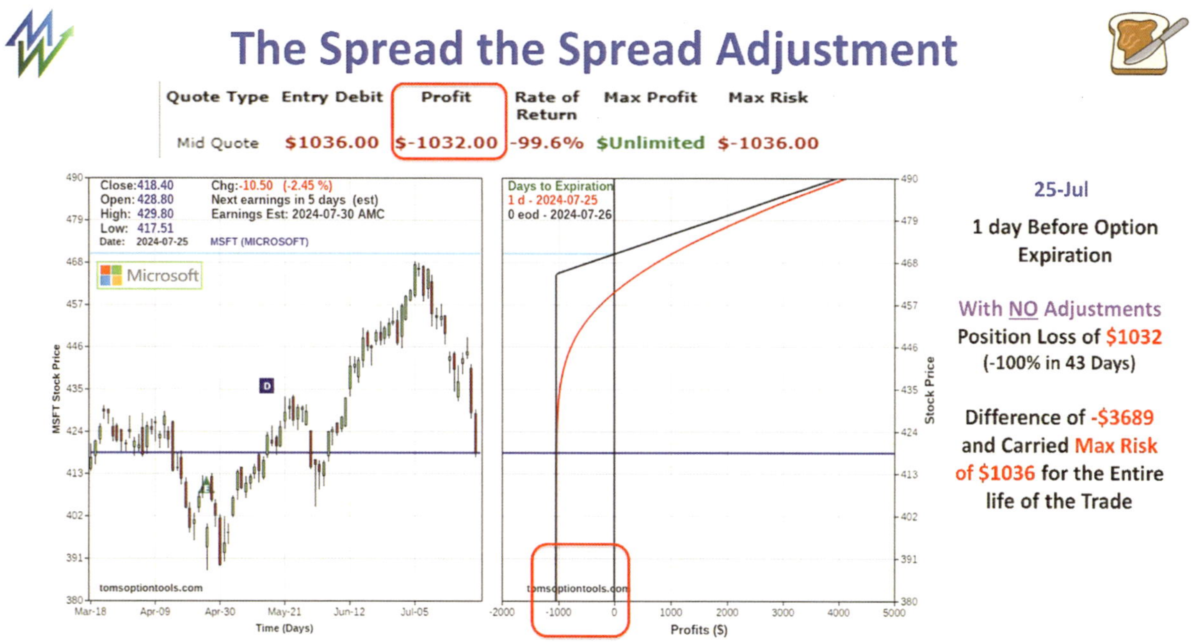

This highlights the incredible power of active risk management through strategic adjustments.

Instead of taking on maximum risk all the time, we minimized risk and secured profits early.

The difference between the adjusted and unadjusted trade? A whopping $3,689.

This is why adjustments matter.

Chapter Summary – Strategic Adjustments in Action

In this chapter, we tracked a live trade from start to finish—making strategic adjustments along the way. We started with a simple long call trade and gradually built it into a multi-leg structure aimed at locking in profits, managing risk, and guarding against market reversals.

Throughout the journey, we demonstrated how to:

- Lock in gains by reducing size
- Add credit by selling spreads
- Defend against reversals with insurance
- Use the power of vertical spreads to dynamically shift probability in our favor

The end result? A +162% profit in just 43 days—with risk eliminated or minimized most of the way. Compare that to the unadjusted version, which lost -100%, and the value of this playbook becomes crystal clear.

This adjustment is about **expanding and repositioning your structure**.

"Spread the Spread" shows how to take an existing spread position and alter its structure to improve probability, adjust risk, or better align with your outlook.

Instead of exiting or overhauling the trade, you evolve it.

By adjusting the spread, you can:

- Reduce risk
- Reposition the profit zone
- Reduce pressure from directional movement

This is a powerful example of structural flexibility:
you're not locked into your original setup—you can reshape it as conditions change.

The deeper takeaway:
A trade is not fixed. It's adaptable.

And with the right adjustments, you can continuously refine it toward a higher-probability outcome.

Now that you can reshape the structure of a trade, the next step is learning how to actively manage risk and preserve profits as the market moves. Get ready for **The "Squeeze Play" Adjustment**.

CHAPTER 15

THE "SQUEEZE PLAY" ADJUSTMENT

CHAPTER 15
The "Squeeze Play" Adjustment

Most option traders have no idea how adjustable simple debit and credit spreads actually are.

These vertical spreads, coupled with this simple yet powerful adjustment, become one of the staples of option trade adjustments.

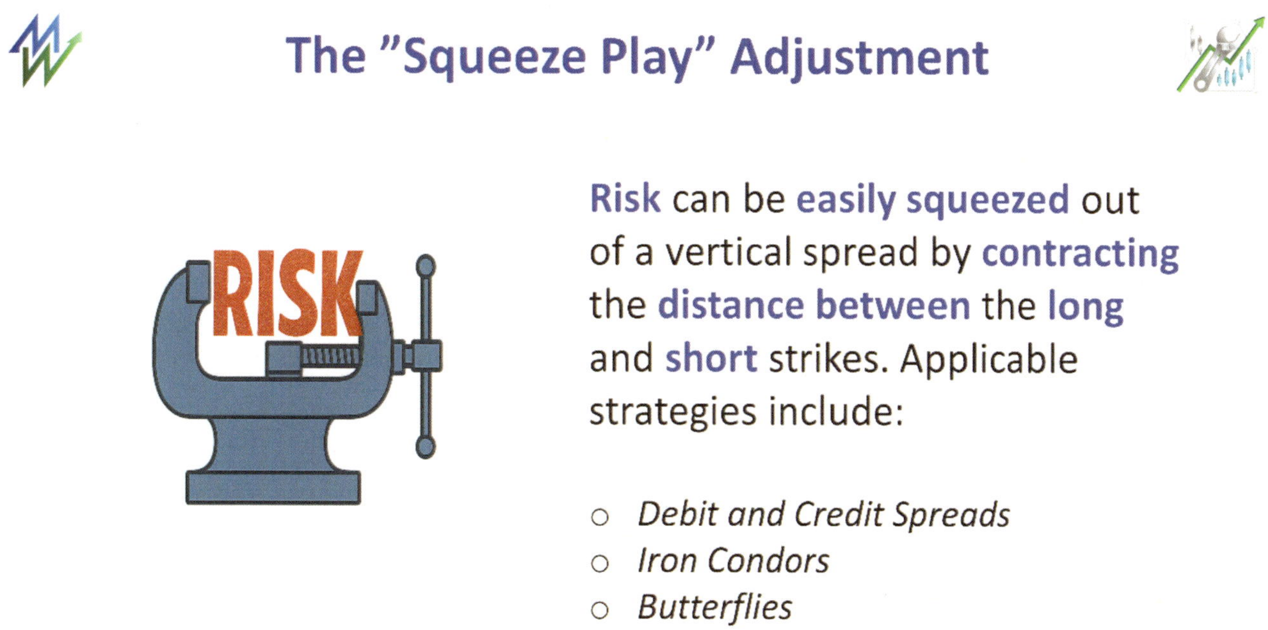

The "Squeeze Play" adjustment is a powerful move that squeezes risk out of a vertical spread by reducing the distance between the strikes.

The "Squeeze Play" Adjustment

Description: *The "Squeeze Play" adjustment is simple yet powerful adjustment to manage risk in any vertical spread. Should you be facing additional loss or you want to lock in a profit, rolling up your long option strike closer to the short option strike will squeeze risk out of your spread. In order to capitalize on this adjustment, you must start with a vertical spread with at least 1 additional strike between the long option and the short option.*

Strategies: *Any vertical spread strategy including debit/credit spreads, iron condors and butterflies.*

Outcome: *This adjustment results in reduced risk in the spread. This can result in a guaranteed profit. The trade-off is that the max profit potential is decreased.*

Timing: *For debit spreads in which the stock is approaching the long strike, this adjustment will squeeze risk out of the trade. The same applies for credit spreads in which the stock approaches or crosses your short strike. It can also be applied to debit and credit spreads to lock in a profit.*

This adjustment is applicable to any position with a debit or credit spread within it.

When used correctly, the "Squeeze Play" enhances your risk/reward profile by shrinking your exposure while keeping control of your directional thesis.

With RISK MANAGEMENT as our mantra, this adjustment is not just optional. It's essential.

Description

The "Squeeze Play" adjustment is a simple yet powerful technique for managing risk in any vertical spread. When facing additional losses or wanting to lock in profits, you can roll your long option strike closer to the short strike to squeeze risk out of the trade. To use this adjustment successfully, start with a vertical spread that has at least one strike between the long and short legs.

Strategies

This adjustment is applicable to any vertical spread strategy, including:

- Debit Spreads
- Credit Spreads
- Iron Condors
- Butterflies

Outcome

The outcome of applying the “Squeeze Play” is lowered risk within the spread. In many cases, it can even secure a guaranteed profit. The trade-off? A lower maximum profit potential. It’s a typical example of sacrificing some upside to eliminate downside.

Timing

Timing is key:

- For **debit spreads**, use the “Squeeze Play” when the stock approaches your long strike.
- For **credit spreads**, apply it when the stock is nearing or crossing your short strike.

In either case, this adjustment can be a proactive way to lock in a profit or squeeze out unnecessary risk before expiration.

The Effect of Spread Strike Distance

Let’s highlight an important vertical spread law:

The distance between the long and short strikes of a debit or credit spread directly impacts the potential ROI of the trade.

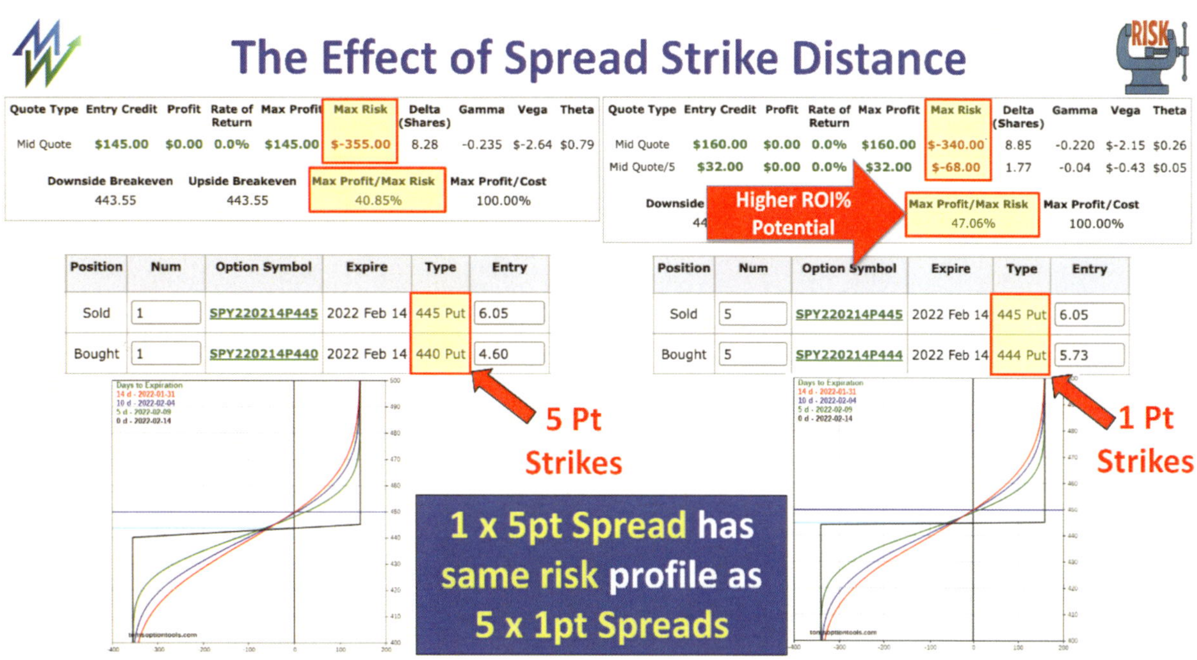

At one end of the spectrum, using consecutive 1-point strikes (the narrowest spread possible) typically offers higher ROI potential than a spread with multiple strikes between the legs.

In the illustration above, we compare two SPY put credit spreads:

- On the left, the spread uses a $445/$440 combination (5-points wide).
  - **Entry credit:** $145
  - **Max risk:** $355
  - **ROI:** 40.85%

- On the right, the spread uses $445/$444, repeated across 5 contracts (1-point wide).
  - **Entry credit:** $160 (total)
  - **Max risk:** $340 (total)
  - **ROI:** 47.06%

At first glance, the 1-point spread appears better: similar risk, more ROI.

But here's the twist—and why the 5-point spread is better when it comes to risk management:

Only the 5-point spread allows room for the "Squeeze Play" adjustment. You can shift your long strike from $440 to $444, reducing the spread and limiting risk. The 1-point spread doesn't provide this option because it's already at its narrowest.

In this game of risk vs. reward, flexibility wins. And the "Squeeze Play" puts that flexibility into action.

Let's now walk through how to apply this adjustment step by step in a real trade.

"Squeeze Play" - Reducing Risk

With risk management job 1 as traders, let's take a look at how the "Squeeze Play" can be used to manage risk.

Here we see a $365/$370 bear call spread (left graphic) in which the stock has moved against the original bearish prognosis. The trade is currently down $59 (a 21.7% loss) with a max risk of $272.

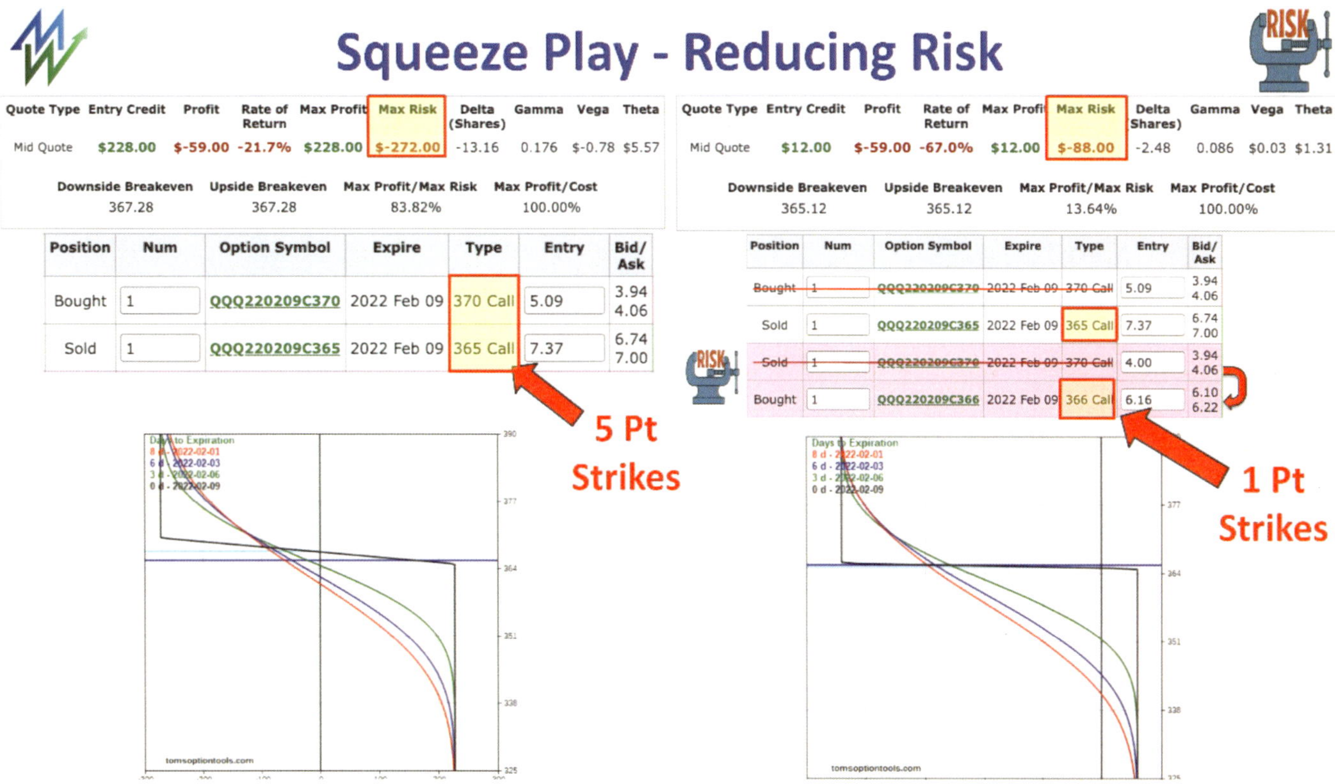

This is where most traders begin inviting Hope and Faith to the party—anticipating the trade will recover and doing nothing. But let me tell you: Hope and Faith will ruin any trader's party.

Always remember: it can get worse. In this case, another $158 of potential loss still exists.

This is THE TIME to adjust.

Manage the risk and let winners take care of themselves.

The trade on the right shows the power of the "Squeeze Play" nicely. We rolled down the $370 call to as close to the $365 short call as we could, resulting in a 1-point wide credit spread.

Now look at the outcome:

- Max risk drops from $272 to just $88
- We're already down $59, so we can only lose another $29
- The trade-off? Our max ROI potential is now just 13.64%, much lower than the original

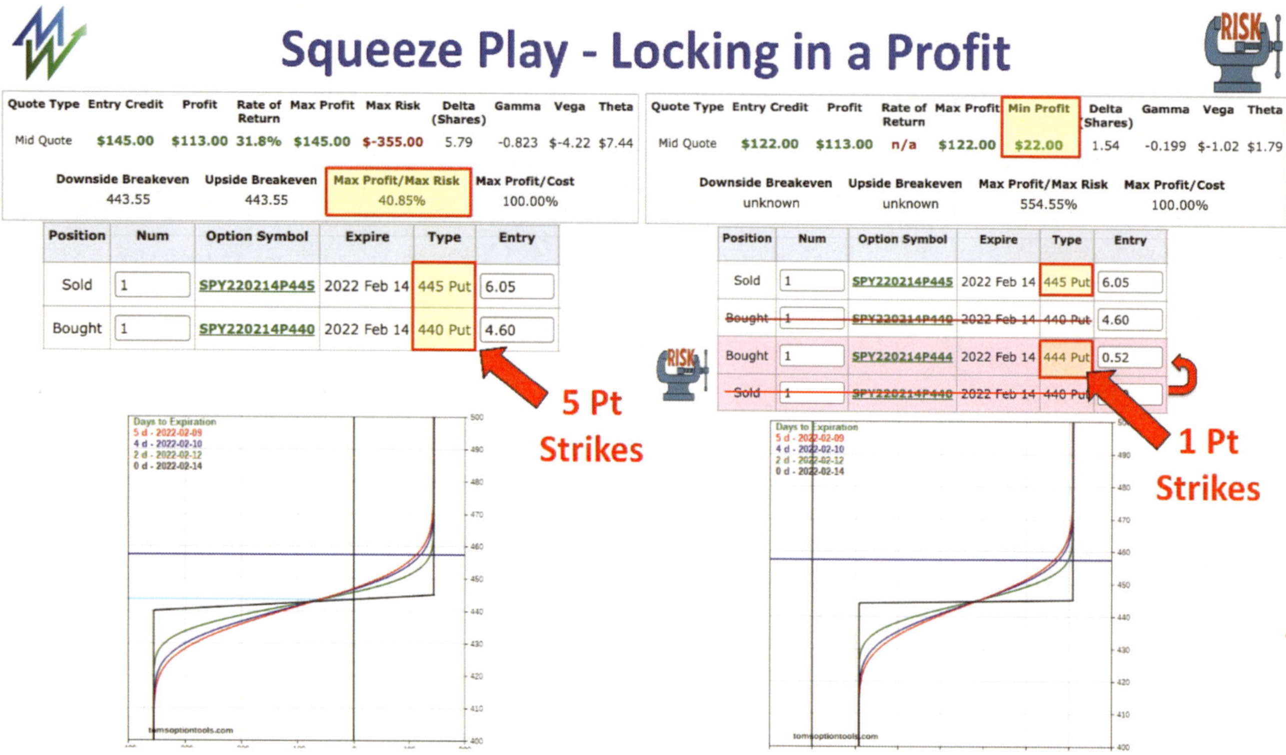

But with risk contained, we regain our most important asset: clarity. From here, we can consider other adjustments—many of which you'll find in this manual.

"Squeeze Play" - Locking in a Profit

Now that we can squeeze risk out of a spread, let's take a look at using the "Squeeze Play" to lock in a profit.

On the left is a bull put spread on the SPYs, created by selling a $445 put and buying a $440 put. Our directional forecast has become reality, and we have a profit of $133 on $355 of risk—a 31.8% return.

Although the max risk is $355, our total risk is $688 when you factor in that if we take a max loss, we lose both our investment and our profit.

The good news is that this spread is 5 points wide, giving us the possibility of mitigating risk in the trade.The trade on the right illustrates how to do exactly that. By rolling the $440 long put up to $444, we convert the spread to a 1-point wide spread.

Here's what changes:

- Max risk drops dramatically
- We lock in a guaranteed profit of $22, with room for additional gains

Squeeze Play Guidelines

1. Initiate the spread with at least **1 strike between** the **long** and the **short** strikes.

TIP

2. This will result in a slightly **lower ROI potential**.

3. However, this extra strike between the long and the short strike will provide the ability to **control risk** and potentially **lock in a profit** with the **Squeeze Play!**

4. To Squeeze, **move** the **long** strike towards the short **strike**.

Imagine a moment being in a trade with locked-in profit.

What would that do to your psychology?

"Squeeze Play" Guidelines

When planning to use the "Squeeze Play", it's important to design your spread with future flexibility in mind. The key is to start your vertical spread with **at least one strike between your long and short legs**. While this may slightly reduce your initial return on investment, it allows for adjustments that can significantly reduce risk—or even lock in profit.This deliberate spacing between strikes is what gives the "Squeeze Play" its power. It enables you to control exposure as the trade unfolds. If the market moves against you or you've already secured most of your profit, you can tighten the spread by bringing the long strike closer to the short. This reduction limits further downside and stabilizes your position.

The takeaway? Give yourself flexibility to adjust. The extra margin in your setup isn't first few moves. You're playing the net, your defensive move, and sometimes your profit safeguard. Like a smart chess player, you're not dedicating all your energy to the first few moves—you're playing the long game with options.

Summary - Squeezing Risk Out of Your Trade

The "Squeeze Play" is one of the most practical and adaptable adjustments available to spread traders. While it may slightly reduce your maximum ROI slightly at entry, the trade-off is well worth it: the ability to reduce risk, prevent large drawdowns, and even lock in profits when the trade moves in your favor.

By building spreads with space between the long and short strikes, you give yourself the power to adjust dynamically as the market moves. You are no longer at the mercy of Hope and Faith. You become the master of your trade's fate.

This adjustment is straightforward in concept, powerful in its effect, and perfectly aligns with our guiding principle: Prioritize managing risk first, and let profits take care of themselves.

Use it wisely, and you'll always have a move to make—just like a chess master with one more piece on the board.

Now that you know how to reduce risk in a winning or losing position, the next step is learning how to handle trades that need more time to work. **The "Kick the Can Down the Road" Adjustment** is next.

CHAPTER 16

THE “KICK THE CAN DOWN THE ROAD” ADJUSTMENT

CHAPTER 16
The "Kick the Can Down the Road" Adjustment

Alright, let's kick it up a notch!

We're stepping into another powerful vertical spread adjustment—and this one's perfect for when things heat up in a losing credit spread.

Because let's face it... We're not always right on direction.

And when the stock begins to surge toward your short strike, those losses can quickly add up. That's exactly when this move steps in to give you some breathing room.

The "Kick the Can Down the Road" Adjustment

A great way to **manage risk** in credit spreads. **Sell** yourself **time to be right** by **moving** your **losing credit spread** farther out in **time** and **strike**. Applicable strategies include:

- *Credit Spreads*
- *Iron Condors*
- *Butterflies*

Just like the old-school phrase "kick the can down the road," this adjustment lets you push the trade forward in time, giving yourself a second chance to be right.

How? You extend the losing credit spread to a later expiration—and sometimes even to a better strike. You're essentially giving yourself more time. Time for the market to settle down. Time for the trade to turn around. Time for YOU to make smarter decisions from a position of strength, not panic.

This technique can be applied to any trade with a credit spread embedded in it, including:

- Credit Spreads
- Iron Condors
- Butterflies

This move isn't about giving up. It's about staying in the game, regrouping, and repositioning like a pro. Let's explore how to make this adjustment work for you—when the market throws a punch, you'll know how to step back, reset, and stay in the fight.

The "Kick the Can Down the Road" Adjustment

Description:	*The "Kick the Can Down the Road" adjustment is simple yet powerful adjustment to manage risk in a credit spread. The basic idea is to move your losing credit spread farther OTM and out in time, kicking the spread down the road.*
Strategies:	*Any trade that has a credit spread within it. Typical strategies include Credit spreads, Butterflies and Iron Condors.*
Outcome:	*This adjustment results in decreasing the probability of loss and increasing the probability of profit.*
Timing:	*Sooner is better than later for this adjustment. As the stock approaches your short strike start considering the adjustment. As support or resistance levels are breached, consider this adjustment. Apply this adjustment no later than a breach of the short strike.*

Description

The "Kick the Can Down the Road" adjustment is one of the most elegant risk-management strategies in our playbook. When a credit spread begins to move against you, this adjustment offers a strong option: extend the trade's time frame and often push it further out of the money. In other words, kick the spread forward to give the market more room and time to cooperate.

It's a deceptively simple tactic. You're not abandoning the trade, you're repositioning it. And when used early enough, it can buy you exactly what you need: Distance from risk and time to be right.

Strategies

You can apply this adjustment to any trade that contains a credit spread, including:

- Standard Credit Spreads
- Iron Condors
- Butterflies

If there's a short option creating pressure in your position, this move can help relieve it.

Outcome

The main advantage of this adjustment is both psychological and practical: It lowers the risk of loss and boosts your chance of profit by moving the trade to a different time and price zone. Yes, the trade may now need more patience—but you'll be in a stronger, more composed position.

Timing

Here's the key: Sooner is better than later.

Don't wait until the short strike is being steamrolled. Start considering adjustments when the stock approaches your short strike, especially if key support or resistance levels are tested.

If a breach is imminent—or just happened—it's not too late, but it's definitely time. Don't hesitate. Don't freeze. Adjust.

Apply the "Kick the Can" adjustment before the market forces your hand. Proactive moves keep you in control—and control is the name of the game.

Real Trade Example – META Bear Call Spread

Here's a real example of the "Kick the Can" adjustment in action.

We've got a bear call spread on META, using the $610/$612.5 strikes. Just one day before, this position was comfortably in profit.

The "Kick the Can Down the Road" Adjustment

Entry Credit	Profit	Rate of Return	Max Profit	Max Risk	Delta (Shares)	Gamma	Vega	Theta
$220.00	$52.00	6.7%	$220.00	$-780.00	-8.53	-0.264	$-3.01	$45.44
$55.00	$13.00	6.7%	$55.00	$-195.00	-2.13	-0.07	$-0.75	$11.36

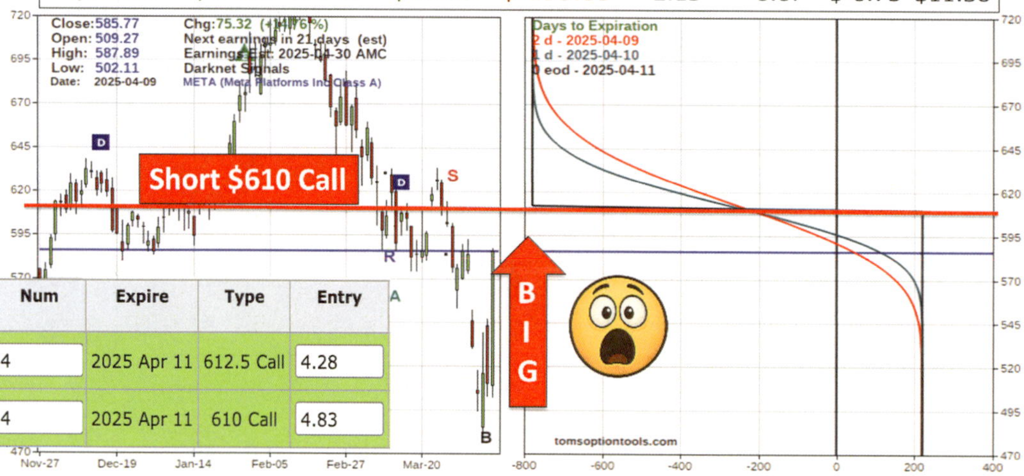

Position	Num	Expire	Type	Entry
Bought	4	2025 Apr 11	612.5 Call	4.28
Sold	4	2025 Apr 11	610 Call	4.83

But on this particular day, META exploded to the upside—making a sharp move directly toward our short $610 call. And we all understand what that means: We're standing right in front of max risk, with little room left to breathe.

The red zone is real. One more pop, and we could be looking at the full $780 max loss. But instead of panicking...

We kick the can.

We roll the entire spread out over time and move up the strike price, giving ourselves more distance, Theta, and a second chance to be right.

This is why we build these adjustments into our toolkit—not just to survive, but to stay in the game with clarity and control.

How the Roll Works – Mechanics in Action

Let's break it down. Here's how the "Kick the Can" adjustment actually works in execution:

We do two things:

Step 1: We roll up the strikes. The new short strike should be placed at a level the stock is less likely to reach—in this case, $615 resistance, which is 5 points higher than our original $610 short call.

Step 2: We extend the expiration. If we stayed with the same expiration, the cost of rolling up would result in a sizable debit. But by going further out in time, we collect more credit. We're literally selling time to be right.

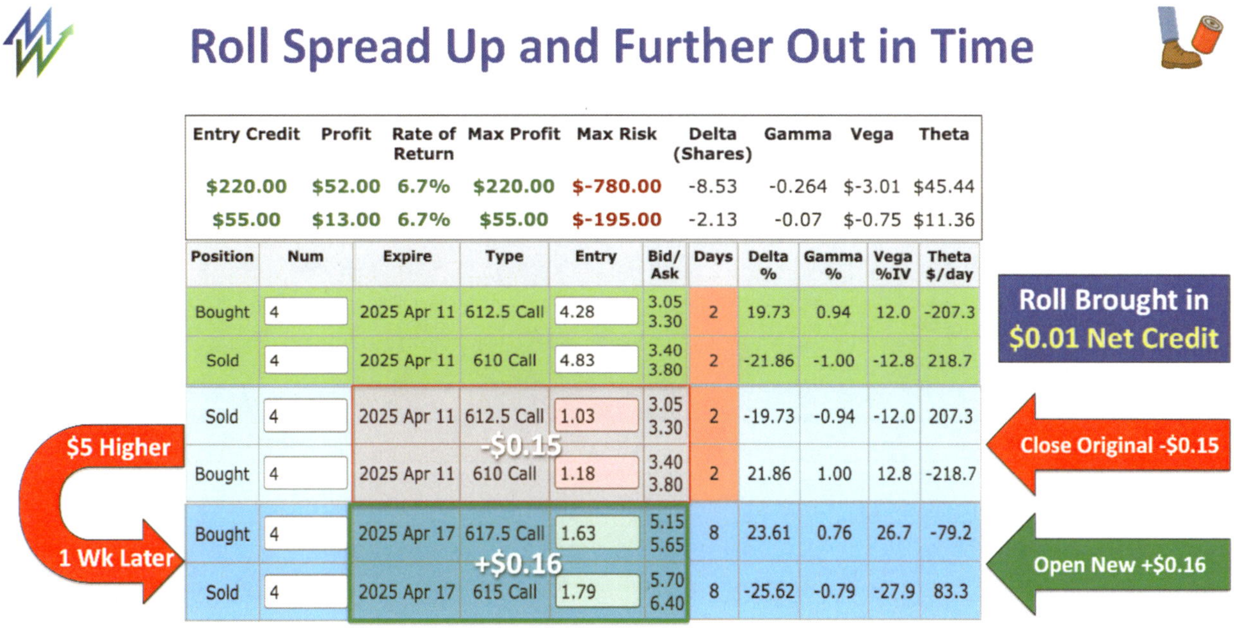

Entry Credit	Profit	Rate of Return	Max Profit	Max Risk	Delta (Shares)	Gamma	Vega	Theta
$220.00	$52.00	6.7%	$220.00	$-780.00	-8.53	-0.264	$-3.01	$45.44
$55.00	$13.00	6.7%	$55.00	$-195.00	-2.13	-0.07	$-0.75	$11.36

Position	Num	Expire	Type	Entry	Bid/ Ask	Days	Delta %	Gamma %	Vega %IV	Theta $/day
Bought	4	2025 Apr 11	612.5 Call	4.28	3.05 3.30	2	19.73	0.94	12.0	-207.3
Sold	4	2025 Apr 11	610 Call	4.83	3.40 3.80	2	-21.86	-1.00	-12.8	218.7
Sold	4	2025 Apr 11	612.5 Call	1.03	3.05 3.30	2	-19.73	-0.94	-12.0	207.3
Bought	4	2025 Apr 11	610 Call	1.18	3.40 3.80	2	21.86	1.00	12.8	-218.7
Bought	4	2025 Apr 17	617.5 Call	1.63	5.15 5.65	8	23.61	0.76	26.7	-79.2
Sold	4	2025 Apr 17	615 Call	1.79	5.70 6.40	8	-25.62	-0.79	-27.9	83.3

The trade mechanics:

- We close the original credit spread (cost: $0.15)
- Then we open a new April 17 $615/$617.50 spread (credit: $0.16)

That's a $0.01 net credit to roll. That's ideal. But even if it were to cost a small debit, the increased distance and time often justify the move.

This is the "Kick the Can" move at its finest—moving your position out of danger while keeping yourself in the game.

Result of the Roll – Comparing Risk and ROI

Original trade: Max risk $780, potential ROI 28.21%

New rolled trade: Max risk $776, potential ROI 28.87%

Better distance. More time. Slightly improved risk/reward profile. We stayed in the game, smartly.

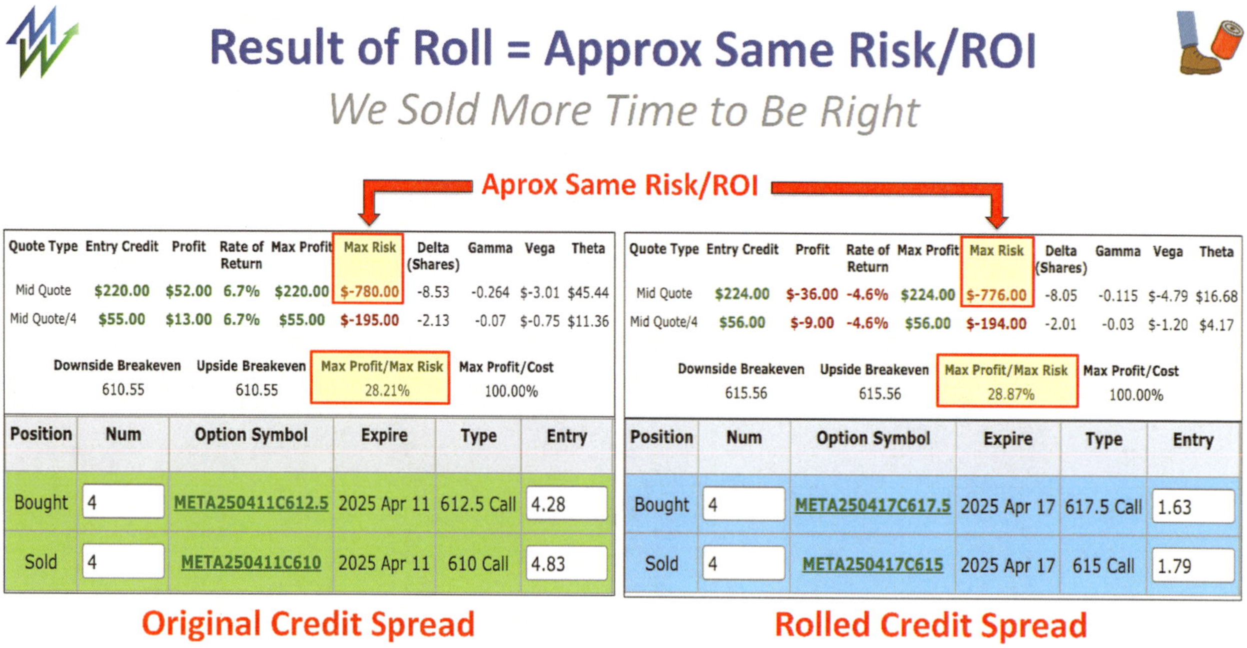

Original Credit Spread

Quote Type	Entry Credit	Profit	Rate of Return	Max Profit	Max Risk	Delta (Shares)	Gamma	Vega	Theta
Mid Quote	$220.00	$52.00	6.7%	$220.00	$-780.00	-8.53	-0.264	$-3.01	$45.44
Mid Quote/4	$55.00	$13.00	6.7%	$55.00	$-195.00	-2.13	-0.07	$-0.75	$11.36

Downside Breakeven	Upside Breakeven	Max Profit/Max Risk	Max Profit/Cost
610.55	610.55	28.21%	100.00%

Position	Num	Option Symbol	Expire	Type	Entry
Bought	4	META250411C612.5	2025 Apr 11	612.5 Call	4.28
Sold	4	META250411C610	2025 Apr 11	610 Call	4.83

Rolled Credit Spread

Quote Type	Entry Credit	Profit	Rate of Return	Max Profit	Max Risk	Delta (Shares)	Gamma	Vega	Theta
Mid Quote	$224.00	$-36.00	-4.6%	$224.00	$-776.00	-8.05	-0.115	$-4.79	$16.68
Mid Quote/4	$56.00	$-9.00	-4.6%	$56.00	$-194.00	-2.01	-0.03	$-1.20	$4.17

Downside Breakeven	Upside Breakeven	Max Profit/Max Risk	Max Profit/Cost
615.56	615.56	28.87%	100.00%

Position	Num	Option Symbol	Expire	Type	Entry
Bought	4	META250417C617.5	2025 Apr 17	617.5 Call	1.63
Sold	4	META250417C615	2025 Apr 17	615 Call	1.79

Before and After – Risk Graph Comparison

A picture paints a thousand words. Before the adjustment, we faced limited time and higher pressure. After the change, we have gained breathing room—increasing the chances of success while keeping the risk under control.

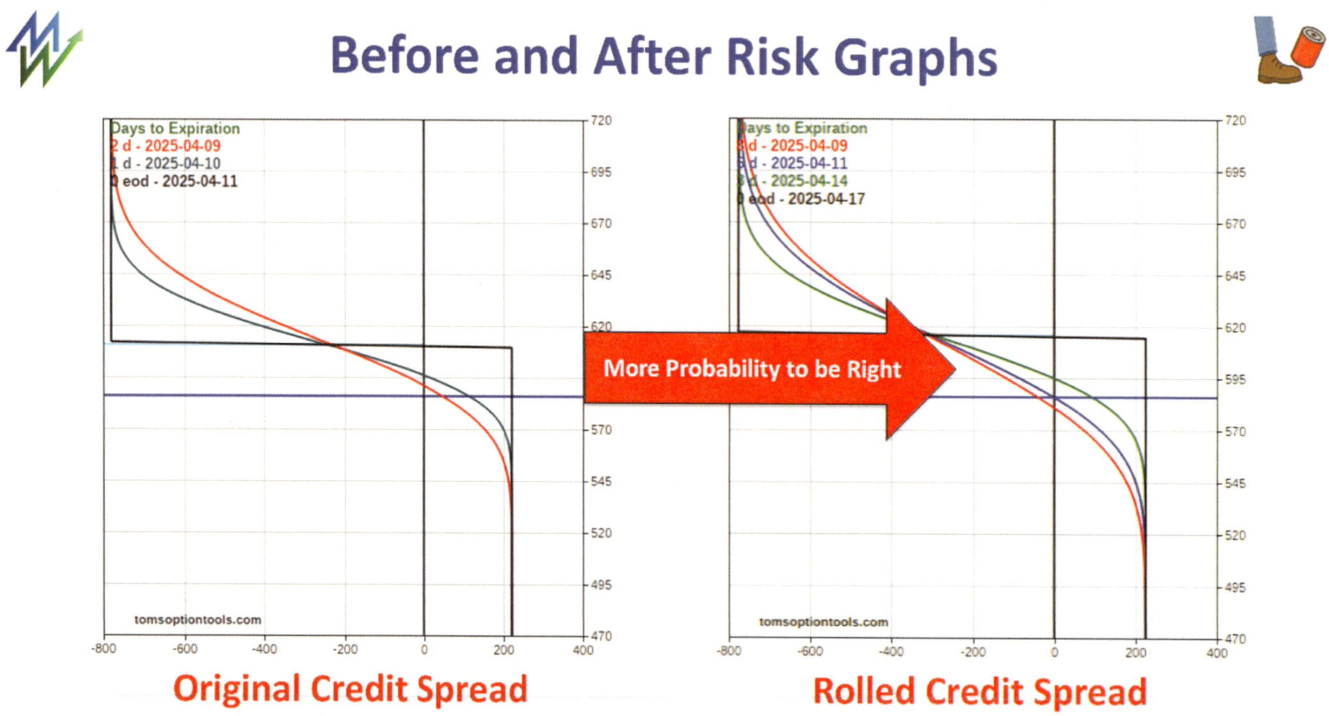

Guidelines to Mastering "Kick the Can Down the Road" Adjustment

Let's talk through how to master the "Kick the Can" adjustment.

Picture this: The stock starts drifting dangerously close to your short strike. That's your cue. Don't wait for it to cross the line—adjust before it breaks through. You want to stay ahead of the move, not react to it in panic.

The "Kick the Can Down the Road" Adjustment

Rules of Thumb

1. Consider this adjustment as stock approaches your short strike.
2. Adjust no later than a breach of the short strike.
3. Early adjustments are better. Use support and resistance breaches as potential early adjustment triggers.
4. For the new credit spread, consider short strikes as far OTM as possible. Usually, 1-2 strikes are available.
5. Consider expiration dates starting at 7-days further out in time. Try longer expirations that match your time prognosis.
6. Roll should result in a small debit or even a credit.

Now, one of the best tools in your kit is watching for support and resistance levels. When those start to crack, it's often a solid signal that it's time to make a move.

And when you do make adjustments, consider giving your new spread some room to breathe. Try to select short strikes that are as far out-of-the-money as the market allows—usually there are one or two good options that provide a margin of safety.

At the same time, give yourself time to be right. Look at expirations that are at least a week out—seven days minimum—and make sure they match your current market prognosis. You're not just rolling out of trouble; you're positioning yourself for a more favorable outcome.

And when you execute the roll, aim for a small debit—or even better, a credit. That way, you're staying in the game without adding unnecessary cost to your position.

That's how you play this move like a pro.

Each of these moves is a strategic choice to stay in the game.

Summary - Buy Time Without Losing the Trade

This chapter introduces one of the most practical survival tools in the playbook.

The "Kick the Can Down the Road" adjustment is about **extending duration when the trade hasn't fully played out yet**. Instead of closing too early or taking unnecessary losses, you roll the position forward to give it more time.

The core idea:
Time can be an asset—if you know how to use it.

By extending the trade, you:

- Delay expiration pressure
- Preserve the original thesis
- Create additional opportunity for recovery or profit

This is especially valuable when your outlook still holds, but the timing was off.

It reinforces patience—but not passive patience:
You're not waiting... you're repositioning.

Now that you can extend time and keep trades alive, we are now going to use spreads to reduce directional and overall risk: **Delta Neutralizing Debit and Credit Spreads with the "Spread the Spread" Adjustment.**

CHAPTER 17

DELTA NEUTRALIZING DEBIT AND CREDIT SPREADS WITH THE "SPREAD THE SPREAD" ADJUSTMENT

CHAPTER 17
Delta Neutralizing Debit and Credit Spreads with the "Spread the Spread" Adjustment

Before we leave the magical world on debit and credit spreads, let's focus on one of the most influential adjustments in our playbook—one we've already covered: The "Spread the Spread" adjustment.

You already know what it is. Now, we're going to show you exactly how it transforms a position.

DNA with "Spread the Spread" Adjustment

A great way to **manage directional risk** in credit and debit spreads. **Reduce risk** and **delta neutralize** a spread by **selling a credit spread** against your credit or debit spread. Applicable strategies include:

- *Credit Spreads*
- *Debit Spreads*

When you apply the "Spread the Spread" adjustment to an existing credit or debit spread, you're not just adding protection. You're fundamentally reshaping the trade.

Adding a second credit spread can significantly reduce directional risk, flatten Delta, lower max risk, and often even boost ROI potential. It's like giving your trade a strong defensive move without sacrificing your offensive approach.

This section is all about visualizing the impact. When you apply this move:

- A credit spread becomes more neutral and better balanced.
- A debit spread gains protection while opening new profit potential.

We're not just learning the move. We're watching it in action. So, buckle up, because what's coming will reveal how strategic this adjustment truly is.

Summary Overview of the Adjustment

This graphic provides a clear summary of what happens when you apply the "Spread the Spread" adjustment to a credit or debit spread.

DNA with "Spread the Spread" Adjustment

Description: *Adjusting a spread into a condor or butterfly has the impact of neutralizing position delta, adding credit and reducing risk.*

Strategies: *Any trade that has a credit or debit spread within it. Typical strategies include credit spreads and debit spreads*

Outcome: *This adjustment results in decreasing risk, the probability of loss and increasing the probability of profit. The adjustment has the impact of neutralizing directional risk (delta) and letting +Theta bring in profits into the position less fettered.*

Timing: *Sooner is better than later for this adjustment. As the stock approaches your credit spread short strike or debit spread long strike, start considering the adjustment. As support or resistance levels are breached, consider this adjustment. Apply this adjustment no later than a breach of the short or long strike in a credit and debit spread respectively*

Adjusting a spread—by turning it into a structure like a condor or butterfly—helps neutralize your position's Delta. This means you're reducing your directional risk. At the same time, you're adding credit and decreasing overall position risk.

The strategies where this applies are straightforward: Any position that has a credit or debit spread embedded in it. That includes classic credit spreads and debit spreads.

What's the outcome? This move can reduce overall risk, lower the chance of loss, and increase the chance of profit. Specifically, it softens the directional bias (Delta) and puts +Theta to work, generating potential profits through time decay.

And when it comes to timing, earlier is better. You want to be thinking about this adjustment as soon as the stock starts approaching your short strike (in a credit spread) or long strike (in a debit spread). If support or resistance levels are being tested or breached, it's time to act. Ideally, make this adjustment before a breach, not after.

GLD Example – Bull Put Spread in Jeopardy

We initiated a $275/$273 bull put credit spread on GLD, expecting it to rise. For a while, it did just that. The trade remained comfortably profitable—until April 4, 2025, when GLD suddenly dropped 2.34% in a single day.

This sharp drop brought GLD right back toward our short $275 put. What had been a winning trade just days earlier suddenly flipped to a -$145 unrealized loss, representing -16.4% of max risk.

But the big concern? Delta spiked to 27.31.

That means for every $1 drop in GLD, we're now at risk of losing an additional $27.31. And of course, GLD could fall more than $1, which would multiply our risk even further.

With risk management always job 1, it's time to act.

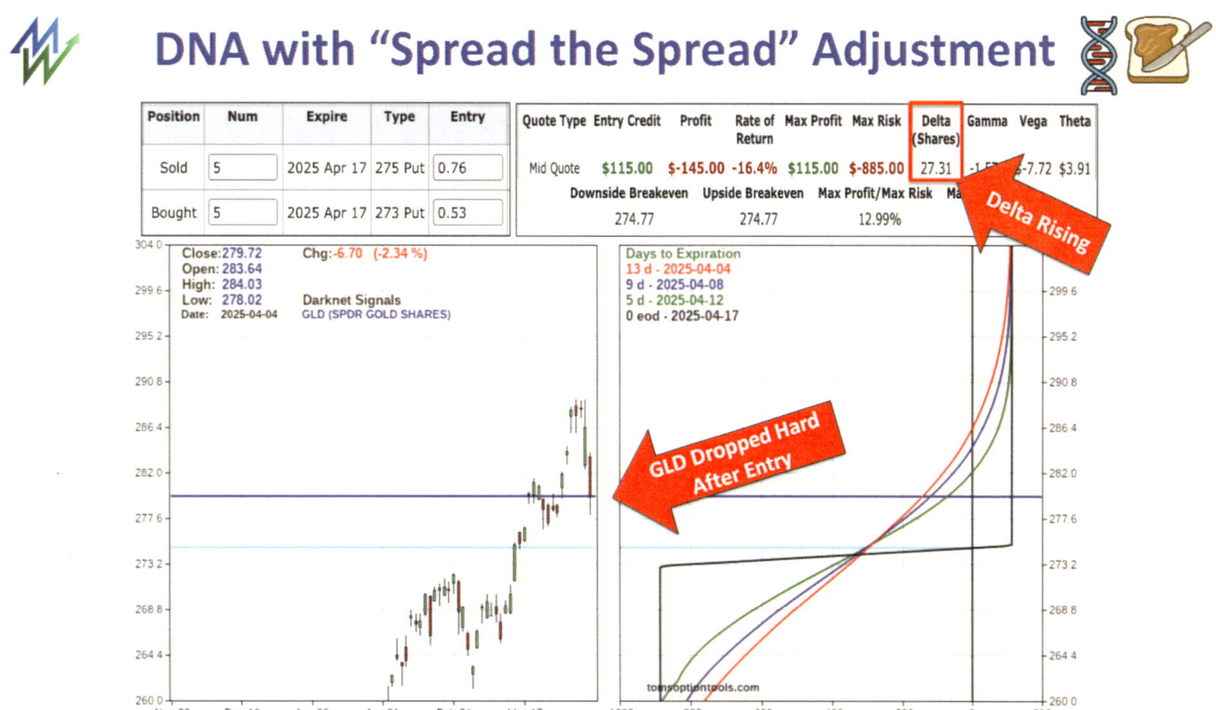

This is the ideal time to flatten out Delta using the "Spread the Spread" adjustment. By adding a second spread, we reduce directional exposure, lower total risk, and—bonus! . We often boost our maximum potential ROI at the same time.

Iron Condor Adjustment – Sell a Bear Call to "Spread the Spread"

We were already managing a bull put credit spread. Now, as GLD was dropping hard and threatening our short strike, we look above the recent high to find resistance. That's where we place our new adjustment.

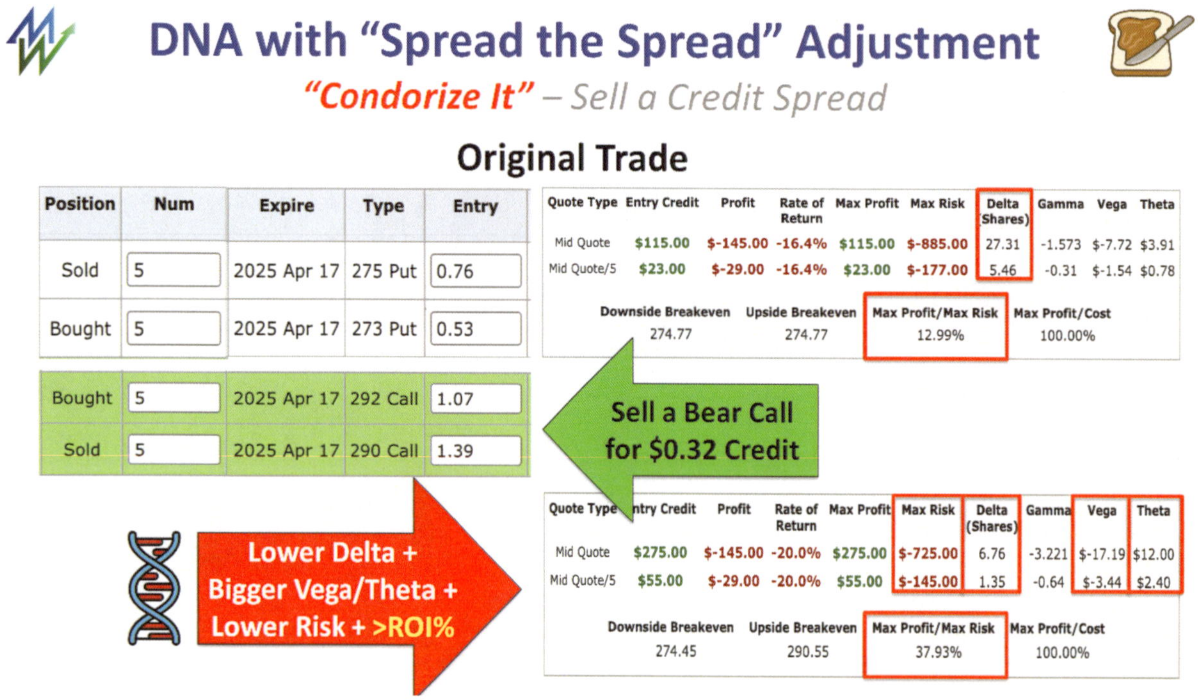

We sell a $290/$292 bear call spread—right at $290 resistance. We collected $0.32 per contract on 5 contracts, generating an additional $160 in credit.

What's that mean for our trade?

- We add that $160 to our maximum profit potential.
- We simultaneously reduce our max risk by $160.
- And—most importantly—we cut our Delta exposure from 27.31 all the way down to 6.67.

This is a textbook example of how the "Spread the Spread" adjustment works. We stay in the trade, reduce risk, increase profit potential, and neutralize our directional exposure.

Resulting Risk Graph – A New Game Board

Now let's take a look at what the trade looks like after the adjustment.

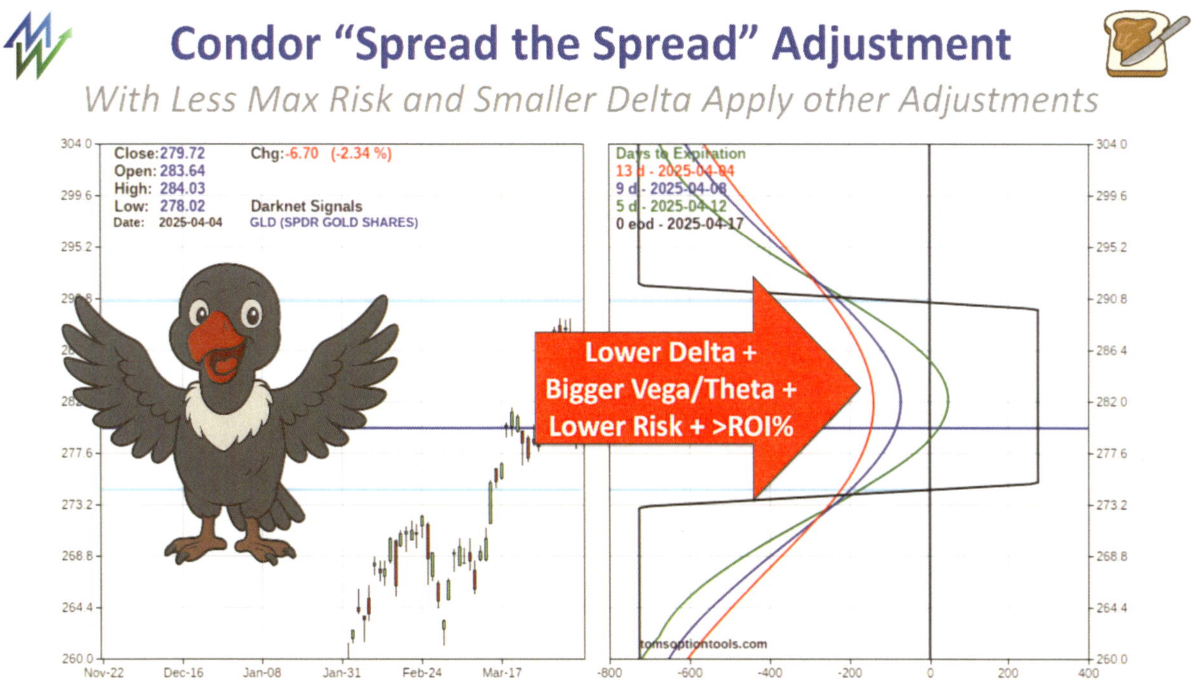

The new iron condor structure gives us a much wider profit zone—GLD can now move within a broader range, and we still have the opportunity to profit.

Take a close look at that red Theta line carefully. It's not falling as sharply into loss territory as GLD fluctuates.

Delta is now neutral. Directional risk has been minimized. And that's not all—Vega is more negative, and Theta is more positive.

That's the ideal setup for a trader who wants time on their side. Since tomorrow is certain to come, Theta will keep working in our favor, adding dollars to the account as each day passes.

Delta has been neutralized allowing **Theta to Do What Theta Do** less encumbered by directional risk

The cherry on top? Risk is lower, and the maximum ROI has nearly tripled.

Butterfly "Spread the Spread" – Lock It Down

If you really want to lock down risk in your trade, you can get more aggressive by using a butterfly-style "Spread the Spread" adjustment. Think of it as battening down the hatches.

DNA with "Spread the Spread" Adjustment

"Butterfly It" – *For Less Risk Than Condor DNA Adjustment*

Original Trade

Position	Num	Expire	Type	Entry
Sold	5	2025 Apr 17	275 Put	0.76
Bought	5	2025 Apr 17	273 Put	0.53
Bought	5	2025 Apr 17	277 Call	6.65
Sold	5	2025 Apr 17	275 Call	7.98

Quote Type	Entry Credit	Profit	Rate of Return	Max Profit	Max Risk	Delta (Shares)	Gamma	Vega	Theta
Mid Quote	$115.00	$-145.00	-16.4%	$115.00	$-885.00	27.31	-1.573	$-7.72	$3.91
Mid Quote/5	$23.00	$-29.00	-16.4%	$23.00	$-177.00	5.46	-0.31	$-1.54	$0.78

Downside Breakeven	Upside Breakeven	Max Profit/Max Risk	Max Profit/Cost
274.77	274.77	12.99%	100.00%

Sell a Bear Call for $1.33 Credit

Quote Type	Entry Credit	Profit	Rate of Return	Max Profit	Max Risk	Delta (Shares)	Gamma	Vega	Theta
Mid Quote	$777.50	$-147.50	-66.3%	$777.50	$-222.50	-1.86	-0.469	$-2.30	$1.52
Mid Quote/5	$155.50	$-29.50	-66.3%	$155.50	$-44.50	-0.37	-0.09	$-0.46	$0.30

Downside Breakeven	Upside Breakeven	Max Profit/Max Risk	Max Profit/Cost
273.45	276.56	349.44%	100.00%

Lowest Delta + Lower Vega/Theta + Lowest Risk + >ROI%

In this case, we use an iron butterfly setup by selling a bear call spread with the short strike matching the original bull put's short strike. For our GLD example, that means selling the $275/$277 bear call.

Selling that spread close to the heat generated a much higher credit—$1.33 per contract, or $665 total. That's a significant premium. It gets added to our total credit and deducted from our maximum risk.

The result? Our max risk was decimated, falling from $885 down to just $222.50.

This is the lowest risk setup we've seen so far—and it's also the most Delta-neutral. Delta fell to just 6.76, making the trade less affected by directional changes.

Plus, Theta increased to +12.00. That means each day that passes moves us closer to breakeven and potential profit—especially since we've already handled the tough part by neutralizing our directional exposure.

The ROI potential has also exploded—from 12.99% to 37.83%.

Keep in mind, this isn't an adjustment with a high-likelihood of profit. It's a loss recovery move, designed to weather the storm and allow for a potential bounce back. You're sacrificing probability for control, lowering risk, and giving the trade space to breathe.

Final Butterfly Risk Graph View – Visualizing Defense

This risk graph for our new iron butterfly quickly reveals all. Notice how the colored lines are nearly vertical, illustrating minimal directional risk—our Delta has been neutralized.

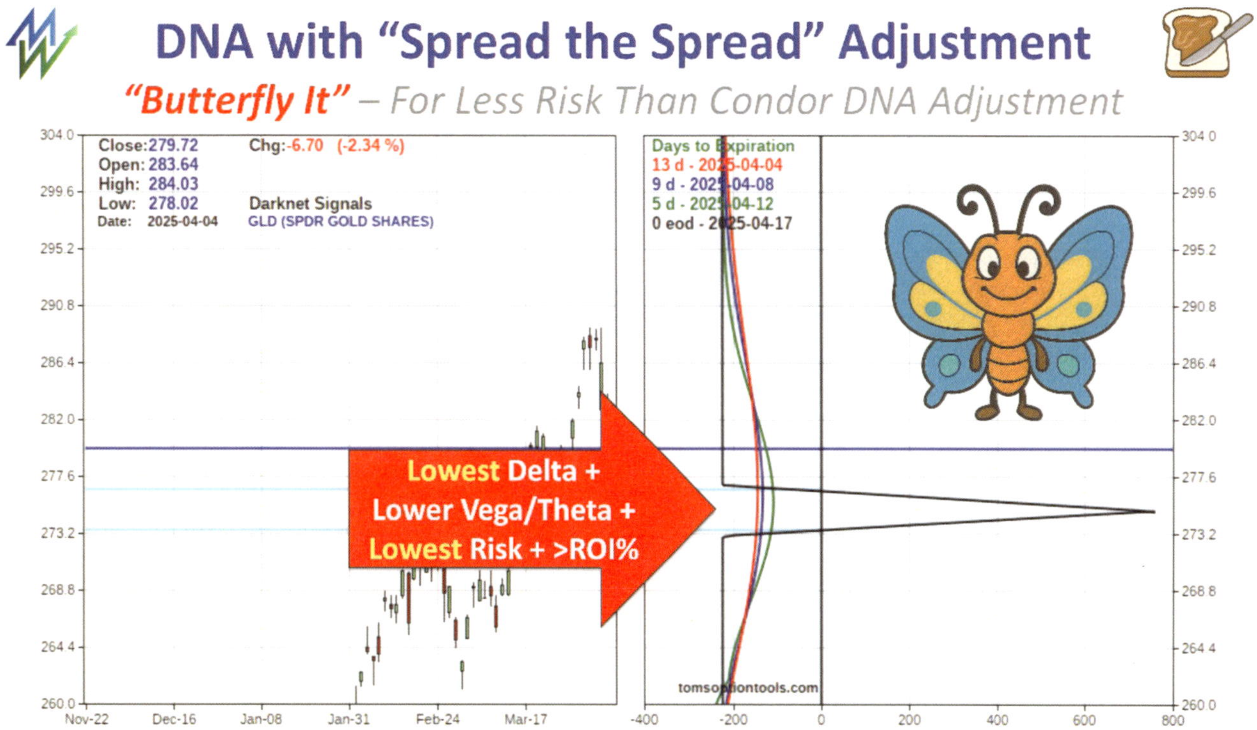

The risk graph also shows the small level of risk relative to the potential maximum profit, which indicates a theoretical—but unlikely—349.44% ROI.

To make money, GLD would need to settle very close to the body of the butterfly at expiration. Is that likely? No. But is that the point? Also, no.

The point is to lose less.

This adjustment helps you significantly manage risk. If GLD keeps moving higher, you can adjust this trade again—maybe by closing the losing side of the butterfly—but that's a discussion for another time.

For now, you've battened down the hatches and weathered the storm and given yourself time to adjust another day.

Summary – Playing the "Spread the Spread DNA" Game Like a Pro

Alright, let's bring it all together.

In this chapter, you learned how to play one of the most powerful cards in the Adjustment Club deck—the "Spread the Spread" move.

You saw how we turned a simple debit or credit spread into something much more resilient and strategic. By adding a second spread, we lowered directional risk, flattened Delta, boosted Theta, enhanced Vega, and tripled our potential ROI. That's a significant win. It's the kind of adjustment that allows you to keep playing your game even when the market tries to knock you out.

DNA with "Spread the Spread" Adjustment

Spreading the Spread Guidelines

1. The main **goal** of the spreading a spread is to **flatten directional risk** (delta/gamma) and **allow Theta to do its work.**
2. The additional spread can be placed **OTM (Condor)** or **ATM (Butterfly).**
3. In both cases, **risk** is **reduced** and **potential ROI** is **increased.**
4. Use the **Butterfly** adjustment to **lock down risk** to it's **lowest** and allow **theta** the opportunity to **reduce your loss** in the trade.
5. Use the **Condor** adjustment to **reduce risk** and allow theta the opportunity to **reduce your loss** with **> probability of profit** than the Fly.
6. Consider Spreading the Spread when **stock approaches** or **crosses** the **short strike** (credit spread) or **long strike** (debit spread).

We explored two flavors of this move:

- **The Iron Condor:** A smart, balanced defense that allows your trade to breathe. It expands your profit zone, reduces risk, and puts the time god (Theta) on your side. Perfect for taking control.
- **The Butterfly Lockdown:** When you need to slam the door shut on risk and stay alive, this is your go-to. You place your short call right on top of your short put, collect premium, reduce your risk, and give yourself a better shot at losing less. It's not about winning big. It's about surviving to play another round.

And that's the spirit of this chapter. It's about staying in the game.

Every great trader knows: The ones who succeed aren't just those who score the most points. They're the ones who last the longest. They adjust. They adapt. They outlast.

You now have a move that helps you do exactly that.

So next time Delta spikes, risk rises, and it seems like the market is pushing your position, don't panic. You have options. You have tools. And now, you have the "Spread the Spread" move in your arsenal.

Now, let's add a new powerful trading strategy to your arsenal that combines 2 vertical spreads: **Butterfly Spreads—The Basics.**

CHAPTER 18

BUTTERFLY SPREADS - THE BASICS

CHAPTER 18
Butterfly Spreads – The Basics

Throughout our journey, we have learned how to transform simple long options into more advanced vertical spreads. Now, we are taking another step forward. We're about to explore how two vertical spreads can be combined into one powerful structure called the butterfly.

Think of this strategy as "Spreading a Spread"—a concept we've already worked with.

At their core, butterfly spreads are created by combining a bullish vertical spread with a bearish vertical spread. As we previously discovered, there are only two types of vertical spreads.:

- Bull Spreads
- Bear Spreads

Each can be constructed with either calls or puts.

And it's the same idea with butterflies.

We can construct a butterfly using either all calls, all puts, or a combination of the two. And here's the key: No matter how you build the butterfly, the resulting risk graph is the same.

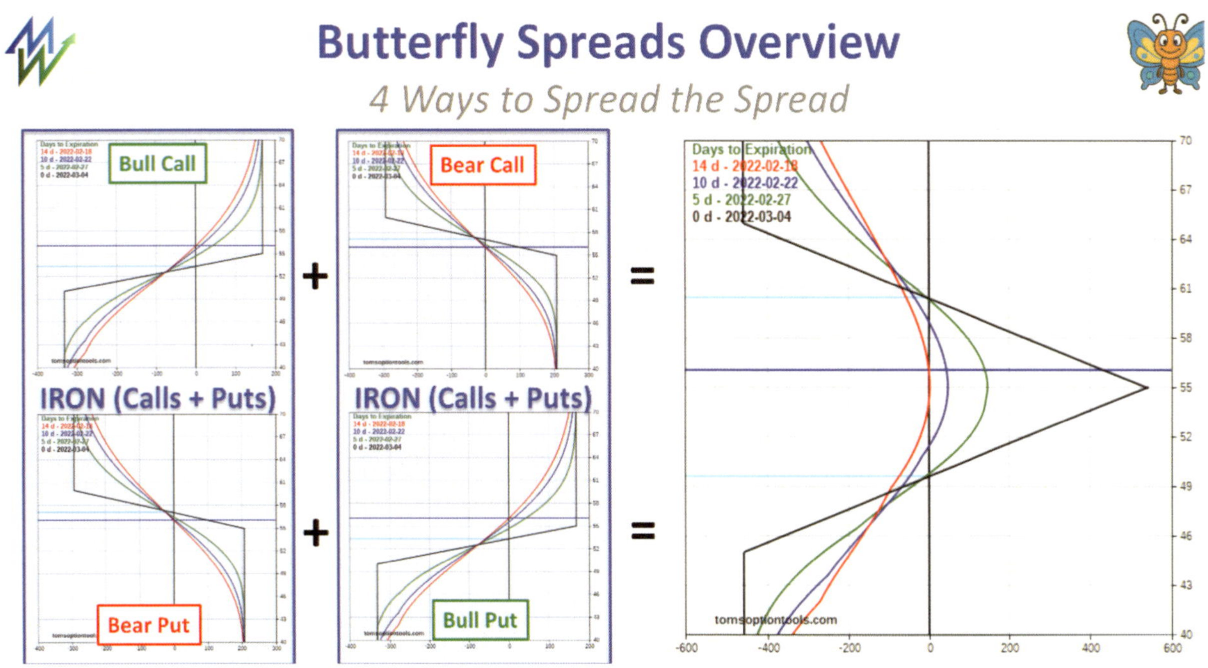

There are 4 unique ways to build a butterfly—all of them create the same payoff profile:

1. Bull Call + Bear Call = **Long Call Butterfly**
2. Bull Put + Bear Put = **Long Put Butterfly**
3. Bull Call + Bear Put = **Iron Butterfly**
4. Bull Put + Bear Call = **Iron Butterfly (Again!)**

These 4 construction methods are visually represented in the graphic above:

Constructing a Balanced Call Butterfly – And Reading the Greeks

Let's now look at a concrete example of a long call butterfly using GLD options.

In this setup, we combine:

- **1 Bull Call Spread:** Buy the $152.5 Call, Sell the $162.5 Call
- **1 Bear Call Spread:** Sell another $162.5 Call, Buy the $172.5 Call

Notice that both spreads share the same short strike ($162.50). This common strike forms the core of the butterfly. The cost to enter the trade is a debit, which also represents your maximum risk.

In the example below, the total debit paid is $500.00, which is the most you can lose.

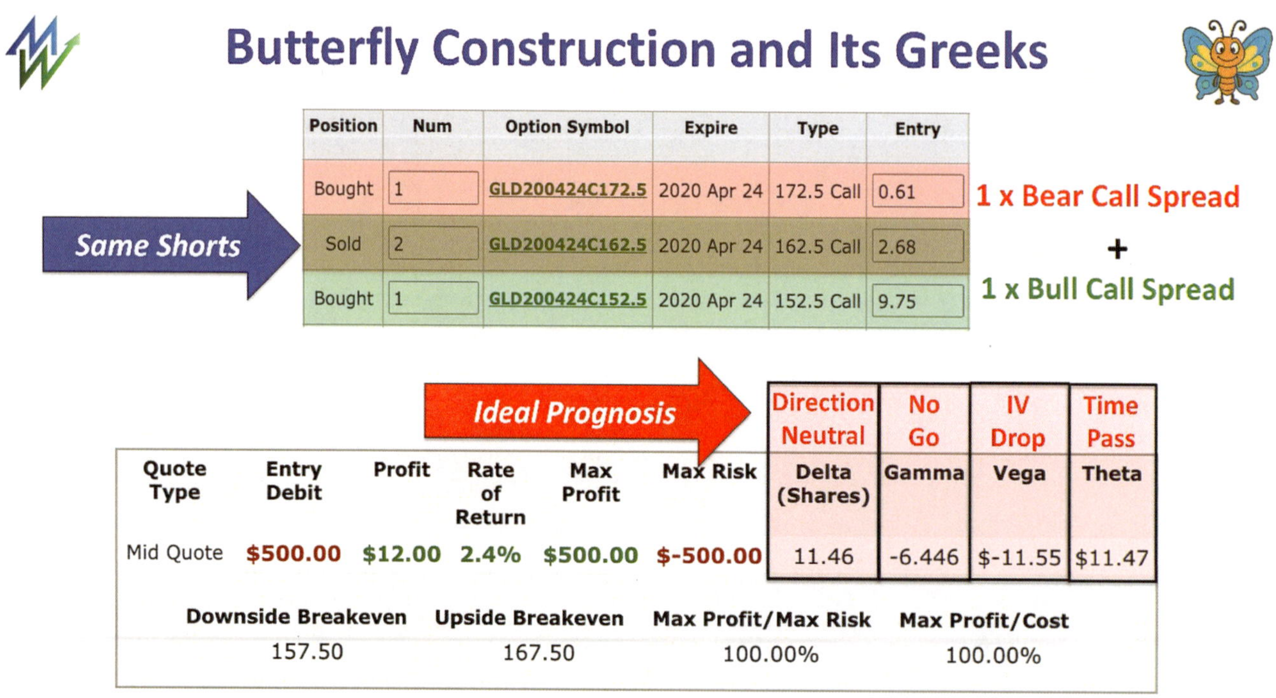

This particular butterfly is centered around the ATM (At-the-Money) strike of $162.50, which means it's designed to profit if the stock doesn't move much—a classic neutral trade.

Here's how the Greeks validate that prognosis:

- **Delta: 11.46**—For a $500 cost, this is nearly neutral. The trade doesn't rely on direction.
- **Gamma: -6.446**—A negative Gamma means the trade benefits if the stock doesn't move. We call this a "No Go" setup.
- **Vega: -11.55**—A drop in Implied Volatility (IV) helps the trade. Perfect for when implied volatility is high and expected to fall.
- **Theta: +11.47**—Time is on your side. With each passing day, the position gains value.

In other words, this trade profits if the stock stays around $162.50, IV drops or stays the same, and time passes.

This is what we call an ideal prognosis: Neutral direction, falling volatility, and time decay.

With only a small risk, this butterfly presents the potential for a 100% return—an attractive risk/reward profile for traders with a neutral outlook.

Butterfly Theta - Varies by Price

Let's now zoom in on Theta, one of the most critical Greeks in butterfly trading.

A butterfly consists of:

- **Two long options (the wings)**—which carry negative Theta
- **Two short options (the body)**—which carry positive Theta

Since Theta measures time decay, and all four options are near expiration, the balance of positive and negative Theta depends entirely on where the stock is trading.

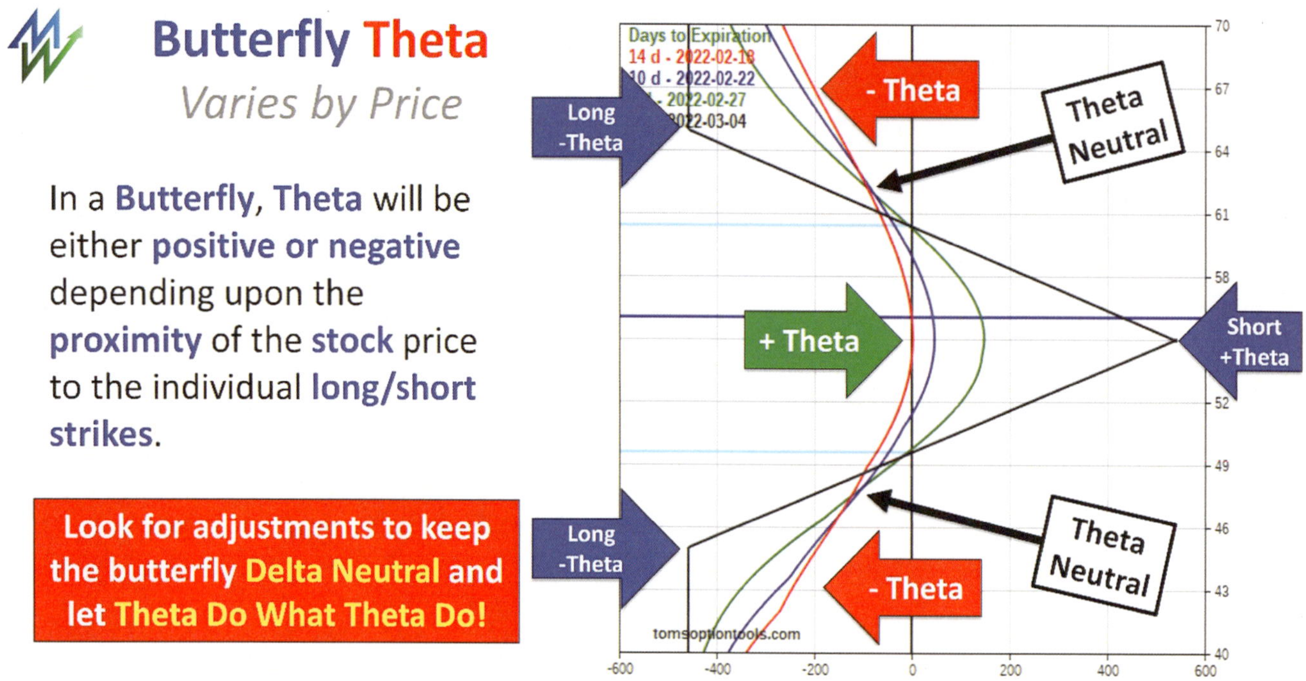

- **In the wings (closer to the outer strikes):** Theta will be negative. The long options dominate.
- **In the body (near the short strike):** Theta becomes positive. The short options dominate.
- **Between the zones:** Theta becomes temporarily neutral. This is where the Theta curves (colored lines) inflect.

The goal of a butterfly is to maintain a Delta Neutral position and to place the stock close to the butterfly's body to benefit from positive Theta—letting time work in your favor.

As the graphic states: **"Let Theta do what Theta do!"**

Later in this guide, we'll discuss smart adjustment strategies to keep your butterfly aligned with this goal—reducing directional risk while maximizing gains from time decay.

Butterfly Vega – Varies by Price

Just like Theta, Vega in a butterfly varies depending on how close the stock price is to the long or short strikes.

Butterfly Vega

Varies by Price

In a **Butterfly**, **Vega** will be either **positive or negative** depending upon the **proximity** of the **stock** price to the individual **long/short strikes**.

Look for adjustments to keep the butterfly Vega as negative as possible with a bearish IV prognosis. Vega is most negative at the short strike.

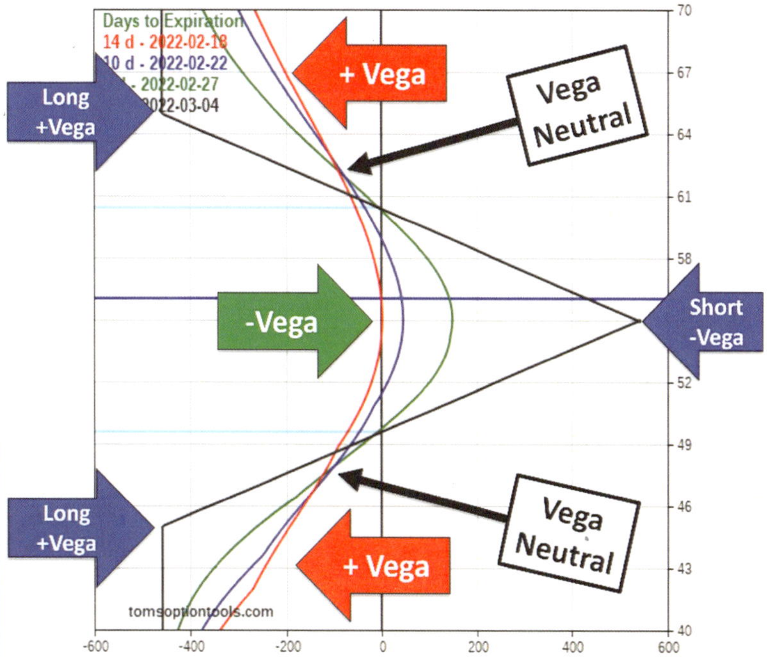

- **In the wings (closer to the long options):** Vega is positive.
- **In the body (at the short strike):** Vega turns negative.
- **Between the legs:** Vega may be neutral at the inflection point of the Theta lines and flips signs as the stock moves about half-way between the long and short strikes. This is because the Greeks mimic the structure of the leg the stock is closest to.

If your stock is in the body of the butterfly, you want a bearish IV forecast, or at least no expectation of an IV increase.

When the stock price sits right at the short strike (ATM), Vega is most negative—reinforcing the bearish implied volatility outlook built into the butterfly.

Adjustments to the butterfly may help you keep Vega negative when your IV prognosis is bearish.

Butterflies and Condors Are Kissing Cousins

Butterflies and condors are constructed nearly the same, except condors have split short strikes. Greeks are nearly identical when centered, but outcomes differ:

Butterfly:

- Less risk
- Lower probability
- Higher ROI

Condor:

- More risk
- Higher probability
- Lower ROI

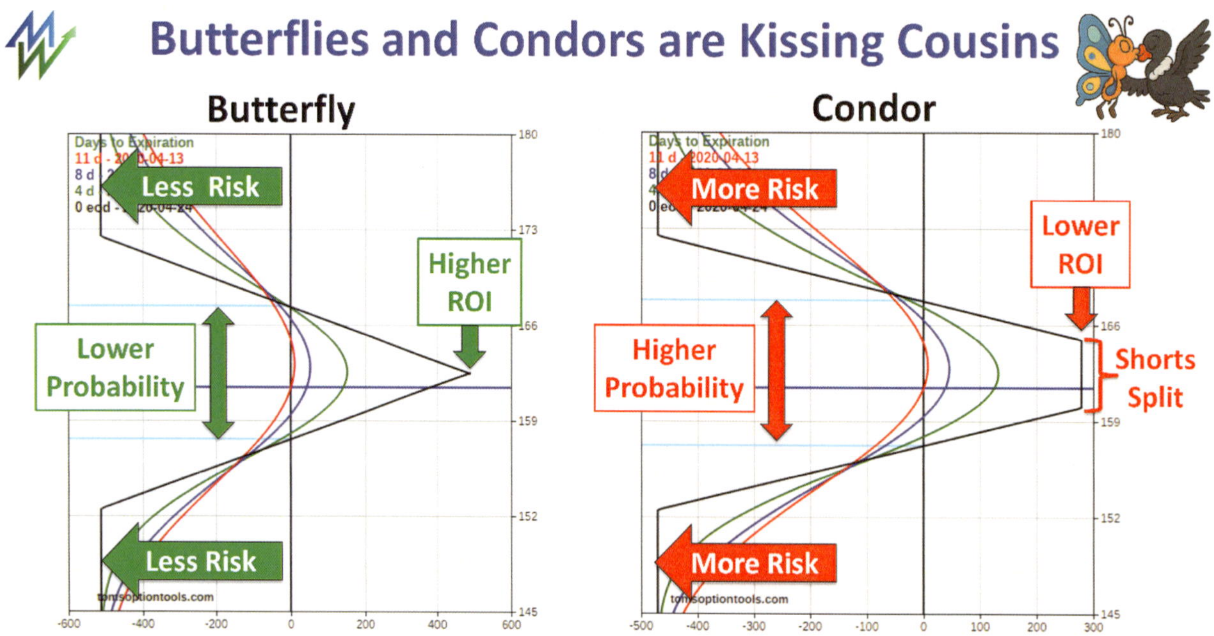

Choose based on prognosis. And remember—butterfly adjustment strategies also work with condors!

Flies & Condors Have Similar Greeks

Let's now look at the numbers behind the inverse relationship between potential return on investment (ROI) and probability of profit (POP) when comparing butterflies and condors.

Flies & Condors Have Similar Greeks

Potential ROI and Prob of Profit (POP) Are Inverse

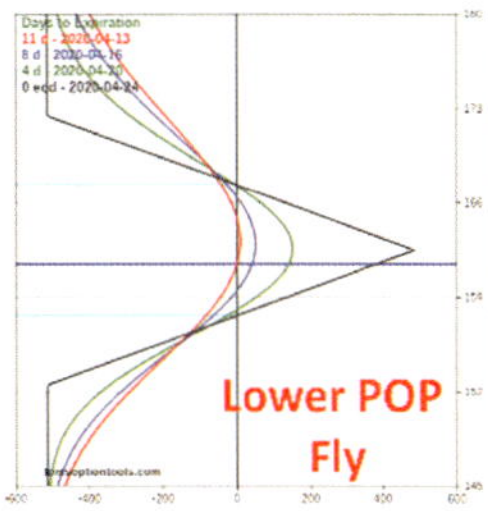

Position	Num	Expire	Type
Bought	1	2020 Apr 24	172.5 Call
Sold	2	2020 Apr 24	162.5 Call
Bought	1	2020 Apr 24	152.5 Call

Delta (Shares)	Gamma	Vega	Theta
11.46	-6.446	$-11.55	$11.47

95.31%

Entry Debit	Profit	Rate of Return	Max Profit	Max Risk
$512.00	$0.00	0.0%	$488.00	$-512.00

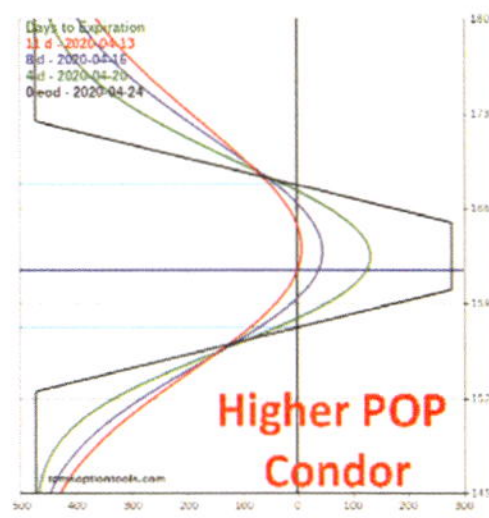

Position	Num	Expire	Type
Bought	1	2020 Apr 24	172.5 Call
Sold	1	2020 Apr 24	165 Call
Sold	1	2020 Apr 24	160 Call
Bought	1	2020 Apr 24	152.5 Call

Delta (Shares)	Gamma	Vega	Theta
9.56	-5.735	$-10.37	$10.45

59.24%

Entry Debit	Profit	Rate of Return	Max Profit	Max Risk
$471.00	$0.00	0.0%	$279.00	$-471.00

Both trades exhibit nearly identical Greeks:

- Delta Neutral
- Negative Gamma
- Negative Vega
- Positive Theta

However, what sets them apart is their risk/reward profile:

- The butterfly setup shown has a **lower probability of profit (POP)**—but offers a **higher potential ROI of 95.31%** (Max Profit / Max Risk).
- The condor setup provides a **higher probability of profit (POP)**—but comes with a **lower potential ROI of 59.24%**.

So, which one is better?

Neither is inherently better. They are simply different. Each has its pros and cons.

In general, POP and potential ROI are inversely related. A higher chance of success typically means a lower reward, and vice versa.

Use this understanding to align your trade choices with your market outlook and personal strategy.

Butterflies and Condors Eat IV for Lunch

Butterflies and condors are powerful structures when it comes to capitalizing on implied volatility decay. They thrive in high implied volatility (IV) environments—especially when IV is expected to fall.

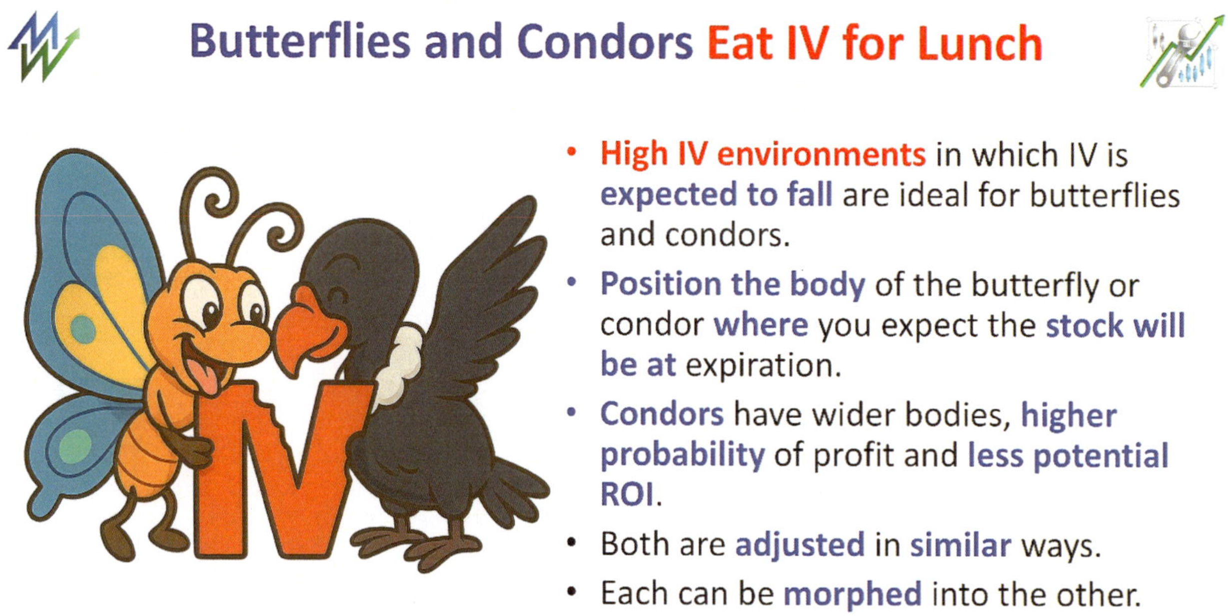

When setting up your trade, it's important to position the body of the butterfly or condor where you expect the stock to be trading at expiration. This approach increases your chances of making a profit.

Condors, with their broader bodies, naturally offer a higher chance of profit but generally deliver less potential ROI compared to butterflies. This provides traders with flexibility based on their risk/reward preferences.

One of the best features of these trades is their flexibility. Both butterflies and condors can be modified similarly, and with a few strategic adjustments, they can be transformed into each other.

That's why we say: Butterflies and Condors eat IV for lunch! When IV is high and expected to fall, these strategies shine.

Summary – The Power of Butterfly Spreads

This chapter introduces butterfly spreads as a **highly structured, probability-focused strategy.**

Butterflies are designed to capitalize on a stock staying within a defined range, offering limited risk with clearly defined reward potential. They bring together many of the concepts already covered—risk control, structure, and positioning—into a single, elegant setup.

The key idea:
You can engineer a trade that benefits from precision, not just direction.

With butterflies, you:

- Define both risk and reward upfront
- Create a targeted profit zone
- Rely on structure and time, not just movement

This chapter lays the groundwork for understanding how butterflies behave and why they are so effective in certain market conditions.

It also sets up the next evolution:
Once you understand the structure, you can begin to **adjust and optimize it dynamically**.

Now that you understand the foundation of butterfly spreads, the next step is learning how to actively shift the risk in a butterfly, conder or credit spread with: **The "Squeeze Play" Adjustment on Butterflies**.

CHAPTER 19

THE "SQUEEZE PLAY" ADJUSTMENT ON BUTTERFLIES

CHAPTER 19
The "Squeeze Play" Adjustment on Butterflies

We've already spoken about the "Squeeze Play"—a simple, elegant technique that contracts the distance between strikes to squeeze risk out of a vertical spread.

But here's the deal: Since butterflies are made from two vertical spreads, this method becomes a great tool to adjust and shift risk within a butterfly.

The "Squeeze Play" Adjustment
Butterflies

Risk can be **easily squeezed** out of a wing of a butterfly or condor by **contracting** the **distance between** the **long** and **short** strikes. This adjustment provides great facility to **move risk** out of play. Applicable strategies include:

- *Iron Condors*
- *Butterflies*

When a butterfly is out of sync with the current price action, instead of tearing it down or starting over, the "Squeeze Play" allows you to reshape one or both of the wings—usually the one closest to the action—and reduce some of that risk.

Why It Works

- A butterfly is made by combining two vertical debit spreads and/or credit spreads.
- When one of those spreads (wings) is no longer serving your prognosis or adds unnecessary risk, you can compress it.
- This contraction reduces risk exposure and keeps your structure nimble.

Risk Shifting Made Easy

Risk can be easily shifted from one side to the other with this move. If one side looks likely to be targeted, why leave it completely exposed?

By pulling the long strike closer to the short strike on that side, you reduce unnecessary risk—and decrease the probability of loss.

Use Cases

The "Squeeze Play" works beautifully with:

- Butterflies – standard or broken wing
- Condors – their close cousin, where each side is already an independent credit spread

It's clean, powerful, and simple to use. The next time your butterfly is becoming too hot to handle or one side starts cooling off—don't panic. Just squeeze.

Summary of the "Squeeze Play" Adjustment

The "Squeeze Play" Adjustment

Butterflies

Description: *The "Squeeze Play" adjustment can be applied to any debit or credit spread. As butterflies are a combination of two spreads, this adjustment applies beautifully to butterflies or condors. Risk can be squeezed out of either wing pushing risk out of the wing and into the other.*

Strategies: *Butterflies and Condors.*

Outcome: *This adjustment results in reduced risk in the spread being squeezed. The squeeze often results in a dramatic reduction in risk. At times numerous squeeze plays can result in a guaranteed profit trade. With practice, risk in a butterfly can be managed, shifted with ease.*

Timing: *Generally, contractions are applied when the stock approaches or crosses the short strike in the butterfly. Should the butterfly have sufficient profit, multiple squeezes can be applied to guarantee a profit.*

Description

The "Squeeze Play" can be used with both debit and credit spreads, making it suitable for butterflies and condors. It works by squeezing risk out of one wing and redistributing or eliminating it.

Strategies

Most often used in butterflies and condors, where wings can be adjusted independently, either symmetrically or asymmetrically.

Outcome

A successful "Squeeze Play" significantly reduces risk in the contracted wing. When done correctly, it can turn a volatile trade into a sure profit. Multiple squeezes are sometimes used in a single trade to secure gains while lowering directional risk.

Timing

Apply this adjustment when the stock price approaches or crosses the short strike of your butterfly. If the trade has enough profit cushion, you can make multiple squeezes, each reducing risk and increasing your chances of keeping your gains.

Real Trade Example: GDX Bullish Broken Wing Butterfly (BWB)

Let's take a look at a bullish broken wing butterfly (BWB) on the Gold Miners ETF (GDX).

- The trade is sitting on a $162 profit, or 32.5% return on the initial $498 risk.
- The butterfly was entered with:
    - 6 long $41.5 calls @ $0.08
    - 12 short $39 calls @ $0.25
    - 6 long $37 calls @ $0.75

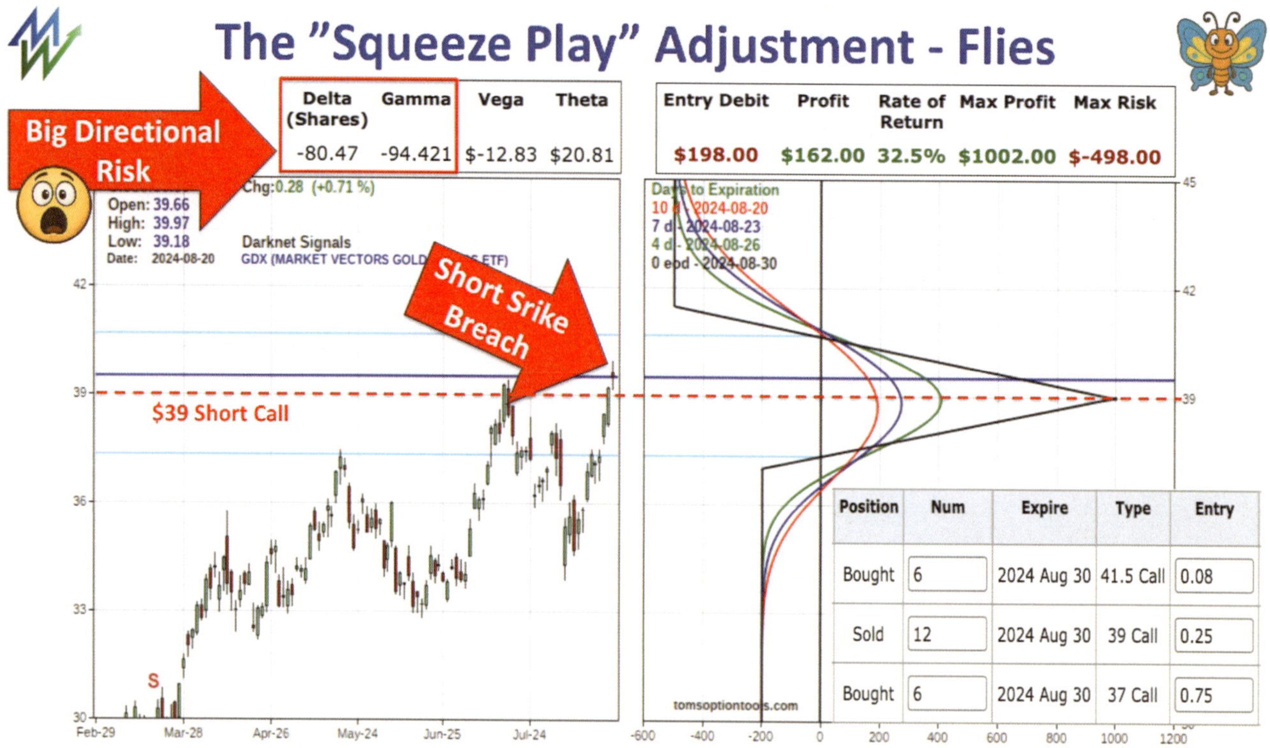

Good stuff—but not without a warning!

The stock has moved up into the body of the BWB, and it looks like it may continue upward.

Here's what we're watching:

- **Delta: -80.47** → If GDX moves up $1, we lose $80.47 of our open profit.
- **Gamma: -94.421** → Delta will worsen with a $1 move. Total directional risk is now over $174 (Delta -80.47 + Gamma -94.421).

Directional Risk Tip:

The absolute value of Delta + Gamma = directional risk. In this case, these two Greeks could erase most or all of your profit if GDX keeps climbing.

Another Tip:

If the short strike is breached (here, the $39 call), the "Squeeze Play" becomes very important.

In this setup:

- GDX blew past the $39 short call.
- With $162 profit at stake, the priority shifts to risk management.

It's time to adjust!

The Adjustment: Applying the "Squeeze Play"

The current risk graph says a lot. We need to reduce this significant amount of directional risk from the trade—specifically, the upper credit spread.

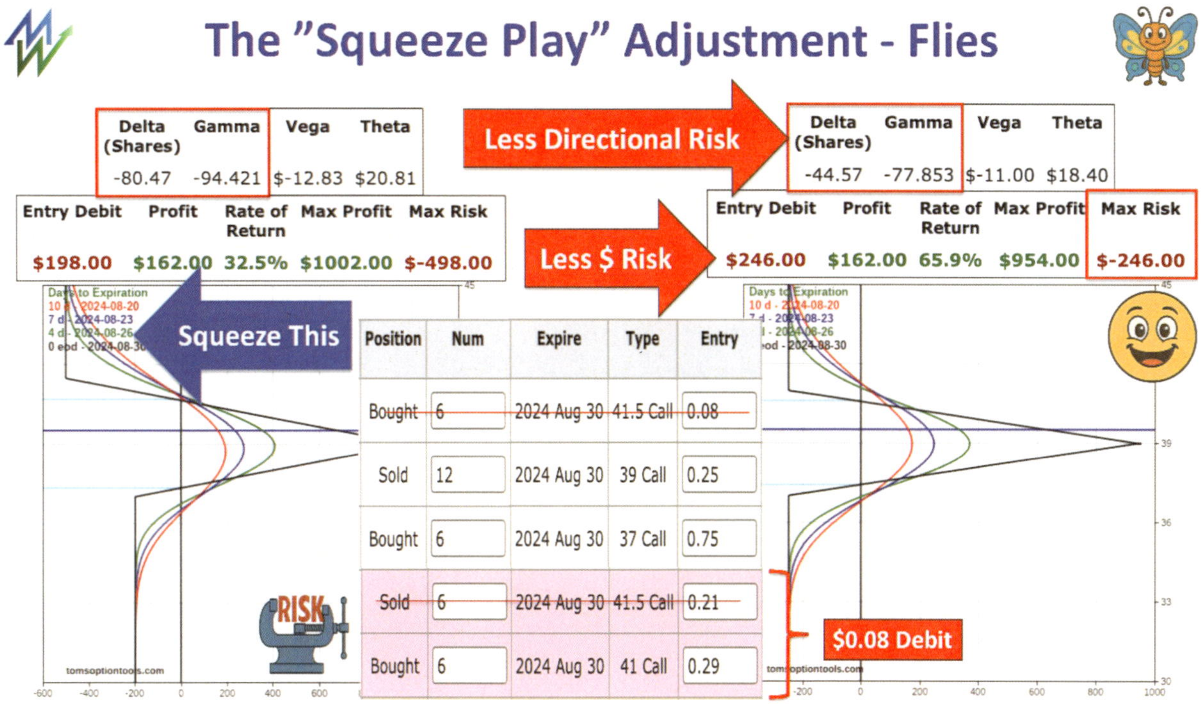

To do this, we simply move the upper $41.5 call down to $41, a $0.50 squeeze.

The resulting trade is a debit spread:

- Sell $41.50 call
- Buy $41 call

This costs us only $0.08 a contract × 6 = $48 total debit.

Here's the magic of this adjustment:

- We spent $48
- Max risk dropped from $498 to only $246 → a $252 reduction in risk
- Delta and Gamma dropped significantly, reducing directional exposure

The result? A balanced butterfly with $246 of risk in both wings.

And remember: This isn't the final move. We can keep using the "Squeeze Play" to shift risk from one side to the other as needed.

Rules of Thumb for the "Squeeze Play"

The "Squeeze Play" Adjustment - Flies

Rules of Thumb

1. The main **goals** of the squeeze play ar to **flatten directional risk** (delta/gamma) and **allow Theta to do its work.**
2. The squeeze play can be **applied to either wing.**
3. Consider squeezing when the **short strike is breached.**
4. Consider squeezing if absolute value of **delta and gamma approach** or **exceed** your **current profit.**
5. **Squeezing** the **bigger wing** will result in a **reduction in risk** and a **higher ROI** on adjusted risk.
6. The squeeze can be **applied multiple times** during the life of the trade.
7. The squeeze play works on **condors** too.

Here are some practical guidelines to help you determine when and how to apply the "Squeeze Play" effectively:

1. The main goal of the "Squeeze Play" is to flatten directional risk (Delta and Gamma) and let Theta do its work.
2. It can be applied to either wing of the butterfly, depending on which side is less relevant or riskier.
3. Consider applying it when the short strike is breached.
4. If |Delta + Gamma| approaches or exceeds your current profit, it may be time to squeeze.
5. Squeezing the bigger wing tends to yield a better reduction in risk and a higher ROI.
6. The "Squeeze Play" is not a one-time tool. It can be used multiple times throughout the trade's lifespan.
7. It's just as powerful for condors as it is for butterflies.

These tips give you a framework to know when the "Squeeze Play" isn't just a clever trick. It's the necessary move to keep your trade alive and thriving.

Summary – Squeezing Risk Out of Your Trade

The **"Squeeze Play" is a precision risk-reduction tool** for butterflies and condors. Instead of closing or rebuilding a trade when price moves against your structure, this adjustment allows you to **reshape the position by compressing one side (wing)** of the trade.

At its core, the concept is simple:

- A butterfly is made of two vertical spreads.
- If one side becomes risky or irrelevant, **you contract that side by bringing the long strike closer to the short strike.**
- This **reduces directional exposure (Delta + Gamma)** and stabilizes the trade.

The chapter emphasizes that this is not just a defensive move. It's a **profit-protection and optimization technique.**

Key Insights

- The **primary objective** is to **flatten directional risk** and allow **Theta to take over**.
- The adjustment is most effective when:
    - Price approaches or breaches the short strike
    - Directional risk begins to threaten open profits
- The **"Squeeze Play"** can:
    - Cut max risk dramatically
    - Reduce Delta and Gamma exposure
    - Balance the structure across both wings
- It is **repeatable**. You can apply multiple squeezes during the life of a trade.

Strategic Advantage

The biggest takeaway:

You don't need to abandon a trade that's getting uncomfortable. You can reshape it.

Instead of reacting emotionally, you act structurally.

If the **"Squeeze Play"** is about **contracting risk,** then the next evolution is the opposite move. **The "Stretch Play" Adjustment on Butterflies** is next.

CHAPTER 20

THE "STRETCH PLAY" ADJUSTMENT ON BUTTERFLIES

CHAPTER 20
The "Stretch Play" Adjustment on Butterflies

Introduction

Just as squeezing a spread reduces risk in a vertical spread, stretching a spread—by increasing the distance between the long and short strikes—increases risk within that spread.

When used within a butterfly structure, this action produces a powerful and elegant side effect: It reduces risk from the opposite wing. This makes it a perfect companion move to the "Squeeze Play".

The "Stretch Play" Adjustment

Butterflies

Risk can be **easily shifted** out of an opposite wing of a butterfly by **expanding** the **distance between** the **long** and **short** strikes. Applicable strategies include:

- *Iron Condors*
- *Butterflies*

Why It Works

- Butterflies are composed of two vertical wings.
- If one spread is expanded (stretched), it absorbs more risk.
- As that occurs, the opposing wing becomes less risky, since the total capital at risk is being redistributed.

Use Cases

This adjustment is especially effective for:

- Butterflies – moving risk to one wing while reducing exposure on the other.
- Condors – same result as with butterflies.

"Stretch Plays" are best used when:

- The stock has shifted toward a risk wing, but profit potential still exists.
- You want to mitigate your directional exposure while staying in the trade.
- The stock is in the body and you want to widen the profit zone.

The "Stretch Play" Adjustment

Butterflies

Description:	*The "Stretch Play" adjustment can be applied to any debit or credit spread. As butterflies are a combination of two spreads, this adjustment applies beautifully to butterflies or condors. Risk can be shifted out of either wing pulling risk out of the wing and into the other.*
Strategies:	*Butterflies and Condors.*
Outcome:	*The stretch can result in an increase in total trade risk and for that reason is often combined with the Squeeze Play. At times multiple stretch and squeeze plays can result in a guaranteed profit trade. With practice, risk in a butterfly can be managed, shifted with ease with a combination of both.*
Timing:	*Generally, the stretch play is applied when the stock approaches or crosses the short strike in the butterfly. Often a squeeze is best applied in conjunction with the stretch play. Should the butterfly have sufficient profit, multiple stretches and squeezes can be applied to guarantee a profit.*

Description

The "Stretch Play" adjustment can be applied to any debit or credit spread. Since butterflies are a combination of two spreads, this adjustment pairs well with butterflies or condors. Risk can be shifted out of either wing, reducing risk on the other side as needed.

Strategies

- Butterflies
- Condors
- Outcome

Stretching increases the risk in the expanded spread, so it's often combined with a squeeze on the opposite wing. This combination allows you to fine-tune risk across the position effectively. When used properly, this balance can sometimes lead to a guaranteed profit trade. With practice, a trader can develop the skill to manage and redistribute risk flexibly using these two tools.

Timing

Typically, the "Stretch Play" is used when the stock nears or crosses the short strike of the butterfly. A squeeze is often best performed together with it. When there's already a profit cushion in the butterfly, multiple stretches and squeezes can be used to systematically remove and neutralize risk.

Real Trade Example: "Stretch Play" Adjustment on a BWB

Let's take a look at a "Stretch Play" applied to a Broken Wing Butterfly (BWB). In this scenario, the stock has broken above the short strike of the BWB. At this point, we're holding a BWB with $498 of risk in the upper wing (which defines the maximum risk for the trade) and $198 of risk in the lower wing.

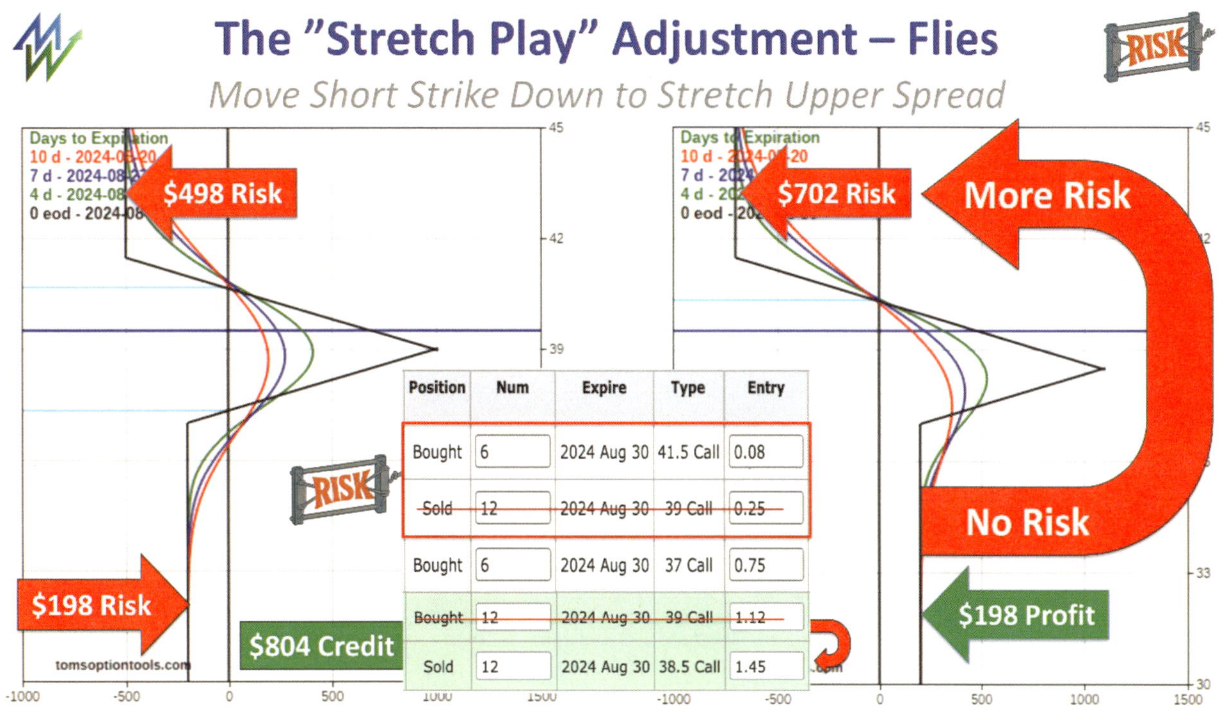

Mechanics of the Adjustment

The move is to add credit to the trade by applying the "Stretch Play", dropping the short $39 calls to $38.50:

- Buy back the $39 short calls
- Sell new $38.5 calls instead

This credit spread sale yields a net credit of $804—effectively generating a cash inflow while restructuring the upper wing.

Results of the Stretch

The adjustment creates a profit of $198 in the lower wing.

- But... it increases total risk in the trade to $702.
- This adjustment could make sense if our outlook turned bearish.

However—and this is key—we do not have a bearish prognosis.

So, while the "Stretch Play" does shift risk, it does so by adding capital exposure to the trade. That's a red flag when your #1 job is risk management.

In this case, we need a different approach to contain the new risk we've taken on... and that's exactly what we'll tackle next.

Houston, We Have a Problem! RISK!

So, the results of the "Stretch Play" put a nice profit in the bottom wing but increased risk in the upper wing. As shown in the risk graph, max risk jumped to $702 and directional exposure also got worse—Delta is now -185.36 with Gamma at -70.988. The combination of those two numbers creates significant directional risk. If the stock moves up another $1, we could lose over $250 in profit. Not good. This is where the "Squeeze Play" comes in. To fix this, we will contract the upper wing and squeeze risk out of the trade. That's up next.

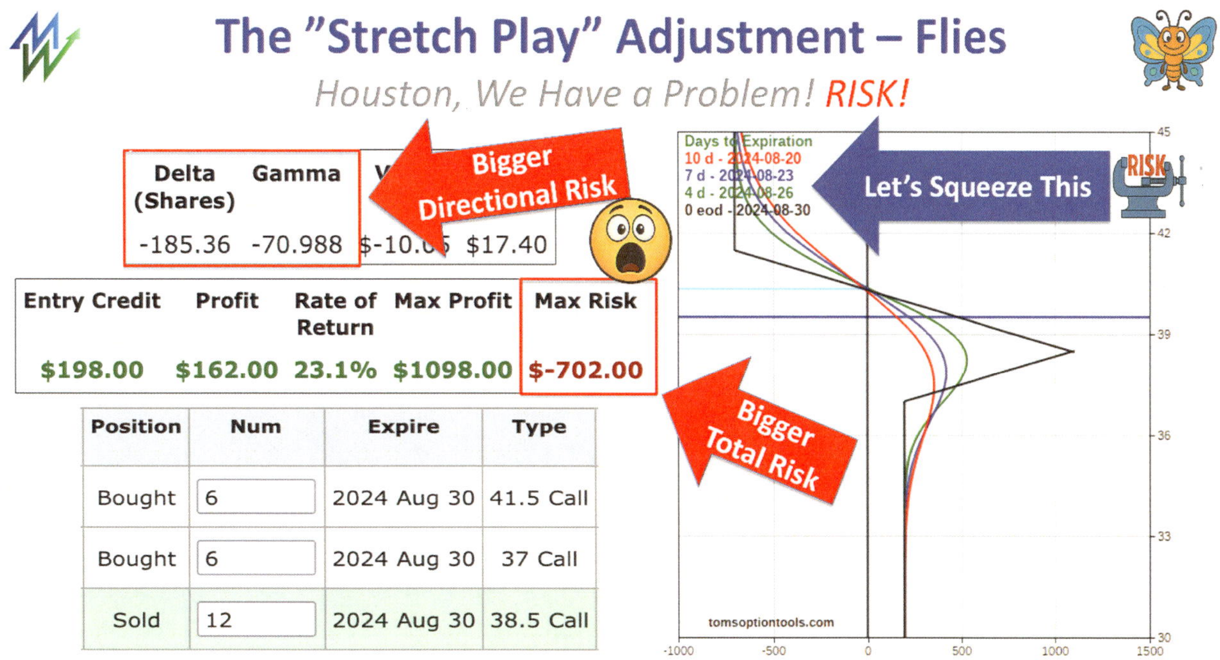

Locking Down the Win: The Squeeze Play on Flies

After executing the "Stretch Play" earlier to push our profit potential onto the bottom wing and take on a bit more risk on the upper wing, it's now time to flip the script and go on defense with the "Squeeze Play."

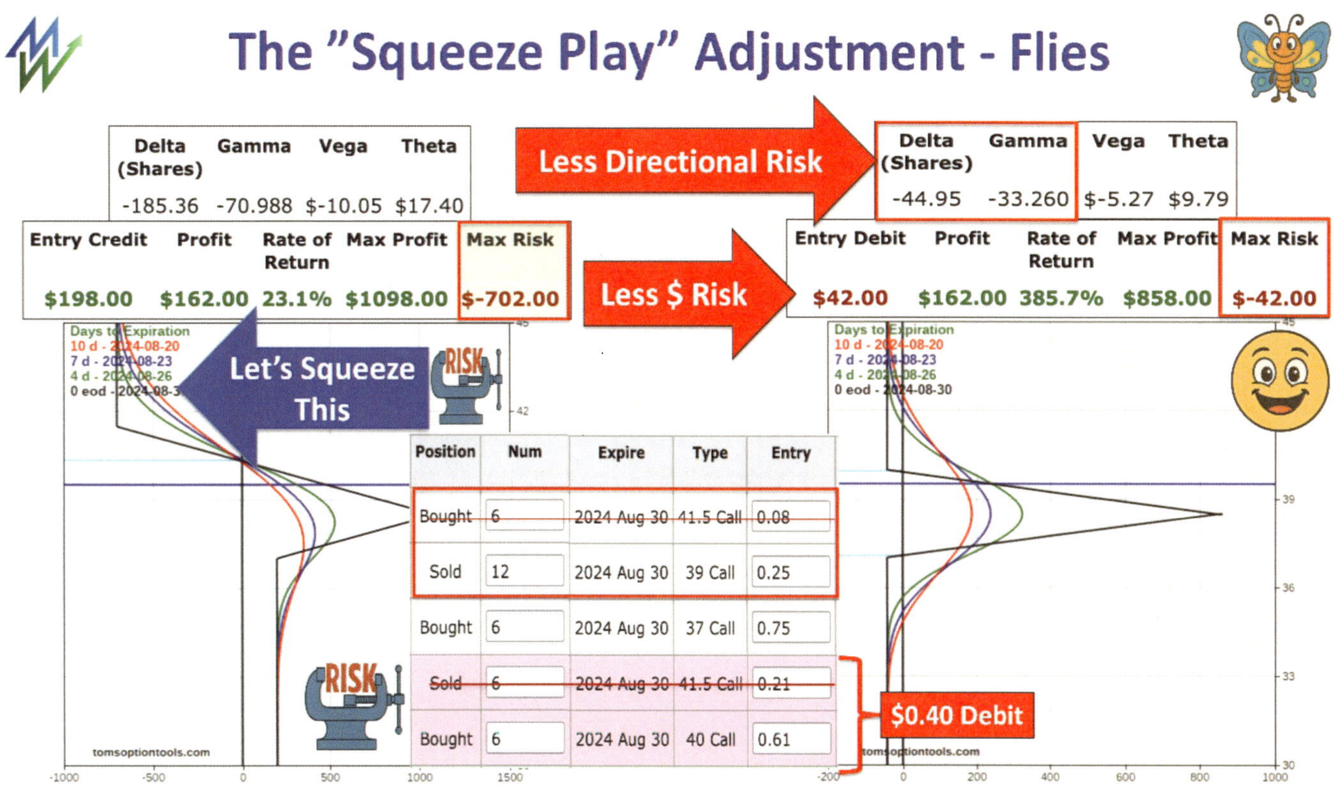

Here's the move: we're taking that long $41.50 call and bringing it down to the $41 call. Think of it as tightening the vice grip on our position—compressing the distance between strikes to concentrate profit in the center and crush unnecessary risk.

This maneuver cost $0.40 per contract—a total debit of $240—but the trade-off is pure gold:

Our max risk shrinks from -$702 to just -$42. That's like going from a full-sized football field to defending a tiny end zone.

Our Delta drops from -185.36 to -44.95 and Gamma falls from -70.988 to -33.260—a huge reduction in directional exposure. Now the market can move without shaking us out of the game.

Theta is still working hard for us at nearly $10/day, while our profit target remains a healthy $162, but now with a stunning 385.7% rate of return.

In trading game terms, this is tightening your defense without giving up your scoring position—the best of both worlds. We've locked down risk, maintained a solid profit zone, and given ourselves a much smoother ride to expiration.

"Stretch Play" Adjustment – Butterflies: Rules of Thumb

The "Stretch Play" Adjustment - Flies

Rules of Thumb

1. The main **goal** of the stretch play is to **flatten directional risk** (delta/gamma) and **allow Theta to do its work.**
2. The stretch play can be **applied to either wing.**
3. Typically, the **short strike** is **moved** to accomplish the stretch, ideally for a **credit.**
4. Used in **conjunction** with the **Squeeze Play** can result in a dramatic **reduction in risk** and even a **guaranteed profit.**
5. The stretch play can be **applied multiple times** during the life of the trade.
6. The stretch play works on **condors** too.

The "Stretch Play" is a versatile adjustment that helps manage directional exposure in butterfly trades. Here are a few guidelines to help you apply it effectively:

The main goal of the stretch play is to flatten directional risk (Delta/Gamma) and allow Theta to do its work.

The "Stretch Play" can be applied to either wing, depending on the market direction and trade shape.

Typically, the short strike is moved farther away from the long strike to accomplish the stretch, ideally for a credit.

Used in conjunction with the squeeze play, this combination can produce a dramatic reduction in risk and even lead to a guaranteed profit in some cases.

The stretch play can be applied multiple times during the life of a butterfly trade as price continues to evolve.

This play is not limited to butterflies—it also works well on condors.

Summary - Spreading Wings Trade to Stay in the Game

This adjustment is about **flexibility under pressure**.

The "Stretch Play" shows how to **widen or reposition a butterfly spread** when the stock moves away from the ideal profit zone. Instead of letting the trade fail, you stretch the structure to bring opportunity back into reach.

By stretching a wing of the butterfly, you:

- Flatten out directional risk
- Reposition the profit zone
- Extend the life and viability of the trade

Now that you've seen how butterfly trades can be built, tightened, and stretched, the next step is doubling down on the "Squeeze Play" to double down on risk reduction: **The "Cocoon the Fly" Adjustment**.

CHAPTER 21

THE "COCOON THE FLY" ADJUSTMENT

CHAPTER 21
The "Cocoon the Fly" Adjustment

Introduction

The "Cocoon the Fly" adjustment is an effective strategy used to lower risk or lock in profits by "cocooning" an existing butterfly or condor. This is achieved by applying the "Squeeze Play" to both wings, narrowing strike distances in both spreads to squeeze risk out of both wings, greatly reducing position risk.

By buying and selling vertical spreads that move both wings closer to the center of the butterfly, the ""Cocoon the Fly" adjustment transforms the position into a safer, often guaranteed-profit setup.

The Cocoon Adjustment

Take an existing Butterfly (or condor) and **morph it to Reduce Risk** and/or **Lock-In a Profit**.

Use the "Squeeze Play" on both wings to contract their width:

- Buying and Selling Vertical Spreads to bring the wings closer to the body.

Strategies:

- Butterflies
- Condors

Description: Used to reduce the risk and/or lock in profit of the original trade by applying the "Squeeze Play" to both wings.

Outcome: Squeezing both wings reduces the overall risk in the trade. When applied to a profitable butterfly or condor, this adjustment often locks in guaranteed profit while still allowing for more gains.

Timing: The best time to apply the "Cocoon the Fly" adjustment is after the trade has become profitable. However, it can be used at any point during the trade. It can also be combined with other adjustments.

The Cocoon Adjustment

Description:	*Used to reduce the risk and/or lock-in profit of the original trade by applying the Squeeze Play (contracting) both wings.*
Strategies:	*Butterflies and Condors.*
Outcome:	*Squeezing both wings results in reducing overall risk in the trade and if applied to a profitable butterfly or condor usually results in a guaranteed profit while providing the opportunity to increase profit.*
Timing:	*Once the existing position moves into profit is best - but can be applied at anytime during the life of the trade. It can also be used in conjunction with other adjustment moves.*

"Cocoon the Fly" Adjustment Case Study – The SPYs

The best way to illustrate the "Cocoon the Fly" Adjustment is with a case study.

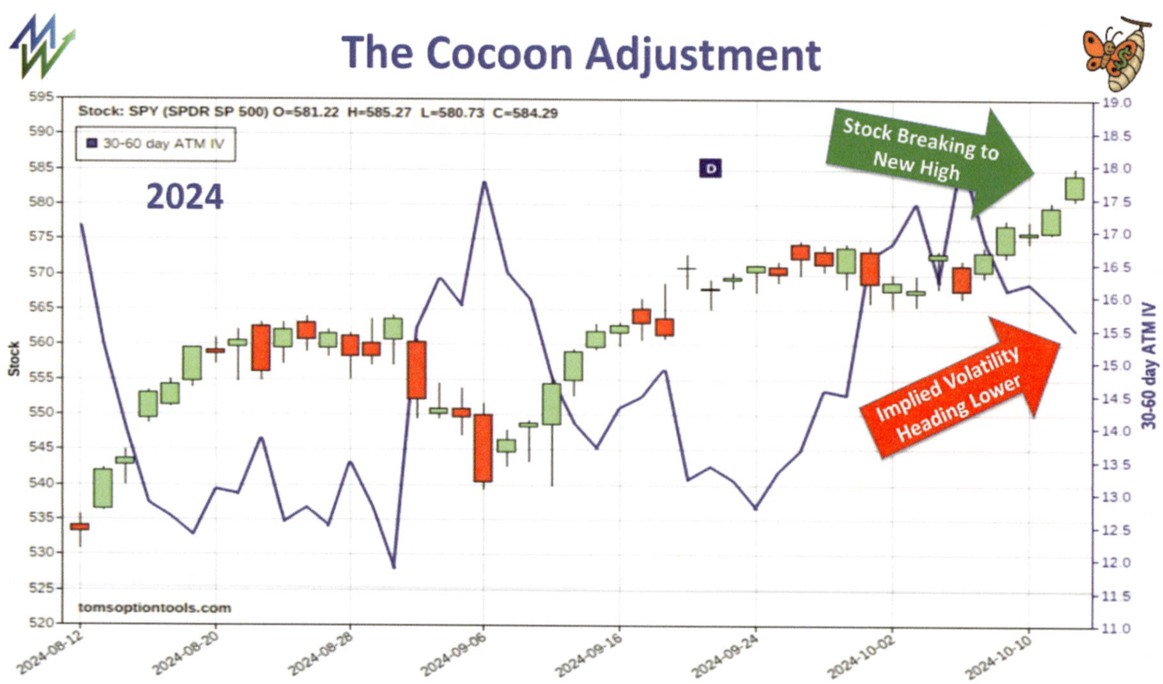

On October 14, 2024, we had a bullish outlook on the S&P 500 ETF (SPY).

Why? Because the SPY had risen to a new high, confirming the bullish trend that began on September 6, 2024. Additionally, we noted a bearish perspective on implied volatility (IV), depicted in blue on the chart. IV was decreasing, which further supported a bullish bias and created opportunities for strategic risk-reduction adjustments like the "Cocoon the Fly".

Constructing the Initial Butterfly

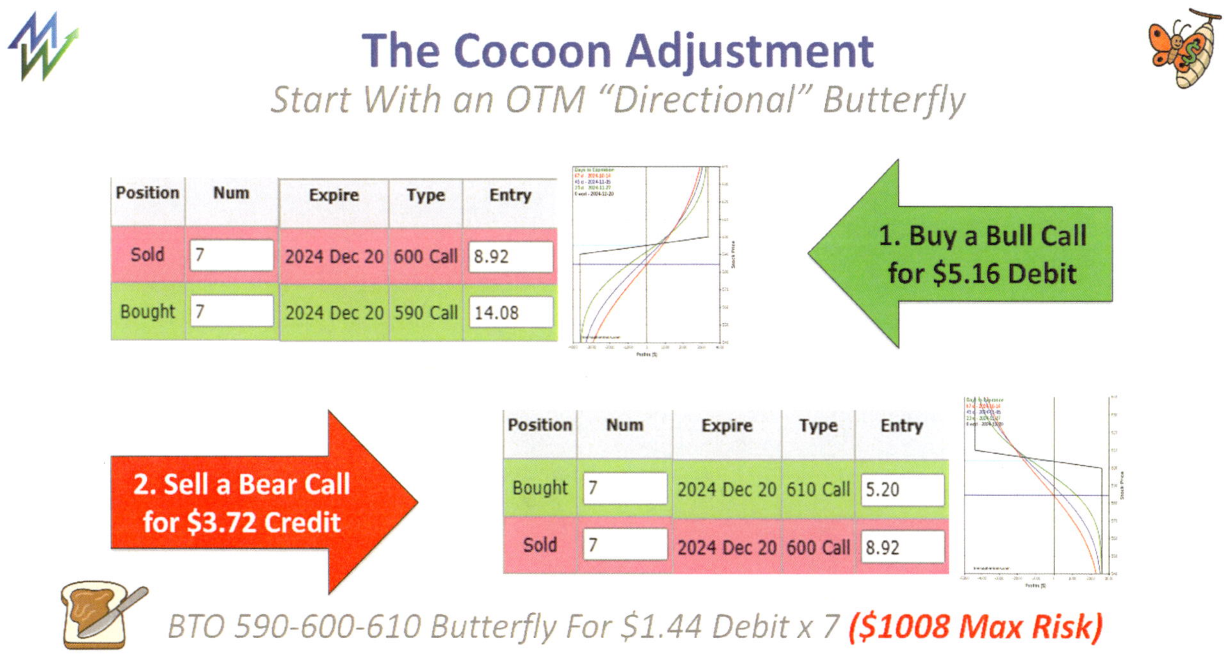

With our bullish stock outlook and bearish implied volatility forecast, we built an Out-of-the-Money butterfly with the short strike set at our resistance target of $600. To create this butterfly, we first purchased the December 20th $590/$600 long call spread for a debit of $5.16. Then, to finish the butterfly, we sold the $600/$610 short call spread for a credit of $3.72. The net cost per spread was $1.44, and we bought 7 of these, resulting in a total maximum risk of $1,008.

Trade Setup and Strategy Commentary

Here's our butterfly trade fully constructed and laid out on the game board.

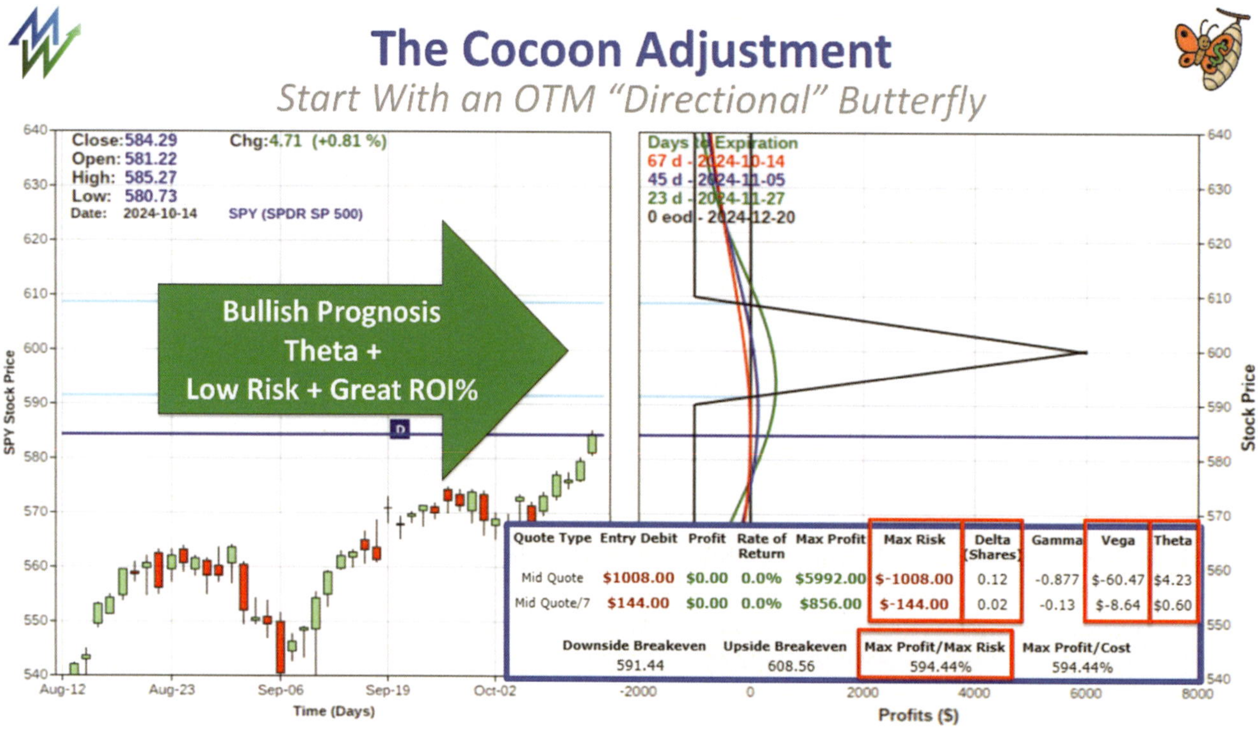

We've positioned the butterfly's core—the sweet spot—precisely at $600, our target resistance. That's where all the value is. If the stock reaches this point at expiration, we net a $5,992 profit on $1,008 at risk. That's a 594% POTENTIAL return.

Now, will we land exactly at $600? Not likely.

But remember, this is a game of probability. You don't need to hit the bullseye to win big. Even grazing the edge of the target pays well. That's the beauty of placing a directional butterfly with a smart prognosis.

And speaking of alignment, this trade is tuned like a concert piano:

- **Delta is positive**. We expect the stock to run higher.
- **Vega is negative**. We expect implied volatility to drop.
- **Theta is $4.23**—yep, we're getting paid daily just to hold this trade.

When your forecast—such as a bullish market with falling IV—matches this structure precisely, you gain the advantage.

The chess piece is in play; the board is set—let's see how this baby performs...

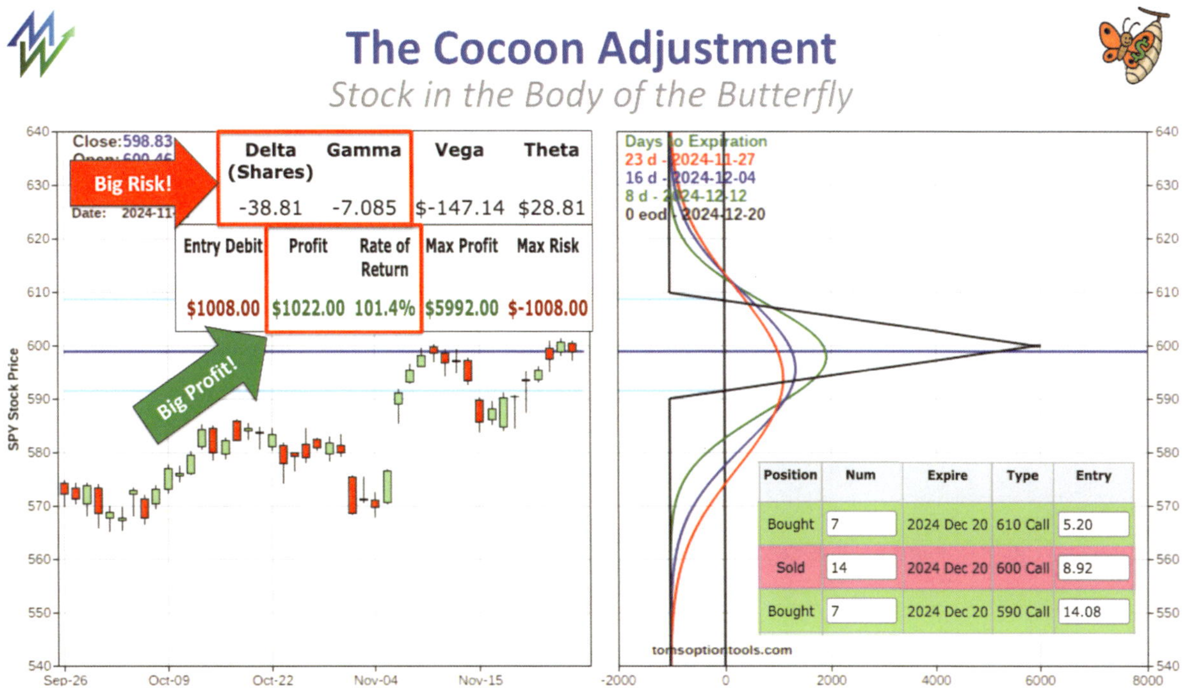

Stock Moves Into the Body of the Butterfly

By November 27, the SPYs had climbed to just under our $600 target, placing the stock right in the body of our butterfly. That's the sweet spot!Our open profit has grown to $1,022, providing a 101.4% return on our original $1,008 risk. With total risk now at $2,016 (our original debit plus the open profit), we are in a strong position—solid gains and potential for more.

But there's a storm cloud on the horizon: Delta and Gamma. Currently, Delta equals -38.81 and Gamma equals -7.085. This means a $1 increase in SPY Delta would cost us nearly $39—and even worse, Delta would become even more negative (Delta + Gamma = -45.90).

If SPY keeps climbing, our beautiful profit could start eroding quickly.

So, here's the million-dollar question:

What if we could reduce that directional risk and lock in a guaranteed profit—while still leaving the door open for more upside?

Who wouldn't take that deal?

Well, good news... that's exactly what we're going to do next.

Applying the "Cocoon the Fly" Adjustment

Time to lock this in.

The "Cocoon the Fly" adjustment involves a classic double squeeze, where we tighten both wings of our butterfly to restore balance and ensure success.

Here's the move:

- Buy the $604/$610 bull call spread for a $2.18 debit
- Sell the $590/$596 bear call spread for a $4.60 credit

Net result? A credit of $2.42 per contract. Multiply that by 7 contracts and you've got $1,694 in cash flowing in. That's real, locked-in premium. And here's the kicker. This adjustment guarantees a minimum profit of $686 no matter what happens next.

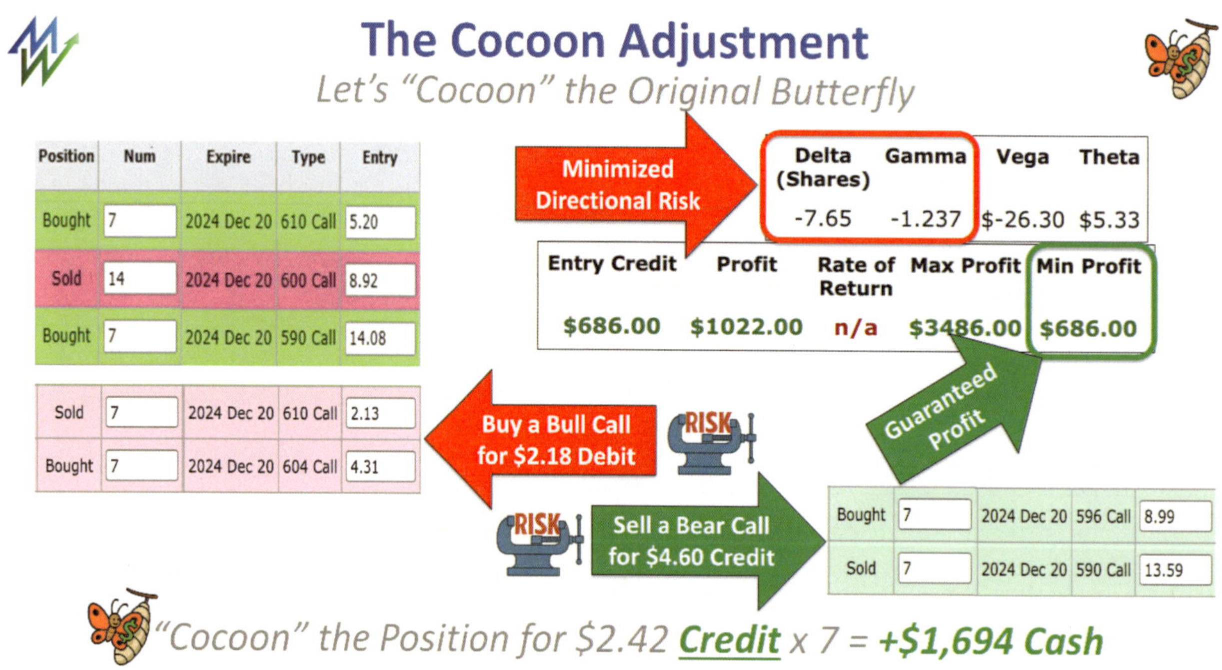

Even better? Our risk is now nearly neutral. Delta has decreased to -7.65 and Gamma is -1.237. That means even if the stock moves a bit, we're not losing much.

The trade is cocooned—secure, profitable, and still capable of flying higher. Game on.

The Cocoon Is Complete

Now this is the part where the crowd goes wild.

Here's the current risk graph—and it tells the full story of a masterfully executed "Cocoon the Fly" adjustment.

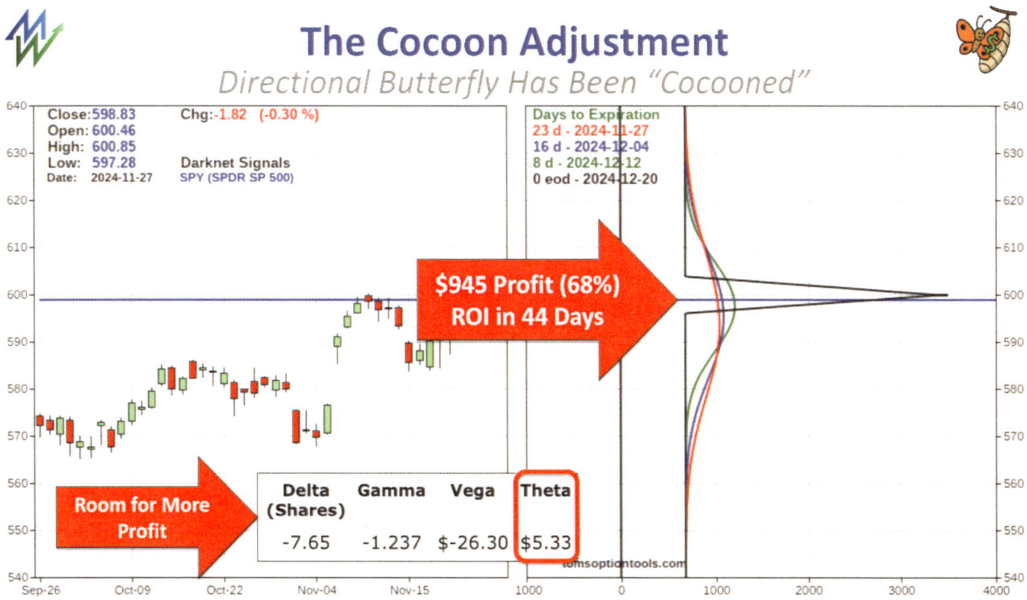

First of all, we've taken risk off the board entirely. That's right—no risk left in the position.

What do we have instead? A guaranteed profit of $686. That's our floor.

But it gets even better. As of this snapshot, we're already sitting on $945 in profit, a 68% return in just 44 days. And we're not done—the graph still shows room to move. That $5.33 in Theta indicates the trade is earning us daily income for holding.Translation: We're still in the game, collecting time decay, with upside potential and no risk to defend. That's how you win before the bell rings.

The Cocoon is sealed; the position is safe—and now we let the clock do the rest.

Summary - The "Cocoon the Fly" Adjustment

The "Cocoon the Fly" adjustment can be applied to any butterfly, not just directional ones. It's a smart defensive move best used once a trade has turned a solid profit and you want to reduce exposure while preserving gains.

- **The strategy:** Apply the **"Squeeze Play"** to both wings of the butterfly—tightening the spreads on both sides.
- **The result:** A safer, balanced butterfly that can result in a guaranteed profit, reduced risk, lower Delta and Gamma, and often positive Theta paying you daily to hold.

"Cocoon the Fly" adjustments are most effective when the stock has made a favorable move and the trade is already in profit. Instead of taking profits and walking away, you lock them in while still leaving room for more upside.

It's like pulling your chips off the table while holding onto a few cards—the market can shift, and you still come out ahead.

The "Cocoon the Fly" adjustment turns your butterfly into a low-risk, high-probability structure that finishes the game strong—with control, confidence, and cash flow.

Now that you know how to protect a butterfly, the next step is understanding another core structure that plays a major role throughout the adjustment playbook: **The "Calendar Spread"**.

CHAPTER 22

THE CALENDER SPREAD

CHAPTER 22
The Calendar Spread

Discover the Calendar Spread, one of the most flexible and sophisticated strategies in an option trader's arsenal.

As the name suggests, a calendar spread involves the strategic use of time. We are literally "spreading the calendar" by selling a short-term option and buying a longer-term option. This strategy is also known as a horizontal spread because both options have the same strike price; therefore, they appear "horizontally" across different expiration dates on an options chain.

Why Use Calendar Spreads?

Calendar spreads shine when your outlook is neutral. You anticipate the underlying stock to stay near a specific price until the short option expires. The profit mainly comes from time decay (positive Theta): The option you sell loses value faster than the one you buy, which is exactly what we want.

But that's not all. Calendars can also be tailored to match directional biases. We'll explore bullish and bearish calendars soon. For now, let's establish the foundation.

Basic Calendar Spread Construction

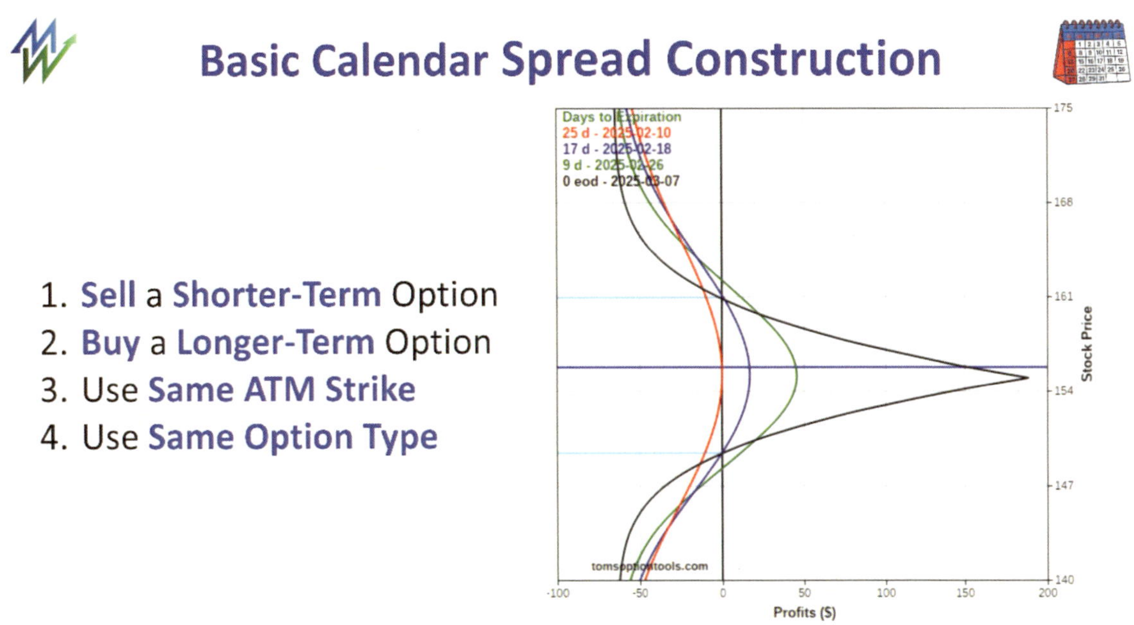

Calls vs. Puts

While both calls and puts can be used for calendar spreads, put calendars are often a bit cheaper. This is due to skew and demand dynamics, especially in highly traded stocks and indexes.

The Calendar Risk Graph

Refer to the chart above. The prominent black peak indicates the risk at expiration of the short option. This represents your maximum profit zone—if the stock ends near your strike price at expiration, you profit.

Each colored curve shows the value of the calendar as time passes. Notice how:

- As time advances, the peaks of the colored lines advance toward profit
- Profit potential increases if the stock stays around the strike
- Risk grows if the stock moves away from the calendar strikes

Summary: Why Trade Calendars?

- Theta positive: Benefit from time decay
- Implied volatility expansion friendly: Rise in IV helps
- Defined risk: Maximum loss is the debit paid
- Adjustable: You can convert to diagonals, butterflies, or double calendars

In brief, a calendar is a wager based on predicting where the stock will not move.

In the next section, we will explore how to tilt the calendar for bullish or bearish setups and how to make adjustments if it moves against you.

Additive Nature of Greeks in Calendar Spreads

Greeks are additive, meaning the long and short legs of a calendar spread have Greeks that sum together, resulting in the overall Greeks of the position.

Calendar Spread Position Greeks

Quote Type	Entry Debit	Profit	Rate of Return	Max Profit	Max Risk	Delta (Shares)	Gamma	Vega	Theta
Mid Quote	$65.00	$0.00	0.0%	$190.88	$-65.00	-0.25	-0.668	$4.00	$1.76

Sum of Leg Greeks

Downside Breakeven	Upside Breakeven	Max Profit/Max Risk	Max Profit/Cost
149.40	160.91	293.66%	293.66%

Leg Date	Position	Num	Option Symbol	Expire	Type	Entry	Bid/ Ask	Leg Profit	IV %	Vol	OI	Days	Delta %	Gamma %	Vega %IV	Theta $/day
2025-02-10	Sold	1	CVX250307P155	2025 Mar 07	155 Put	3.25	3.15 3.35	$0.00	22.34	1	220	25	45.40	-4.34	-16.1	7.2
2025-02-10	Bought	1	CVX250321P155	2025 Mar 21	155 Put	3.90	3.80 4.00	$0.00	21.13	31	2804	39	-45.66	3.67	20.1	-5.4

In the calendar position shown above, Vega is +$4.00, which means this trade benefits if implied volatility (IV) increases. Finally, the calendar spread's main contributor is Theta at +$1.76, indicating that by tomorrow, time decay will add $1.76 of value to the trade. Additionally, Theta increases as the trade approaches expiration.

Among the Greeks, Theta is the most dependable because time decay is assured. However, predicting the stock's direction or the movement of IV is never completely certain.

Calendar Spread Risk Graph

A picture—or a risk graph—paints a thousand words. The graphic shown below illustrates the power of the calendar spread:

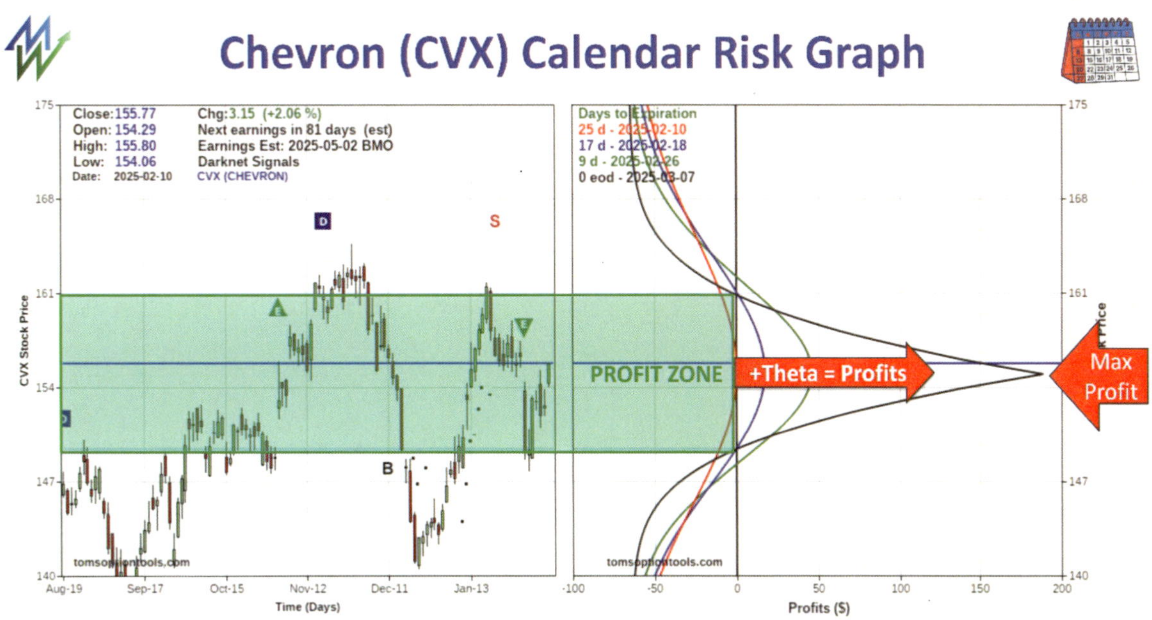

The calendar establishes two breakeven points that define a profit zone, often called the "backyard." As long as the stock remains in the backyard, Theta will continually and increasingly generate profits. Maximum profit is achieved at the strike price used at expiration.

The colored lines represent different timeframes:

- **Red** = Today
- **Blue** = 1/3 of the time elapsed
- **Green** = 2/3 of the time elapsed
- **Black** = Expiration

Notice how the gap between the lines widens as time passes. This demonstrates how Theta grows stronger over time. Another advantage of calendars is that even if the stock moves past the breakevens and you decide to exit, the loss is usually very small.

Lining Up Your Prognosis with the Calendar Greeks

The ideal prognosis for a calendar spread is that the stock remains flat or moves sideways, implied volatility (IV) will not decline, and time will pass—which is always the case.

The Greeks of this calendar reveal:

- **Delta** is -0.25 (essentially neutral)
- **Gamma** is -0.668 (the negative sign indicates "No Go")
- **Vega** is +$4.00
- **Theta** is +$1.76

Calendar Spread Position Greeks

How Do Calendars Makes Money?

Delta Neutral	No Go!	IV Up	Time Passes
Delta (Shares)	**Gamma**	**Vega**	**Theta**
-0.25	-0.668	$4.00	$1.76

The game of calendar spreads is to ***keep delta neutral*** *and* ***let Theta*** *(passage of time)* ***bring in profits.***

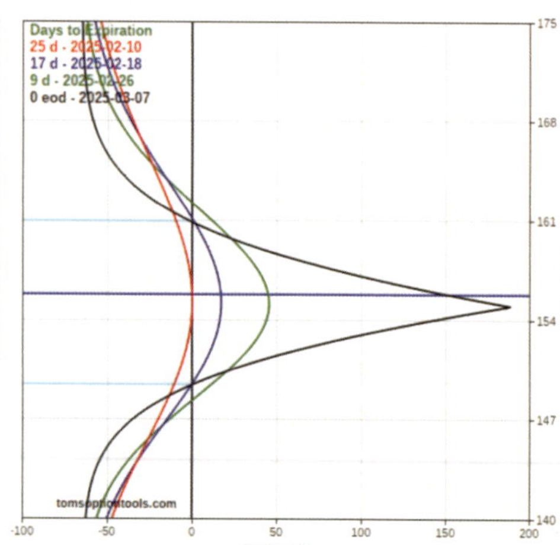

If your forecast indicates the stock will remain flat, implied volatility (IV) will increase, and time will advance, then the calendar spread is an ideal trade.

The goal of calendar spread trading is to keep directional risk (Delta) as low as possible and let Theta do its work—unburdened by directional movement.

How Theta Works in a Calendar Spread

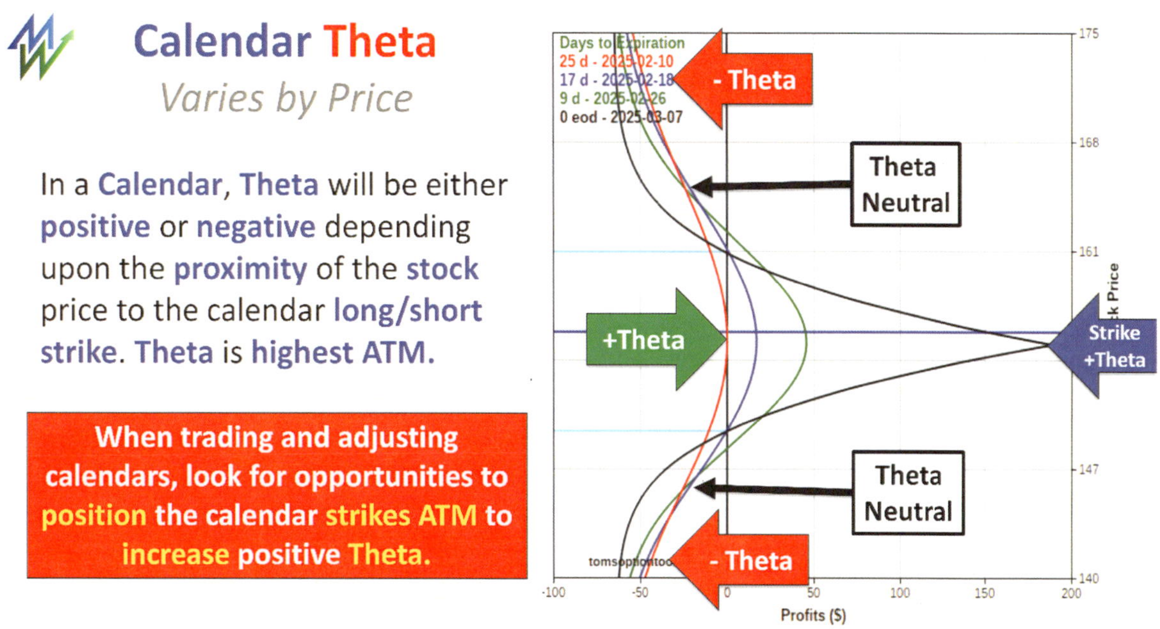

Like most spreads, Theta can be either positive or negative depending on how close the stock is to the strikes in the calendar spread. Theta is positive within the body of the calendar and turns negative at the wings. Theta remains neutral where the colored lines inflect.

Theta is most positive ATM (at the money)—when the stock is near the strike price. So, a good practice is to keep your calendar strikes close to the stock price. We will reveal an adjustment later to achieve that.

Calendar Spread Vega Behavior

Unlike Theta, Vega is consistently positive in a calendar spread regardless of the stock price's position relative to the strike price. This occurs because the +Vega of the longer-term long option will always be greater than the negative Vega of the shorter-term short option.

Calendar Vega

Varies by Price

Unlike a vertical spread, **Calendars**, will have a **positive Vega** in **all parts** of the risk graph. The **+Vega** of the long-term long option will always **exceed** the **-Vega of** the short-term short option.

When trading and adjusting calendars, be sure to have flat or up IV prognosis. OTM/ITM calendar Vega is smaller making the trade less sensitive to IV drops.

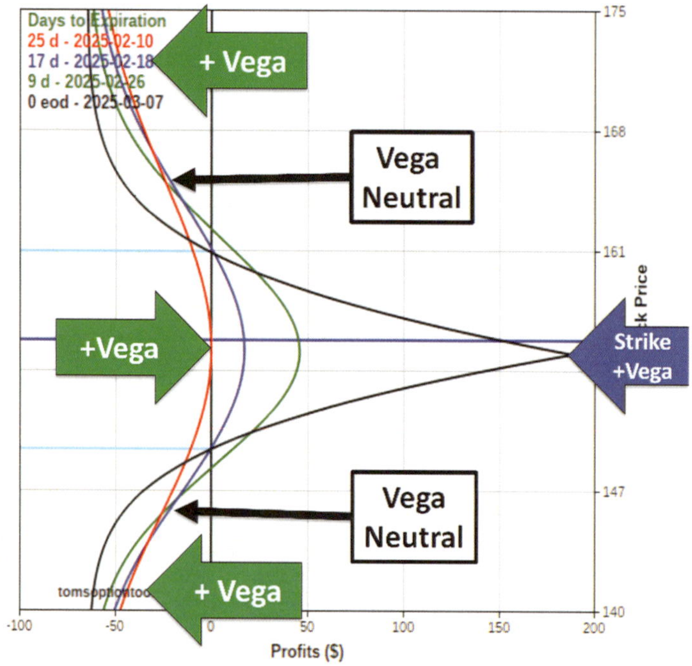

Since Greeks are additive, the calculation will always yield a net positive Vega for the position.

This makes calendars a great strategy when your IV (implied volatility) outlook is at least "not down," and ideally "up." If IV increases, the calendar gains value thanks to its positive Vega. Even if IV remains flat, positive Vega won't hurt. But if IV drops, the calendar could lose value. That's why aligning your Vega exposure with your IV forecast is essential.

A special note for OTM/ITM calendars: These tend to have lower Vega values and are therefore less sensitive to drops in IV.

Calendars vs. Butterflies – Vega Behavior

The main difference between calendar spreads and butterfly spreads is their Vega exposure.

- Calendars have positive Vega, meaning they benefit when implied volatility (IV) increases.
- Butterflies have negative Vega, meaning they benefit when IV decreases.

Both strategies have a positive Theta in the trade's body, so they both gain value if the stock remains flat. This makes either strategy appealing with a sideways stock outlook.

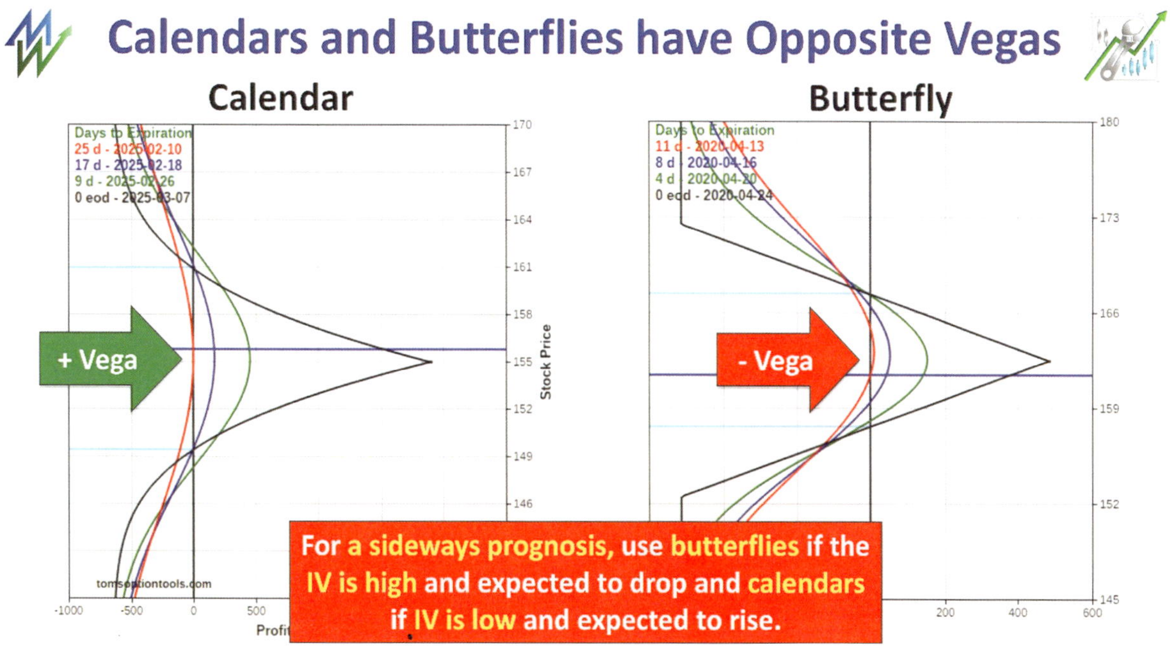

Your implied volatility outlook becomes the decisive factor.:

- If your IV outlook is up, use a calendar spread.
- If your IV prognosis is down, use a butterfly spread.
- If IV is expected to stay stable, either approach is acceptable.

Avoiding IV Skew Risk

A key yet often overlooked aspect of successful options trading is grasping how implied volatility (IV) works. Many option traders know nothing about IV, even those familiar with it often lack understanding of how IV varies over different time frames.

Typically, implied volatility (IV) is higher for shorter-term options compared to longer-term options. In the graphic, the red line indicates the shortest-term option, while the other lines represent options with more time until expiration. This phenomenon is known as IV Skew.

IV skew actually benefits a calendar spread when entering the trade.

Why? Because it involves selling the more expensive short-term option and covering it with a cheaper long-term option. As long as both IVs move up or down proportionally, the position stays balanced.

However, a problem can occur when the IV rushes more quickly in the short-term option than in the long-term one after entering the trade. This may cause the short-term option to become more costly than when it was initially sold, potentially resulting in a loss.

Avoiding IV Skew Risk

What is IV Skew?

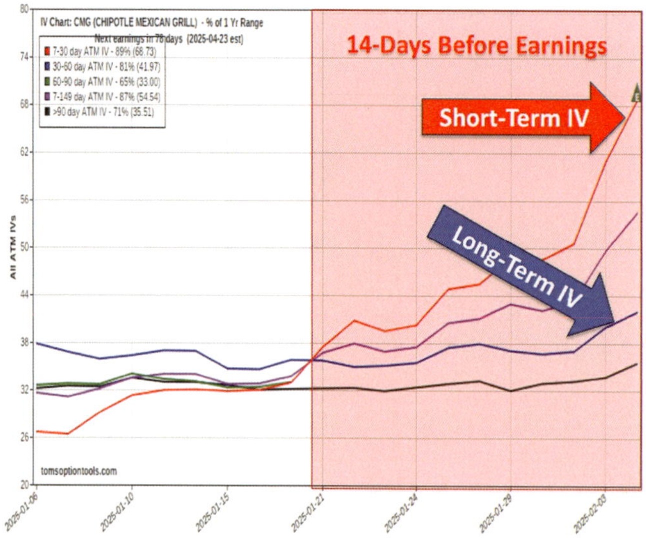

Short-term options typically have **higher IV** than **longer-term** options.

IV typically **rushes more** in **shorter-term** options than in **longer-term** options as expiration approaches.

This is particularly true the **14-days before earnings.**

So, when does this IV skew become dangerous? The answer is: earnings season. About 14 days before an earnings announcement, IV skew tends to increase significantly as the earnings date approaches. Short-term IV starts to spike, while long-term IV stays relatively stable. This disrupts the balance of the calendar and can cause unexpected losses.

The solution: Don't trade calendars during the 14-day window leading into an earnings event.

Vega in the Long and Short Options of a Calendar Spread

A closer look at the individual Vegas of the two legs in a calendar spread reveals an important relationship.

IV Skew Impact on a Calendar

Position	Num	Option Symbol	Expire	Type	Delta %	Gamma %	Vega %IV	Theta $/day
Sold	10	CMG250404C50	2025 Apr 04	50 Call	-52.15	-6.84	-5.2	4.9
Bought	10	CMG250425C50	2025 Apr 25	50 Call	53.34	5.65	7.0	-3.3

-Vega for Short Option

+Vega for Long Option

IV rush ***hurts short-term*** *options* ***(- Vega)***
IV rush ***benefits long-term*** *options* ***(+ Vega)***

- The **short option has a negative Vega**. It gains in value when IV falls and loses value when IV increases.
- The **long option has a positive Vega**. It gains in value when IV rises and loses value when IV drops.

Since a calendar spread has a positive net Vega, it benefits when implied volatility (IV) increases at a similar rate on both legs. This is because the long option's positive Vega will surpass the short option's negative Vega, leading to a net profit for the spread.

However, if IV increases more in the short option than in the long option, the short side becomes more costly than when it was initially sold—and this can turn a potentially profitable trade into a loss.

IV Crush Risk

So, what occurs if we encounter an IV rush skew?

Bad things, man!

In fact, this circumstance has an ominous name: **IV CRUSH!**

The risk graph on the left side of the image shows a calendar spread that does not experience an IV rush skew. In this case, the trader makes a nice profit of $750.

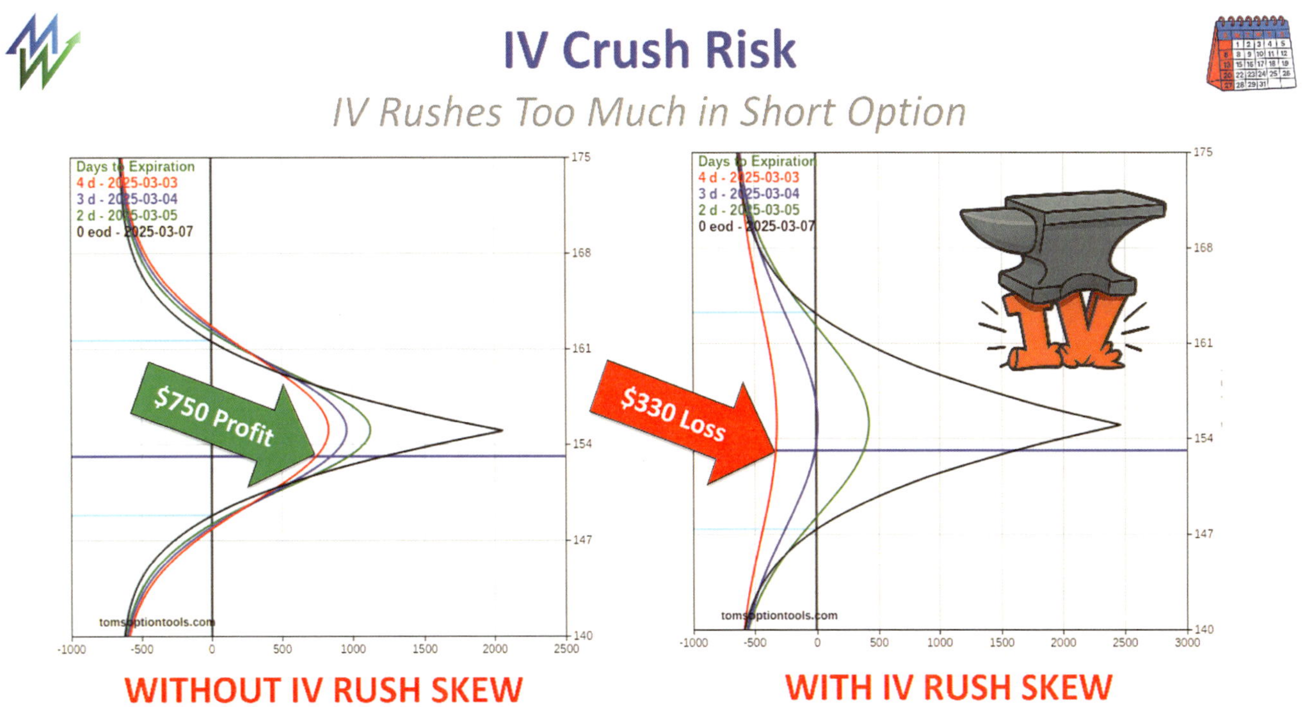

However, the graph on the right presents a different perspective. It illustrates the impact when IV suddenly increases mainly in the short option, distorting the overall trade.

Even though the stock behaved similarly in both trades, the one on the right experienced an IV crush caused by IV skew. Instead of making a profit, the trade resulted in a $330 loss—turning what could have been a $750 gain into a painful loss. That's an $1,080 turnaround solely due to implied volatility skew.

Avoiding IV Crush Risk the Smart Way

A simple and powerful way to avoid IV crush risk is this:

DON'T BE IN A CALENDAR SPREAD WITHIN 14-DAYS OF AN EARNINGS ANNOUNCEMENT

This single rule helps you avoid most IV rush skew events.

Why? Because earnings announcements act like a magnet for implied volatility. Traders expect movement, demand rises, and short-term IV begins to increase faster than long-term IV.

When you're in a calendar that experiences IV skew, it's a recipe for disaster.

Short-term options with negative Vega become more costly as IV rises. Long-term options with positive Vega don't always keep pace. The result? A calendar that looked well-positioned on the chart suddenly appears underwater—even if the stock moves exactly as you expected.

Although earnings are often the main cause, they are not the sole factor. Any known catalyst—like an anticipated product launch, regulatory decision, or significant economic report—can also cause a similar IV increase.

So, what's the bottom line?

Avoid opening or holding calendar spreads in the final two weeks leading up to earnings or other known catalysts.

The best calendars are built in calm waters, not in the volatility storms of the news cycle.

Calendars Can Be Used Directionally

While calendars are most commonly used to profit from range-bound stocks, they also provide a powerful and often overlooked advantage: They can be used as directional strategies.

Think of a directional calendar as a method to lower the cost of a long call (bullish outlook) or long put (bearish outlook) by selling a shorter-term option at the same strike price. This reduces the overall cost of the trade while keeping a favorable exposure to time and volatility.

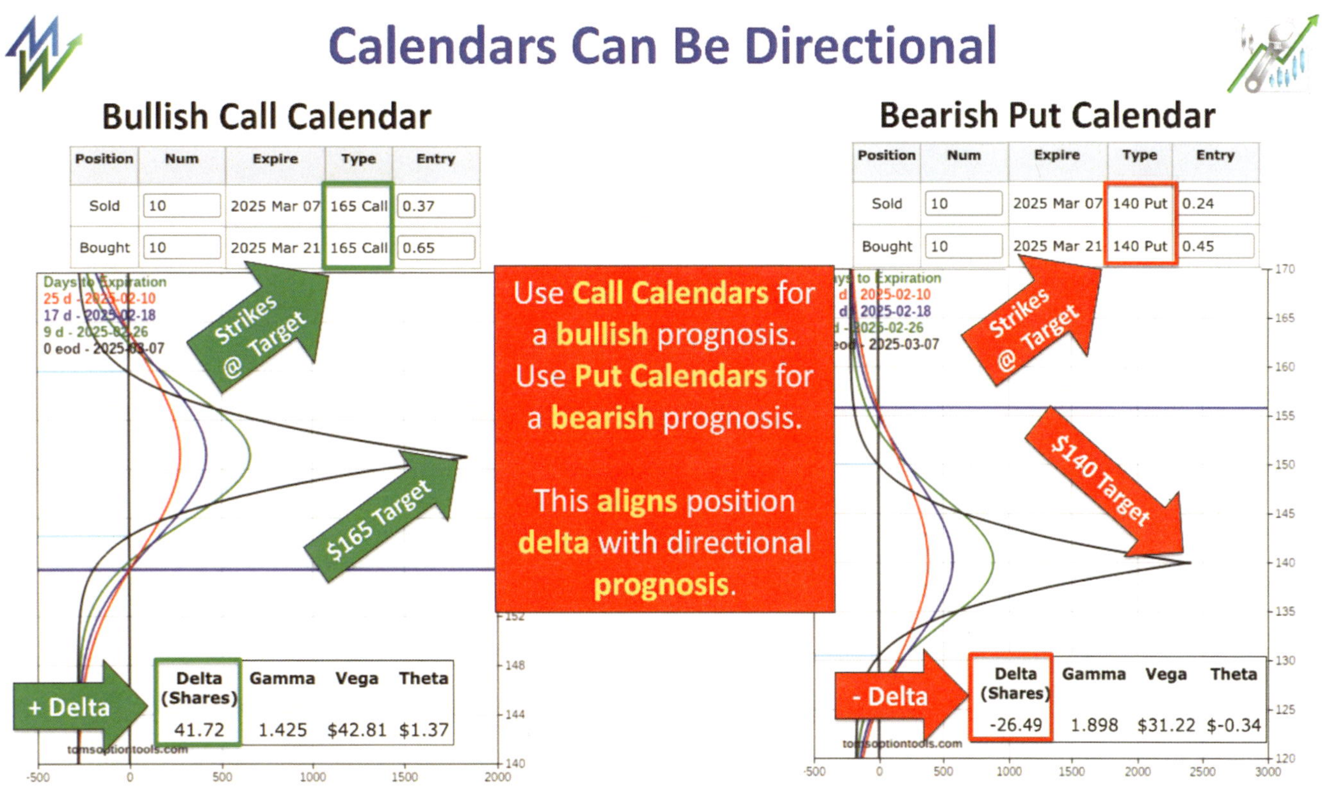

Let's analyze the bullish call calendar shown on the left side of the graphic above. In this setup, the trader has a target price of $165. Instead of choosing At-the-Money strikes, both the short and long options are set at the $165 strike. The long position involves buying 10 March 21 $165 calls at $0.65 each, costing $650. To reduce the cost, 10 March 7 $165 calls are sold at $0.37, bringing in $370 in premiums. This reduces the net cost of the position to $280.

As the stock approaches the $165 target, Theta becomes positive—letting time work in our favor. The risk graph indicates a positive Delta of +41.72, which supports the bullish outlook.

The same principle operates in reverse for a bearish outlook. On the right side of the graphic, the trader anticipates a move down to $140. They create a put calendar with both options at the $140 strike. This involves buying 10 March 21 $140 puts at $0.45 each (total $450). To offset this, they sell 10 March 7 $140 puts at $0.24 each, earning $240 in premium. As a result, the overall cost of the trade drops to $210.

As with the bullish calendar, this trade gains value as the stock approaches the target strike. The position Delta is -26.49, aligning with the bearish forecast.

In both scenarios, the trader employs the calendar structure to lower costs, preserve favorable Greeks, and capitalize on directional moves.

Use call calendars for bullish positions and put calendars for bearish ones.

Directional calendars offer a cost-effective and strategic method to express market outlook while leveraging Theta and cost advantages.

Summary - Harnessing Time with "Calendar Spreads"

Calendar spreads are a basic options strategy that uses time decay and implied volatility changes across different expiration dates. Although often viewed as neutral strategies, calendars are flexible, adaptable, and highly effective when used skillfully.

Core Concepts

- A calendar spread consists of selling a short-term option while purchasing a longer-term option at the same strike price.
- Calendars are Theta-positive and Vega-positive, meaning they profit when time advances and implied volatility increases.
- The position is Delta-neutral by default, which makes calendars ideal for range-bound markets.

Strategic Applications

- Use sideways (ATM) calendars when your stock outlook is sideways and your IV forecast is stable or rising.
- Avoid calendars during the 14 days before earnings, as IV skew can cause the short option's value to inflate and turn a good setup into a loss.
- IV rush skew is genuine—and risky. Safeguard yourself by monitoring news cycles and steering clear of brief IV spikes.

Understanding the Greeks

- The short leg has a negative Vega and is adversely affected by increases in IV.
- The long leg has higher positive Vega and benefits from rising IV.
- The position has a net positive Vega and benefits from rising IV.
- When IV rushes more into the short option than the long, the calendar can experience IV Crush Risk.
- Use this knowledge to time entries wisely and manage implied volatility exposure effectively.

Directional Calendars

- Calendars aren't just neutral. They can be directional.
- Use call calendars when your prognosis is bullish and put calendars when it's bearish.
- Place your strikes at the price target, not necessarily ATM.
- Benefit from cheap directional exposure and positive Theta—all in one trade.

Final Word

Calendar spreads benefit those who grasp the interaction between time and implied volatility. Whether used for neutral strategies or directional trades, the key advantage lies in aligning the Greeks, implied volatility forecast, and time frame.

Trade with precision. Let Theta and Vega work for you. And never trade a calendar blindly without considering the power of timing.

Now that you understand the calendar structure, the next step is learning how to actively adjust it as the stock begins to move. **The "Kite String Pull" Adjustment** is next.

CHAPTER 23

THE "KITE STRING PULL" ADJUSTMENT

CHAPTER 23
The "Kite String Pull" Adjustment

Calendar spreads start with built-in advantages. They provide excellent risk management and allow you to fine-tune the Greeks—especially Theta—to your benefit. What really makes calendars powerful is how easy they are to adjust during the game.

The "Kite String Pull" Adjustment

Risk can be **easily shifted** between the wings of a calendar spread, **pulling wings into profit,** by:

- *Ratioing the # of Shorts and Longs*
- *Diagonalizing (Different Strikes)*
- *Adding Insurance Adjustment*
- *Reducing Short Calls and Puts*

Let's start our adjustment toolkit with one of the most versatile moves in the calendar playbook: The "Kite String Pull" adjustment.

Imagine you're flying a two-stringed kite. With just a gentle tug on one of the strings, you can change the angle, steer the kite, and catch a better wind. That's exactly what we're doing here—shifting risk away from danger and pulling profit toward the side that needs it most.

The "Kite String Pull" helps you reshape your calendar spread wings and realign your position when the price begins moving toward the edge. It's a proactive step that safeguards your downside while opening opportunities for new upside—without abandoning your original strategy.

You can apply this adjustment using a variety of in-game tactics:

- **Ratioing the number of shorts and longs** – selling fewer options than you buy (a.k.a. a ratio calendar) to favor one side of the trade.

- **Diagonalizing** – shifting the strike of the short leg to a further Out-of-the-Money (OTM) level to shift risk opposite to the stock's move and adding profit possibilities.
- **Adding Insurance** – layering in protection using the Insurance Policy Adjustment to guard your unprotected side.
- **Buying Back Shorts** – removing short exposure to reduce directional risk.

The beauty of the "Kite String Pull" is that it doesn't require a dramatic shift. It's about precision. One smart move, and suddenly, you've shifted risk to a different part of the board and added new profit potential.

"Kite String Pull" Adjustment – Overview

Description

Calendar spreads are among the most flexible trade strategies in the options trading game. From the moment they're initiated, they present a high-probability setup with one of the clearest risk profiles. But that's just the start. When price begins to move, you have options—literally.

The "Kite String Pull" Adjustment

Description: *Calendar spreads are highly adjustable. From initiation, calendar spreads offer a high probability of profit with one of the best risk profiles of numerous option strategies. Wings can be pulled towards profit in numerous ways including ratioing longs and shorts, diagonalizing strikes, adding long options. They can even be repositioned to encompass stock movement for low cost.*

Strategies: *Calendar spreads and other time spreads.*

Outcome: *Risk is easily moved in the risk graph providing an exceptional ability to control risk, achieve desired directional bias **(Delta)** and greatly increase the probability of profit.*

Timing: *These adjustments can be applied on trade inception and anytime throughout the life of the trade. The game is to keep directional risk **(Delta)** neutral while allowing the passage of time **(Theta)** to bring in profits into the trade. Generally, if the delta to theta ratio approaches or exceeds 2:1, kite string pulls become reasonable. Additionally, technical analysis is used to signal an adjustment.*

The "Kite String Pull" adjustment allows you to smoothly shift risk and bring the wings of the calendar into profit. This can be achieved by:

- Ratioing longs and shorts
- Diagonalizing strike prices
- Adding protective long options
- Repositioning the calendar with minimal cost

Think of it as guiding the kite mid-flight. Small adjustments, clever tweaks, and suddenly the wind is on your side again.

Strategies

This adjustment applies not only to calendar spreads but also to any time-based spread that benefits from Theta and requires risk management.

Outcome

Risk can be effectively managed throughout the risk graph. You can modify your exposure, fine-tune your Delta to align with a market bias, and significantly boost your chances of profit—all without making major changes to your position.

Timing

The "Kite String Pull" can be used at the beginning of a trade or in the middle as the price starts to move against one side. The goal is to keep directional risk (Delta) neutral and let time decay (Theta) do its work. If Delta becomes too large compared to Theta—say, approaching a 2:1 ratio—it's time to consider pulling that string. Technical analysis can also help signal when to make the move.

Types of "Kite String Pull" Adjustments

Types of "Kite String Pull" Adjustments

Ratio: *The simplest way to **adjust directional bias (delta)** in a calendar spread. This is by accomplished adjusting the ratio of longs and short strikes.*

Diagonal: ***Selling further OTM short options** shifts directional **(delta)** bias. **Call Calendars** lend themselves well for **bullish** adjustments and **Put Calendars** lend themselves well for **bearish** adjustments.*

Seagull: *Combining one of the above with the **Insurance Policy Adjustment** will **pull BOTH wings towards profit** creating the **seagull**. Seagulls are **HIGHLY sensitive to IV fluctuations!***

TIP: ***These adjustments can be applied on trade inception or during the life of the trade.***

There are three main ways to pull the wings of a calendar spread toward profitability. Each method provides a different way to adjust directional bias, manage risk, and increase flexibility in the trade.

Ratio

The simplest form of pulling a kite string is to sell fewer options than you buy, forming a ratio calendar spread. This subtly shifts your risk position to one side, providing directional bias without disrupting the overall structure.

Diagonal

This version offsets risk against your directional outlook by selling your shorts further out of the money than your longs. This maintains your Delta aligned with your directional view with unlimited upside potential, while generating profit if the stock remains still.

Call calendars perform well for bullish diagonal setups. Put calendars excel when you're betting on the downside.

Seagull

The Seagull, the most dynamic of the three strategies, merges a ratio or diagonal calendar with the Insurance Policy adjustment—buying long calls or puts for extra protection. This combination enhances the profit potential of both wings and results in an engaging payoff structure.

Be aware—Seagulls are extremely responsive to IV movement. With significant ability comes heightened sensitivity.

And here's the key point: You can make these adjustments at the beginning of the trade or at any time during its duration. This flexibility is what makes calendars so powerful. Already a strong strategy—now you've unlocked their true potential: They are highly adaptable.

The Bullish Ratio "Kite String Pull" Adjustment

Let's start with a simple call calendar positioned at the money (ATM), shown on the left of the graphic. This setup has a modest, nearly neutral Delta of 11.94 and a total risk of $516. In this layout, the calendar aims to profit if the stock remains within a narrow range.

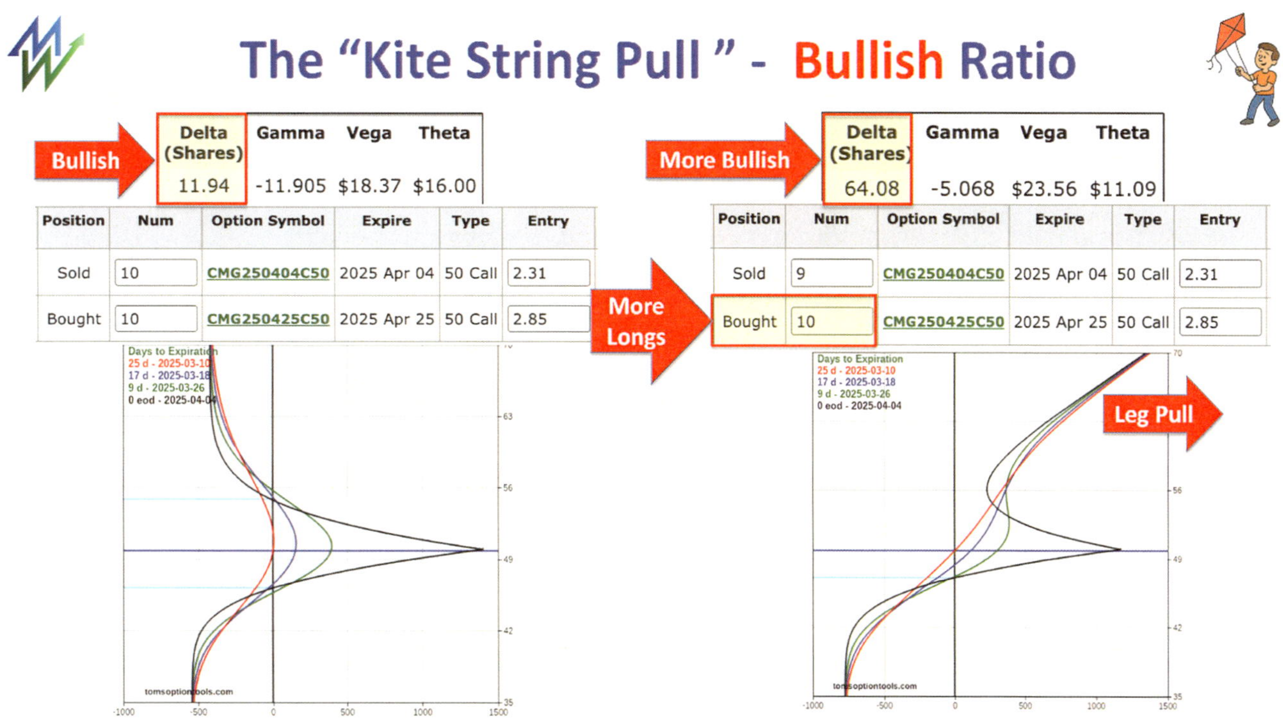

But what if your outlook is somewhat more optimistic—neutral to bullish? You aim to profit whether the stock stalls or rises. It might sound like having your cake and eating it too, but in the world of options, it's possible.

By simply adjusting the balance of shorts and longs—selling one fewer short call—you bring the upper wing into profit. This is the core of the Bullish Ratio "Kite String Pull".

On the right side of the graphic, it shows that the trader now has 10 long calls but only 9 short calls. This minor adjustment significantly impacts the position by raising the Delta from 11.94 to 64.08, creating a stronger bullish bias.

Here's the advantage: If the stock remains flat, the trade still makes a profit as before. But now, if the stock surges upward, the position gains even more. You've transformed a neutral calendar into a double-edged winner—all with just one simple leg adjustment.

Simple, powerful, and among the easiest kite pulls to master.

The Bearish Ratio "Kite String Pull" Adjustment

Just as you can adjust a call calendar to favor a bullish outlook, you can use the same approach with a put calendar to favor a bearish outlook.

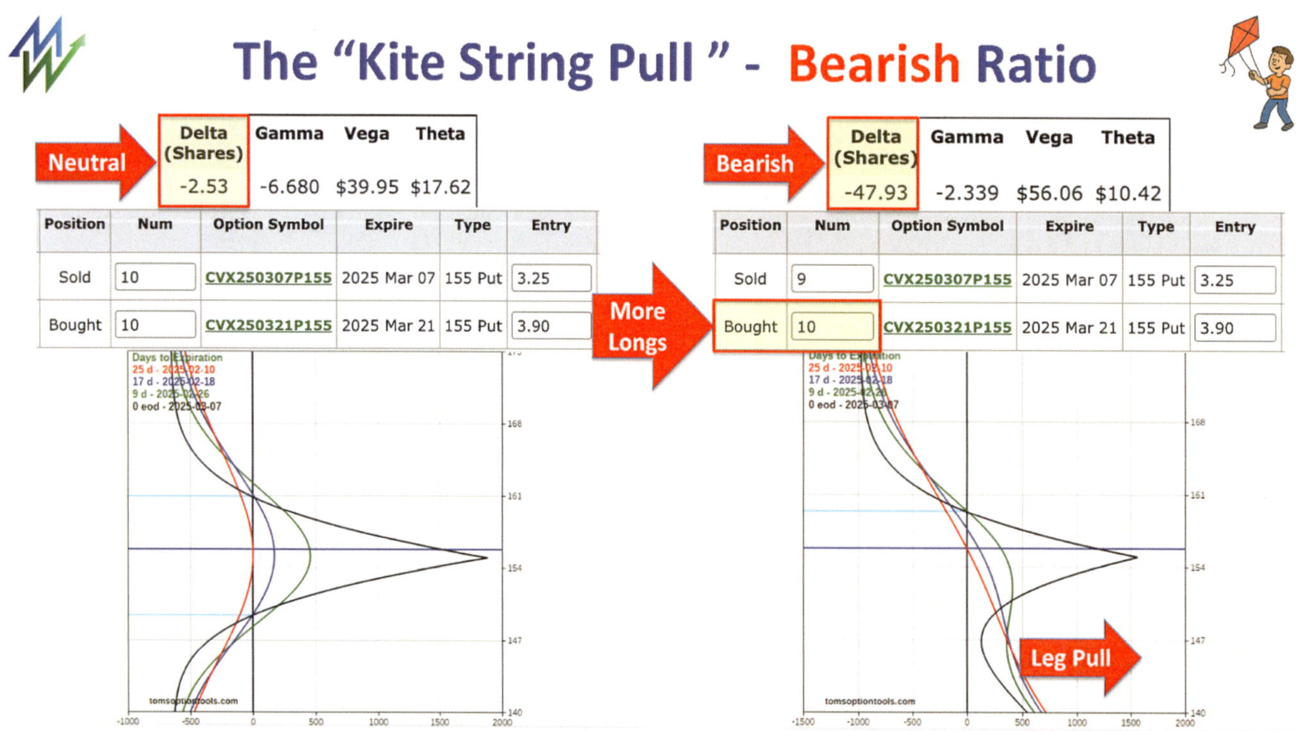

The trade on the left features a simple, neutral calendar using puts, with both legs at the $155 strike. Here, Delta is a modest -2.53, indicating a primarily range-bound profile.

Now let's say your outlook shifts. You believe the stock could decline further, or maybe even drop quickly. By adjusting the ratio—selling one fewer short put—you bring the lower wing into profit and reshape the profile for a more bearish scenario.

As the graph on the right shows, selling 9 short puts against 10 long puts significantly increases Delta to -47.93. The payoff? You now have a trade that can still profit sideways but also has unlimited potential for profit to the downside.

This is the real power of pulling the kite string. It allows you to play both defense and offense without resetting the board.

The Bullish Diagonal "Kite String Pull" Adjustment

Another way to turn part of your calendar into profit is by making a diagonal move—selling your short option at a strike price further out of the money than your long option. This change cleverly adjusts your risk profile, making it more adaptable.

Start with the setup on the left: A balanced April 4 / April 25 call calendar at the $50 strike. This position is fairly neutral with a Delta of 11.94. It will perform well if the stock stays near the $50 mark.

But if you have a sideways-to-bullish outlook, you can use the "Kite String Pull" adjustment to unlock even greater potential. By simply selling a higher-strike short-term call—in this case, the $51 call expiring April 4—you pull the upper leg into profit.

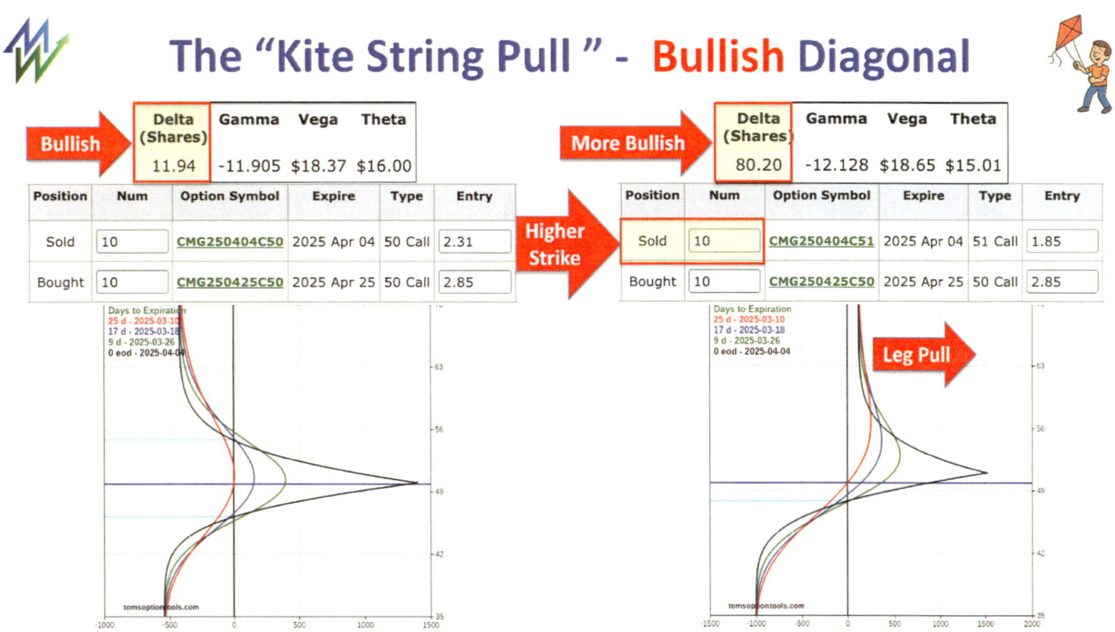

The risk graph on the right reveals the complete picture. You are currently long the $50 call (expiring April 25) and short the $51 call (expiring April 4). Consequently, the entire upper wing is profitable. Even if the stock remains stable, you will earn Theta. And if the stock rises, this setup is poised to increase in value along with it.

Take a look—Delta has risen to +80.20, indicating a strong bullish bias. You didn't add extra funds or rebuild the position; you simply made a small adjustment.

The Bearish Diagonal "Kite String Pull" Adjustment

The same diagonal adjustment method used to tilt a calendar bullish can also be applied downward. By modifying the structure, you can introduce bearishness into a range-bound calendar—allowing you to profit from both sideways and downward movements.

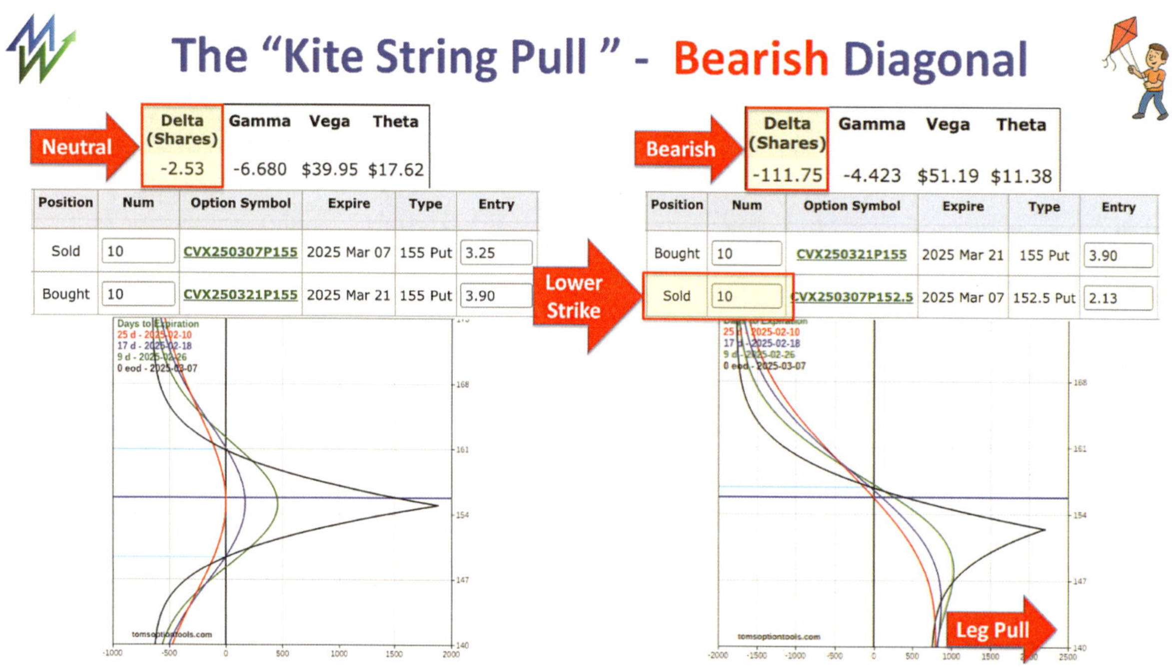

Begin with the calendar spread on the left: A balanced put calendar with both legs at the $155 strike. This setup is fairly neutral, showing a Delta of -2.53 and designed to profit most if the stock remains flat.

But what if your read indicates the stock might decline? No problem. You can execute a bearish diagonal "Kite String Pull" by selling a short put at a strike price lower than the long.

The graphic on the right shows exactly that: Selling the March 7 $152.50 put against a March 21 $155 long put. This small adjustment pulls the lower wing into profit, setting you up for gains if the stock trades sideways or moves lower.

Another clever tool in your adjustment arsenal—and an additional "Kite String Pull" arrow in your quiver.

The "Insurance Policy" "Kite String Pull" Adjustment

Another simple and effective way to make both wings of a calendar spread profitable or very low risk is to buy a small amount of insurance—literally. We do this by adding Out-of-the-Money (OTM) long calls and puts to offset directional risk on both ends of the trade.

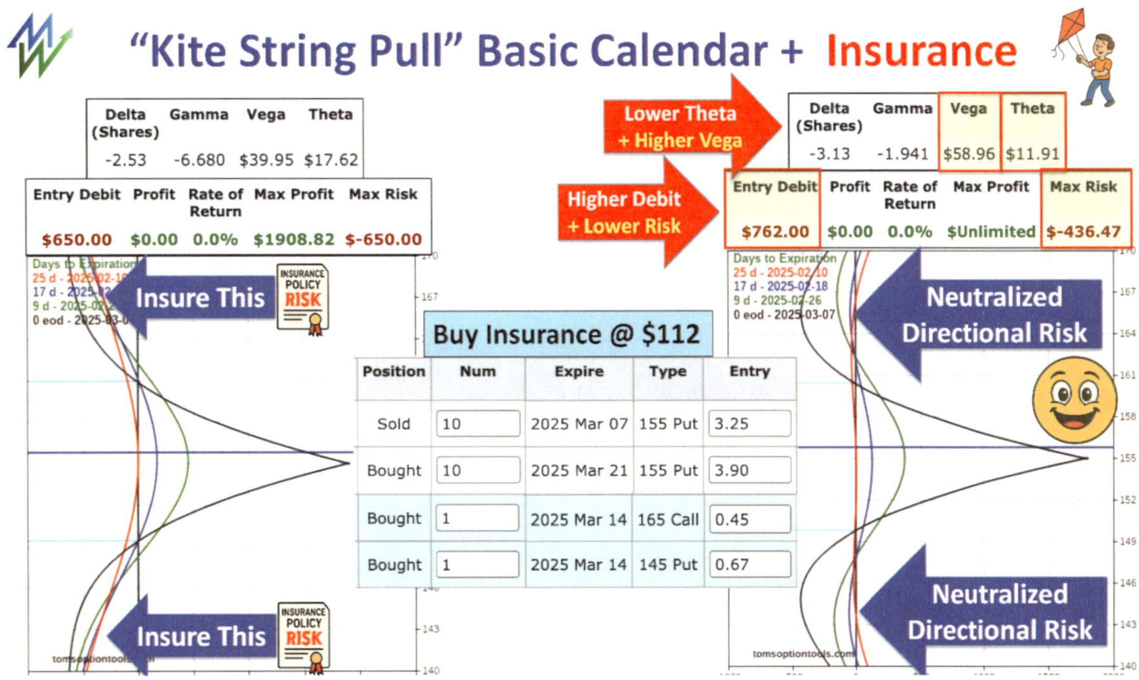

Starting with the setup on the left: A simple balanced calendar created using puts. We sell 10 March 7 $155 puts and cover this short by buying 10 March 21 $155 long puts. The overall cost of the trade is $650, which also represents the total directional risk if the stock moves significantly in either direction.

This position will perform well if the stock remains near $155. However, if there's a gap up or down, we face exposure. That's when the Insurance Policy Adjustment steps in.

To insure this calendar, we purchase a March 14 $165 call for $45 and a March 14 $145 put for $67. This amounts to a total cost of $112 to hedge $650 of risk—an excellent risk-to-coverage ratio.

The results are impressive. On the right-side risk graph, you can see that both wings have been pulled toward profit. Risk at expiration has been reduced from $650 to $437, a $213 decrease. And that's just at expiration—if a gap occurs before expiration, the pre-expiration lines (red, green, blue) show that losses will also be substantially lowered.

And let's not forget the Theta: It's still positive at $11.91. That means if the stock remains near your calendar body, time decay continues to benefit your position.

Simple. Clever. Secure.

Now, you've included insurance in your toolkit—another "Kite String Pull" to master.

The "Kite String Pull" - Seagull Adjustment

Things become even more engaging when you combine two of the most effective tools in the calendar strategy: The ratio or diagonal adjustment and the Insurance Policy Adjustment. Welcome to the Seagull.

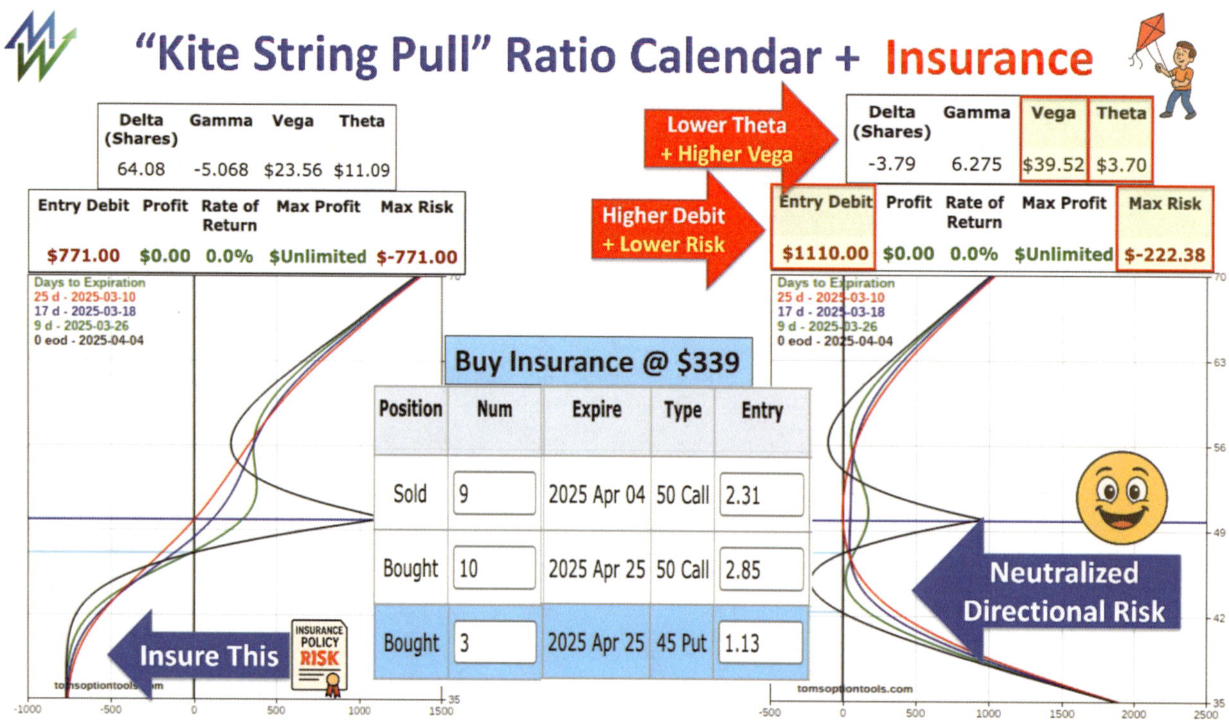

Start with a bullish ratio calendar like the one shown on the left. Here, we've sold 9 April 4 $50 calls and bought 10 April 25 $50 calls. This setup provides us with a nice sideways-to-bullish outlook. However, there's a problem: We're exposed to $771 of risk in the lower wing. If the stock drops, that risk becomes very real.

The fix? Insurance. By purchasing 3 April 25 $45 puts for a total of $339, we significantly reduce the lower wing into profit territory. The result is remarkable: Total risk drops from $771 to just $222.30 at expiration.

Examine the risk graph on the right carefully. The colored lines show how time progresses. By March 26—the green line, which represents two-thirds of the trade's duration—the entire profile is to the right of the zero-profit line. That means if you exit the trade around this point, assuming IV stays steady, you'll walk away a winner.

This trade is excellent: You gain profit whether the stock remains flat, gaps up, or gaps down. It resembles a straddle but benefits from positive Theta.

Of course, there's no free lunch. This trade carries another Greek risk—Vega. And that's exactly what we'll cover next.

Seagull Adjustments – Vega Risk and IV Sensitivity

This graphic displays two of the Seagull trades we discussed earlier—each combining a ratio or diagonal calendar with the Insurance Policy Adjustment. They're called "Seagulls" because the shape of their risk graph looks like a bird in flight: The center peak is the head, and the two extended wings resemble outstretched feathers.

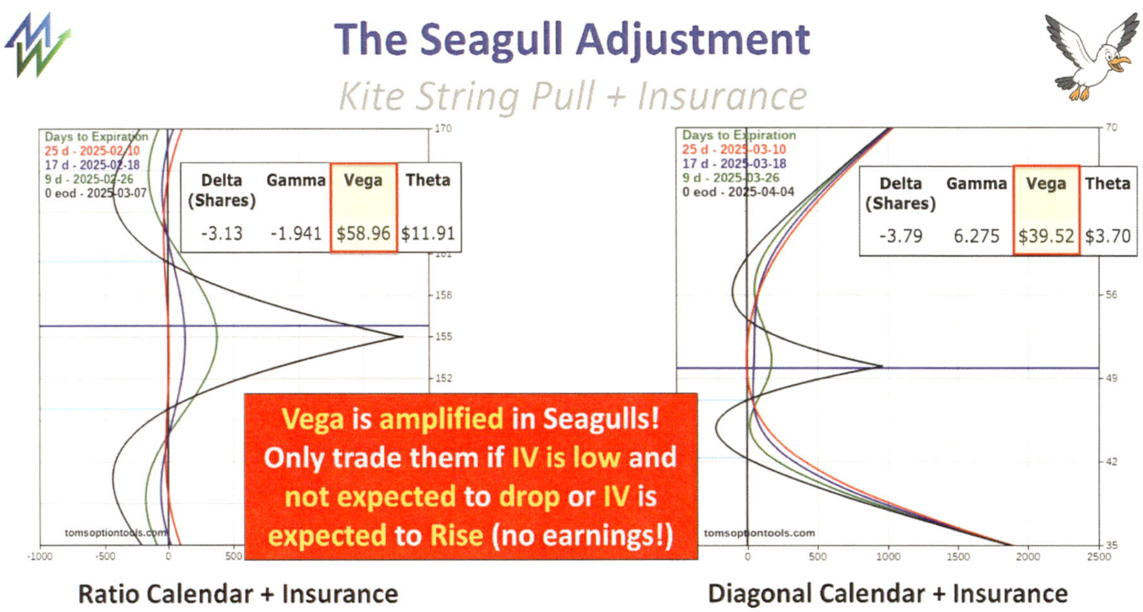

They seem almost too good to be true—and often, they are. The Seagull setup can profit whether the stock stays flat, rises, or falls. However, their main weakness is IV Crush.

By choosing more long options than shorts, you're increasing your exposure to implied volatility. That means Vega is amplified. In the graphic above, the Seagull on the left shows a Vega of $58.96, and the one on the right has $39.52. That's beneficial—if implied volatility goes up.

But if IV drops—especially if we get an IV Rush Skew—these birds get crushed. Even with a perfect price move, falling IV can wipe out the trade's edge.

So, what's the rule?

Only trade Seagulls when IV is low and anticipated to remain steady or increase. During earnings season? Steer clear of them.

However, with accurate IV analysis and well-timed entries, Seagulls can turn into high-probability, high-reward trades. Approach them with care, and they could become your preferred strategy.

Seagulls with IV Rush – The Power of Vega

Let's show what happens when volatility behaves exactly as you expected—rushing upward. This graphic demonstrates the effect of a 25% IV surge on two Seagull positions.

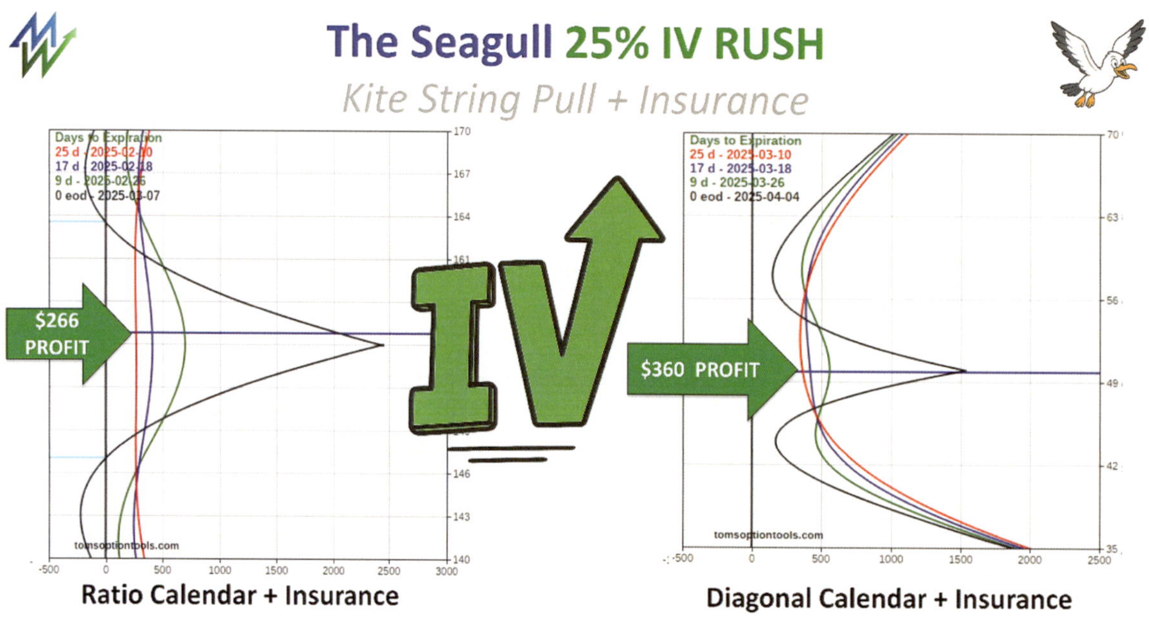

On the left, we see a Seagull built with a balanced calendar and an Insurance Policy Adjustment. With the 25% IV pop, this setup earns a solid $266 profit. That's strong performance and confirms the effectiveness of pairing a ratio or diagonal calendar with the Insurance Policy Adjustment.

On the right, we see a Seagull created from a ratio calendar plus insurance. This version has higher Vega, as explained earlier. Thanks to that additional Vega, a 25% IV spike pushes this bird even higher—resulting in a $360 profit.

This is the power of correctly applied Seagulls: When you get your IV call right—not down, but up—you unlock one of the most probable option trades available.

Stack Theta, control Delta, and ride the Vega wave. If you learn to identify low IV conditions poised for expansion, these trades won't just fly. They'll soar.

Seagulls with IV Crush – The Risk of Flying Too High

As exciting as a Seagull with IV Rush can be, the opposite is just as true—and much more painful. A high-flying Seagull can come crashing down to earth when an IV Crush happens.

The graphic below shows the result of a 25% drop in implied volatility on two Seagulls. The Seagull on the left, built with a ratio calendar and insurance, takes a hit: $241 loss. Ouch.

But the Seagull on the right—built with a diagonal calendar and more positive Vega—gets hit even harder. That same 25% IV crush leads to a sharp $341 loss.

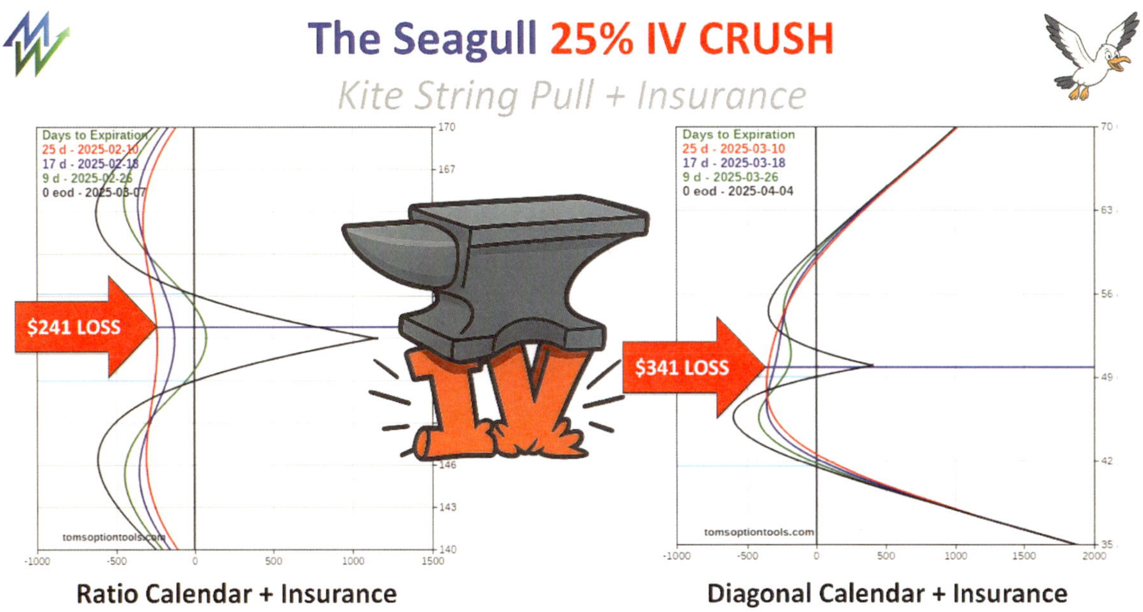

The bottom line? **Only trade Seagulls when IV is at or near historical lows.** That significantly reduces the chance of an IV drop during the trade's lifespan.

Respect implied volatility. Analyze your IV conditions before entering. Do that, and your Seagulls will soar where they belong—high above the danger zone.

Review: The 10 Basic Calendar Adjustment Moves

The "Kite String Pull" Adjustments

10 Basic Moves (6 Adds + 4 Closes)

Adjustment Moves	Delta	Vega	Theta
Add Long Call *(Close Short Call)*	*Positive*	*Positive*	*Negative*
Add Long Put *(Close Short Put)*	*Negative*	*Positive*	*Negative*
Add Short Call *(Close Long Call)*	*Negative*	*Negative*	*Positive*
Add Short Put *(Close Long Put)*	*Positive*	*Negative*	*Positive*
Add Long Stock	*Positive*	*N/A*	*N/A*
Add Short Stock	*Negative*	*N/A*	*N/A*

TIP

Use these basic moves + consider moving strikes to diagonalize your calendars

We discussed this in an earlier chapter, but now is the ideal time to revisit it. The above graphic is your essential guide for calendar adjustments.

It describes the 10 fundamental moves you can use to adjust your trade's risk profile as conditions change. There are six addition moves—buying options or stock—and four closing moves—buying back short options. Each one impacts your Delta, Vega, and Theta in different ways.

Begin with your 3-part prognosis—direction, IV, and time—to steer your initial trade. As your outlook changes, refer to this chart to determine the best way to adjust your Greeks and refine your edge.

Each move provides a precise lever to pull, whether you need to neutralize Delta, amplify Theta, or manage Vega risk. And remember the final pro tip at the bottom: Consider moving strikes to diagonalize your calendars. This offers even more flexibility in your risk management toolkit.

Learn these 10 moves to become skilled at adjusting your calendar effectively.

"Kite String Pull" – Strategic Guidelines

Before we finish this chapter, let's go over the key guidelines for effectively using the "Kite String Pull" adjustments. Think of this as your coaching on the sideline—knowing when to act, what your targets are, and how to stay in the game when market conditions change.

"Kite String Pull" Guidelines

1. The **Kite String Pull** can be applied upon **inception** of the trade or as a **later adjustment.**
2. Consider **reducing gap risk** in any variation of calendar with the Insurance **Policy adjustment.**
3. **Wings** can be **pulled** by **adjusting ratios** of **longs/shorts**, **sliding shorts further OTM** or buying Insurance.
4. The desired **outcomes** of these adjustments are to **neutralize directional risk (delta)** and keep **Theta** as **positive** as possible.
5. Calendars and seagulls are **very sensitive** to **IV fluctuations**, so be sure to derive a **solid prognosis** that **IV will not drop** AND that you are **outside** of the **14-days pre-earnings** window.

1. You can run the "Kite String Pull" at trade inception or mid-game.

Some players prefer to incorporate the adjustment into the opening trade, while others wait and respond to the stock's behavior. Both approaches are fair—choose based on your setup and forecast.

2. Protect against big gaps with insurance.

If your calendar looks good but has too much downside or upside risk, use the Insurance Policy Adjustment. It's a smart way to reduce gap risk and keep your head in the game.

3. Pull those wings by tweaking ratios or strike locations.

You've seen it all in this chapter—pull one side by reducing the number of shorts, pull the other by shifting them further OTM. Or pull both by layering on some insurance.

4. Your objective: Neutralize Delta and maximize Theta.

Every "Kite String Pull" should bring your Delta closer to zero while keeping Theta positive. This maintains your edge growing day by day—no matter what the stock does.

5. Be IV-smart: Avoid Seagulls when IV is high or earnings are near.

Calendars, especially Seagulls, are highly sensitive to implied volatility changes. You need a reliable forecast that IV will remain stable or increase—and that you're outside the 14-day pre-earnings risk zone where IV skew risk usually occurs.

Use these guidelines as a game plan. They won't just keep you in the trade. They'll help you turn adjustments into high-probability plays.

Summary - "Kite String Pull"

The "Kite String Pull" is one of your most flexible, powerful, and elegant tools in adjusting your calendar spread. In this chapter, we learned how to use it to manage risk, unlock profit potential, and navigate market conditions with accuracy.

Core Concept

Think of the "Kite String Pull" like flying a two-stringed kite—by tugging on one string, you change its shape and direction. In trading terms, this means adjusting the Greeks (Delta, Vega, Theta) to match your changing outlook.

Adjustment Tools Covered

- **Ratio Adjustments:** Reducing the number of shorts to create directional bias.
- **Diagonal Adjustments:** Shift short options OTM to adjust Delta and widen wings.
- **Insurance Policy Adjustment:** Add long OTM puts/calls to cap risk and pull both wings toward profit.
- **Seagull Adjustment:** Combine a ratio or diagonal calendar with insurance for wide-range, high-Theta, low risk trades.

Managing Risk

These adjustments can be made at trade inception or mid-life. Always aim to:

- Neutralize Delta (directional risk)
- Maximize Theta (time decay benefit)
- Protect Vega (volatility risk) in high-sensitivity setups like Seagulls

The Vega Trap

Derivatives of calendars have positive Vega, and changes in IV can help or hurt your position. Seagulls look great—but they come with a catch: **Vega amplification.** If IV drops or IV skew appears, your high flyer could turn into a crash landing. Only trade Seagulls and any calendar derivatives when IV is historically low and expected to stay flat or increase.

Your Playbook

Use the 10 Basic Moves chart and the strategic guidelines to keep your adjustments precise, responsive, and well-planned. This chapter provided you with the playbook—now go make things happen and take control of your trades.

Now that you can guide your trade back into position, the next step is doubling down on Calendar Spreads to greatly improve probability of profit: **The "Double-Wide" Adjustment**.

CHAPTER 24

THE "DOUBLE-WIDE" ADJUSTMENT

CHAPTER 24
The "Double-Wide" Adjustment

What's better than one well-placed calendar spread? Two of them stacked together.

The "Double-Wide" adjustment is a strong strategy that involves placing two calendars at different strikes—either right at the start of the trade or as a mid-trade adjustment. This approach significantly lowers the chance of loss and gives your trade more statistical flexibility.

The "Double Wide" Adjustment

Calendar spreads can be **stacked** atop each other to **reduce** the **probability of loss** and **greatly increase** the statistical **probability of profit.**

When executed properly, stacking calendars broadens the profit zone and balances out directional risk. It's like placing two overlapping safety nets—if the stock moves away from one, the other can still catch it.

Use this play to move from high conviction to high probability. Whether you're reacting to market changes or creating broader coverage from the start, the "Double-Wide" adjustment has you covered.

"Double-Wide" Adjustment – Strategy Overview

The "Double-Wide" adjustment isn't just about gaining more space. It's about increasing flexibility, coverage, and staying power in the game. When you stack a second calendar on top of the first, you widen your breakevens and expand the range of profitability. That means you don't need to be precise. You just have to stay within a broader zone.

You can set up a call calendar at the higher strike and a put calendar at the lower strike. This creates a broad range to capture movements in both directions, while letting Theta work for you. And the best part? You can build this at trade inception or add the second calendar later as the stock starts to drift.

The "Double Wide" Adjustment

Description: *Calendar spreads can be stacked to widen the resulting breakevens and providing a large range in which the stock can move and still realize profit. To accomplish this, use call calendars for the higher strike and put calendars for the lower strike. This adjustment can be made on trade inception or during the life of the trade.*

Strategies: *Any type of calendar spreads or derivation of time spreads.*

Outcome: *The adjustment will result in a wider profit zone. The cost of the resulting double calendar will result in a higher trade cost and a lower ROI potential. In exchange, the resulting trade will have a higher probability of profit.*

Timing: *This adjustment can be placed on trade inception. An ATM or OTM call calendar can be added during the life of the trade if the stock approaches the upper breakeven and an ATM or OTM put calendar can be added if the stock approaches the lower breakeven.*

Remember, it's not free. Adding a second calendar will cost extra and lower your potential ROI, but it raises your probability of profit. It's the classic trade-off: Sacrifice some potential upside to reduce your downside and improve your win rate.

This move works with any calendar or time spread variation. The main idea here is adaptation: Stack broadly and play smart to give yourself more ways to win.

Calendar in Trouble – Time to Adjust

Let's examine a real-world example where a calendar spread begins to wobble. In this case, the stock has moved down to the lower breakeven point of the calendar. If it drops any further, the trade will start losing money.

The "Double Wide" - Initial Calendar

Quote Type	Entry Debit	Profit	Rate of Return	Max Profit	Max Risk	Delta (Shares)	Gamma	Vega	Theta
Mid Quote	$23.00	$0.00	0.0%	$69.33	$-23.00	8.05	-2.487	$0.40	$0.55

Bullish

Downside Breakeven	Upside Breakeven	Profit/Max Risk	Max Profit/Cost
8.22	12.60	301.44%	301.44%

Position	Num	Option Symbol	Expire	Type	Entry
Sold	1	RUN250228C10	2025 Feb 28	10 Call	0.28
Bought	1	RUN250321C10	2025 Mar 21	10 Call	0.51

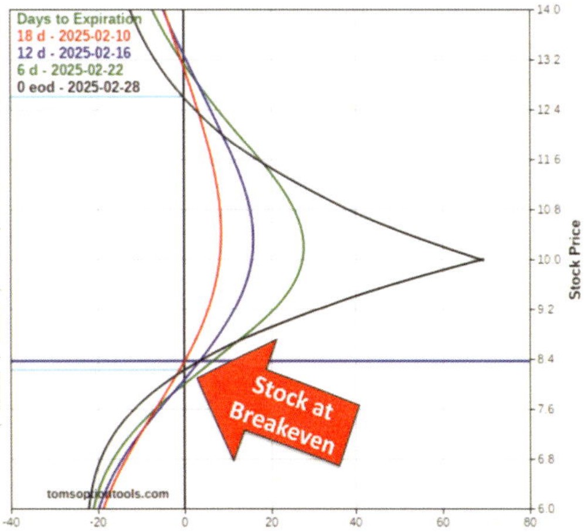

TIME TO ADJUST:

1. *Stock approaching lower risk wing*
2. *Delta Bullish (+$8.05)*
3. *Breakevens $4.38 wide ($12.60 - $8.22)*

The Delta is reading +$8.05, which means we'll lose about $8 for every $1 the stock drops. Not catastrophic by itself, but if the decline speeds up, this calendar could fall apart—and quickly.

In fact, if the stock continues to decline without intervention, we're facing a potential 100% loss.

Now, a good move here would be to add some downside protection using the Insurance Policy Adjustment. That would lower directional risk and allow Theta to work its magic, but there's another option...

In the next play, we'll learn how to stack a second calendar below the first and use the "Double-Wide" adjustment to expand the reach and reduce our loss risk.

"Double-Wide" Adjustment – Applied in Action

So, the stock's drifting lower and you're nearing the edge of your calendar's comfort zone. What do you do when you want to open up the downside and give yourself more room to win?

Easy. You drop in a second calendar.

The "Double Wide" - Adjustment 1

Quote Type	Entry Debit	Profit	Rate of Return	Max Profit	Max Risk	Delta (Shares)	Gamma	Vega	Theta
Mid Quote	$44.00	$0.00	0.0%	$55.23	$-44.00	4.19	-4.822	$0.73	$1.07

Downside Breakeven	Upside Breakeven	Max Risk	Max Profit/Cost
6.46	11.51	125.52%	125.52%

Less Bullish

Position	Num	Option Symbol	Expire	Type	Entry
Sold	1	RUN250228C10	2025 Feb 28	10 Call	0.28
Bought	1	RUN250321C10	2025 Mar 21	10 Call	0.51
Sold	1	RUN250228P7	2025 Feb 28	7 Put	0.27
Bought	1	RUN250321P7	2025 Mar 21	7 Put	0.48

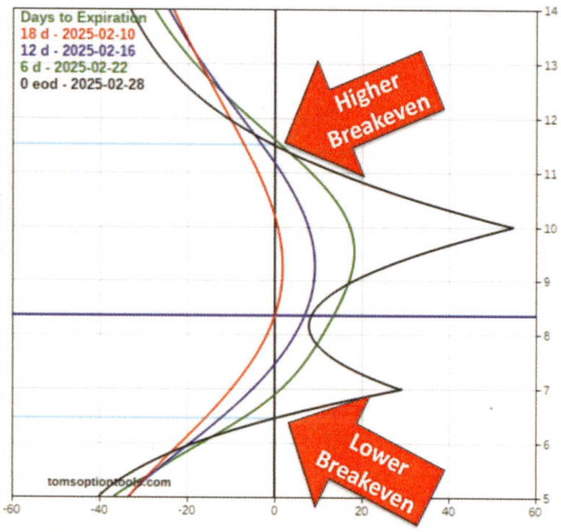

DESIRED OUTCOME:
1. *Reduce Delta*
2. *Widen Breakevens*

1. *Add OTM Put Calendar (blue legs)*
2. *Delta reduced to $4.19*
3. *Wider profit zone of $5.05 ($11.51 – $6.46)*

In this example, we added a brand-new calendar at the $7 strike using the same expiration dates. The result? A cleaner, wider profit zone and a softer Delta—now down to +4.19. If the stock keeps dropping, we're still in the game with a better chance to finish strong.

The downside breakeven also decreased to $6.46, while the upside breakeven remains at $11.51, creating a profit zone that's now over $5 wide. That's some serious space to breathe and let time decay work its magic.

Yes, the trade cost has gone up. You've basically doubled the debit. But what you've gained is a much higher chance of making a profit. Now, all the other strategies you know—insurance, diagonals, ratio adjustments—can be used on either or both calendars.

Simple. Powerful. Smart play.

"Double-Wide" Adjustment – Game Plan Guidelines

Here are your official sideline guidelines for running the "Double-Wide" adjustment. This isn't a gimmick. It's a legit power move. But like any good strategy, you need to know when and how to use it.

"Double Wide" Guidelines

1. The **Double Wide** is best applied upon **inception** of the trade or as a useful **later adjustment.**
2. **Max risk and ROI** are **exchanged** for a **higher probability of profit**.
3. The Double Wide can be **coupled** with **other calendar adjustments** like the Kite String Pull, and Insurance Policy adjustments.
4. Combining two calendars **increases Vega.** This is especially true with adjusted calendars with **more long options** than shorts. Be sure to **have a strong "not down" IV prognosis**.
5. Do **NOT** hold a calendar and any of its derivations **during the 14-days** prior to an **earnings announcement** to avoid IV Skew Risk.

1. Best played early, but great as a comeback move too.

You can launch the "Double-Wide" adjustment immediately or add it later when your first calendar begins to feel the pressure. Use it as a proactive strategy or a reactive fix. It's flexible.

2. Yes, you're spending more. But you're buying better odds.

Max risk and ROI do take a hit, but in exchange, you gain breathing room. You're trading some upside potential for a better win rate—smart tradeoff if your game is consistency.

3. The "Double-Wide" adjustment stacks well with other adjustments.

Use it along with the "Kite String Pull" or add an "Insurance Policy" on top and or bottom. This isn't a one-trick move. It's part of a bigger playbook.

4. Two calendars = more Vega.

When you stack, you increase your exposure to IV changes, especially if one or both spreads have more longs than shorts. So, you better have a solid NOT DOWN IV forecast in your pocket.

5. Never, ever hold a calendar through earnings.

Don't even think about it. The 14-day pre-earnings window is an IV skew trap. Don't step into it—your calendars will get crushed.

Play it smart. Play it wide. And keep that profit zone open like a championship end zone.

Summary – The "Double-Wide" Adjustment

The "Double-Wide" adjustment focuses on broadening your advantage and reducing your risk. By stacking calendars—either at trade inception or during a mid-game adjustment—you create a larger profit zone, diminish your directional bias, and boost your chances of making a profit.

Key Takeaways

- Use a second calendar (call or put) to widen breakevens and flatten Delta.
- This strategy can be initiated right away or used reactively if the stock pushes toward one side.
- You're trading a higher cost and lower ROI for more flexibility and a stronger win rate.
- The "Double-Wide" adjustment plays nicely with the "Kite String Pull" and the "Insurance Policy" adjustments, and all your core adjustment moves.

Reminders

- Watch your Vega—stacking calendars increases sensitivity to IV.
- Only use this strategy with a solid 'not down' IV prognosis.
- Never hold into earnings—IV skew risk is too high in the 14-day lead-up.

Bottom Line

The "Double-Wide" adjustment is a powerful move in your trading toolkit. When you need space to breathe and a better chance of success, this is how you get it. It's about consistency, adaptability, and setting yourself up for a win—every time.

Now that you can widen your trade for more flexibility, the next step is learning how to actively reposition it as the market trends. **The "Move the Catcher's Mitt" Adjustment** is next.

CHAPTER 25

THE “MOVE THE CATCHER’S MITT” ADJUSTMENT

CHAPTER 25
The "Move the Catcher's Mitt" Adjustment

In baseball, catchers don't wait for the ball to magically find their glove. They position the mitt where they expect the pitch to land. That's exactly the mindset behind this next adjustment.

The "Move the Catchers Mitt" Adjustment

Calendar spreads can be cheaply **moved up and down** along with the stock to **reduce** the **probability of loss** and **greatly increase** the statistical **probability of profit.**

With calendar spreads, your catcher's mitt is the body of the calendar—the strike price where you're positioned to catch profit. And when the stock starts moving elsewhere, you don't just sit and hope. You move your mitt. You shift the calendar.

This adjustment allows you to cheaply reposition your entire calendar up or down to follow the stock. You're not trying to guess. You're adjusting your aim to match where the pitch is going.

Most of the time, you can do this for a small debit, and what you gain is significant: Lower risk of loss and a greatly increased chance of profit.

It's straightforward, strategic, and keeps you in the game with your mitt ready—right where the action is headed.

"Move the Catcher's Mitt" Adjustment - Overview

This adjustment is among the most intuitive and effective tools in your trading strategy. Just as a catcher moves the mitt to frame the pitch, you're repositioning your calendar spread to target the stock's movement.

When the stock makes a decisive move—especially toward or beyond your breakeven point—it's time to adjust your position. You shift the entire calendar up or down in strike to align it with the new stock price. This aligns the risk profile, helps neutralize Delta, and creates a new profit zone.

The "Move the Catchers Mitt" Adjustment

Description: *Calendar spreads can be moved up and down in strike to center the calendar around the stock price. This is particularly useful when the stock makes a move towards or beyond either of the breakevens. The bonus is that this adjustment results in a small debit keeping the additional risk incurred minimal.*

Strategies: *Any type of calendar spreads or derivation of time spreads.*

Outcome: *This adjustment will result in a calendar centered at the current stock price. Sliding the calendar up or down along with the stock move will usually only incur a small debit and result in neutralizing Delta. Risk will be slightly increased in exchange for effective risk management and a higher probability of profit.*

Timing: *Generally, this adjustment is made when the stock begins to make a strong move or approaches/crosses either of the breakevens.*

The advantage of this move? It typically costs very little. Most "repositionings" can be made for a small debit. And the reward is significant: Improved risk management and a higher chance of profit without overloading your account.

You can use this move on any type of calendar or time spread variation. It's especially helpful when the stock makes a sharp directional move. Instead of hoping it rebounds, you go along with it.

It's about staying agile, centered, and always ready for the next pitch.

Time to Adjust - Calendar in Trouble

This setup should sound familiar. You're in a calendar, the stock drifts too far, and suddenly you're leaning way off course.

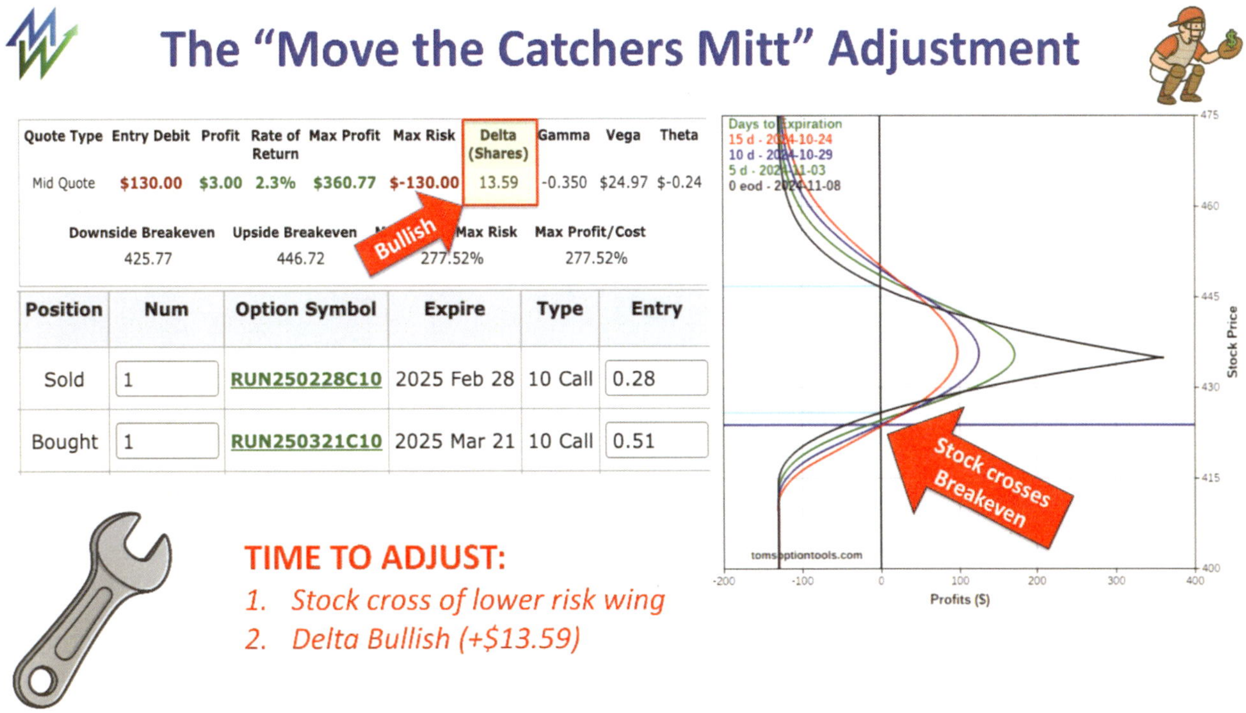

Quote Type	Entry Debit	Profit	Rate of Return	Max Profit	Max Risk	Delta (Shares)	Gamma	Vega	Theta
Mid Quote	$130.00	$3.00	2.3%	$360.77	$-130.00	13.59	-0.350	$24.97	$-0.24

Downside Breakeven	Upside Breakeven	Max Risk	Max Profit/Cost
425.77	446.72	277.52%	277.52%

Position	Num	Option Symbol	Expire	Type	Entry
Sold	1	RUN250228C10	2025 Feb 28	10 Call	0.28
Bought	1	RUN250321C10	2025 Mar 21	10 Call	0.51

Here, the stock has just dropped below the lower breakeven. That's your cue to act.

Delta at +13.59 indicates that we're poised to lose $13.59 for every $1 the stock declines. Our maximum risk is $130. That might not seem like much, but when the stock starts moving against us, time also quickly works against you.

The trade is still on, but it's near the profit zone's edge. You have a choice: Wait and hope the ball comes back into reach or move your glove and catch it where it's going.

Next, we will implement the "Move the Catcher's Mitt" Adjustment—repositioning the entire calendar to focus on the new stock price and returning the risk zone to your control.

Applying the "Move the Catcher's Mitt" Adjustment

Here's where the mitt actually moves. When your calendar spread drifts out of the money—like this one did at $435—and the stock falls to $424, you don't stay still. You move with it.

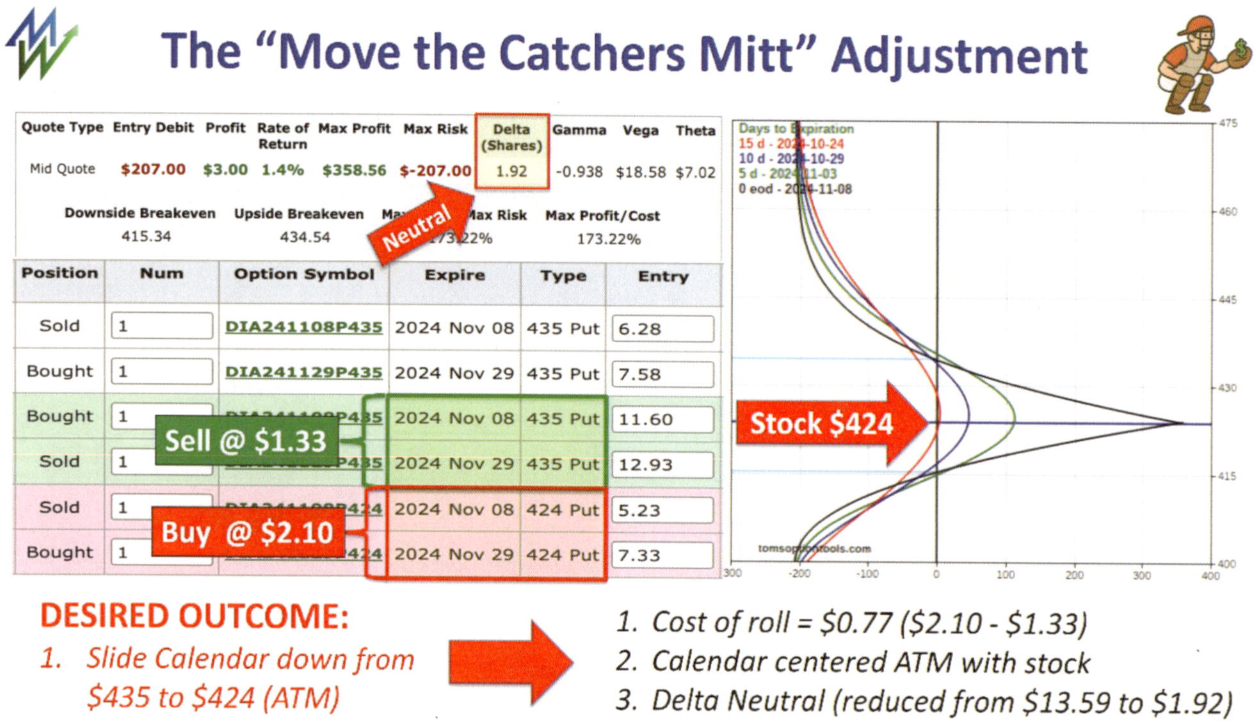

Quote Type	Entry Debit	Profit	Rate of Return	Max Profit	Max Risk	Delta (Shares)	Gamma	Vega	Theta
Mid Quote	$207.00	$3.00	1.4%	$358.56	$-207.00	1.92	-0.938	$18.58	$7.02

Downside Breakeven	Upside Breakeven	Max Profit/Max Risk	Max Profit/Cost
415.34	434.54	173.22%	173.22%

Position	Num	Option Symbol	Expire	Type	Entry
Sold	1	DIA241108P435	2024 Nov 08	435 Put	6.28
Bought	1	DIA241129P435	2024 Nov 29	435 Put	7.58
Bought	1	[illegible]	2024 Nov 08	435 Put	11.60
Sold	1	[illegible]	2024 Nov 29	435 Put	12.93
Sold	1	[illegible]	2024 Nov 08	424 Put	5.23
Bought	1	[illegible]	2024 Nov 29	424 Put	7.33

This move is very simple: Close the old calendar for a credit and open a new one closer to the current stock price for a debit. In this example, we sold the original $435 calendar for $1.33 and bought the new $424 calendar for $2.10. That results in a net debit of $0.77, or just $77 to re-center your risk and improve your chances.

More importantly, look at what happened to the Delta. It dropped from $13.59 to just $1.92, removing directional risk and putting the stock firmly back in the strike zone.

You're still in the game. The chance of making a profit has increased. And all you paid was a small fee to maintain the advantage.

That's why we love calendars. Adjustments like this are simple, strategic, and they keep your mitt right where the ball is headed.

"Move the Catcher's Mitt" Adjustment – Guidelines

This move is all about positioning—keeping your glove where you expect the ball is likely to land. When the stock breaks outside your calendar's breakevens, you don't wait for the market to come back to you. You adjust the entire trade to meet it.

"Move the Catchers Mitt" Guidelines

1. Consider the **"Move the Catchers Mit"** adjustment when the stock has **broken outside** of the calendar's **breakevens**. **Sooner** is **better** than later.
2. Moving the calendar will **cost a debit**, usually a **small** one.
3. When moving the calendar be sure that your **adjusted max risk** does **not exceed** your **maximum** position size **limits**.
4. Consider the **"Kite String Pull"** or the **"Insurance Policy"** adjustment when moving your calendar.
5. Use **support and resistance** as guidelines to reposition your calendar spread.

Here are your in-game guidelines:

1. **Pull the trigger early**—when the stock hits your breakeven or even before, act quickly. Waiting raises the risk. A well-timed adjustment gives you the best chance to recenter your profit zone.
2. **Expect to pay a small fee**—usually modest—but it's the cost of staying in position to win.
3. **Always stay aware of your new total risk.** When adjusting the calendar, ensure you're still within your permitted position size.
4. **Combine this move with other strategies.** A "Kite String Pull" or "Insurance Policy" adjustment can add flexibility and hedge directional exposure.
5. **Use support and resistance levels as your field markers.** They help you decide where to position your mitt next.

Like any great player, you stay ready and mobile. The calendar doesn't have to stay in one place. You move it with the game—and win more consistently doing it.

Summary – The "Move the Catcher's Mitt" Adjustment

This reminder shows you're not stuck at the starting point of the trade. You're an active participant. As the stock moves, you adjust your calendar spread accordingly, just like a catcher shifting the mitt to frame the next pitch.

The goal here is simple: Keep the calendar body aligned with the stock's direction. When the stock crosses a breakeven point and directional risk activates, close your current calendar and open a new one centered on the new stock price.

The result? You reduce Delta, realign your Theta engine, and restore a high-probability trade setup. And the cost is usually minor—often just a small debit to roll. It's a trade-off worth making to stay in control.

This move performs well in trending markets. When a stock isn't staying put, neither should you. Let your calendars move with the game.

Combine this with the "Kite String Pull" and "Insurance Policy" adjustments, and your risk management rules, and you'll stay ahead of the game. The mitt doesn't catch the ball by accident. It's because you moved it exactly where it needed to be.

This adjustment is all about staying in sync with price movement.

"Move the Catcher's Mitt" teaches you to reposition your calendar as the stock trends—shifting your center point to follow the action rather than resisting it.

The key concept:
Don't wait for the market to come back—move with it.

By relocating the structure, you:

- Realign your profit zone
- Reduce directional risk
- Keep Theta working efficiently

This move is particularly effective in trending markets where staying static leads to increasing pressure.

Now that you can move your structure with the market, the next step is learning how to take a directional stance while still maintaining a high probability of success. **The Risk Reversal** spread is next.

CHAPTER 26

THE RISK REVERSAL - PLAYING DIRECTION WITH A HIGH PROBABILITY OF PROFIT

CHAPTER 26
The Risk Reversal – Playing Direction with a High Probability of Profit

In this game of options, directional trading is like calling your shot in a pool hall. You don't just say you'll make the 8-ball. You specify which pocket it will go into. And if you're wrong? You lose your turn... and maybe the match.

Now let's relate this to trading. A straightforward long call or put—your typical directional move—is like that bold 8-ball shot. You only succeed if the stock does what you expect and moves favorably. But what if it doesn't? What if it stays flat... or worse, moves against you?

Here's the harsh truth: Stocks can move in three ways—up, down, or sideways—and a simple long option only profits in one of those (up). That means a statistical 33% chance of success. Not the best odds when your capital is at risk.

And sure, you can adjust. You should adjust. But wouldn't it be better to start the game with the odds stacked in your favor—right out of the gate?

Enter the Risk Reversal. This is your secret weapon—a strategic combination that allows you to aim for directional profits while still maintaining a high 80% chance of winning. It's like calling your shot and having two extra balls fall into the pocket just because you played smart.

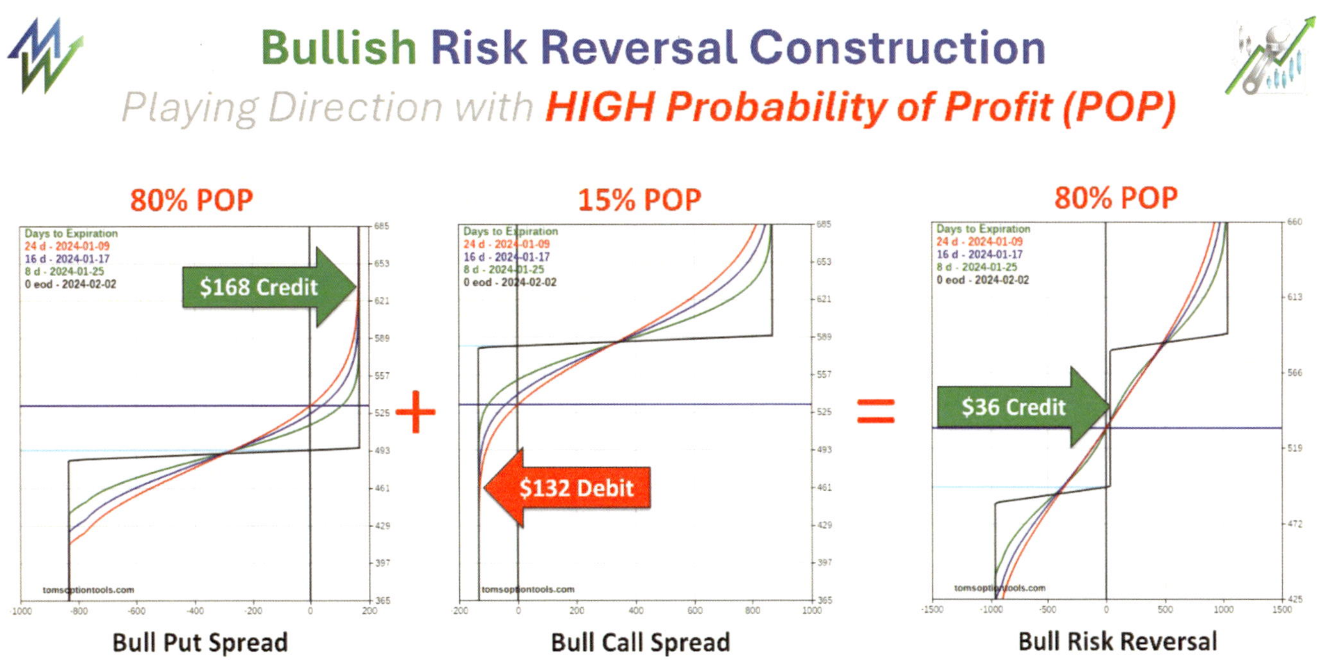

Here's how it works...

- Start with a Bull Put Spread. In our example shown above, we're collecting a $168 credit and entering a trade that already has an 80% probability of profit (POP). That alone gives us room to win if the stock rises, stays the same, or even dips slightly—down to our short put strike at $495. That's coverage in two-and-a-half directions. Solid ground.
- But if you're feeling more bullish and want to juice the upside, you can use that credit to fund an OTM Bull Call Spread. Sure, this one only has a 15% POP on its own, but we're not paying for it out-of-pocket. The $168 credit covers the $132 debit, leaving us with a net credit of $36 and keeping our overall POP at 80%.

The result? You're playing direction... but with a far better setup than your average long call.

Instead of relying on a one-way bet, the Bullish Risk Reversal allows you to strategically play the market—covering multiple scenarios, controlling risk, and positioning for high-probability directional gains.

It's not just smart trading. It's elite-level gameplay.

How to Construct a Bullish Risk Reversal

Here's an example of a Bullish Risk Reversal on Nvidia (NVDA). We start by selling a $495/$485 Bull Put Spread, earning a $168 premium. That premium is then used to finance the purchase of a $580/$590 Bull Call Spread, which costs $132. The result? A net credit of $36.

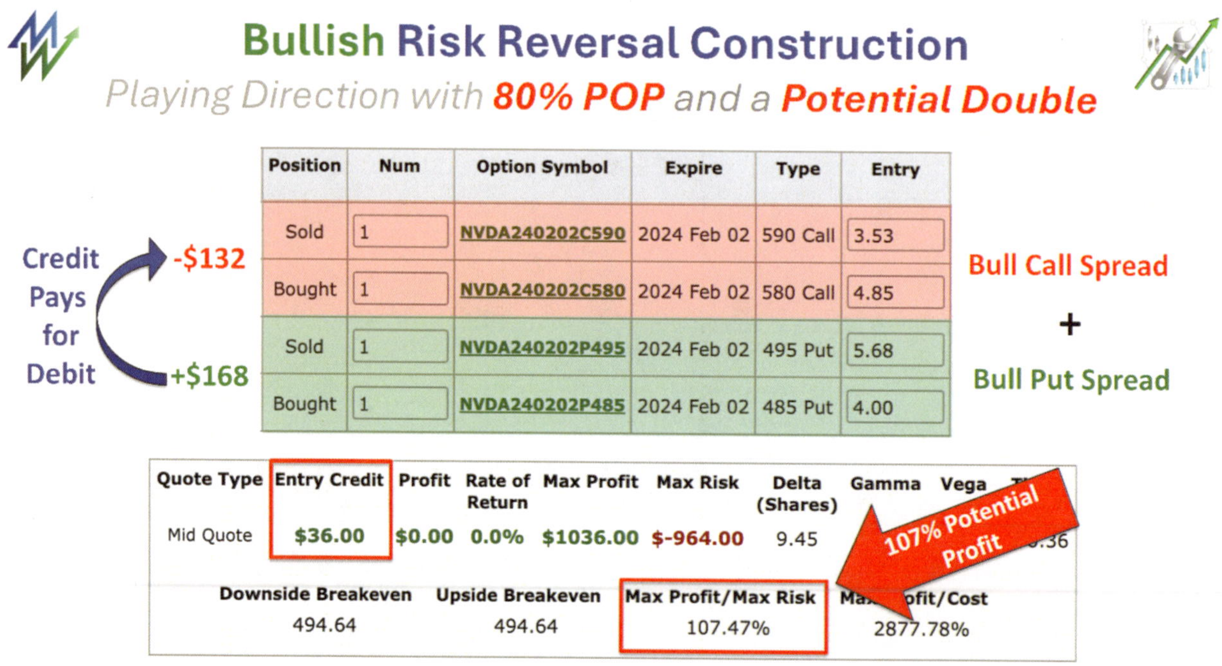

Position	Num	Option Symbol	Expire	Type	Entry
Sold	1	NVDA240202C590	2024 Feb 02	590 Call	3.53
Bought	1	NVDA240202C580	2024 Feb 02	580 Call	4.85
Sold	1	NVDA240202P495	2024 Feb 02	495 Put	5.68
Bought	1	NVDA240202P485	2024 Feb 02	485 Put	4.00

Quote Type	Entry Credit	Profit	Rate of Return	Max Profit	Max Risk	Delta (Shares)	Gamma	Vega	[illegible]
Mid Quote	$36.00	$0.00	0.0%	$1036.00	$-964.00	9.45	[illegible]	[illegible]	[illegible].36

Downside Breakeven	Upside Breakeven	Max Profit/Max Risk	Ma[illegible]ofit/Cost
494.64	494.64	107.47%	2877.78%

So, what does that mean for you as a trader? First, you now have a trade with an 80% chance of profit. That's a big improvement from the 33% odds of a simple long call or put. And here's the kicker—if your bullish outlook is correct, this trade can give a 107.47% return on investment.

Think about it... You're betting on the outcome, but even if you're wrong, you still win four out of five times. And when you're right, you more than double your money. That's what I call playing the game with style and an edge.

Bearish Risk Reversals

Are you prepared to flip the battery in backwards and play the downside? That's exactly what a Bearish Risk Reversal does—a strategic approach to betting on a decline while increasing your chances of success.

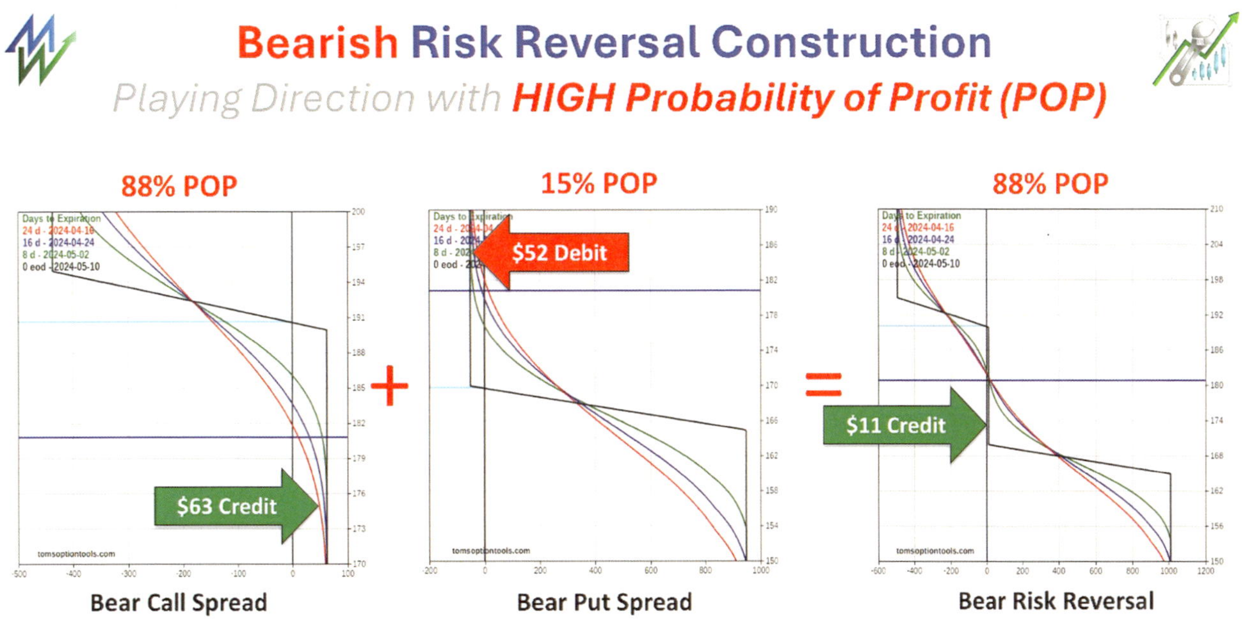

Bearish Risk Reversals are created by selling an Out-of-the-Money (OTM) Bear Call Spread and using the proceeds to fund an OTM Bear Put Spread. In this example, we sell a bear call spread for a $63 credit and use that to pay for a bear put spread that costs $52. This results in a net credit of $11.

Now look at the probabilities. The bear call spread has a strong 88% chance of profit. The bear put spread? Only 15% chance. But when you combine them, the trade keeps the 88% probability of success while offering the chance to make big gains if your bearish prediction comes true.

It's a well-constructed bearish position: Low risk, high odds, and explosive potential. When you want to confidently aim downward, this is the move that smart players make.

How to Construct a Bearish Risk Reversal

A bearish risk reversal involves combining a bear call credit spread (to collect premium) with a bear put debit spread (to profit from a decline).

In this case, we're consolidating everything on NVIDIA (NVDA) with options expiring on February 2, 2024.

Here's an example of a Bearish Risk Reversal on Nvidia (NVDA). We start by selling a $580/$590 Bear Call Spread, which generates a $63 credit. That credit is then used to finance the purchase of a $580/$590 Bear Put Spread, which costs $52.

The result?

A net credit of $11 with an 87% probability of profit.

This trade is a smart move for high-probability traders who still seek serious upside if the decline occurs.

Even if the move never happens. We still win.

That's risk reversal power. That's thinking like a pro.

Strategic Spread Placement in a Bullish Risk Reversal

When constructing a bullish risk reversal, we can increase our edge by using statistics to guide our strike placement.

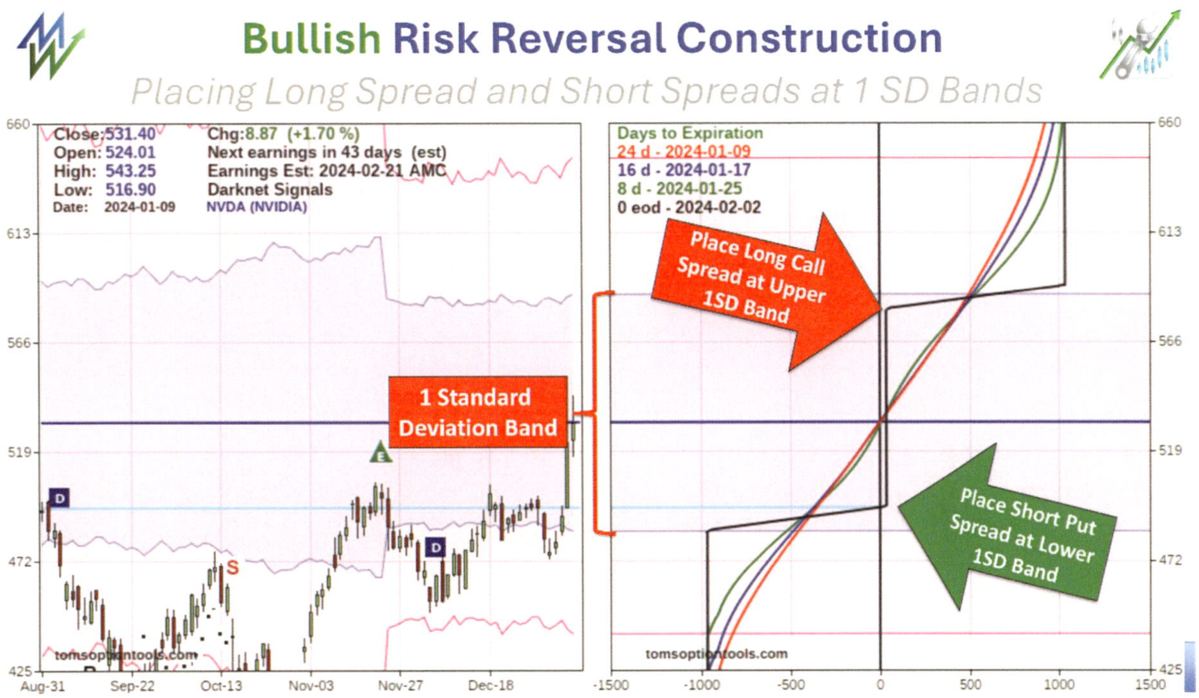

To ensure the best statistical accuracy, we use 1 standard deviation (1-SD) bands as a placement guide.

- Place the short strike of the bull put credit spread near the lower 1-SD band
- Place the long call strike of the bullish debit spread near the upper 1-SD band

This method helps limit losses if the stock drops to the lower edge of the expected range, while positioning us to make enough profit to adjust and remove risk if the move works in our favor.

Strategic Spread Placement in a Bearish Risk Reversal

When creating a bearish risk reversal, we again rely on statistics to help us position the spreads wisely.

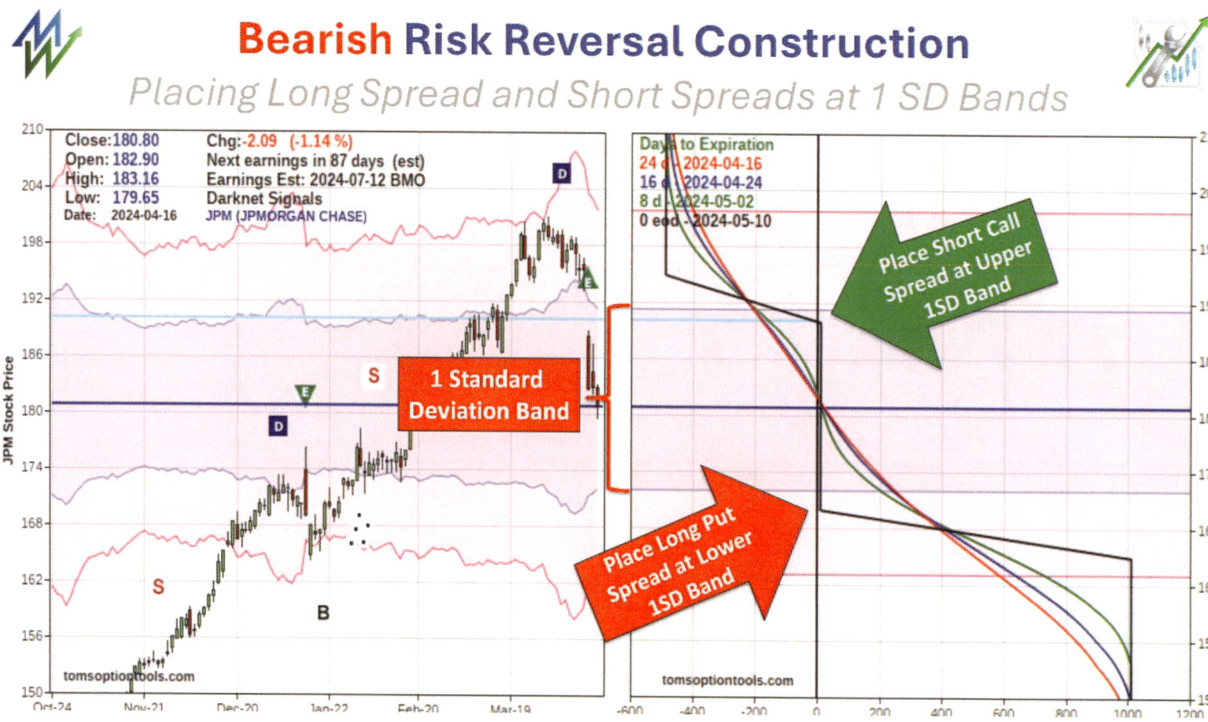

To optimize the trade:

- Place the short call spread at the upper 1-SD band
- Place the long put spread at the lower 1-SD band

This placement approach does two important things:

1. Limits potential losses if the stock pulls back toward the lower band
2. Creates the opportunity to generate enough profit to remove all risk with an adjustment (which we'll cover later)

Using statistics is the foundation of the Risk Reversal game. We're not guessing. We're leveraging probability as our advantage.

The result?

A directional trade that offers us the highest likelihood of profit, with built-in protection and flexibility.

Risk Reversal Theta: Varies by Price

One of the nice things about risk reversals is that for most of the trade's movement, Theta remains fairly flat.

In essence, a risk reversal is synthetic stock between the inflection points of the risk graph.

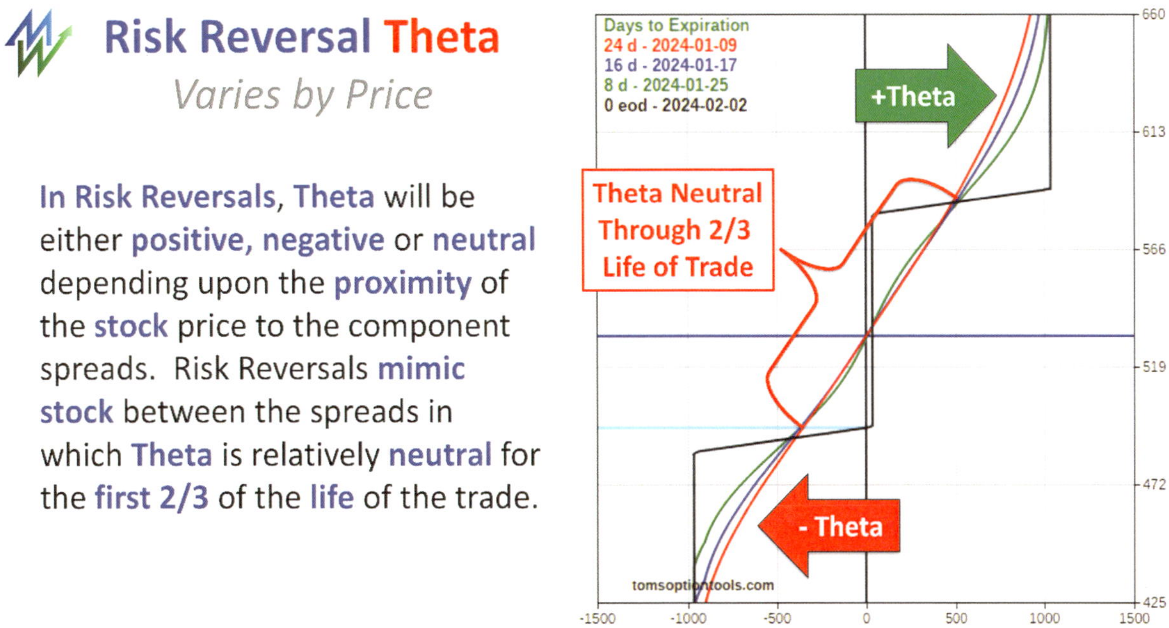

Notice that Theta remains neutral (little space between the colored Theta lines) between the spreads for roughly two-thirds of the trade's duration.

That means Theta isn't your enemy—or your ally—during the majority of the trade.

However, once price starts to move:

- If the stock falls and the credit spread goes in the money Theta turns negative.
- If the stock rises and enters the body of the debit spread, Theta turns positive.

And that's a big deal.

Positive Theta in the winning debit spread gives us an advantage. It helps us leverage time and positions us to make more effective adjustments—which we'll explore in detail in the Adjustment section.

Risk Reversal Vega: Varies by Price

Like Theta, Vega in a risk reversal acts in a distinct and strategic manner.

For most of the trade, Vega is relatively flat—especially between the spreads.

Why? Because between the inflection points, the risk reversal acts like synthetic stock. That means we're relatively protected from implied volatility changes while the stock remains within that zone.

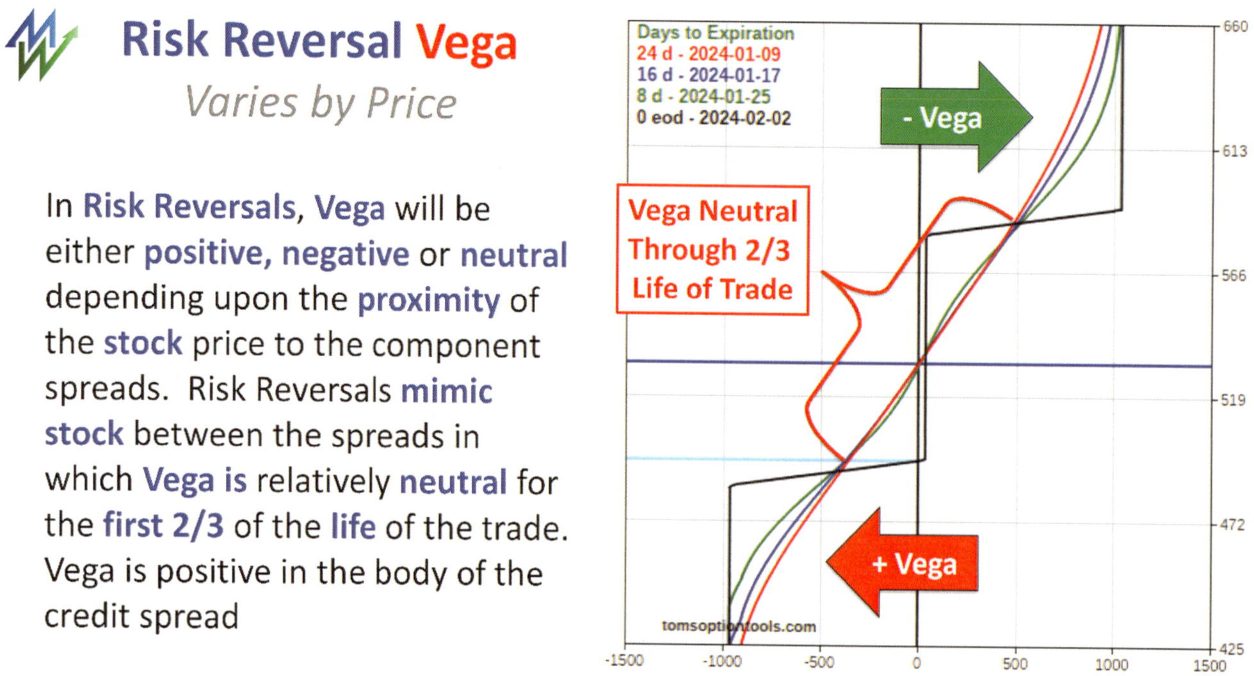

But here's where it gets interesting:

- If the stock drops into the credit spread, Vega turns positive
- If the stock rises into the debit spread, Vega turns negative

Since IV typically moves opposite to price, Vega actually works in our favor for us at both extremes.

Risk Reversals allow us to use Vega as a silent partner—neutral when needed, and supportive when it matters.

Risk Reversal Construction: Rules of Thumb

Risk Reversal Construction
Rules of Thumb

1. Sell **credit spread** about **1 SD** away from stock and at **support/resistance.**
2. Buy **debit spread** about **1 SD** away from stock and at **support/resistance.**
3. Receive a **net credit** or at least **a $0 debit**. **Higher credits** are **better.**
4. Receive at least a **100% potential ROI.**
5. Consider **closing** the trade **for a loss** should stock **cross** the **short strike** of the credit spread.
6. **Adjust** them with the **"Spread the Spread"** adjustment that follows.

1. Explore options analysis tools
2. Sell a credit spread roughly 1 standard deviation (1 SD) away from the stock price, ideally aligning with key support or resistance zones. This creates a solid base with a high probability.
3. Buy a debit spread also about 1 SD away from the stock price, and again, aim to place this around support or resistance for additional structure and edge.
4. Always aim to receive a net credit, or at minimum, initiate the trade for a $0 debit. The higher the credit, the better the trade—giving you more room for profit and easier adjustments later.
5. Look for trades that offer at least a 100% potential ROI. If you're risking $500, you want the potential to make $500 or more.
6. If the trade moves against you and the stock crosses the short strike of your credit spread, consider closing the position to protect your capital and wait for a better entry.
7. Finally, when a trade needs help—adjust it using the "Spread the Spread" method, which we'll break down in the next section.

Summary - High Probability Directional Trading with Risk Reversals

Risk reversals are like a two-sided chessboard—one side attacks, the other defends. When played right, you stay in control no matter where the opponent (stock price) moves.

This chapter demonstrated how to build the trade in the right spot on the board, position your pieces, and predict your opponent's moves with statistical accuracy.

- You learned to place your spreads like a pro, using 1 standard deviation bands as your game boundaries.
- You discovered how Theta and Vega are neutral allies during most of the game—but come alive with Vega in your favor when the market makes its move.
- You saw that the credit side pays for your offense, and the debit side fuels your upside should the stock move your way.

And now you know that adjustments are your secret weapon—coming soon with the "Spread the Spread" move.

The power of a Risk Reversal is that it resembles stock trading—but with a twist: It can give you multiple ways to succeed. You earn credit, reduce risk, and still go for big gains with the odds in your favor.

In short?

You're not just trading in the market. You're playing a more intelligent game.

Now get ready—because in the next section, we show you how to make mid-game adjustments that can wipe out risk and even lock in profit with the opportunity to make more using **The "Spread the Spread" Adjustment**.

CHAPTER 27

APPLYING THE "SPREAD THE SPREAD" ADJUSTMENT TO RISK REVERSALS

CHAPTER 27
Applying the "Spread the Spread" Adjustment to Risk Reversals

Risk reversals already have a built-in advantage—a high likelihood of profit from the beginning.

But when you add the "Spread the Spread" adjustment, your probabilities don't just improve. They skyrocket.

The Spread the Spread Adjustment

Risk Reversals

Take an existing Vertical Spread position and **morph it into a Butterfly or Condor** position by selling or buying vertical spreads. With **Risk Reversals** this adjustment can be applied to the credit spread to **eliminate/reduce risk** and on the debit spread to **guarantee a profit.**

Some ways to do so:

- Selling ATM Credit Spreads
- Buying OTM Long Spreads

The "Spread the Spread" adjustment involves adding a second spread—either a credit or debit—to your existing vertical spreads to significantly improve your chances.

You've already seen how powerful this move can be in reducing risk or locking in gains. Now we're going to apply it directly to our Risk Reversal strategy.

Here's how it works:

Apply the adjustment to the credit spread, where the risk of the trade lies, to reduce or even eliminate that risk.

Apply it to the debit spread to help guarantee a profit when the stock moves favorably.

To execute this, we'll strategically use OTM credit spreads and OTM debit spreads—layering them over the core risk reversal like a tactical overlay.

This is how you trade like a pro—transforming high probability into top performance.

"Spread the Spread" Adjustment - Risk Reversals

The "Spread the Spread" adjustment is one of the most versatile and effective tools you can use for Risk Reversals. Its main goal is to reduce or eliminate risk on the credit spread side and to ensure a profit on the debit spread side.

The Spread the Spread Adjustment

Risk Reversals

Description: *Applying the "Spread the Spread" adjustment to the 2 spreads of a Risk Reversal to reduce or eliminate risk and guarantee a profit.*

Strategies: *Risk Reversals*

Outcome: *There are 2 primary adjustments. First, the credit spread can be converted to a butterfly to greatly reduce or eliminate the risk in the trade. Second, the debit spread can be converted into a butterfly or condor to guarantee a profit.*

Timing: *Timing on the risk elimination move is done whenever a debit spread can be bought for the original credit of the risk reversal. Do this with a GTC order. The guaranteed profit move, selling a credit spread on the debit spread is typically applied when the desired stock direction has stalled.*

There are two primary adjustments involved:

Risk Elimination - Convert the credit spread into a butterfly or condor by buying an additional debit spread. This move can often be made for the same credit you received from the original trade. Once completed, it eliminates or dramatically reduces risk.

Profit Lock-in - Transform the debit spread into a butterfly or condor by selling an extra credit spread. This adjustment when coupled with the risk elimination can guarantee a profit and is usually used when the stock has made a favorable move and is consolidating.

Timing is critical.

The risk elimination move should be executed as soon as the debit spread can be purchased for the same credit (or less) as the original trade. This is a great way to use a GTC (Good-Til-Canceled) order.

The guaranteed profit move typically occurs after the stock's direction has played out and starts to stall.

When used correctly, this adjustment turns a high-probability trade into a precise tool—reducing risk and maximizing gains with skill and confidence.

Risk Reversal Adjustment Rules – Job 1

As the stock moves in the expected direction of a Risk Reversal, the initial credit spread starts to lose value. This is exactly what we want—because we sold the credit spread for a credit, a decrease in its value means that the credit spread is earning us money.

Risk Reversal Adjustment Rules

Job 1: *Convert Winning Credit Spreads to Butterflies*

Convert Winning Credit Spread into a butterfly by ***buying a debit spread*** *resulting in $0.00 trade risk or a guaranteed profit.*

BULL PUT: ***Buy Higher Strike Put***
Sell Lower Strike Put *<< Same as current short strike*

BEAR CALL: ***Sell Higher Strike Call*** *<< Same as current short strike*
Buy Lower Strike Call

Once this occurs, we can convert that credit spread into a butterfly by using the credit from the original trade. If done correctly, this adjustment removes the risk of the position, leaving you with either a risk-free trade or a guaranteed profit.

Here's how to do it for each setup:

- **For a bullish Risk Reversal with a bull put spread, you:**
  - Sell a lower strike put at the same strike as your original short put
  - Buy a higher strike put above that

This creates a bear put spread for a debit. Make sure to use the same strike width as the original credit spread.

- **For a bearish Risk Reversal with a bear call spread, you:**
  - Buy a lower strike call
  - Sell a higher strike call at the same strike as the original short call

This establishes a bull call spread for a debit. Make sure to use the same width as the original credit spread.

In both cases, if you can add this new debit spread to your existing credit spread at a cost equal to the original credit received (or less), you create a risk-free trade. That's Job 1 in the adjustment game: Turn risk into safety, and safety into strength.

"Spread the Spread" Adjustment – Eliminate Risk Example

Let's take a look at a real example of how to apply the "Spread the Spread" adjustment to eliminate risk on a bullish risk reversal.

In this trade on Nvidia (NVDA), the position was constructed by:

- Selling 2 Feb 2 $495/$490 bull put spreads
- Buying 1 Feb 2 $580/$590 long call spread

The original trade credit was $60. We will use that credit to set up a butterfly around the credit spread, effectively removing all downside risk in the trade. That's the power of spreading the spread.

RR Adjustment 1: Eliminate Risk

Quote Type	Entry Credit	Profit	Rate of Return	Max Profit	Max Risk	Delta (Shares)	Gamma	Vega	Theta
Mid Quote	$60.00	$333.00	35.4%	$1060.00	$-940.00	10.00	0.007	$0.46	$-1.42

Downside Breakeven	Upside Breakeven	Max Profit/Max Risk	Max Profit/Cost
494.70	494.70	112.77%	1766.67%

Leg Date	Position	Num	Option Symbol	Expire	Type	Entry
2024-01-09	Sold	1	NVDA240202C590	2024 Feb 02	590 Call	3.50
2024-01-09	Bought	1	NVDA240202C580	2024 Feb 02	580 Call	4.80
2024-01-09	Sold	2	NVDA240202P495	2024 Feb 02	495 Put	5.85
2024-01-09	Bought	2	NVDA240202P490	2024 Feb 02	490 Put	4.90

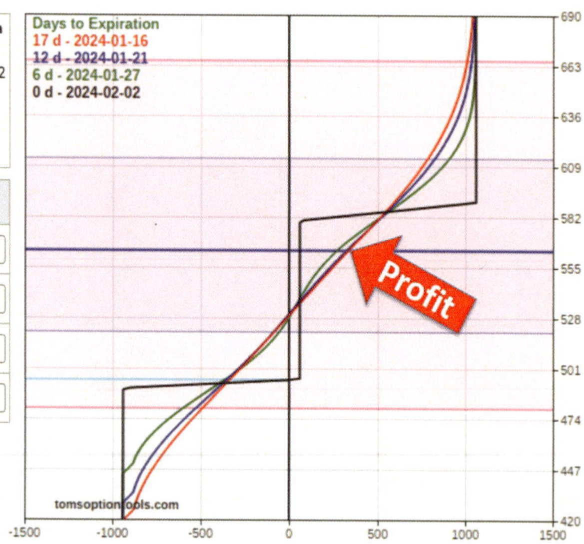

At the time of the adjustment, NVDA had increased in value, approaching our long call spread—just as we intended. The trade was showing a $333 profit, which is a 35.4% return, while still carrying a remaining risk of $940.

But we're not going to leave that risk unaddressed. Next, we'll eliminate it completely using the original $60 credit. This is where the adjustment game becomes enjoyable— and profitable.

RR Adjustment Example: Risk-Free Trade Achieved

To reduce the risk, we bought a Feb 2 $500/$495 long put spread for $0.30 per spread, or a net debit of $60—exactly our original position credit.

RR Adjustment 1: Butterfly Credit Spread

Quote Type	Entry Debit	Profit	Rate of Return	Max Profit	Min Profit	Delta (Shares)	Gamma	Vega	Theta
Mid Quote	$0.00	$329.00	n/a	$1000.00	$0.00	7.66	0.088	$4.76	$-5.70

Downside Breakeven	Upside Breakeven	Max Profit/Max Risk	Max Profit/Cost
500.00	580.00	9999.99%	9999.99%

Leg Date	Position	Num	Option Symbol	Expire	Type	Entry
2024-01-09	Sold	1	NVDA240202C590	2024 Feb 02	590 Call	3.50
2024-01-09	Bought	1	NVDA240202C580	2024 Feb 02	580 Call	4.80
2024-01-09	Sold	2	NVDA240202P495	2024 Feb 02	495 Put	5.85
2024-01-09	Bought	2	NVDA240202P490	2024 Feb 02	490 Put	4.90
2024-01-16	Bought	2	NVDA240202P500	2024 Feb 02	500 Put	1.70
2024-01-16	Sold	2	NVDA240202P495	2024 Feb 02	495 Put	1.40

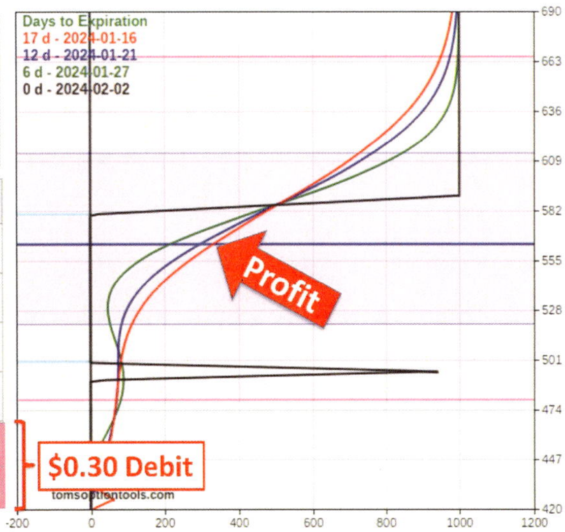

$60 Debit to Eliminate $940 of Risk!

The risk graph on the next page shows the entire picture: Our new maximum risk is actually a minimum profit of $0.

We just spent $60 to completely eliminate $940 in risk—a trade any savvy trader would take immediately.

And here's the best part: We didn't give up a single dollar of the current profit. We secured our position, protected the downside, and kept the upside fully open.

This is what trading like a pro looks like—turning risk into power while preserving profit.

RR Adjustment Job 2: Converting the Winning Debit Spread to a Butterfly

The second of the two "Spread the Spread" adjustments is to turn the winning debit spread into a butterfly or condor.

Risk Reversal Adjustment Rules

Job 2: *Convert Winning Debit Spreads to Butterflies/Condors*

*Butterfly credit spread for $0.00 position risk, then **sell credit spread** to convert long spread to a butterfly or condor*

Bull Call: ***Buy Higher Strike Call***
Sell Lower Strike Call *<< Same or higher than current short*

Bear Put: ***Sell Higher Strike Put*** ***<< Same or lower than current short***
Buy Lower Strike Put

For a bull call spread, sell another short call at the same strike as the original short call and buy a higher strike call with the same width as the initial debit spread.

This creates a bull call credit spread over your initial debit spread. If you've already eliminated risk with Job 1, this move ensures a profit in the trade.

For a bearish risk reversal, do the same with puts: Sell another put at the short strike of your current long put spread, and buy a lower put with the same strike distance.

This creates a bullish short put spread—which adds more credit to the trade, increasing the guaranteed return. Again, if you've already eliminated risk, this move guarantees a profit in the trade.

RR Adjustment 2: Butterflying the Debit Spread for a Guaranteed Profit

Now that Job 1 has eliminated all risk from the trade, it's time for Job 2: Locking in a guaranteed profit by turning the debit spread into a butterfly.

With 15 days to expiration, NVDA had moved higher, pushing our risk-free trade to a $363 profit.

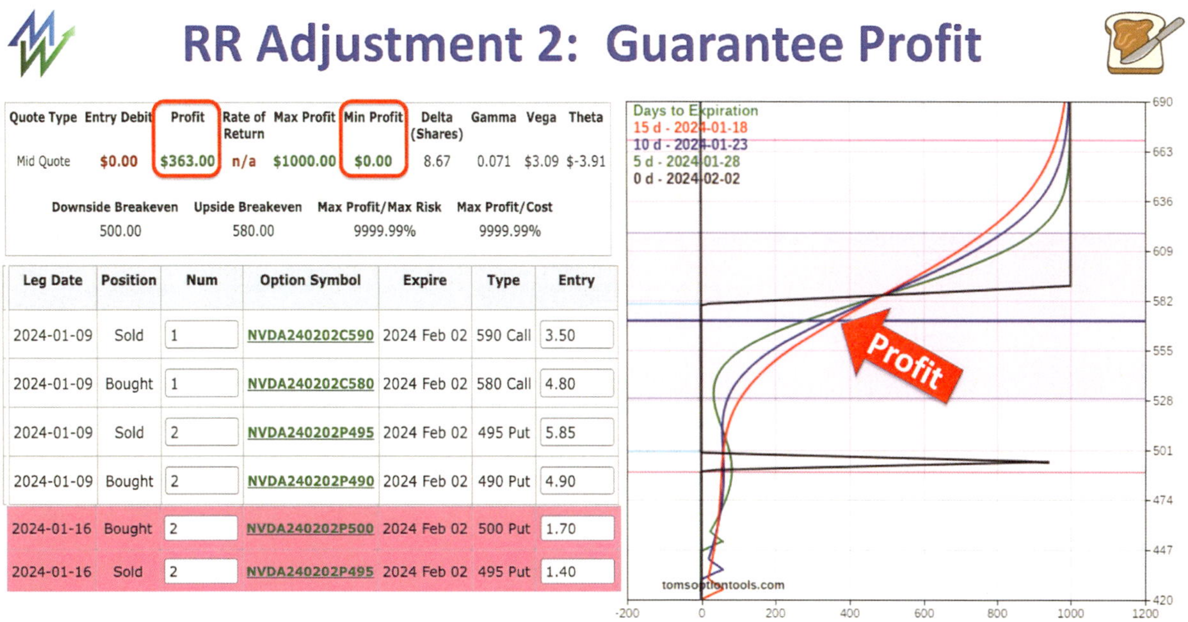

Quote Type	Entry Debit	Profit	Rate of Return	Max Profit	Min Profit	Delta (Shares)	Gamma	Vega	Theta
Mid Quote	$0.00	$363.00	n/a	$1000.00	$0.00	8.67	0.071	$3.09	$-3.91

Downside Breakeven	Upside Breakeven	Max Profit/Max Risk	Max Profit/Cost
500.00	580.00	9999.99%	9999.99%

Leg Date	Position	Num	Option Symbol	Expire	Type	Entry
2024-01-09	Sold	1	NVDA240202C590	2024 Feb 02	590 Call	3.50
2024-01-09	Bought	1	NVDA240202C580	2024 Feb 02	580 Call	4.80
2024-01-09	Sold	2	NVDA240202P495	2024 Feb 02	495 Put	5.85
2024-01-09	Bought	2	NVDA240202P490	2024 Feb 02	490 Put	4.90
2024-01-16	Bought	2	NVDA240202P500	2024 Feb 02	500 Put	1.70
2024-01-16	Sold	2	NVDA240202P495	2024 Feb 02	495 Put	1.40

To secure that profit, we will add a credit spread on top of the existing debit spread—converting it into a butterfly. This final step turns a strong position into a guaranteed win.

RR Adjustment 2: The Guaranteed Profit Move

To lock in a profit on this bullish risk reversal, we sold a Feb 2 $590/$600 bear call spread for a credit of $278.

This credit becomes your guaranteed profit—with the added potential to make even more if the stock ends within the range of either butterfly.

RR Adjustment 2: Butterfly Debit Spread

Quote Type	Entry Credit	Profit	Rate of Return	Max Profit	Min Profit	Delta (Shares)	Gamma	Vega	Theta
Mid Quote	$278.00	$363.00	n/a	$1278.00	$278.00	0.68	-0.026	$-1.45	$1.93

Downside Breakeven	Upside Breakeven	Max Profit/Max Risk	Max Profit/Cost
unknown	unknown	459.71%	459.71%

Leg Date	Position	Num	Option Symbol	Expire	Type	Entry
2024-01-09	Sold	1	NVDA240202C590	2024 Feb 02	590 Call	3.50
2024-01-09	Bought	1	NVDA240202C580	2024 Feb 02	580 Call	4.80
2024-01-09	Sold	2	NVDA240202P495	2024 Feb 02	495 Put	5.85
2024-01-09	Bought	2	NVDA240202P490	2024 Feb 02	490 Put	4.90
2024-01-16	Bought	2	NVDA240202P500	2024 Feb 02	500 Put	1.70
2024-01-16	Sold	2	NVDA240202P495	2024 Feb 02	495 Put	1.40
2024-01-18	Bought	1	NVDA240202C600	2024 Feb 02	600 Call	6.75
2024-01-18	Sold	1	NVDA240202C590	2024 Feb 02	590 Call	9.53

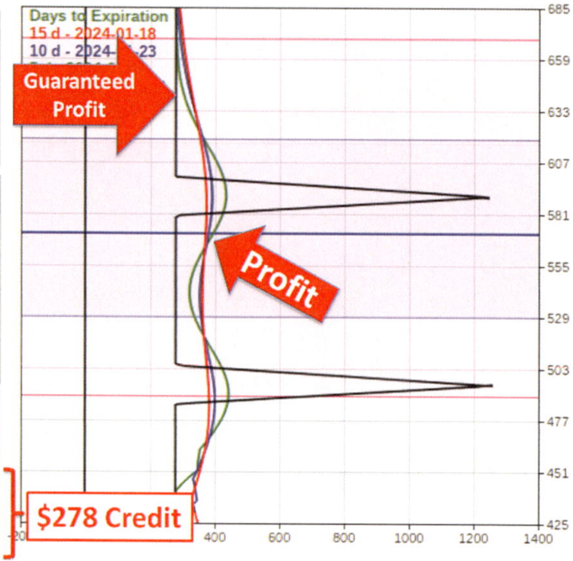

That guaranteed profit represents a 29.5% return on the original $940 risk in the trade.

Imagine how it feels to lock in profits like this—confidently walking away with a win, while still leaving space for more gains!

There are even more adjustments you could make from here to boost your potential. But with this setup, it's a winning position created through precision, practice, and a bit of trading brilliance.

Chapter Summary – "Spread the Spread": Locking in the Win

In trading, just like in games, the top players don't just make a good first move… they know how to adapt during the game and secure the win.

That's exactly what you've learned in this chapter.

Risk Reversals are already highly effective—with high probability, clear direction, and intelligent design.

But what makes them elite is what occurs after the entry.

That's where the "Spread the Spread" adjustment kicks in—and that's where the real game starts.

You now have two game-winning adjustments in your toolkit when using Risk Reversals:

Job 1: Butterfly the Credit Spread

Like building a strong defensive wall, this move removes your risk out of your original credit spread and, therefore, the entire trade. It's the same as saying, **"No matter what happens next—I can't lose."**

"Spread the Spread" Adjustments on Risk Reversals

Rules of Thumb

1. The primary adjustment is to **butterfly out the risk** in the credit spread of a **Risk Reversal.**
2. Place a **GTC order** to butterfly the credit spread for a **total debit not to exceed** the **credit** of the original **Risk Reversal** to **eliminate risk**
3. Consider **selling** an **OTM credit spread** to convert the long spread into a **butterfly** or **condor**. This will result in a **guaranteed profit** if risk has been butterflied out of the credit spread. Do no later than **10-days before expiry.**
4. Do this if your **stock hits and/or reverses** from support or resistance.
5. Consider **other adjustments** to manipulate the Greeks.

Job 2: Butterfly the Debit Spread

Once the defense is in place, it's time to switch to offense. This move ensures a profit by adding credit on top of a risk-free position. That's not just good trading. That's "checkmate".

You also explored examples that showed how to:

- Use OTM spreads to manage risk and generate profit
- Time adjustments based on support/resistance
- Lock in a $278 profit on a $940 risk—with zero downside left

Here's the truth: The entry gets you in the game.

But adjustments? That's how you win.

Now you're not just holding a high-probability trade. You're designing outcomes, managing risk like a pro, and playing the long game with strategy and confidence.

The game board is set.

The pieces are moving.

And now... you control the board.

Now that you can refine directional structures, the next step is learning how to protect stock positions using options. **Collars** are next!

CHAPTER 28

THE COLLAR - HEDGING STOCK WITH OPTIONS

CHAPTER 28
The Collar - Hedging Stock with Options

In this chapter, we move to the next level of trading: Protecting stock positions with options—a strategy called The Collar.

A collar is a defensive options strategy aimed at protecting a long stock position by doing two things at once: Selling a call (covered call) and buying a protective put.

It's like outfitting your king with armor before moving him across the board. You're still in the game, still playing offense, but now with added defense.

As illustrated in the graphic above, the Collar enables you to:

- **Reduce Risk** –by limiting downside using a protective put.
- **Build a Long-Term Portfolio** – by creating a structured position that can weather market swings.

Here's what we'll cover in this chapter:

- **Long "Naked" Stock**
- **The Covered Call**
- **Protective "Married" Put**
- **The Collar**

Each of these is a key part of the puzzle—and when combined, they give you the confidence to hold your position while protecting your capital like a grandmaster guards their queen.

The Collar – Hedging Stock with Options: Strategy Overview

The Collar isn't just a strategy. It's your stock's suit of armor. This move combines owning stock with options to provide protection, consistency, and sometimes even more shares—without needing to spend more cash.

The Collar – Hedging Stock with Options

Description: *The Collar and its siblings (The Covered Call and Married Put) are simply combining Stock ownership with Option contracts. These strategies are a form of hedging long Stock positions.*

Strategies: *Stock (or equity) ownership. Add long and/or short Option positions.*

Outcome: *To reduce risk and market exposure. Also to acquire additional shares as the market gyrates – financed by the trade itself.*

Timing: *Upon entering a long Stock position, risk reduction is critical to avoid adverse down moves in Stock price. Typically adjusted at least once per month. Adjustments are done at or near Option expiration. In addition, intra-month adjustments are often used. The Collar can also be applied in conjunction with other adjustment moves.*

Here's how it works:

Description: The Collar, along with its close cousins the Covered Call and the Married Put, involves pairing your stock position with options. You're not abandoning ownership. You're enhancing it with strategic option contracts. This is hedging with precision.

Strategies: Begin with stock (or equity) ownership, then add long and/or short option positions. It's like building an army around your king—combining pieces for maximum coverage and offense.

Outcome: The goal is to lower risk and market exposure. But here's the catch: You might also end up buying more shares along the way—financed by the trades themselves. That's turning defense into opportunity.

Timing: As soon as you buy stock, focus on defense. Risk reduction starts immediately to protect against sudden drops. Usually, collars are adjusted monthly or near option expiration, but don't hesitate to pivot mid-month. Flexibility is part of the strategy. And yes, the collar can be combined with other adjustment tactics too—because chess champions don't depend on just one move.

The Collar - Comparing Three Investor Approaches

Before we put on the collar, let's quickly review the playing field. There are three ways investors approach long stock positions—and each one is like playing a different level of the game.

1. **Naked Stock (Buy and Hold)** – This is your basic traditional investor. You buy the stock and hope it climbs. Maybe you sell a call against it to generate a little income (that's your covered call). But you've got no safety net if things fall apart. You're playing without armor.
2. **Protective Put (Insurance)** – A smarter investor says, "If I'm in the market, I want protection." So, they buy a Put option as insurance. Now they have downside coverage, and they can weather volatility much better.
3. **The Collar** – This is where savvy investors live. You own the stock, buy a put for protection, and sell a call to help offset the cost of the put. You've got built-in defense and some credit generation too. It's controlled risk, with a chance to build long-term success.

So, here's the real question—when opening a new stock position, how can you reduce risk and maximize your dollar investment?

If you're serious about playing this game, you can't ignore risk. And the collar? It's the most well-rounded move on the board—combining offense, defense, and smart strategy all in one.

Owning Stock – "Naked Stock" Strategy

Welcome to Level 1 of the investing game—the classic move: Owning Stock, also called Naked Stock. It's the most common starting point, and for many investors, it's the entire game plan.

The idea is simple. You:

- Buy low and hold.
- Collect the dividends (if the company pays them).

- Sell high and book your profit.It's simple—and it works. But here's the catch... You're playing without any armor. If the stock drops sharply, you're exposed. Naked, just as the name suggests.

You've got unlimited reward—but also unlimited risk down to $0. That's like sending your king across the board with no defense in place. Bold? Maybe. Smart? Not always.

As we advance this chapter, we'll learn how to incorporate strategic defenses—and eventually transform this basic opening move into a position that's both strong and secure.

Owning Stock – The Risk Profile Revealed

Here's what the raw numbers show when you start with only stock ownership—no options, no protections, just your shares.

In the example shown below, we purchased 500 shares at $39.82 each. That amounts to a total investment of $19,910, which also represents our maximum risk.

If the stock drops to zero, you lose everything. That's not just a theoretical risk. It's a real possibility. Granted, stocks don't often fall to $0, but they can drop significantly.

You're walking into the trading arena wearing nothing but optimism.

Now, the upside remains limitless. If the stock rises to $45, $50, $60, and beyond. You're earning money all the way up.

But the tradeoff is clear: Unlimited Reward / Unlimited Risk down to $0.

This is what I call Level 1 play. You're in the game, but you're not strategizing yet. You're rolling the dice, hoping the market favors you—and "hoping" isn't a strategy.As we move forward, we'll examine how to

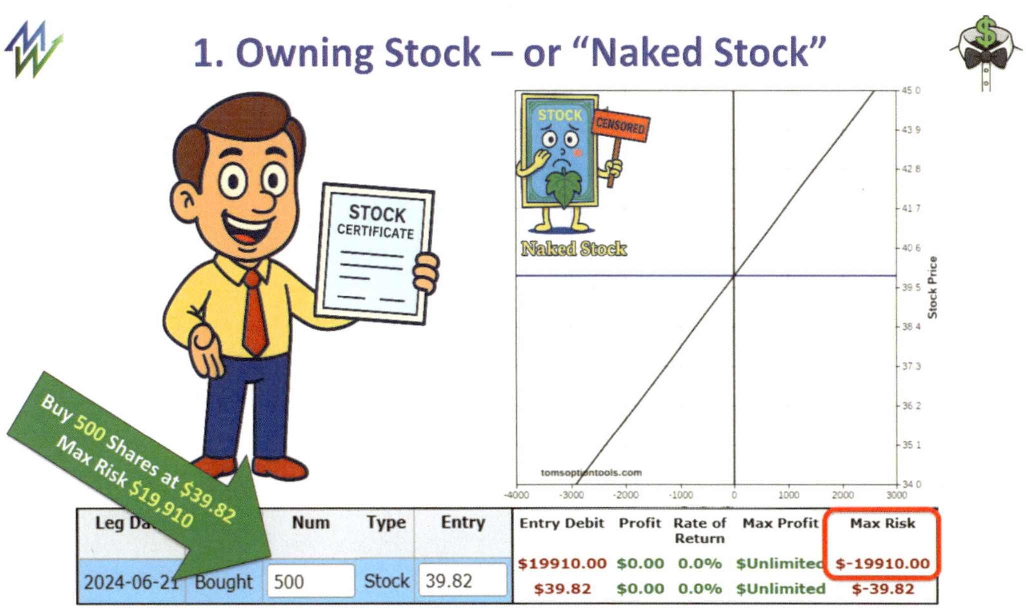

make smarter moves—those that protect your capital and create opportunities. Because a real player doesn't just hope to win. They play with protection, positioning, and purpose.

The Covered Call – Collecting Rent on Your Stock

1a. The Covered Call

AKA: Synthetic Short Put

The most popular form of Option trading by amateur investors is selling **Covered Calls**. The plan is to:

- **BUY** and hold the Stock.
- **Collect the Dividends** if paid.
- **SELL Calls** to make money by collecting Option premium.

Some say it's like collecting rent on a house

Covered Calls are among the most popular strategies on the options chessboard—especially for beginners just starting out. The Covered Call is straightforward, dependable, and effective (to a limited degree). Some even compare it to collecting rent on a house you already own.

Here's how it works:

- Buy and hold the stock
- Collect dividends
- Sell calls against the stock to earn extra income from option premium

This strategy is so popular that it's practically the default setting for stock owners dipping their toes into the options world. It's called a Synthetic Short Put in technical terms, but don't let the name distract you—the concept is clean and powerful but has limitations.

What you're doing is giving someone else the right to buy your stock at a specific price—and they're paying you for that privilege. As long as you're comfortable selling the stock at that level (or continue to collect premiums), it's a smart way to increase your returns.

Think of this as playing offense while on defense. You have the stock. Now you're monetizing it like a rental property and building small wins as you wait for the next big opportunity.

The Covered Call – Risk Profile and Play Setup

Let's examine how this play actually appears on the board. In this example, we're implementing a classic Covered Call setup. We buy 500 shares at $39.82 and simultaneously sell 5 call options at the $42 strike for $0.80 each.

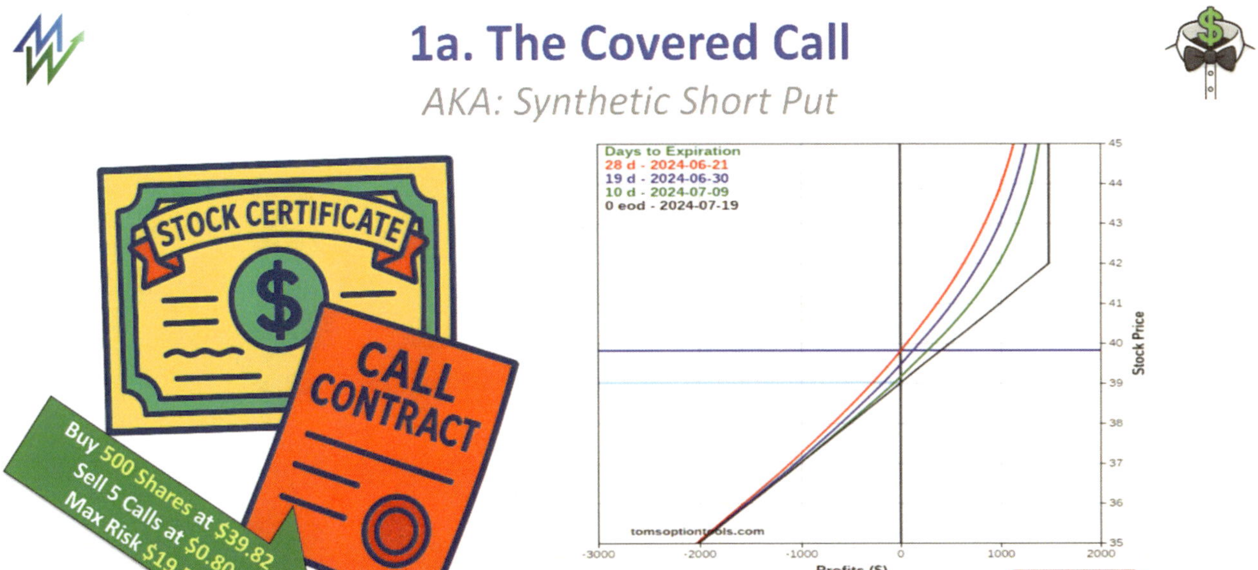

Leg [illegible]		Num	Type	Entry	Entry Debit	Profit	Rate of Return	Max Profit	Max Risk
2024-06-[illegible]	Sold	5	42 Call	0.80	$19510.00	$0.00	0.0%	$1490.00	$-19510.00
2024-06-21	Bought	500	Stock	39.82	$3902.00	$0.00	0.0%	$298.00	$-3902.00

That call premium generates extra income—a small bonus to offset your stock risk. It's like having a tenant pay rent while you own the property.

Now let's look at the numbers: You've still got a total cash outlay of $19,510, which is also your maximum risk if the stock drops to zero. But your maximum profit is capped at $1,490. That's the premium collected plus the move up to $42.

As the risk graph illustrates: Steady, increasing profit until you reach the call strike, then it levels off. Why? Because if the stock rises above $42, it can be called away—and you've reached your limit.

This is a solid trade for stable or slightly bullish markets where you want to generate cash flow rather than chase big gains.

The Protective Put - Insuring Your Position

This is where smart players begin applying strategy to the game. The Protective Put— also known as the Married Put—occurs when you move from gambling to hedging.

Instead of just owning the stock and hoping for the best, you pair it with a put. That put acts like a shield, kicking in to limit your losses if the market turns against you. It's the same idea as buying insurance for your car—and just as important if you want to keep playing long-term.

The plan is simple:

- Buy and hold the stock
- Collect dividends
- Buy puts to reduce risk and protect your downside

You maintain your equity position and upside potential, but now you have defined risk. This shifts everything. You're still aiming to win—but now there's a safety net beneath you.

This strategy transforms you from an optimistic participant into a strategic investor. And once you realize the difference it makes when things go sideways. You'll never go back to being unprotected.Protective Put – Risk Profile and Strategic Upgrade

Now this is where the strategy becomes real. In this example, we're still buying 500 shares at $39.82, but this time, we're not going in unprotected.

Instead, we add a layer of protection by buying 5 puts at the $38 strike for $0.83. That put locks in our floor, which dramatically changes the shape of our risk profile.

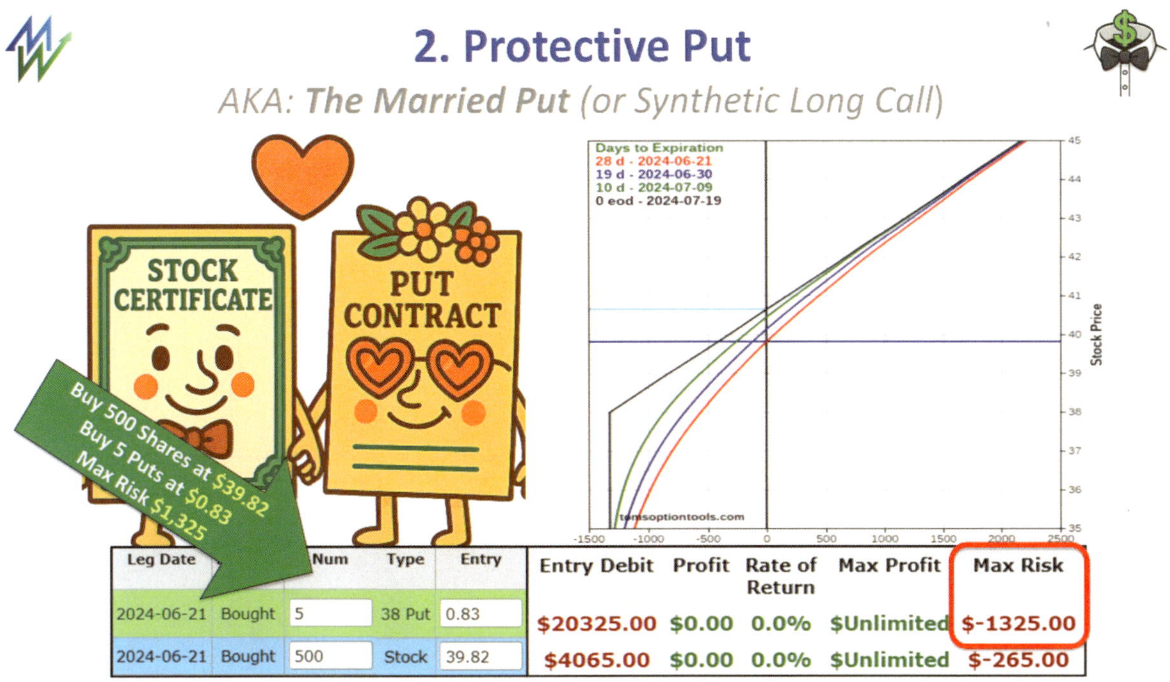

Look at the numbers: Our total investment is just over $20,325, but our maximum risk is limited to $1,325. That's a HUGE improvement compared to the unlimited risk of owning stock alone.

With this setup, your losses are controlled, your upside stays unlimited, and your mind is free to concentrate on smarter adjustments. This is the tactical difference between a good trader and a great one.

You're still playing to win—but now you have a safety net that allows you to stay in the game even when the situation becomes difficult. This is what true trade positioning looks like. Strategic. Thoughtful. Protected.

The Collar - Smart, Balanced, and Strategic

Now this is how you play like a pro. The Collar strategy combines everything we've discussed—but with one clever twist: You're not paying for the protection yourself.

You buy the stock, purchase a put to limit the downside, and then sell a call to help cover the cost of that protection.

You've essentially built a defensive and offensive setup using stock and two option legs. It's often called a Synthetic Long Call Spread—but the actual name you should remember is the Collar, because it does exactly that: Surrounds your position to enforce discipline and control.

3. The Collar

AKA: Synthetic Long Call Spread

Stock ownership at it's best. Protected against **bearish** market conditions with the insurance cost offset by selling Call options. The plan is to:

- **BUY** and hold the Stock.
- **Collect the Dividends** if paid.
- **BUY Puts** to protect the position and **SELL Calls** to reduce the cost of the Puts.

It's like buying insurance with someone else's money

Here's the basic game plan:

- Buy and hold the stock
- Collect dividends
- Buy puts and sell calls to structure risk and reduce net cost

Think of it like this: You're buying insurance with someone else's money. That's a veteran move.

The Collar gives you confidence to withstand pullbacks, generate passive income, and protect your capital. That's not just playing. That's playing with purpose.

The Collar - The Ultimate Risk Graph

Now this is what a pro-level move looks like on the board. We're creating the ideal combo of stock ownership, protection, and strategy—all in one compact, efficient package. This is the Collar.

In the play shown below, we're buying 500 shares at $39.82, buying 5 puts at the $38 strike, and selling 5 calls at the $42 strike—both for about $0.83.

The result? Maximum risk is just $925. That's a small part of the full stock position. You have solid protection on the downside, while still maintaining room for gains on the upside.

The payoff graph illustrates the situation. You have defined your trade within clear limits: Restricted risk, capped profit, but also massive clarity. You know your worst-case scenario. You've insulated your capital. You're no longer reacting to market changes, you're strategically managing the trade with the precision of an experienced tactician.

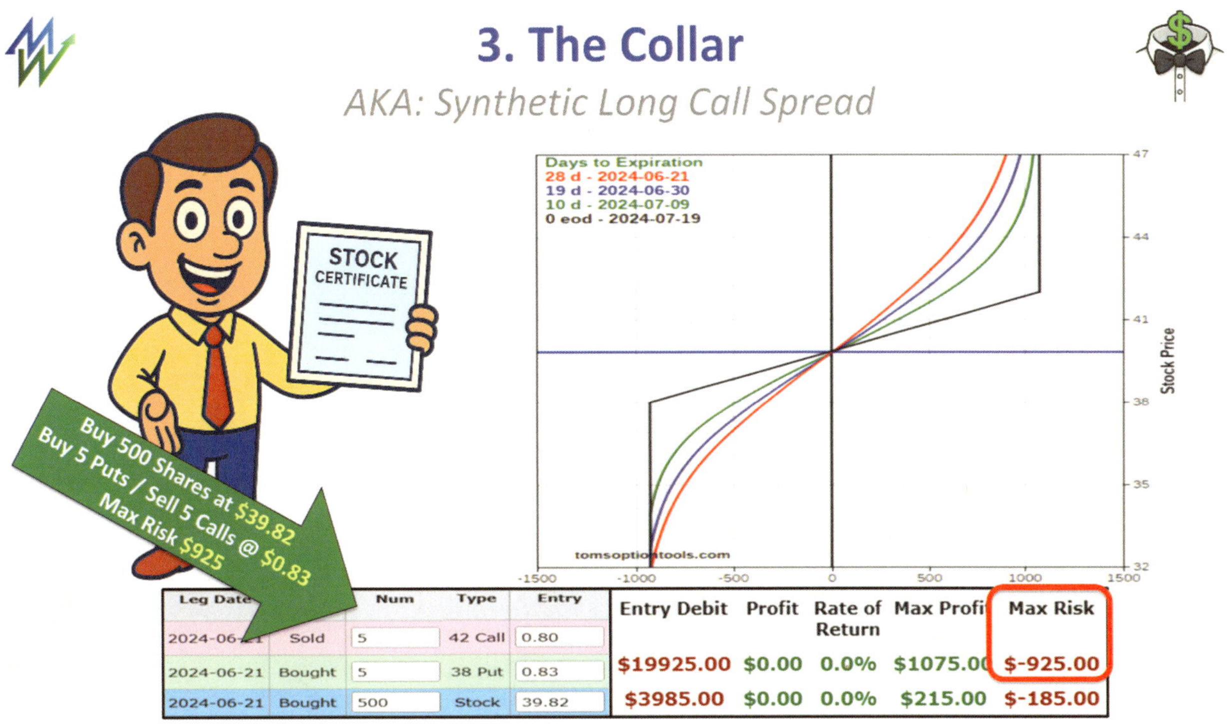

That's what sets apart the casual player from the disciplined strategist. The Collar is chess, not checkers.

The Collar – Protect Stock, Lower Cost, Stay in the Game

Whether you're starting fresh or already holding a stock, the Collar isn't just a tactic. It's your go-to strategy for maintaining control. You're not just watching the board... you're actively managing it.

Step one: Buy puts to protect your stock and mitigate risk. Think of this as your shield, insurance, or safety parachute.

Step two: Sell calls to lower the cost of those puts. You're collecting rent—a little income to fund your defense. We call that smart positioning.

This version of the "Collect the Rent" adjustment is the same as before—now it's integrated into the core trade. Instead of just defending, you're transforming it into a profit.

This is what distinguishes the amateur from the strategist: Creating a position with layered logic, not just hope. The Collar ensures every move counts.

Collar Case Study – Ally Financial (ALLY), June 21 Entry

Alright, let's bring this strategy to life with a real-world example. On June 21, we implemented the Collar strategy on Ally Financial (ALLY) with a bullish outlook. This isn't just theory. This is real gameplay in action.

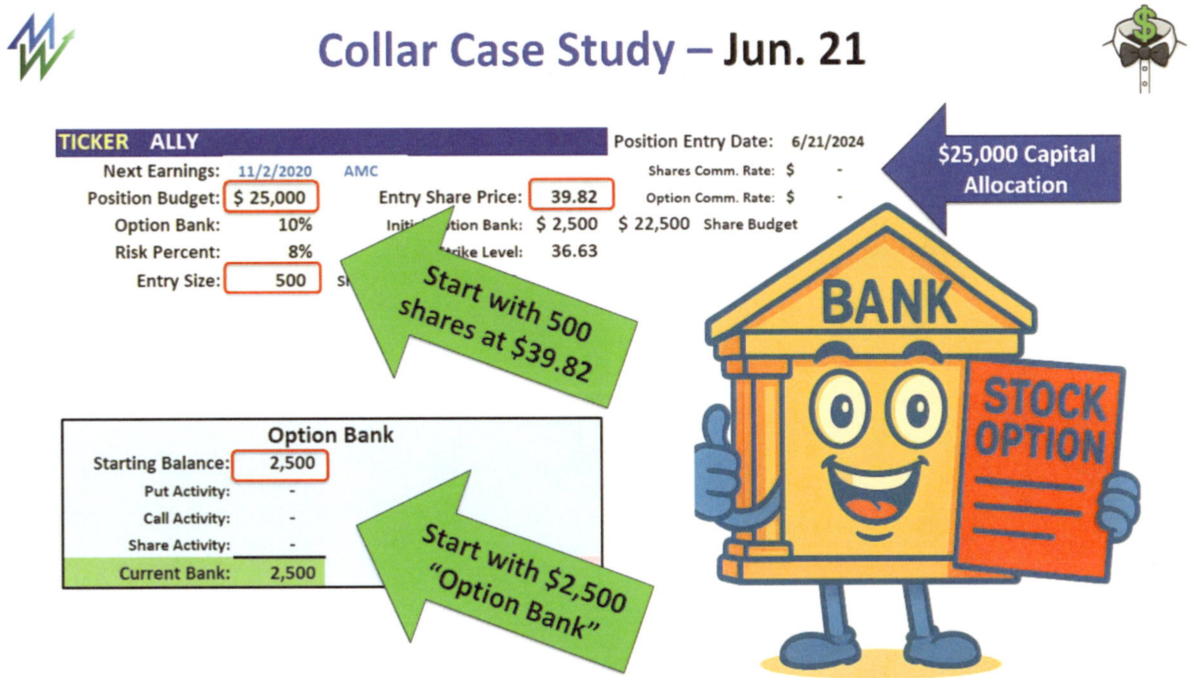

We began with a capital allocation of $25,000. From that, we purchased 500 shares at $39.82, deploying most of our capital into equity ownership.

But here's where strategy aligns with structure. We allocate 10% ($2,500) as our dedicated Option Bank. This isn't merely a reserve for purchasing puts; it's a flexible fund we'll utilize to:

- Finance protective puts
- Capture call premium
- Track net cash flow from adjustments
- And—if the stock drops—buy more shares at lower prices

This is our flexible ammunition. Every adjustment we make—every premium collected —flows through this bank. It gives us visibility, precision, and power to scale when the market presents opportunity.

As we walk through this example, we'll make real-time adjustments and manage this trade like a portfolio expert. Because Collars aren't just about protection. They're about playing the long game with full control.

Collar Case Study – Jun. 21 Setup Breakdown

Let's examine the details of our ALLY Collar position and walk through the exact setup we executed on June 21. This is where the strategy aligns with the structure—and where your plan materializes.

Collar Case Study – Jun. 21

Leg Date	Position	Num	Action	Expire	Type	Entry		
2024-06-21	Sold	5	To Open	2024 Jul 19	42 Call	0.80	X 5 = 4.00	+ $400
2024-06-21	Bought	5	To Open	2024 Jul 19	38 Put	0.83	X 5 = 4.15	- $415
2024-06-21	Bought	500	To Open		Stock	39.82	X 500 = 19910	- $19910
							Total	- $19925

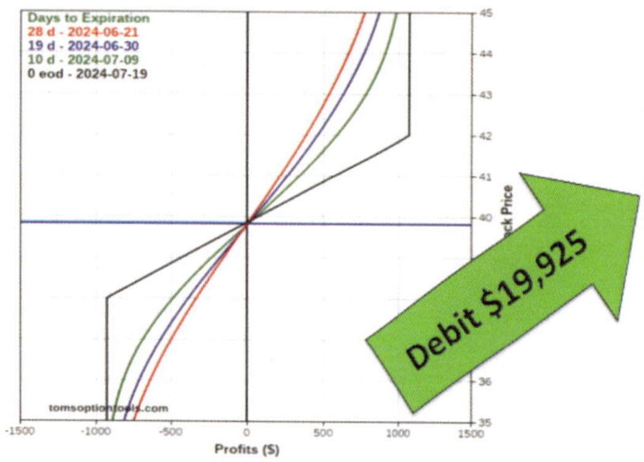

Entry Debit	Profit	Rate of Return	Max Profit	Max Risk
$19925.00	$0.00	0.0%	$1[illegible]	$-925.00
$3985.00	$0.00	0.0%	[illegible]	$-185.00

Max Risk $925

We bought 500 shares at $39.82, costing us $19,910.

To create the Collar, we bought a protective put at the $38 strike for $0.83 (total cost $415), and offset that by selling a $42 call for $0.80 (receiving $400).

The result? Our total entry debit was $19,925, which includes the cost of the stock and the net option position.

Most importantly, our maximum risk is now capped at $925, which protects over 95% of our capital while still allowing room for further gains and future adjustments.

The risk graph illustrates how this works in practice: Downside is limited, upside has potential, and you're no longer vulnerable to market chaos. You're protected, structured, and ready to act—just like a serious player should be.

Collar Case Study – Jun. 21 Risk Graph & Structure

This is where the Collar reveals its true strength. On the left, we see our entry and setup details for Ally Financial (ALLY) on June 21. And on the right—the visual payoff: The risk graph. This is your strategic battlefield view.

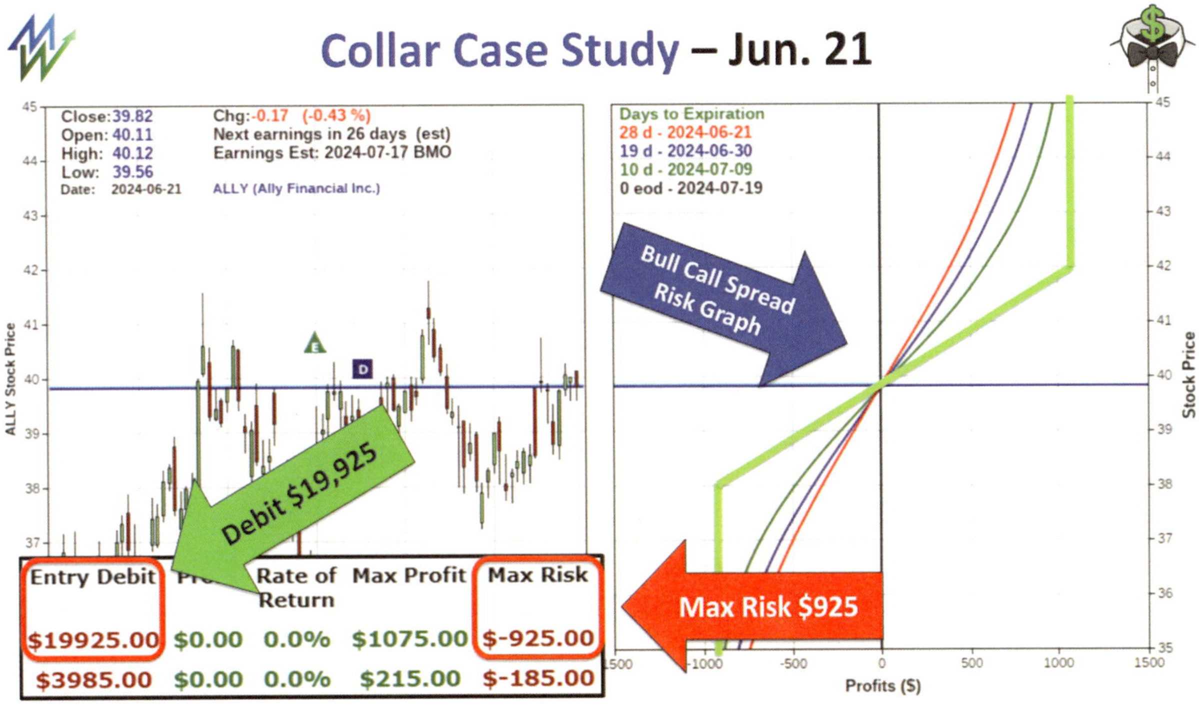

With a total debit of $19,925 to initiate the trade, and a maximum risk of just $925, our downside is boxed in tight—and that's by design.

Notice how the risk graph looks similar to a bull call spread. That's because this Collar setup functions like a synthetic long call spread. It's a smart structure: By owning the stock, buying puts, and selling calls, it replicates the payoff of a long vertical call spread, while also providing the tax advantages and flexibility of stock ownership.

That's the brilliance of the Collar. You get the defined risk and profit potential of an option spread but embedded into a stock position you control. You're not just in a trade. You're in charge of it.

And now, as the market moves, we'll start adjusting this position—locking in profits, scaling shares, and strengthening our setup.

Collar Case Study – Jul. 19 Option Expiration: Time to Adjust

It's July 19, and we've hit a critical point in the Collar journey—option expiration. This is where the game changes, and your next move becomes most crucial.

The position has fulfilled its role. We secured premium, limited downside, and managed risk carefully. Now, it's time to adapt. This isn't the conclusion of the trade. It's the next strategic move.

Look at the numbers: The position shows a profit of $1,005 with a maximum profit of $1,075. That's a 108.6% return on the original Collar risk.

But here's the kicker—our maximum risk remains $925. So, if we don't make an adjustment now, we're losing control. That's not how we operate.

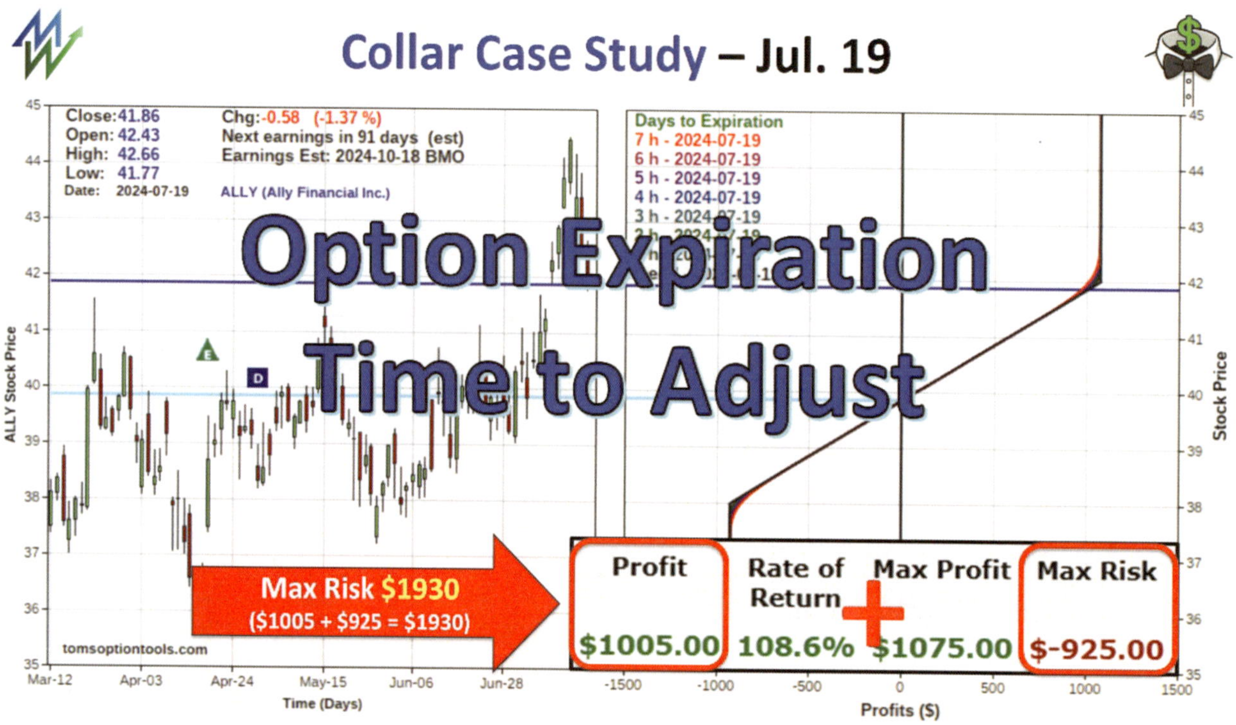

This is the moment to re-energize the trade. You've taken the value from the first move—now it's time to reload: Add a new put, sell a new call, lock in profits, or scale the position. You're not cashing out. You're strengthening your advantage.

Think of it like chess—the opening was successful, your midgame is on track, and now it's time to position for the endgame with an upgrade in protection, income, or size. Let's move forward and confidently adjust this Collar.

Collar Case Study – Jul. 19 Adjustment and Option Bank Update

It's Friday, July 19—and this marks a crucial point in the Collar lifecycle. The options we initially opened are expiring today, and this is where a disciplined trader steps in to manage risk and adjust positions.

We're performing a re-collar: Closing the July $42 call and $38 put, and opening new August $44 calls and $40 puts. This keeps our hedge active and our income strategy moving forward.

Why not let the options expire? Because if either leg is in the money (ITM), you introduce assignment risk and lose control. We always aim to exit smoothly and reset deliberately.

Here's what the adjustment looked like: We closed the July $42 call for $0.05 and opened the August $44 call for $0.43—generating a net $215 in premium. We bought new August $40 puts for $0.60—costing $300. The original $38 puts expired worthless. Total net debit from this roll: $110.

That leaves our Option Bank at $2,375, down just $125 from the initial balance. We're still in great shape, ready for the next move.

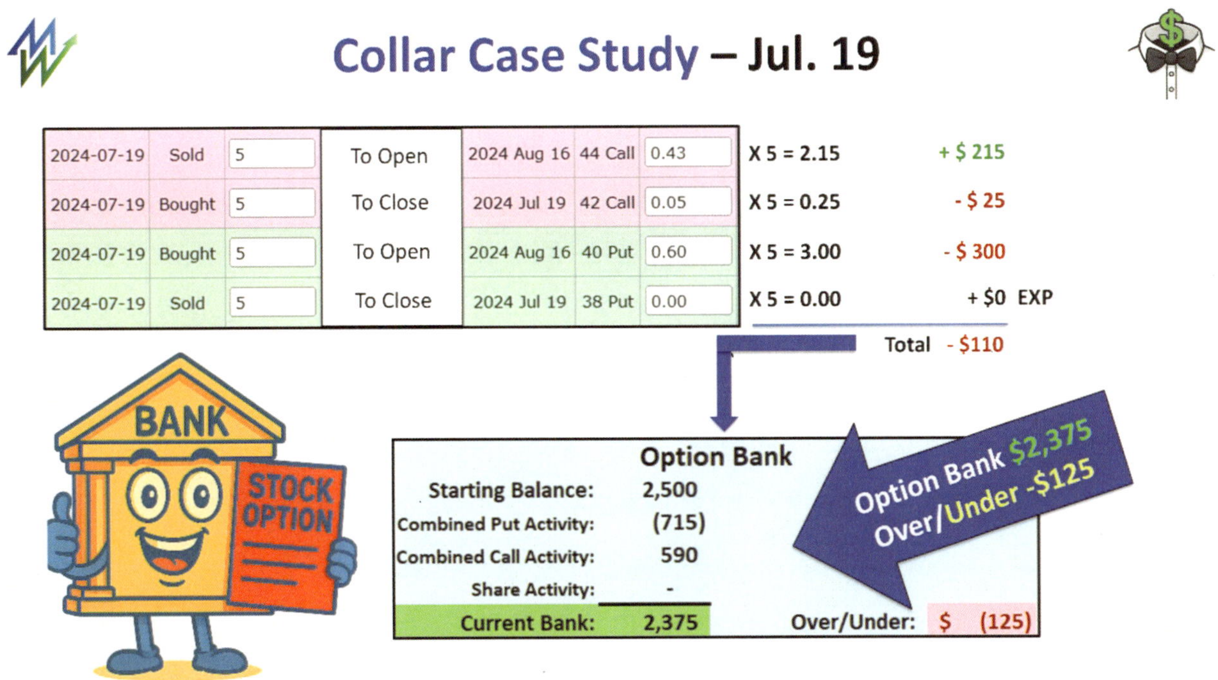

This is the rhythm of the Collar strategy: Manage at expiration, control your rolls, track the budget, and always stay one step ahead of the market.

Collar Case Study – Jul. 19: New Risk Graph with Epic Risk Control

Now, this is what Collar mastery looks like. Just hours after our re-collar on July 19, the new risk graph is in—and it's a thing of beauty. Structured, powerful, and shockingly efficient.

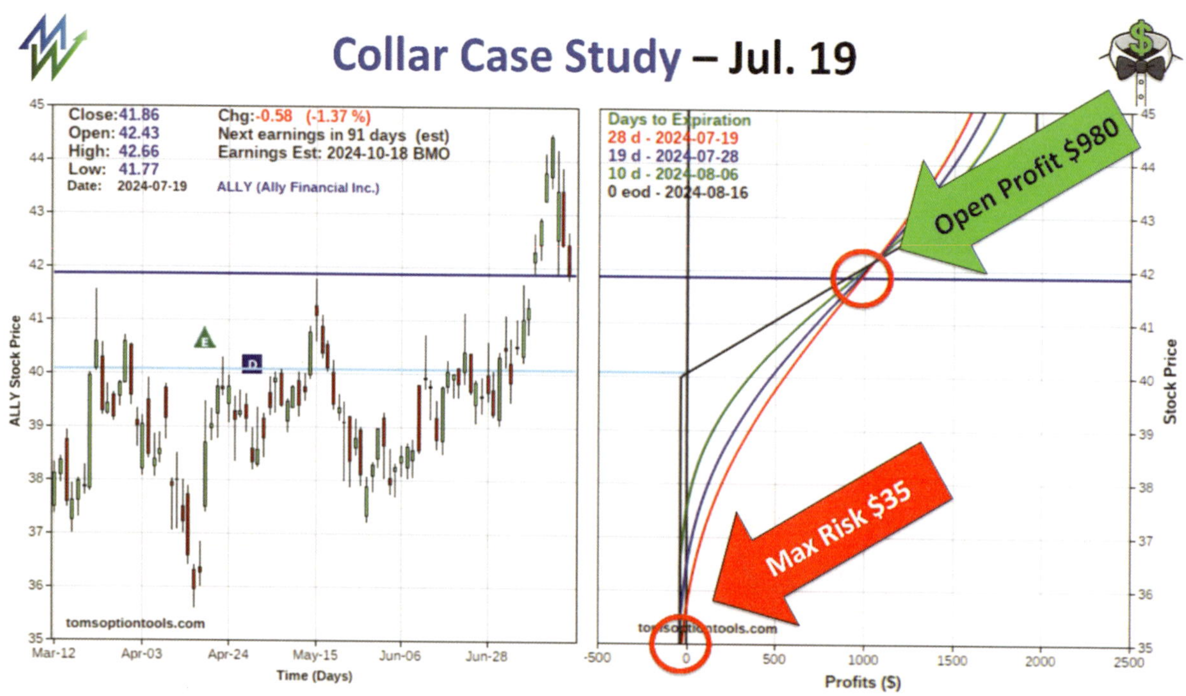

Let's begin with the most important number—maximum risk: $35. That's right. With this Collar adjustment in place, we've lowered downside exposure to the cost of dinner and a tip.

Look at the risk graph above, it curves upward gracefully, showing a solid open profit of $980, while maintaining our capital with strict discipline.

This is what makes Collars such a powerful tool. They're not passive hedges; they're active profit engines. Every move we've made has sharpened the edge, and this risk profile is the payoff.

We're up nearly a grand, and our worst-case scenario - just a scratch—a $35 loss on a $25,000 position. This is the kind of risk/reward setup professionals dream of.

At this point, we allow the trade to breathe. The protection is set. The upside remains open. And our next step? Continue managing, keep observing... and prepare to adjust again when the opportunity presents itself.

Collar Case Study – Aug 16 Adjustment

It's expiration day—and you know what that means in our game: It's time to make our next move.

On August 16, our collar options will expire. And here's a golden rule of collars you should always remember:

"Never let your collar options expire without managing them!"

Why? Because if either leg of your collar ends in the money, you could be assigned on your short options OR be automatically exercised on your longs – which would have you wake up with surprises Monday morning—and we don't gamble with our trades.

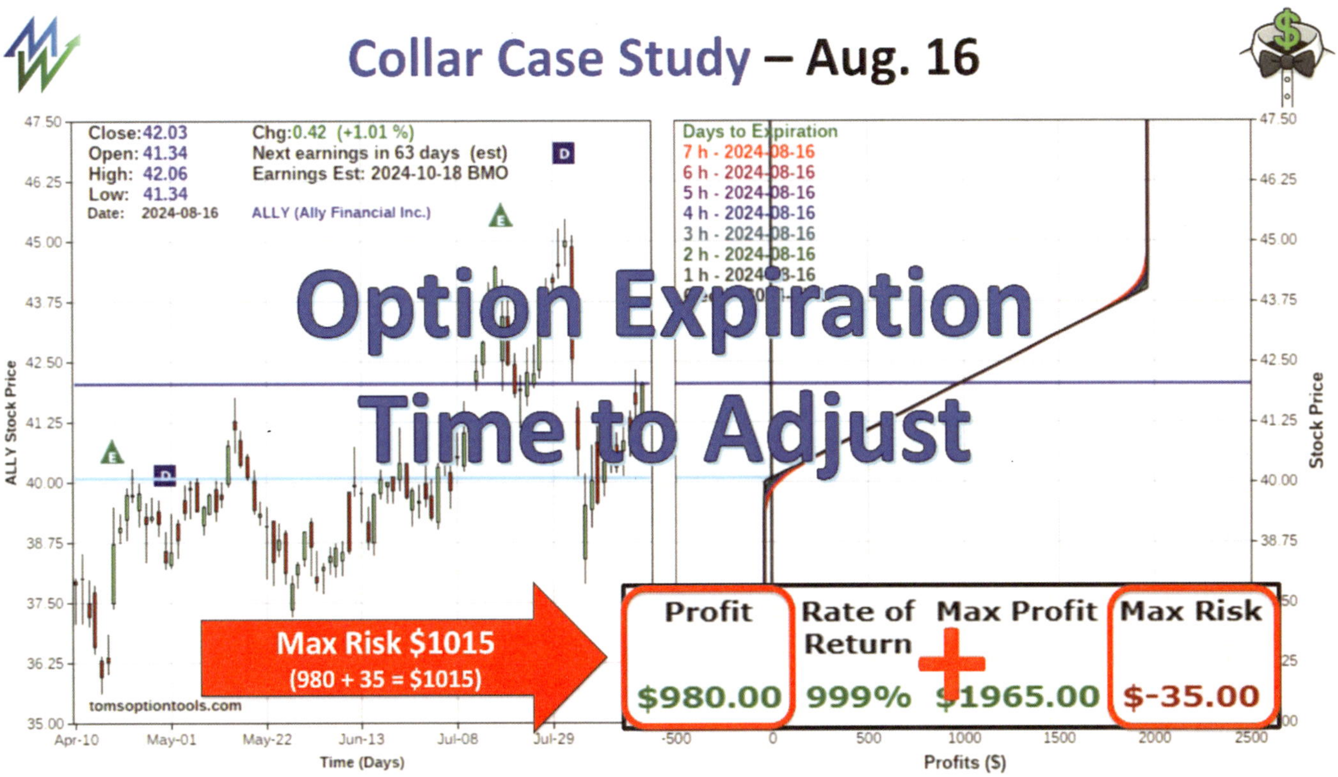

So, here's our next move:

1. Close the current collar before market close.
2. Re-collar by buying a new put and selling a new call —one month out.

This roll isn't just a habit. It's a key part of the system. You stay in control, stay protected, and stay in the game.

How did we do?

Let's break it down:

- Stock moved in our favor since the last re-collar.
- Our trade delivered a $980 profit.
- We only had $35 of risk left on the table from the last re-collar.
- That gives us a total risk of $1,015—which, considering the return, is a big win. That's a 999% rate of return on the final leg of the collar.

Game Insight

This is the exciting part. We're now working with house money. We're not just making adjustments to survive, but to grow, safeguard, and multiply.

So, grab your scorecard, mark this as a win, and prepare for the next round. You're becoming skilled at the collar game, one expiration at a time.

The August 16 Adjustment—Re-Collaring with a Full Bank Audit

It's time to roll the collar forward and check in with our Option Bank to ensure we stay in balance.

Here's the move:

- We closed our expiring collar (Aug 16 $44 Call @ $0.05 and $40 Put @ $0.00).
- We opened a new collar one month out (Sep 20 $44 Call @ $0.70 and $40 Put @ $0.65).

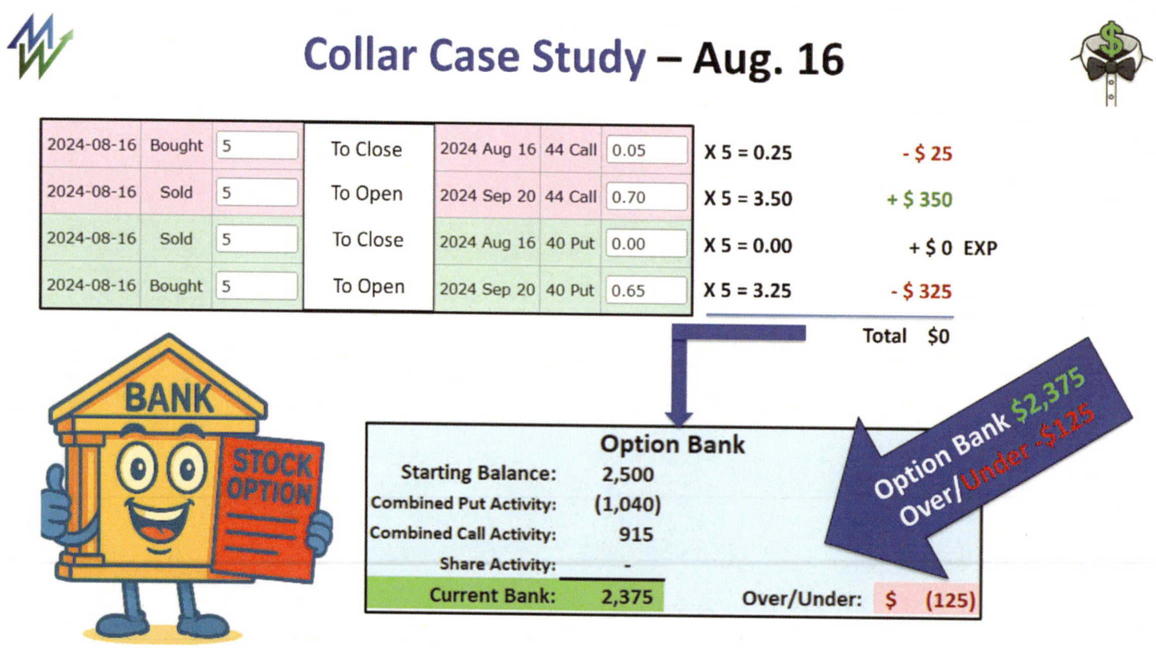

Let's talk numbers:

- Closing the old call cost us $25.
- Opening the new call brought in $350.
- The old put expired, worthless.
- Buying the new put cost us $325.

The cost of this full re-collar? Zero dollars out of pocket.

And that leads us to the Option Bank, our ongoing record of all trades and activities.

- **Starting Balance**: $2,500
- **Put Activity:** ($1,040)
- **Call Activity:** $915
- **Share Activity:** $0

Current Bank Balance: $2,375

But here's the catch: we're coming in $125 under budget—and that means we'll need to make smart adjustments to recover that.

This is the kind of tracking that separates the rookies from the pros.

Stay focused on the game. The next move is always imminent, and each adjustment brings you closer to mastering this system, much like a chess champion.

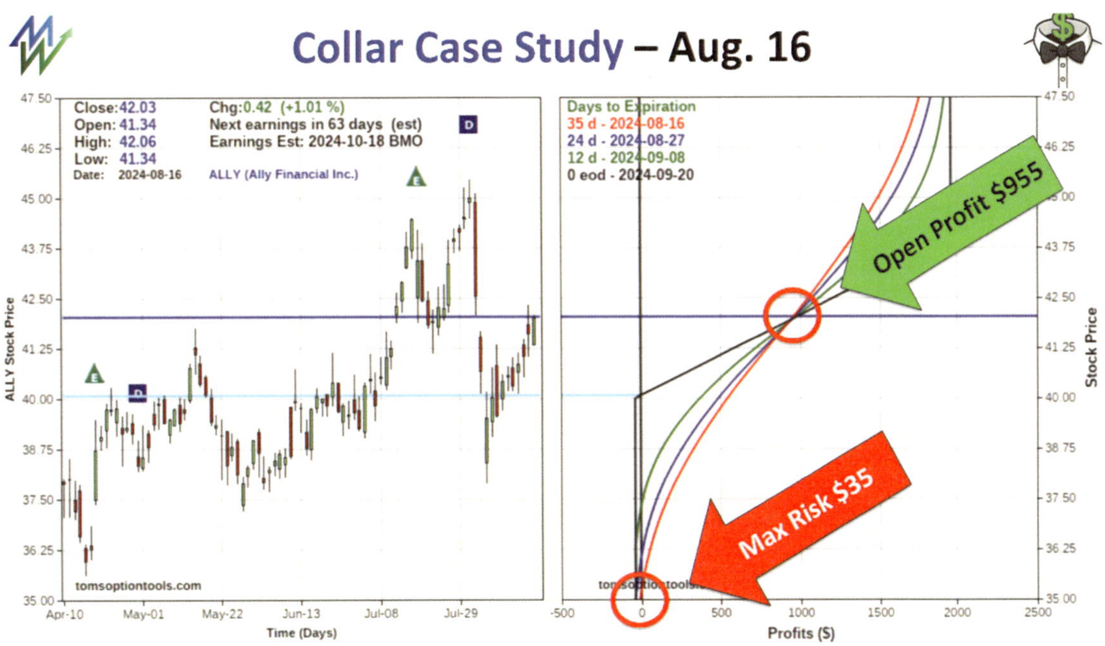

The New Risk Graph—Playing With Virtually No Risk

Here's where the game board resets—and the power of adjustment becomes clear. We've just re-collared our position, and this is what our new risk graph looks like. The stock is sitting at $42.03, and our new September collar is locked in.The result:

- An open profit of $955, already built into the position.
- A maximum risk of just $35, thanks to smart management and prior gains.That tiny red zone at the bottom left of the graph? That's all we're risking now. Everything else—the green curve climbing to the right—is pure opportunity. We're playing with house money, and the odds are stacked in our favor. Keep adjusting. Keep compounding. You're not just managing risk. You're building a masterpiece.

September 20 Expiration – The Power of the Collar When the Stock Tanks

September 20 was one of those trading days you'll never forget. The stock dropped sharply, falling all the way to $34.48. For anyone holding the naked stock, this would have been a brutal wake-up call.

Let's break it down:

- **Original purchase:** 500 shares at $39.82 = $19,910
- **Stock price on Sept 20:** $34.48
- **Naked stock value:** 500 × 34.48 = $17,240
- **Total loss without protection:** $2,670

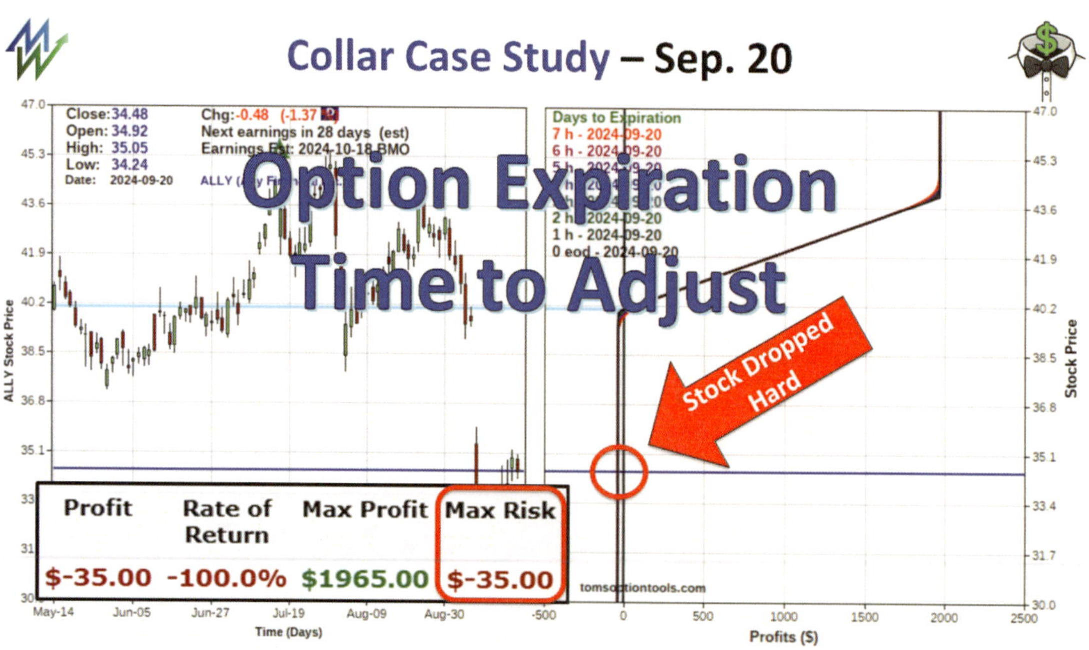

That's a gut-wrenching 13% loss in one move. Now, here's the power of smart trading: With our collar in place, the maximum loss was only $35.

That's right—instead of a multi-thousand-dollar disaster, we limited our risk with a simple adjustment. This is what strategic defense looks like in trading. The collar didn't just protect our capital. It kept us in the game. Because when the market turns against you like this, survival becomes THE real victory.

You don't always know when a stock will drop—but you can always choose to protect yourself.

September 20 – Option Bank Payday: Puts Save the Day

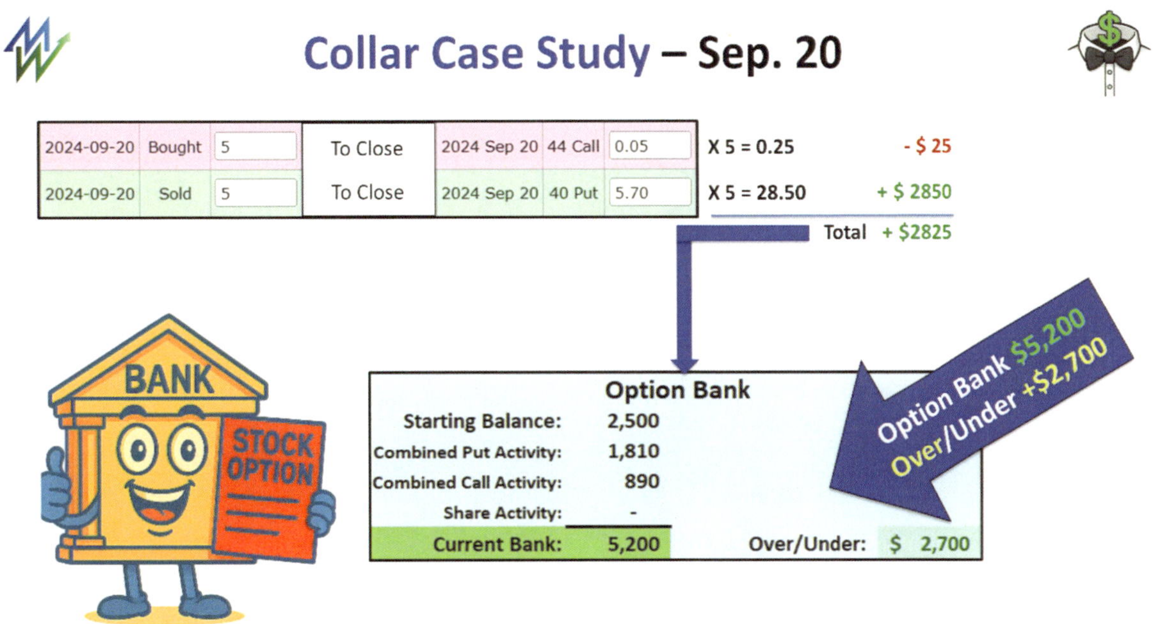

On September 20, we finalized our position by selling the 40 puts for an impressive $5.70 each and covering the short $44 calls for only $0.05. After 5 contracts, the net profit was a solid $2,825 added to our Option Bank.

This is where risk-managed trading really stands out. The puts soared in value as the stock plummeted—turning what could have been a big loss into a significant profit. That $2,670 drop in the stock... it was almost a dollar-for-dollar offset by the gain in the puts.

Our Option Bank, which started at $2,500, now stands at $5,200, showing a gain of $2,700 total. That Over/Under figure is what counts: It proves that by managing risk carefully, we didn't just protect our account. **We grew it**.

September 20 – Cash In, Double Down, Re-Collar

With the market crash behind us, we've officially cashed in our insurance policy—those puts we bought for protection just handed us $2,850 in pure defensive profit.

Now, we shift from defending to attacking. The premium earned from the puts becomes capital that we use to purchase additional shares. This strategy is the key to successful trading: Leveraging volatility and smart protection to expand your position while others are exiting.

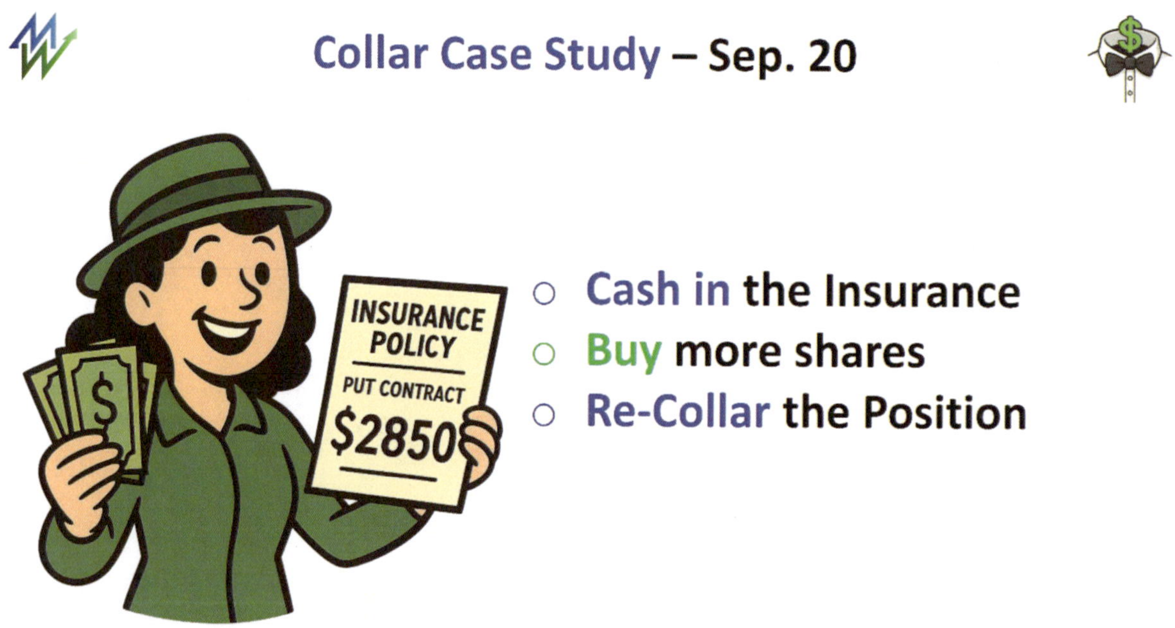

Once those shares are added, we don't just cross our fingers. We promptly re-collar the new position to keep our risk tight and our strategy intact.

In short, we didn't just survive the drop. We reinvested the insurance payout to grow our stake and stay protected for the next round. That's how you trade like a pro.September 20 – Re-Collar Executed: Risk Back in Check

Right after cashing in the puts, we reloaded with 100 new shares at $34.48 and reaffirmed our protection. We sold 6 x October 18th $37 calls and bought 6 x October 18th $33 puts, forming our next collar.

The total cost of this move was $3,586, drawn from our Option Bank. After accounting for the credits from the short calls and the cost of the new puts, our Option Bank balance decreased to $1,614, resulting

Collar Case Study – Sep. 20

2024-09-20	Bought	100	To Open		Stock	34.48	X 100 = 3448	- $ 3448
2024-09-20	Sold	6	To Open	2024 Oct 18	37 Call	0.45	X 6 = 2.70	+ $ 270
2024-09-20	Bought	6	To Open	2024 Oct 18	33 Put	0.68	X 6 = 4.08	- $ 408
							Total	- $3586

Option Bank

Starting Balance:	2,500
Combined Put Activity:	1,402
Combined Call Activity:	1,160
New Share Activity:	(3,448)
Current Bank:	**1,614**

Over/Under: $ (886)

Option Bank $1,614
Over/Under -$886

in an Over/Under of -$886.But here's the key: Risk is now managed again. We've lowered the collar range to match the new market reality. Yes, it cost us some cash from the bank—but we're playing for long-term survival and opportunity, not for short-term savings.

This embodies the discipline of advanced options trading: Even after a win, we stay vigilant—re-collaring to safeguard against the next significant move.

September 20 – The New Collar: Bigger Position, Capped Risk

This is where things get exciting. After a tough drop, we've rebuilt—and not just recovered, we've expanded. We now own 600 shares, up from our original 500, and the average cost basis is now $38.93.

That extra 100 shares? They were funded by our previous insurance payout—proof that defensive trading can generate offensive opportunities. We turned protection into power.

Looking at the new collar's risk graph, we're already sitting on an open profit of $30, and our max risk is capped at $996. This is the beauty of the collar strategy in action. We hold a larger position, and our downside is clearly defined and limited.

We're now ideally positioned for the next move, with more shares working for us and a risk profile that keeps us calm under pressure. Growth with guardrails—that's how we trade.

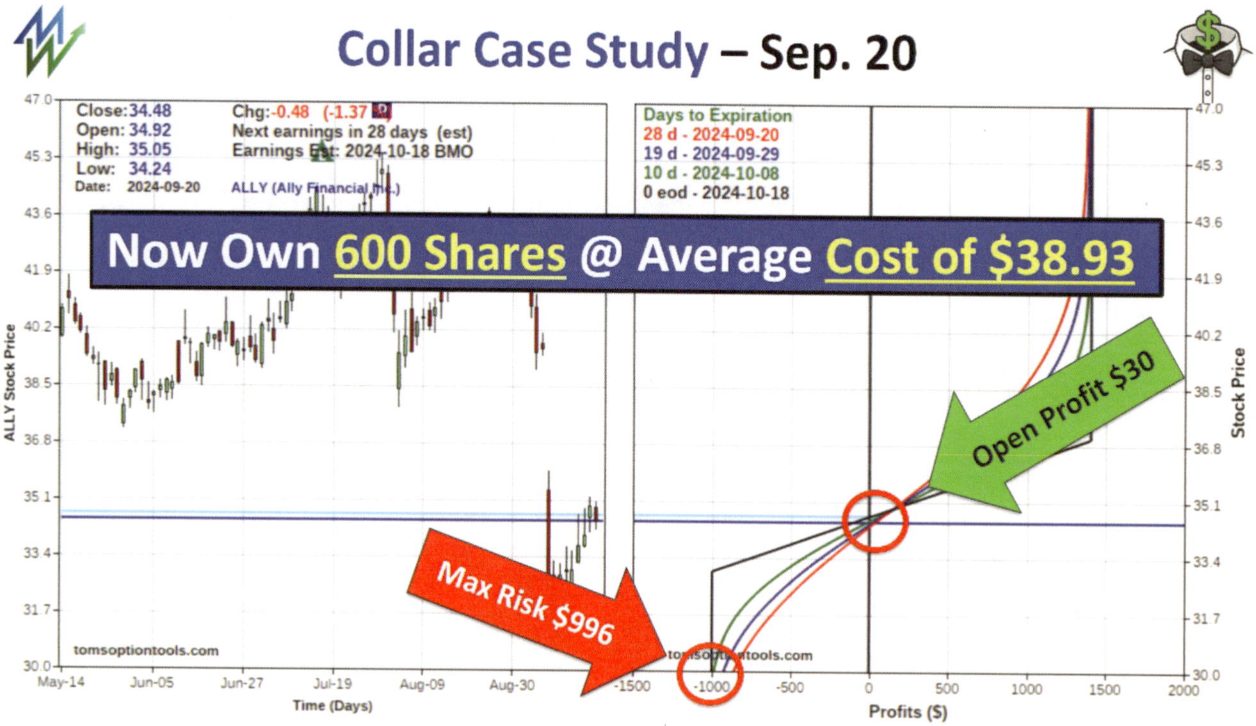

March 21 – The Cost of Doing Nothing

Let's pause to consider the do-nothing approach—the typical buy-and-hope tactic. On June 21, you purchased 500 shares at $39.82 each. You held on through every twist and turn, waiting for the rebound.

Fast forward 9 months to March 21—the stock trades at $36.44. That's a $3.38 decrease per share, or 8%. Your account now shows an unrealized loss of $1,690.

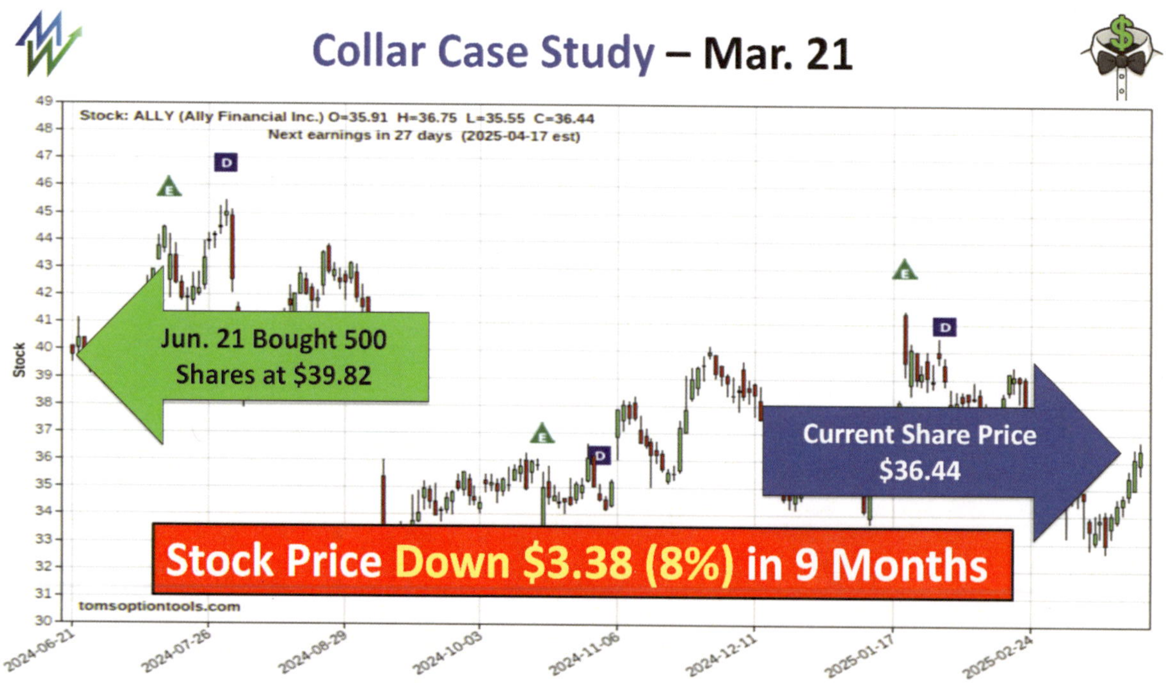

This is the danger of passively holding in a volatile market. Without protection, you endure every dip, hoping for a rebound. But time keeps passing, and the loss—while seemingly small—gradually erodes both your capital and your confidence.

That's why we use collars. Not just to protect against large drops, but to handle the small losses that add up over time. Smart traders don't just wait. They take action… and that makes all the difference.

March 21 - The Collar Wins: The Power of Smart Adjustments

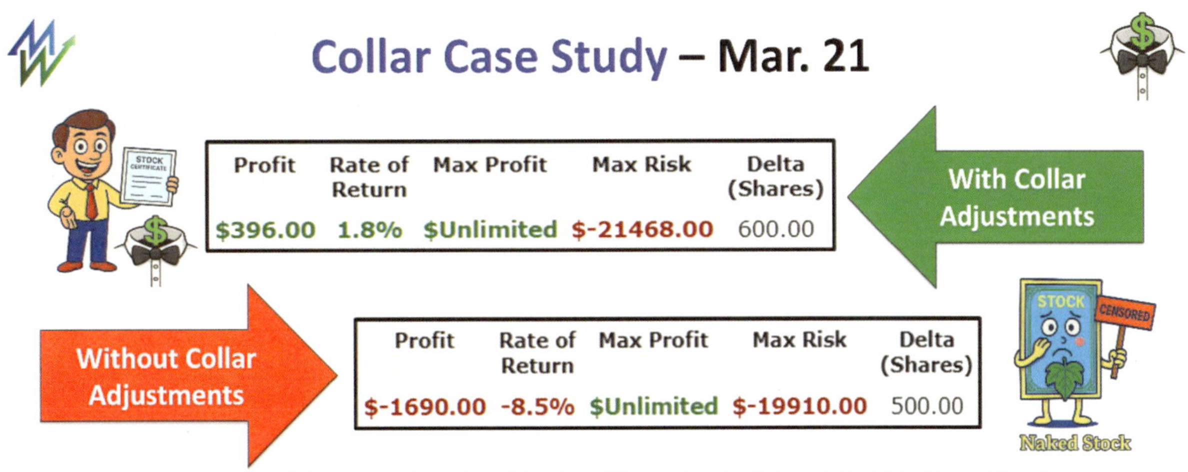

Strategy	P/L $	ROI %	Shares	Position Value
Naked Stock	$-1,690	-8.5%	500	$18,220
Collared Stock	$396	1.8%	600	$21,864
Collar Difference	$2,086	10.3%	+100	+$3,644

Let's compare two parallel worlds: One where you simply bought and held the stock, and another where you followed the collar strategy taught in this chapter.

The result? The naked stock trader has lost $1,690 over nine months, which is an 8.5% decrease. Meanwhile, the collar trader made a $396 profit—plus 100 more shares and an extra $3,644 in position value.

That's a 10.3% performance swing just by using a simple rule-based adjustment method—proof that defense doesn't just protect… it can grow your portfolio.

And look at the kicker—the collar strategy had lower maximum risk than the naked position, even though it was holding more shares! That's not just smart… that's how the pros play.

March 21 – Pros and Cons: Collared vs. Naked

Let's lighten things up with a side-by-side of the pros and cons of following the collar strategy versus just holding the naked stock—because, yes, you can trade smart and have fun doing it.

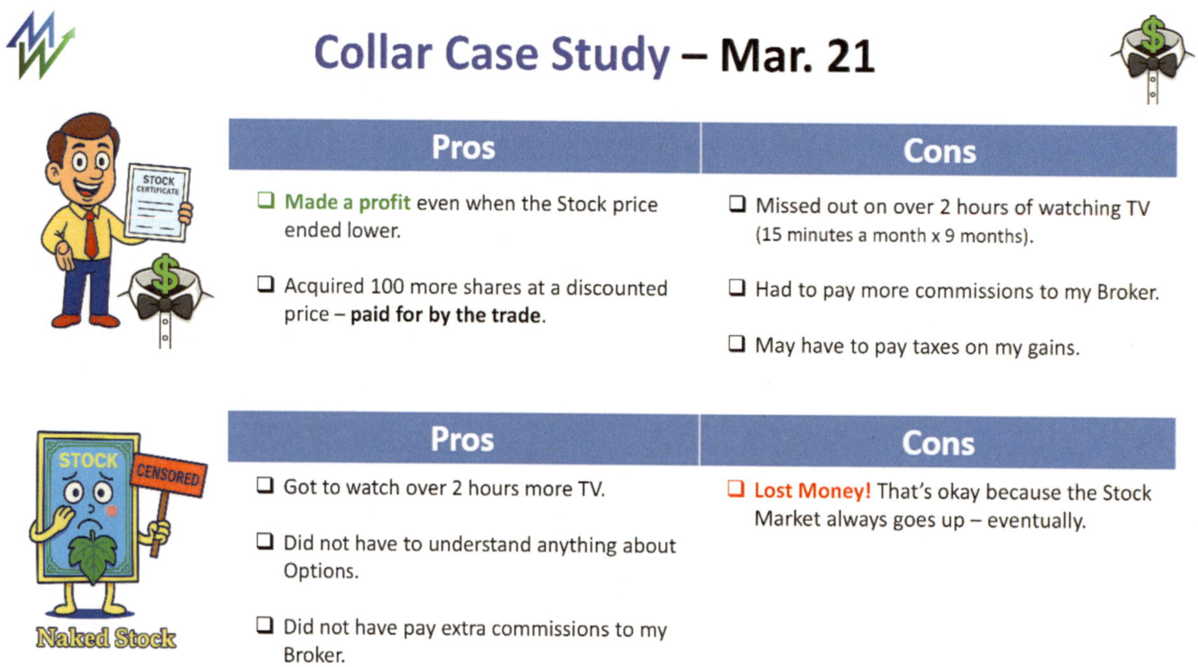

With the collar, the pros speak for themselves:

- You made a profit even though the stock dropped.
- You ended up with 100 more shares, paid for by the trade itself.

But of course, nothing comes free... You lost about 2 hours of TV time (15 minutes a month), paid your broker more in commissions, and—worst of all—you may owe taxes on your gains. A tragic price to pay for being a profitable, proactive trader.

On the other hand, the naked stockholder had some... unique advantages:

- Watched more TV.
- Didn't have to learn options.
- Avoided extra commissions.

But the con list hits hard: Lost money. As the slide jokingly notes, "That's okay because the stock market always goes up—eventually." (Spoiler: That's not a valid strategy.)

Bottom line? Active, protective trading wins. And if you're laughing a little right now, good—because the best trades are the ones that make you smile in the end.

April 17 – But Wait, There's More...

Just when you thought you had collars mastered, we unveil the next chapter in your strategy playbook. There is more than one way to run a collar—and your adjustments can totally change your trading experience.

April 17 – Lazy vs Dynamic Collar Results

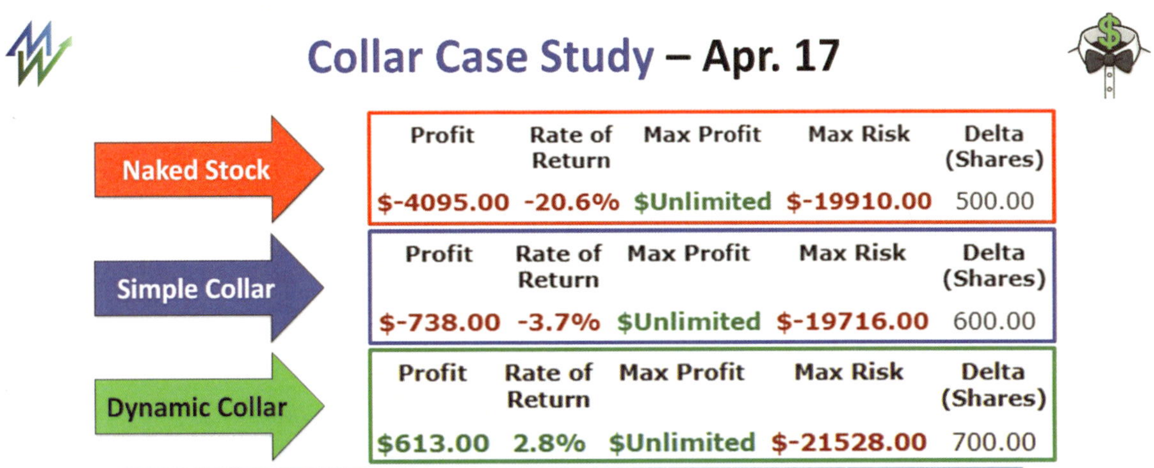

Strategy	P/L $	ROI %	Shares	Position Value
Naked Stock	$-4,095	-21%	500	$15,815
Collar - Simple	$-738	-4%	600	$18,978
Collar - Dynamic	$613	+3%	700	$22,141

There isn't just one way to run a collar—and how you choose to adjust can completely change your trading experience.

On one side, there's the **Simple or Lazy Collar**: Low-maintenance, one adjustment per month. Great for busy traders who still want downside protection and defined risk.

On the other, we have the **Dynamically Hedged Collar**: Actively managed with multiple adjustments each month. It demands more attention, but can respond to fast-moving markets with precision.

Both approaches work. The key is understanding which one fits your life style—and knowing that mastering collars means you've got options within your options.

The results are in—and the difference is clear.

The Naked Stock trader took a severe hit, losing $4,095 and ending with a -21% return. That's the cost of doing nothing—and hoping. The Simple Collar eased the impact significantly. With just one adjustment per month, the trader lost only $738 (a -4% return), while increasing the position to 600 shares. But the top performer is the Dynamic Collar strategy. With more active adjustments, this trader secured a $613 gain and a +3% return—while expanding to 700 shares valued at $22,141.

Same stock. Same starting point. Very different outcomes—all driven by how actively you manage the collar.

The Collar - Chapter Summary

Throughout this chapter, we traced a complete collar case study—from the initial stock purchase, through major market drops, multiple adjustments, and a final comparison of results. Here are the key takeaways:

- **Collars protect your downside**
  Even during a big stock decline, the collar limited losses to just $35—while the naked stock position would have lost $2,670 or more.
- **Adjusting the collar unlocks growth**
  By cashing in the puts and buying more shares at a discount, we grew the position from 500 to 600 shares and stayed protected with a re-collar.
- **The power of the Option Bank**
  Each adjustment—buying shares, selling calls, buying puts—was tracked with our Option Bank. It revealed the true cost and gains from each move, and kept us disciplined.

- **The collar turned a potential loss into a gain**
  While a passive investor would've ended with a $1,690 loss, our dynamic collar trader ended with a $396 profit and an even stronger position.

- **Lazy vs Dynamic collaring matters**
  The simple collar outperformed the naked stock easily, but the dynamic collar delivered the biggest win—$613 in profit and a 3% return with 700 shares in hand.

- **Collars offer clarity, confidence, and control**
  Instead of riding emotional waves, the collar approach provided us with structure—knowing when to enter, when to adjust, when to re-collar, and how to measure performance.

Bottom line: This isn't just a protective strategy. It's a strategic growth engine for smart traders. And when played right, it's a game you can win.

With collars now under your belt, let's switch gears and return to a powerful way to stack butterflies for an ultra-wide profit zone and probability of success: **The "Flock O' Flies".**

CHAPTER 29

THE FLOCK O' FLIES

CHAPTER 29
The Flock O' Flies

The Flock O' Flies strategy expands on the butterfly trade by using multiple butterflies across various strikes and expirations to create a broader net of opportunities.

The Flock O' Flies

Use **multiple butterflies** to create **wide coverage** over time and strike to greatly **increase** the **probability of profit** and **reduce** the **probability of loss**.

By spreading your risk over time and different price levels, you create broad coverage that helps increase the chances of making a profit and decrease the chances of losing. Like a flock of butterflies fluttering together, this strategy focuses on movement, balance, and smart spacing. You're not trying to land on a single perfect strike. You're surrounding the target zone with layers of profit potential.

Flock O' Flies – Strategy Overview

Description: The Flock O' Flies strategy involves using two or more butterfly spreads on the same underlying asset, spread out across different strike prices or expiration dates. This layered approach creates a web of opportunities over time and price.

Strategies: It works on any optional instrument and can be positioned for bullish, bearish, neutral—or even mixed directional moves.

Outcome: Think of this as setting up multiple traps on the chart. You might only trigger one or two, but when you do, the payoff can be significant. Since butterflies are so cost-effective, missing a few doesn't matter much—and a single successful hit can more than make up for the others.

Timing: This strategy can be used across various timeframes (multiple expirations) and strike levels. It becomes especially effective when combined with other adjustment tactics—enabling you to defend or improve positions dynamically.

The Flock O' Flies

Description:	*The Flock O' Flies strategy is a combination of two or more Butterfly positions applied to the same instrument (Stock) at different strike levels and/or expiration dates.*
Strategies:	*Can be used on any "Optionable" instrument to profit with bullish, bearish or neutral (or any combination of) price movement.*
Outcome:	*To set multiple "traps" at different locations on the price chart. Ideally, the profit to risk ratio on each butterfly is quite high (very low risk coupled with high potential reward). This provides big profits when one or more are hit, while losing a very small amount on the ones that don't.*
Timing:	*Can be applied across multiple times frames (expiration dates) and/or multiple price levels – all on the same instrument. Other adjustment moves can also be applied in conjunction with The Flock O' Flies for more risk reduction and/or profit-making opportunities.*

The Butterfly Strategy – Target Practice Explained

Butterflies—like their cousins, Calendar spreads—are best thought of as a form of target practice. They aren't about betting randomly... they're about aiming. You're choosing a price you believe the stock will reach—or stay near—at a specific future date.

The Butterfly Strategy

Keep in mind, **Butterflies** *(as with Calendar spreads)* are like playing **"target practice"** with price and time on a stock chart.

For optimal results and profitability, you need to determine a **price target** for the underlying instrument will be **at/on specific date** in the future.

For the strategy to work best, you need to set a clear price target and adjust your strike placement and expiration accordingly. The closer the stock ends up near your central strike at expiration, the more profitable it is. Precision counts. That's why butterflies reward traders who are not only directionally correct but also accurate in both price and timing.

Flock O' Flies – Netting Profits with Strategic Placement

The Flock O' Flies strategy focuses on setting traps—butterflies positioned at various strike levels and expirations—to capture profits from a range of price targets. It's like casting a broad net across your forecast, giving yourself multiple opportunities to make a profit. You don't need to hit the exact target each time. Instead, you "net the profits" from any strike the market reaches. With careful placement, one successful trade can outweigh several small losses.

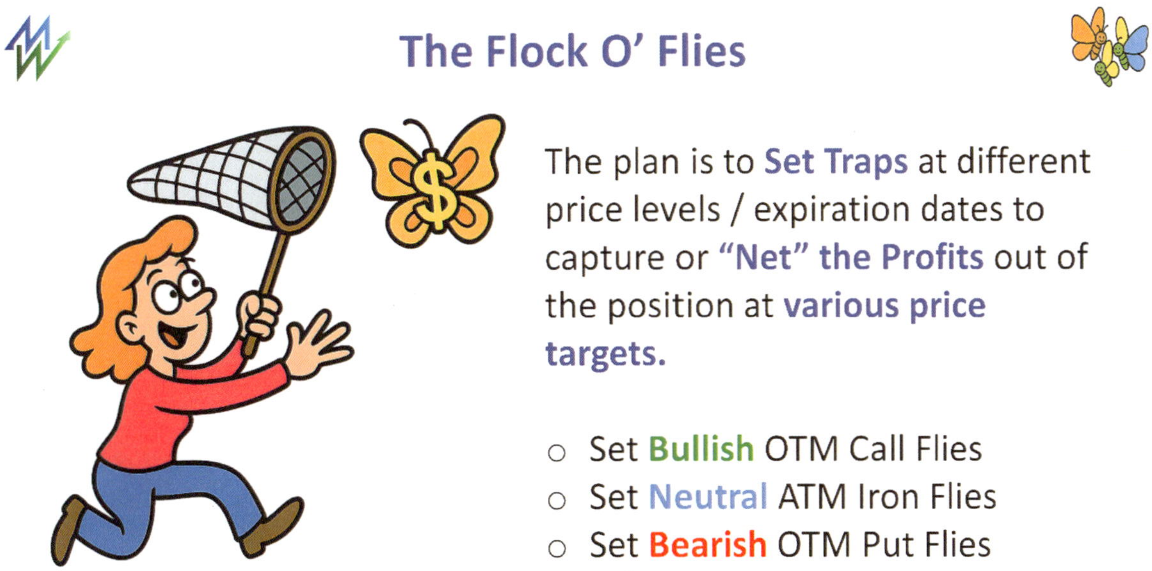

There are three ways to fly:

- **Bullish Flies**—Use OTM Call Butterflies to target upward movement.
- **Neutral Flies**—Use ATM Iron Butterflies when you expect the stock to hover near the current price.
- **Bearish Flies**—Use OTM Put Butterflies to profit from downward moves.

Step 1 – Start the Flock with a Bullish Fly

The first step in building your Flock O' Flies is to deploy a bullish Out-of-the-Money (OTM) Call Butterfly. This structure is perfect when your outlook is positive and you expect the stock to rise. By placing the butterfly above the current price, you're setting a trap to profit if the market rallies into your chosen range. As shown in the risk graph, the payoff zone peaks right at the upper strike target—offering a favorable risk/reward setup if the market moves in your favor.

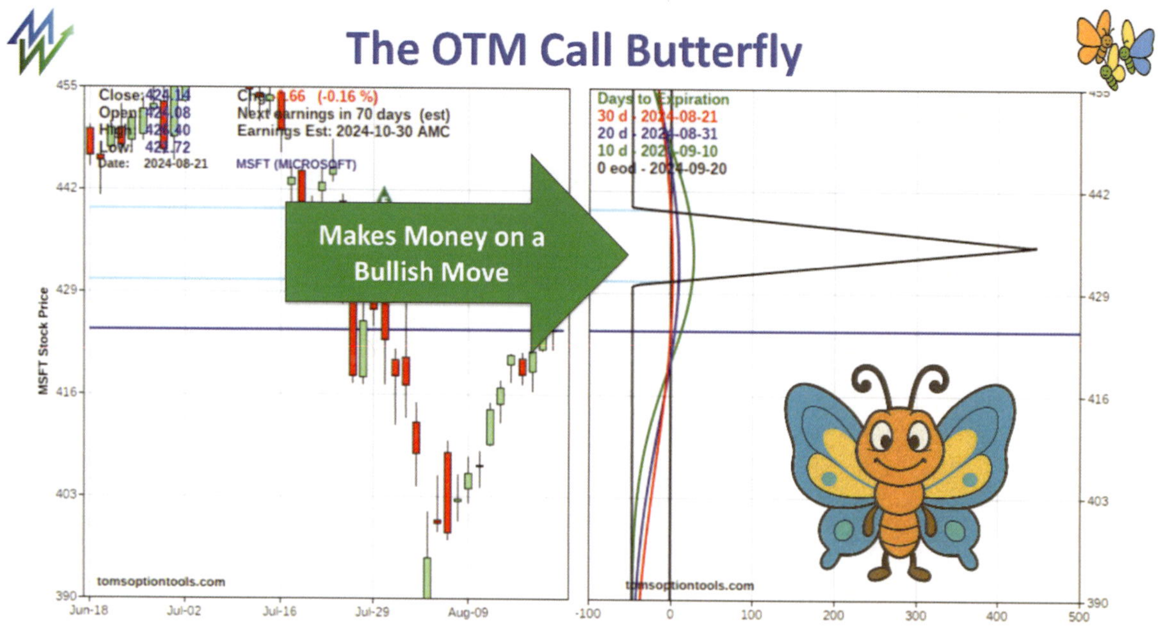

This bullish fly becomes the first wing of your strategic net—designed to catch profits on the upside.

Step 2 – Add a Neutral Fly for Sideways Profits

The second step in building your Flock O' Flies is to add a neutral At-The-Money (ATM) Iron Butterfly. This butterfly is placed right at the current stock price and is designed to profit if the market remains flat.

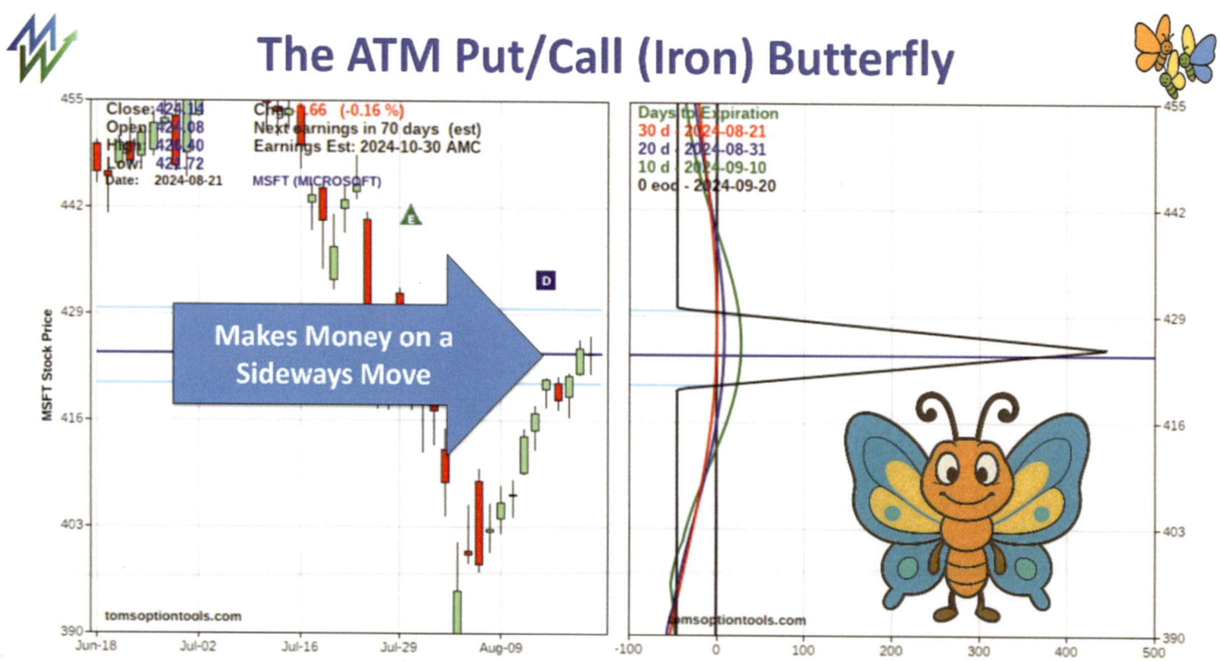

It works best in sideways markets, capturing time decay and implied volatility crush as expiration nears. The payoff graph shows a peak directly at the strike price—providing maximum profit if the stock price stays put. Even slight movements around that level can still generate a decent return.

This fly adds a strong layer of non-directional profit potential to your strategy, boosting the likelihood that one of your flies lands in a profit net.

Step 3 – Add a Bearish Fly for Downside Coverage

To finish your Flock O' Flies, add a bearish Out-of-the-Money (OTM) Put Butterfly. This strategy aims to profit from a downward move by placing it below the current market price, effectively setting a trap for a bearish decline.

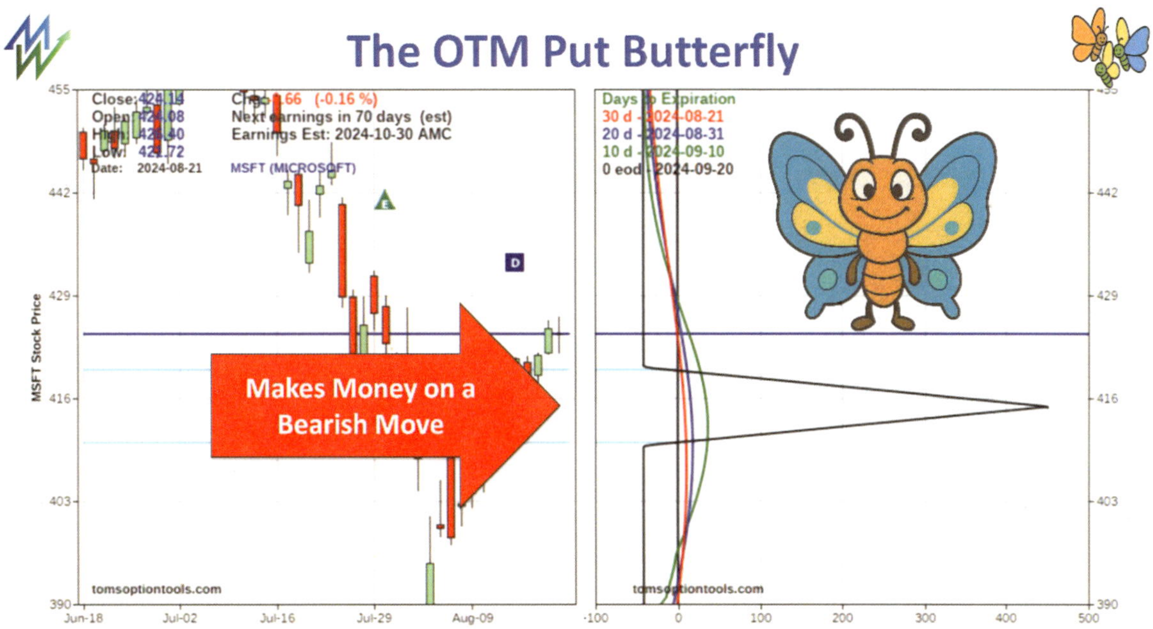

If the stock drops toward your target zone, this fly becomes highly profitable—while your other bullish and neutral flies remain intact. This diversification of positions makes the overall strategy much more resilient. By having bullish, neutral, and bearish flies in place, your position is now surrounded—ready to profit from multiple directions. This demonstrates the true power of the Flock O' Flies strategy in action.

Bullish Fly Construction – The Bullish Net is Set

Here's the detailed setup of a bullish call butterfly—the first trap in our Flock O' Flies strategy. This trade is executed above the current stock price and aims to profit if the market rallies.

The setup involves:

- Buying 1 $430 Call
- Selling 2 $435 Calls
- Buying 1 $440 Call
- All expiring on September 20, 2024

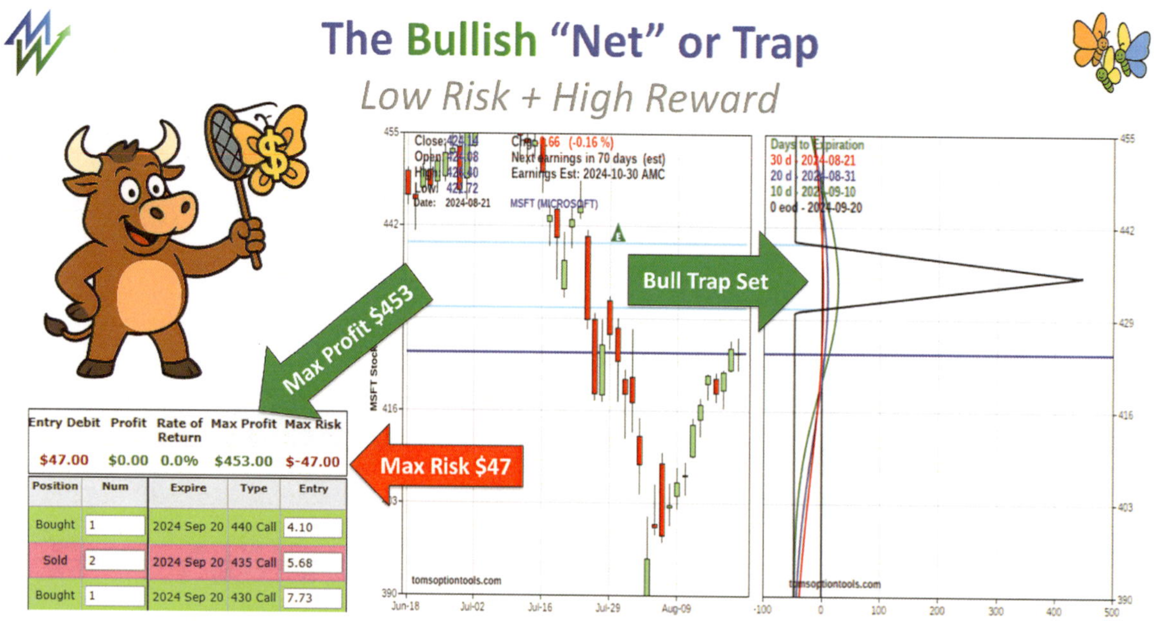

This entire trade costs $47. That's the maximum risk. The reward? Potentially earning up to $453 if MSFT closes exactly at the middle strike of $435. This risk/reward ratio is what makes butterflies so effective. A small, defined risk with the potential for a significant payout. This is the first net in our system—and it's ready to catch the bull.

Neutral Fly Construction – Trapping Sideways Profits

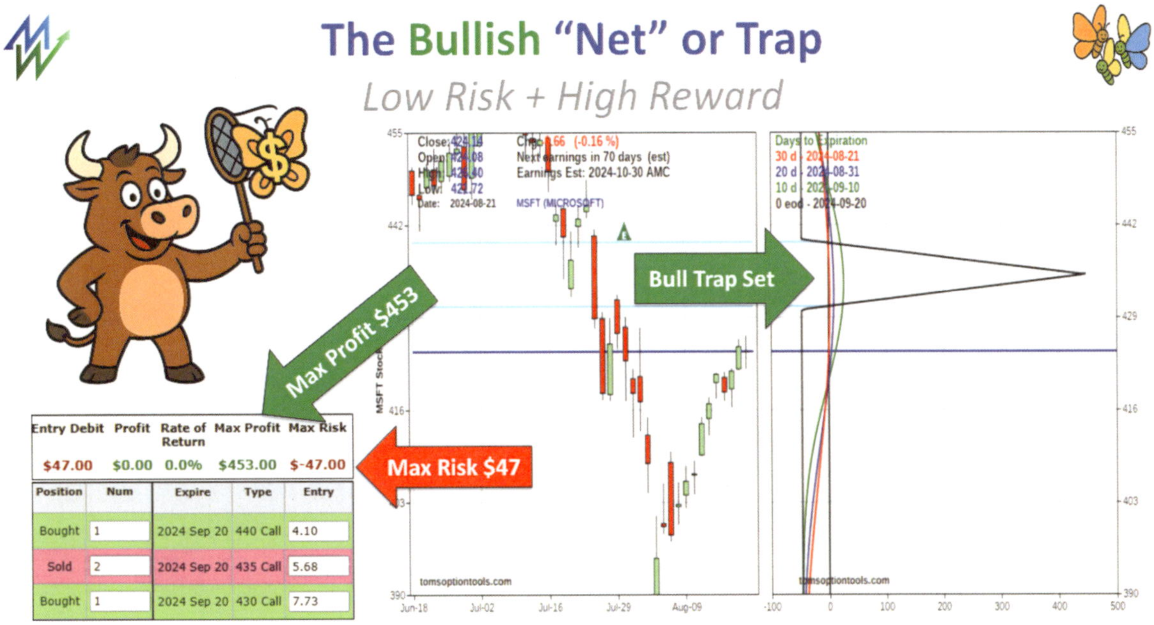

This section explains the ATM Iron Butterfly—your neutral position in the Flock O' Flies. It's meant to profit if the stock remains flat.

This setup includes:

- Buying 1 $430 Call
- Selling 1 $425 Call
- Selling 1 $425 Put
- Buying 1 $420 Put

All expiring on September 20, 2024

This position earns a $455 credit and carries a maximum risk of only $45. That's nearly a 10-to-1 reward-to-risk ratio—and it activates if MSFT finishes near $425 at expiration. This trap catches your profit in sideways market moves. When the market stalls, this fly pays off.

Bearish Fly Construction – The Final Trap

To complete your Flock O' Flies, the final net is a bearish OTM put butterfly. This trade is set below the current market price to profit if the stock declines.

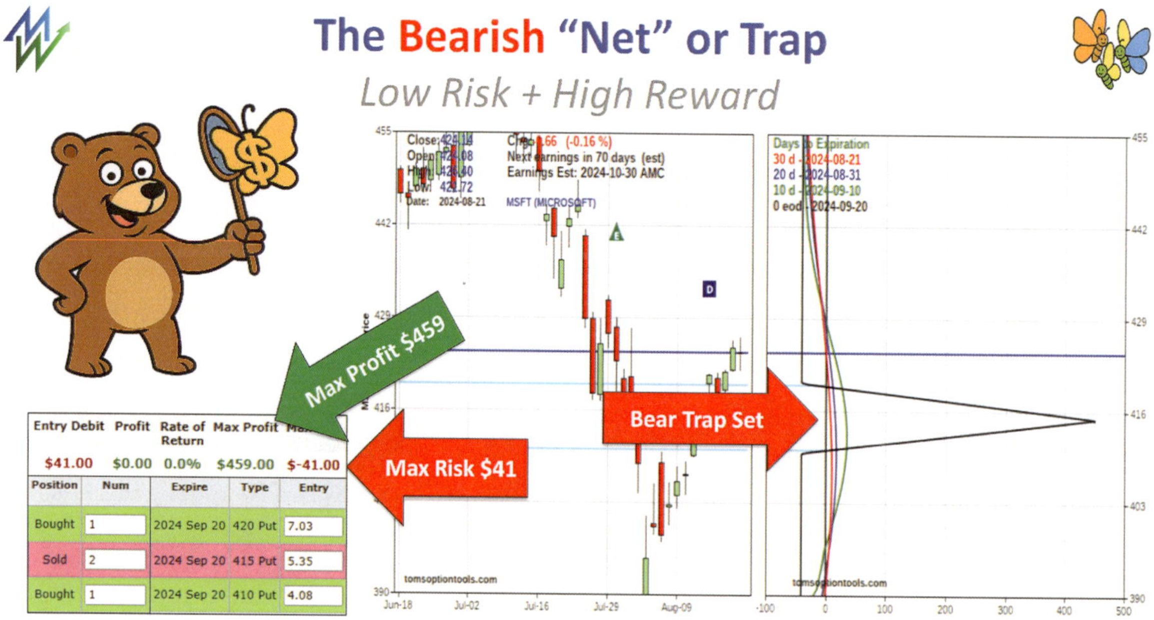

The setup includes:

- Buying 1 $420 Put
- Selling 2 $415 Puts
- Buying 1 $410 Put
- All expiring on September 20, 2024

This bearish fly costs only $41 and offers a maximum profit of $459 if MSFT drops and lands near the $415 strike at expiration. It's the ideal low-risk, high-reward tool to capitalize on bearish momentum, completing the trifecta by providing full directional coverage—up, down, or sideways.

The Flock O' Flies – Net Position Summary

Here's the completed Flock O' Flies position—a three-part setup with a bullish call fly, a neutral iron fly, and a bearish put fly. These three carefully positioned nets surround the price action and create multiple profit zones.

The total position results in a credit of $367, with a maximum risk of only $133. This means you're risking a small amount for three different ways to profit—upward, sideways, or downward movement.

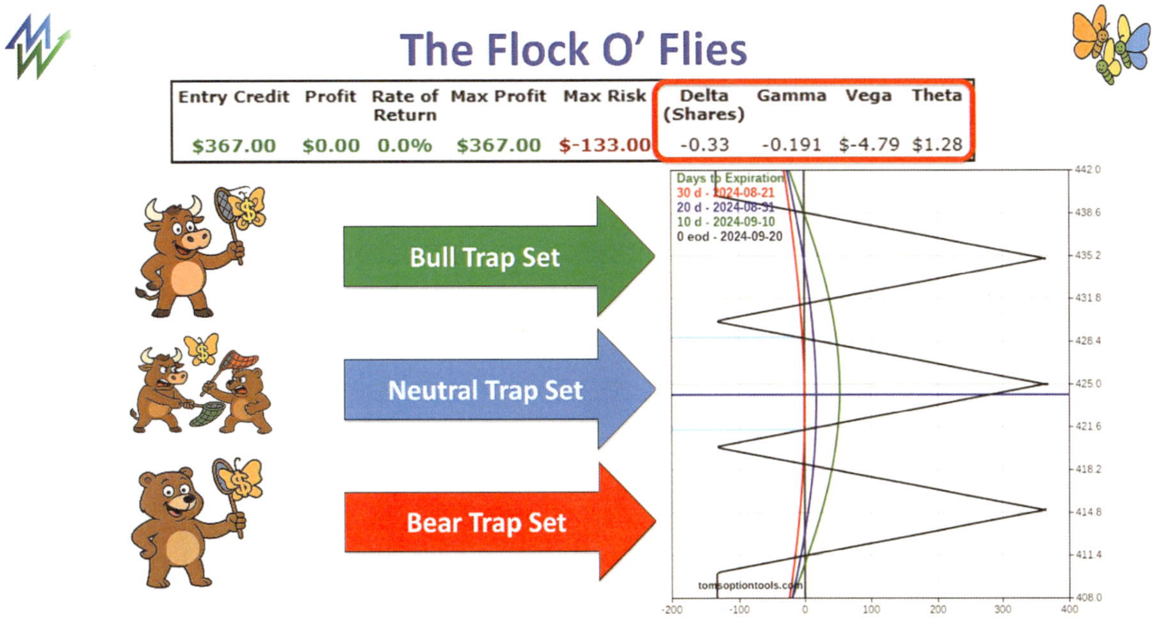

The combined position Greeks tell a powerful story:

- **Delta is close to zero (-0.33)** → This eans the position has nearly no directional bias.
- **Gamma is low (-0.191)** → Little change in Delta as the stock moves—a calm, controlled setup.
- **Vega is negative (-$4.79)** → The position benefits slightly from volatility contraction.
- **Theta is positive ($1.28)** → The position earns money with the passage of time.

Most importantly, the colored Theta lines on the risk graph indicate a stable risk profile during the first two-thirds of the trade's life. Directional risk is neutralized early, allowing time decay to work in your favor despite short-term market fluctuations. With all three traps set, your flock is in flight—ready to catch high-probability profits.

The Flock O' Flies at Expiration – Bullseye Hit!

It's expiration day—and the bullish fly hit the target! MSFT finished just above the center of our bullish butterfly, triggering the trap and locking in a $340 net profit on a position that only risked $133. That's a 255.6% return on risk.

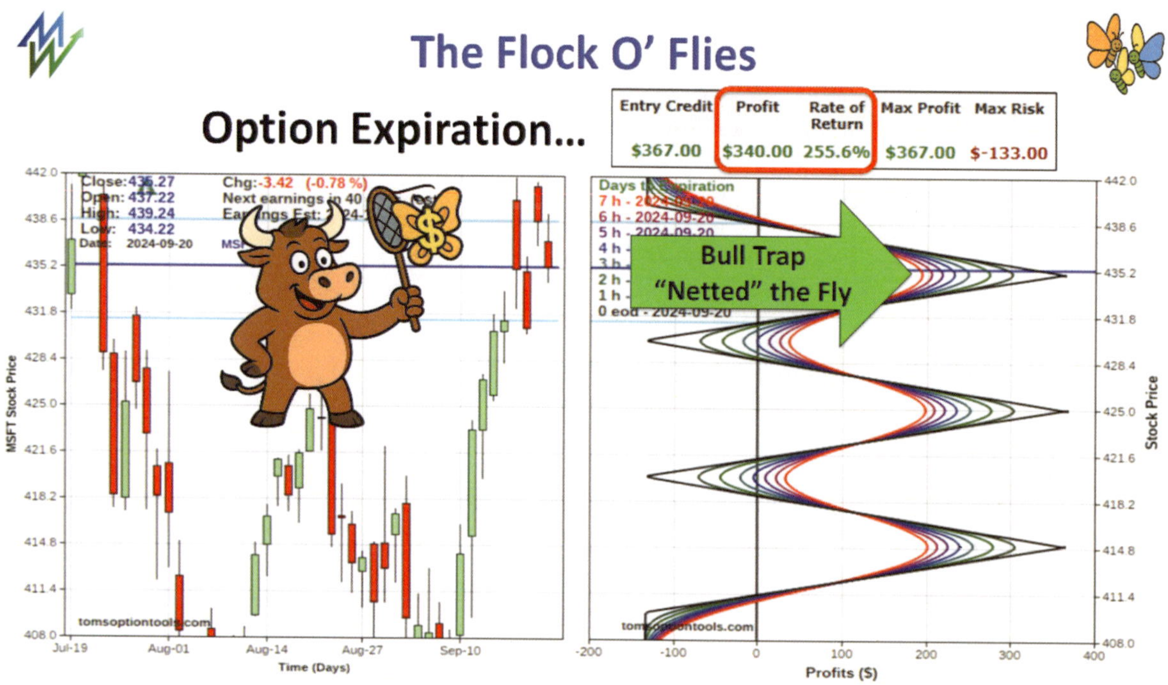

What if MSFT had gone the other way? No problem. The maximum loss was always capped at just $133 thanks to the defined-risk nature of the butterflies.

This result comes from a static flock setup—meaning no adjustments were made. Later in this chapter, we'll look at how active management and dynamic tweaks can boost results even more. For now, this straightforward win is a perfect example of why the Flock O' Flies is such a strong risk-controlled strategy—designed to profit without needing to predict any specific outcome.

Layering Flies Over Strike AND Time

Just when you believed the Flock O' Flies strategy couldn't get any more effective... there's still more to discover.

Besides stacking butterflies at various price points to form both directional and non-directional traps, you can also layer them across multiple expiration dates.

This approach introduces a new aspect of trade design. By combining expiration cycles, you gain:

- **Greater Theta decay collection at multiple points in time**
- **More chances to hit a profit zone**
- **The ability to adjust and reposition traps as time passes**

It's like layering nets along a jungle path, not just at one spot—but across the whole trail. The more structure you add, the greater the potential profit—all while managing limited, calculated risks.

In the next example, we'll show you exactly how this works—stacking butterflies across three expirations and different strikes to create a deep, multi-layered opportunity.

Case Study Setup – Bear Signal on ENPH

In this real-world case study, we focus on Enphase Energy (ENPH). The chart has shown a clear bearish signal after breaking below support on above-average volume.

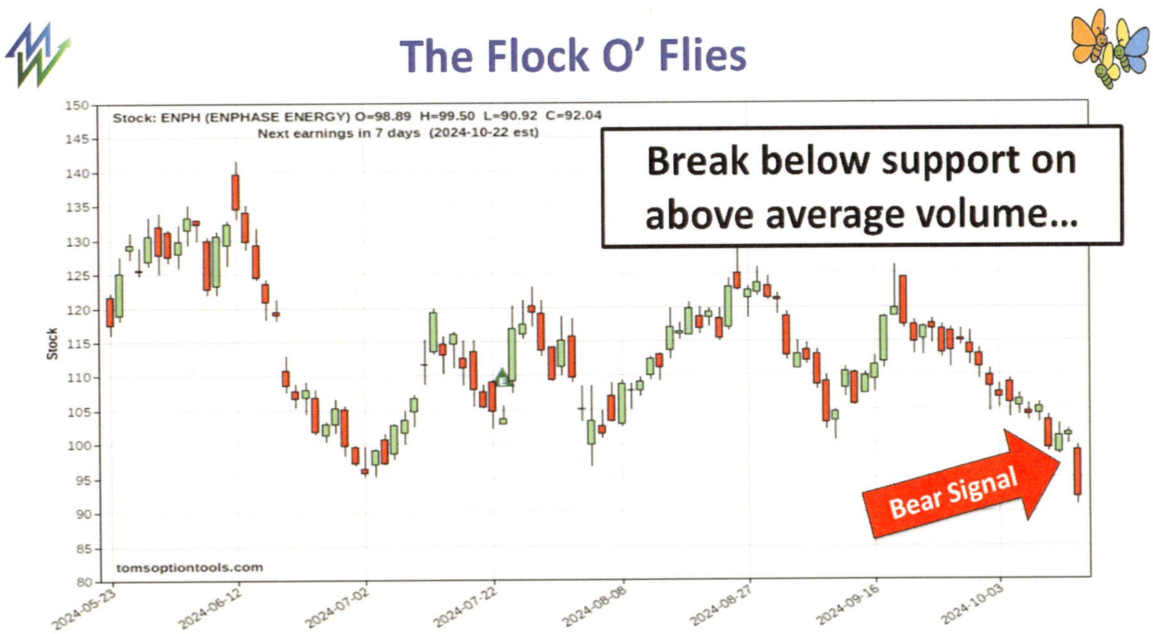

When volume spikes during a breakdown like this, it shows strong conviction by sellers—and that momentum might keep driving the price downward.

The timing is ideal:

- **The stock just broke below a key support zone**
- **Volume confirms the move**

We'll use this setup to show how to create a layered Flock O' Flies strategy for bearish follow-through—including expiration staggering and strike selection for optimal risk/reward.

OTM Put Butterfly #1 – Near-Term Trap

Our initial move in the ENPH bearish case study is to establish a near-term OTM put butterfly expiring in 31 days (Nov 15). This sets the first trap in our layered strategy—in line with the recent breakdown below support.

This butterfly is structured as follows:

- Buy 1 Nov 15 $80 Put
- Sell 2 Nov 15 $75 Puts
- Buy 1 Nov 15 $70 Put

The entry cost is $42, and the maximum possible profit is $458. That results in a reward-to-risk ratio over 10:1—an excellent setup for strong directional moves. As the stock declines, this butterfly positions us to profit if ENPH drops quickly toward the $75 range in the coming weeks.

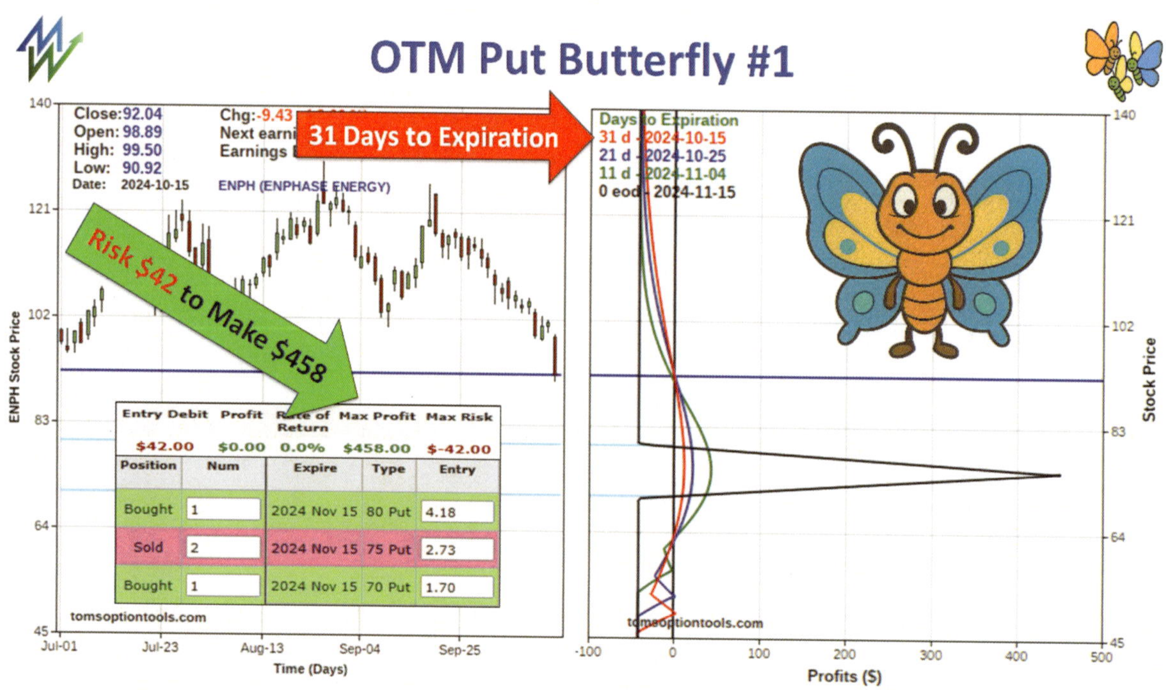

OTM Put Butterfly #2 – Further Out in Time, Further OTM

The second layer of our bearish ENPH strategy is a longer-dated, deeper Out-of-the-Money put butterfly. This fly expires in 66 days (Dec 20) and extends our coverage to lower prices and further out in time.

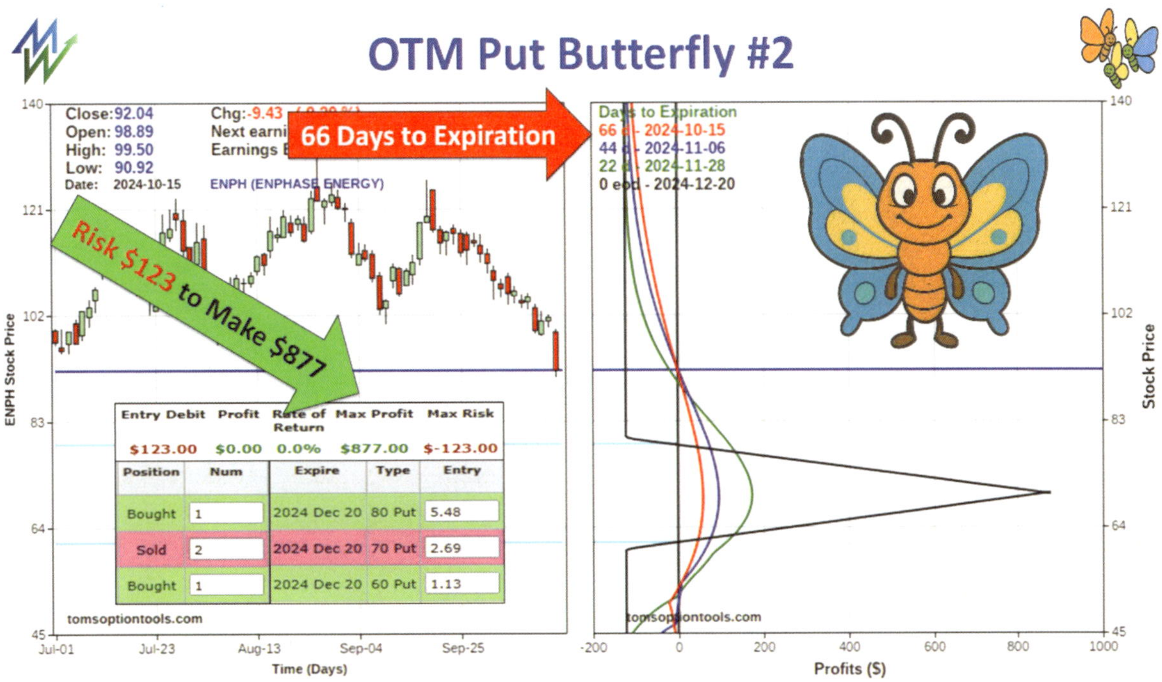

Here's the setup:

- Buy 1 Dec 20 $80 Put
- Sell 2 Dec 20 $70 Puts
- Buy 1 Dec 20 $60 Put

The entry cost is $123, with a maximum profit potential of $877—offering a strong reward-to-risk ratio of over 7:1. This second butterfly provides the trade with more time to develop and a profit zone further down the chart. It complements the first fly by adding duration and range, creating a more solid bearish position.

OTM Put Butterfly #3 – Deep OTM, Longest Duration

The third butterfly in our layered bearish ENPH setup is positioned further out of the money and farther in the future. It expires in 94 days on January 17, 2025, providing the broadest profit zone and the longest period for the price to move into the optimal range.

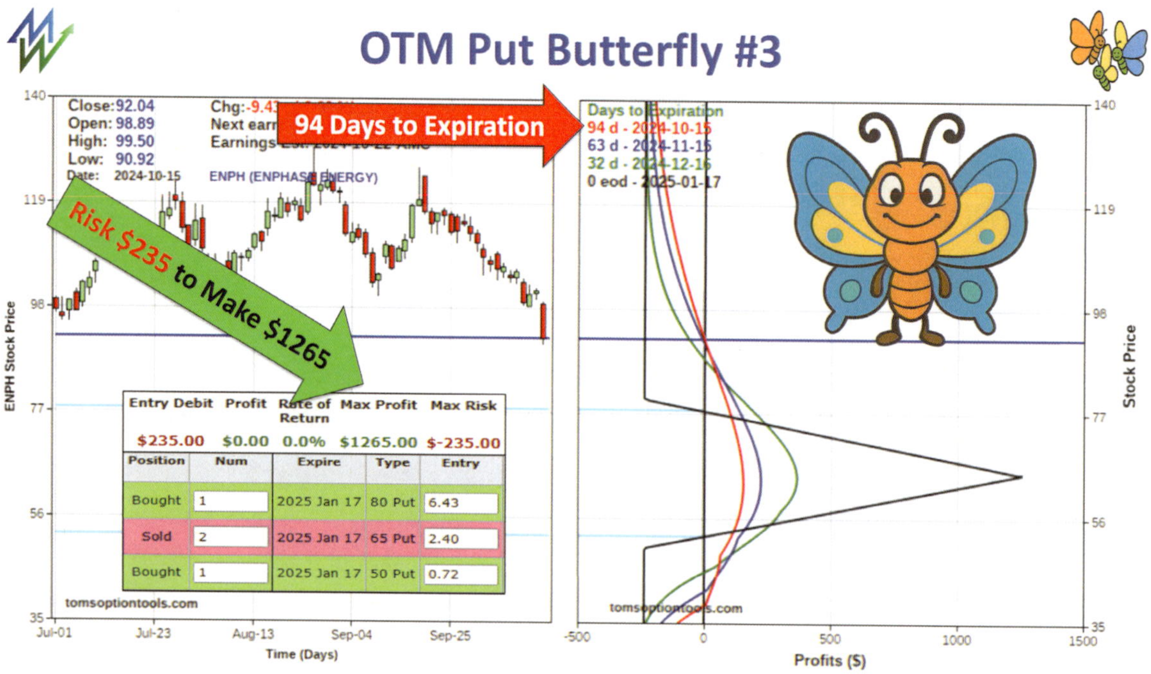

Here's the trade setup:

- Buy 1 Jan 17 $80 Put
- Sell 2 Jan 17 $65 Puts
- Buy 1 Jan 17 $50 Put

The total cost to enter is $235, with a potential maximum profit of $1,265—a very attractive reward-to-risk ratio of nearly 5.4 to 1. This third fly adds more depth to the overall flock, offering an extended profit range into early next year. It's the final wing in this multi-fly strategy, created to profit if ENPH continues to decline—especially if it takes time to unfold.

The Flock O' Flies – Final Numbers Recap

Here's the full picture: Three OTM Put Butterflies, all set as bearish traps over different expiration dates (31, 66, and 94 DTE). Each trade was built with a low-risk, high-reward setup, with risks ranging from \$42 to \$235 and maximum profits from \$458 up to \$1,265. Together, this layered approach across time and strike can generate up to \$2,600 in profit while risking only \$400 in total across all three trades.

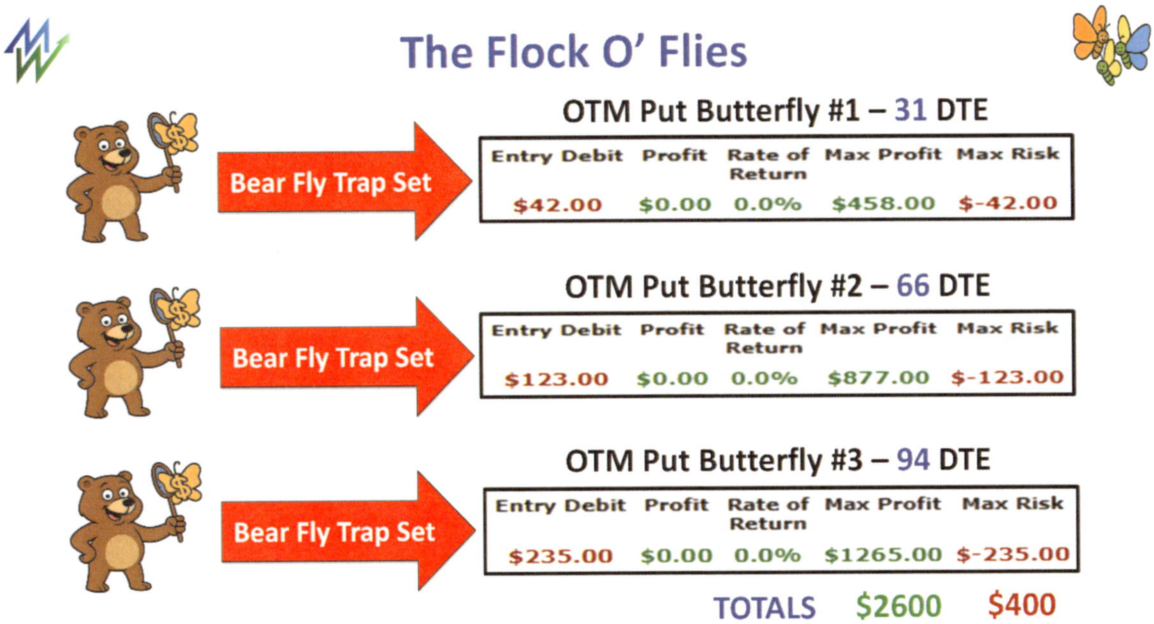

This is the strength of The Flock O' Flies: Shared risk, multiple chances to win, and strategic coverage that adjusts to market timing. Whether one, two, or all three trades succeed, you're equipped with power and protection.

The Flock O' Flies – 2 Lot Setup

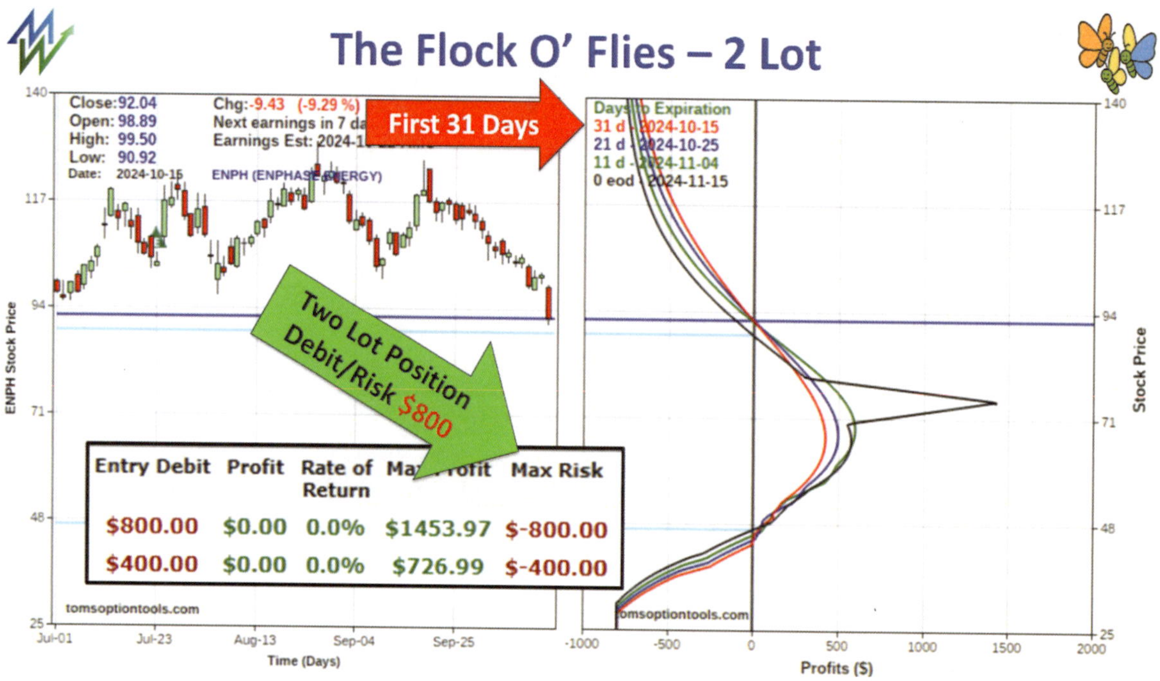

To kick off this campaign, we entered a 2-lot version of Fly #1. Why two lots? Simple: It provides more flexibility for adjustments later. With more contracts, we can partially unwind or tweak the position as needed—a key part of strategic maneuvering in advanced fly trading.

This first fly expires in 31 days, and we're risking $800 total across both lots. The chart shows the overall risk graph—illustrating how the position changes over time as we get closer to expiration. The red, green, blue, and black curves represent the changing profit/loss profile as days pass and time decay occurs.

Key Stats for the 2-Lot Setup:

- **Entry Debit:** $800.00
- **Max Profit:** $1,453.97
- **Max Risk:** $800.00
- **Rate of Return:** 0% (at setup, this will change)

With this structure in place, we're ready to watch, adjust, and capitalize as the market unfolds over the next month.

The Flock O' Flies – Fly #1, 15-Days into the Trade

We're officially halfway through the first leg of our Bear Fly setup, and something exciting has happened: Fly #1 has doubled in value—a 100% return with a gain of $84 on a $42 entry.

You can see in the risk graph that the stock has drifted toward our sweet spot, and with 16 days left to expiration, this is our cue: Time to Adjust!

We're sitting on unrealized profits, but the current shape of the risk curve makes us vulnerable. Without an adjustment, the stock could drift up and wipe out our gains.

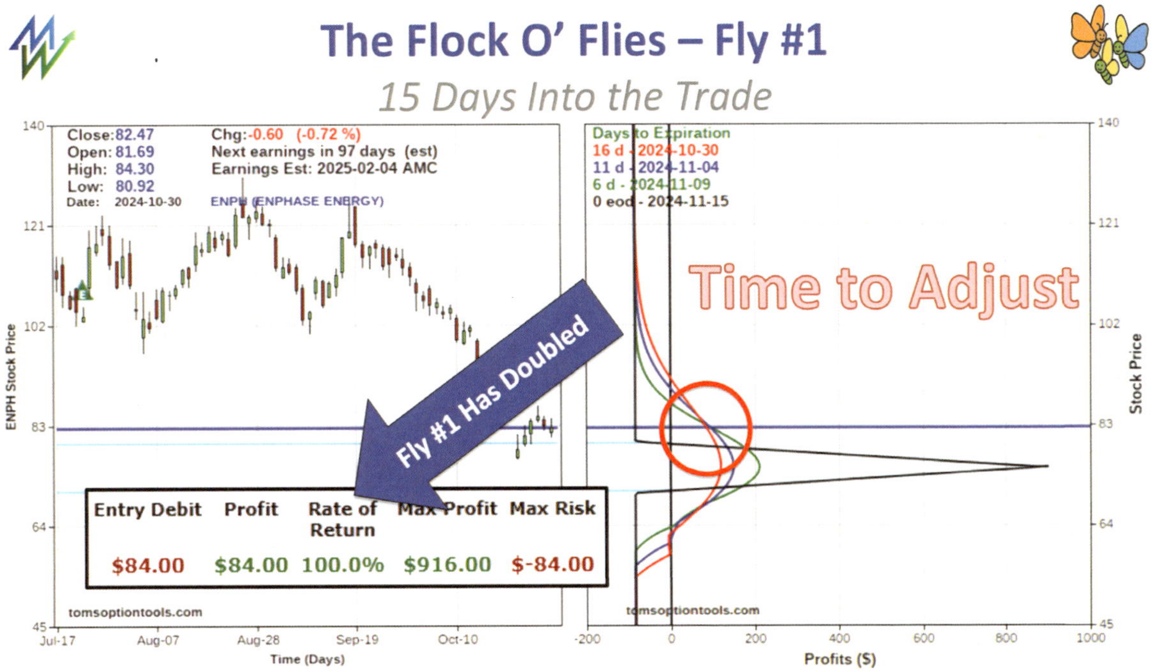

In short:

- **Entry debit:** $84
- **Current profit:** $84
- **Rate of return:** 100%
- **Max profit potential:** $916
- **Remaining risk if unadjusted:** $84

We're in an ideal position to lock in gains and adjust our stance. The next section will walk through the adjustment step and explain how we protect the win and stay in the game.

The Flock O' Flies – Fly #1: "House Money" Adjustment

Fifteen days into the trade, Fly #1 has already doubled in value.

The Flock O' Flies – Fly #1

15 Days Into the Trade…Close ½ at a Double

House Money Adjustment

Entry Debit at $0

Position	Num	Expire	Type	Entry
Bought	2	2024 Nov 15	80 Put	4.18
Sold	4	2024 Nov 15	75 Put	2.73
Bought	2	2024 Nov 15	70 Put	1.70
Sold	1	2024 Nov 15	80 Put	3.58
Bought	2	2024 Nov 15	75 Put	1.75
Sold	1	2024 Nov 15	70 Put	0.76

Entry Debit	Profit	Rate of Return	Max Profit	Min Profit
$0.00	$84.00	n/a	$500.00	$0.00

To lock in profits and reduce risk, we perform a classic "House Money" adjustment:

- We close half of the original position at twice the price, recovering our full entry debit of $84.
- That means we are now trading with the house's money—our remaining position has zero cost basis.
- The table shows the updated position after selling half of the fly. One of two contracts was closed, leaving one-lot equivalents to run.
- The updated debit entry is $0.00, with a guaranteed minimum profit of $0 and a maximum potential profit of $500.

This adjustment locks in gains while keeping the trade alive for additional upside—a zero-risk, all-reward opportunity.

The Flock O' Flies – Fly #1 Risk-Free "House Money" Adjustment

After locking in a 100% return on half of the position, we've now shifted to a house money setup, effectively eliminating all risk from the remaining trade.

This revised risk graph tells the full story:

- No matter what happens, this fly cannot lose.
- Maximum profit potential is still alive and well, even though we already took gains off the table.
- Theta is working in our favor, and we still maintain a defined reward zone.

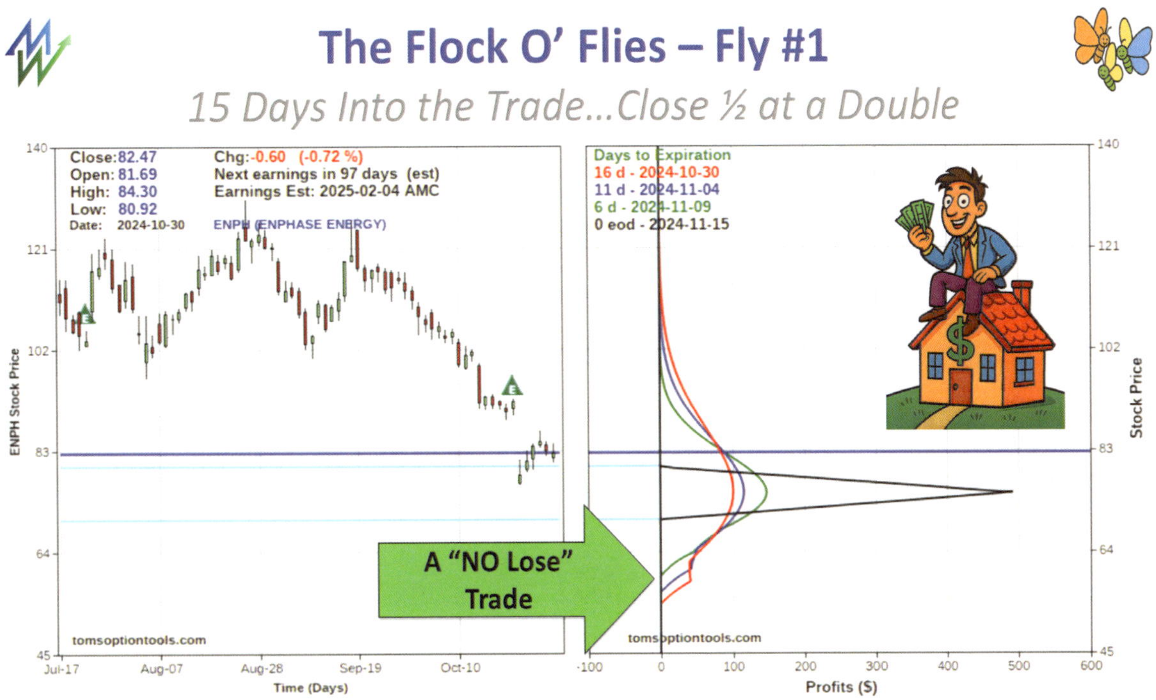

This is the ideal adjustment scenario:

- We've eliminated risk.
- We've locked in profit.
- We're still in the game.

Welcome to the power of risk-managed Flock O' Flies trading. Remember, we haven't checked on the other two flies that are also in profit.

The Flock O' Flies – Fly #1, 9-Days to Expiration

With just 9 days left until expiration, Fly #1 continues to perform well. The stock price has fallen further and is now within the body of the butterfly spread, prompting a second adjustment opportunity. We are showing an open profit of $131 with no risk on the trade due to the earlier "House Money" adjustment.

Since the stock is now near the peak profit zone, time decay will quickly impact the position over the final week. This is an ideal time to consider a follow-up adjustment to lock in gains or expand the profit zone, especially with the stock trading right inside the structure's body.

With $131 of profit, it's time to adjust!

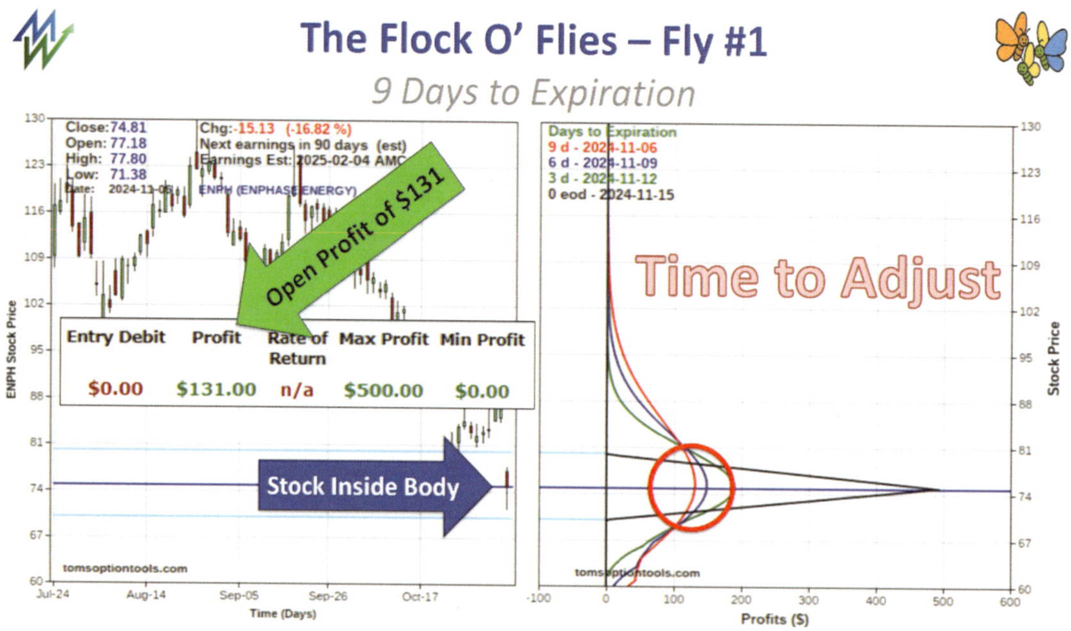

Fly #1 – "Cocoon the Fly" Adjustment (9-Days to Expiration)

With just over a week remaining and profits increasing, now is the time to reduce risk and secure gains—and we do it with a move you've seen before: The "Squeeze Play".

But this time, we double it.

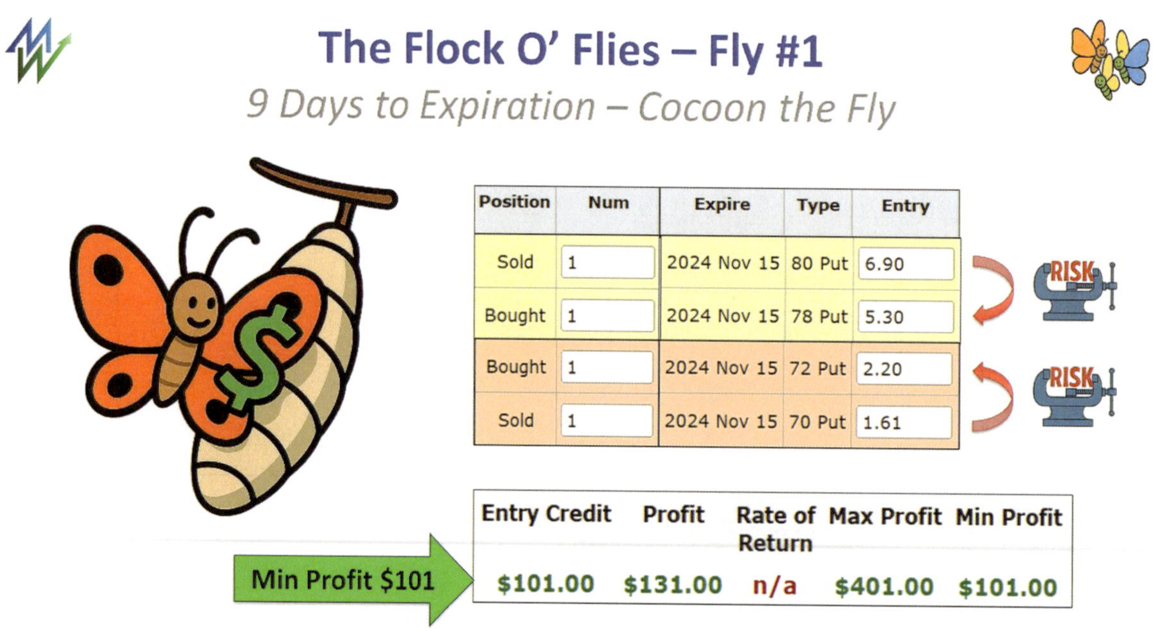

The "Cocoon the Fly" adjustment is just two "Squeeze Plays", one on each wing of the original butterfly. By tightening both sides, we reduce the risk while securing a guaranteed win.

Here's what we've done:

- On the **upper wing**, we converted the $80/$75 put spread into a tight $80/$78 put spread.
- On the **lower wing**, we adjusted the $75/$70 into a $72/$70 put spread.
- Both are classic **"Squeeze Plays"**—squeezing both spreads by $3

This results in a new trade structure that has:

- An entry credit of $101
- A minimum profit of $101, even if nothing else happens
- A maximum potential profit of $401 if the stock finishes near the center of the new zone

This is risk management at its best. We've cocooned the fly, protecting what we've earned and setting up a safe path to a strong finish.

The Flock O' Flies – Fly #1: Cocooned Risk Graph

With only 9 days left until expiration, our "Cocoon the Fly" adjustment has turned Fly #1 into a guaranteed winner. The latest risk graph shows that regardless of where the stock moves, this trade will turn a profit. The main move was reducing the risk with two "Squeeze Play" adjustments—one on each side—locking in a minimum profit while keeping the potential for more. This demonstrates the power of strategic adjustments: You now have a risk-free trade with a guaranteed outcome.

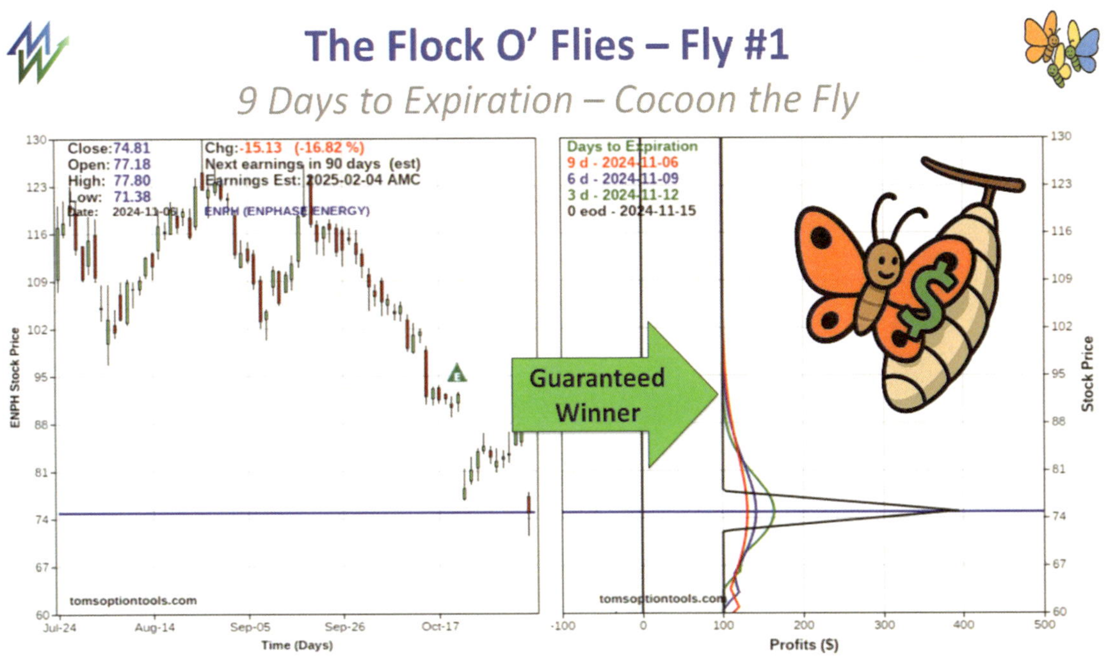

The Flock O' Flies – Fly #1 at Expiration

At expiration, Fly #1 yielded a guaranteed profit despite the underlying stock surpassing the target. Thanks to the earlier "Cocoon the Fly" adjustment, which secured a minimum profit, the trade closed with a solid gain.

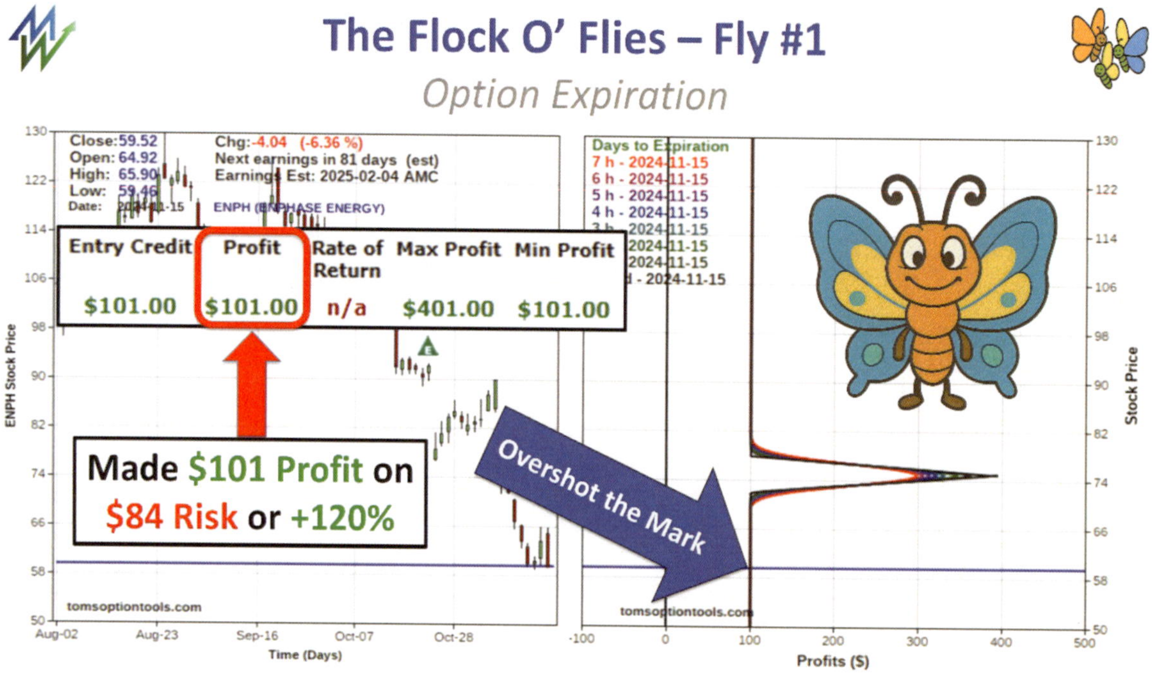

The final outcome:

- **Entry Credit:** $101.00
- **Profit:** $101.00
- **Maximum Profit Potential:** $401.00
- **Minimum Profit:** $101.00
- **Initial Risk (before adjustment):** $84.00
- **Final Return on Risk:** +120%

Although the stock dropped well below the body of the butterfly (highlighted on the chart as "Overshot the Mark"), the risk had already been minimized through the "Squeeze Play" method. This adjustment turned the trade into a "No Lose" scenario with guaranteed profit, exemplifying proactive risk management.

The Flock O' Flies – Fly #1 (No Adjustments)

In this final slide, we see what would have happened if no adjustments were made to Fly #1.

The stock greatly overshot the downside, closing well below the target range at $59.52. With no defensive action taken, the original butterfly expired worthless, resulting in a total loss of the entry debit.

Loss: $84 on $84 Risk, representing a -100% return.

This emphasizes the importance of timely adjustments. Compared to the $101 profit gained earlier through cocooning, it shows how crucial proactive management is. Without it, even a well-constructed setup can lead to maximum loss.

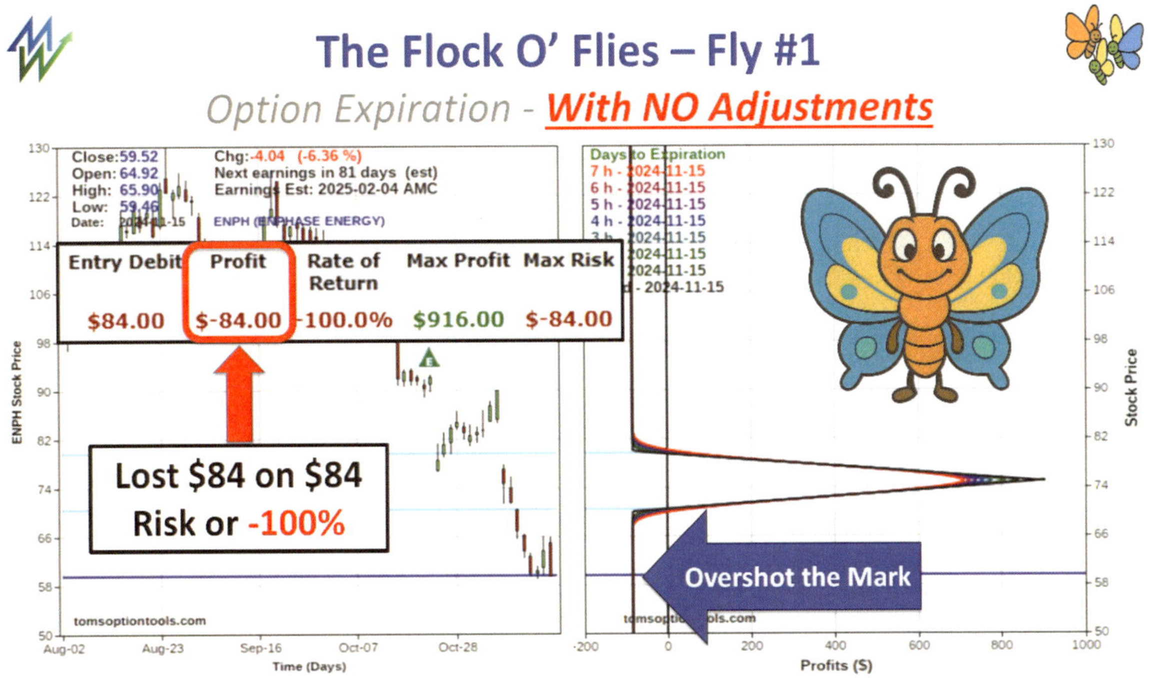

The Flock O' Flies – Final Results Comparison

This concluding section summarizes everything. It compares the results of the Flock O' Flies trade, both with and without adjustments, at the expiration of Fly #1.

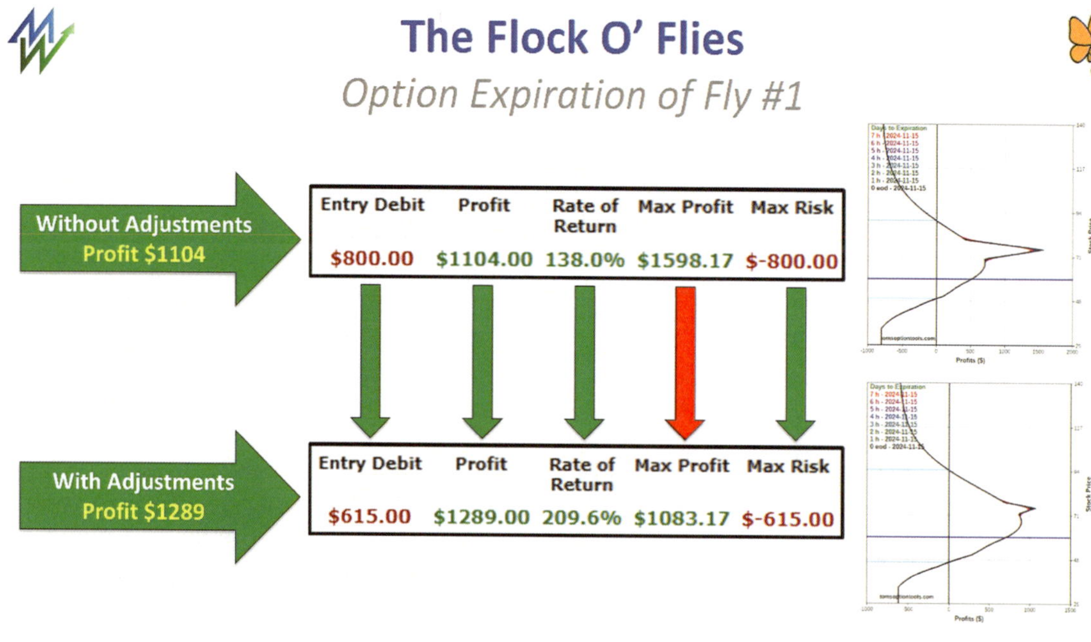

Without Adjustments:

- The composite position made a strong $1,104 profit on an $800 risk.
- Max return potential was $1,598.17 with a 138% rate of return.

With Adjustments:

- The profit jumped to $1,289 on a reduced risk of $615.
- This pushed the return up to an impressive 209.6%.
- Although max profit was reduced slightly, the overall profit and risk/reward were better.

This shows the power of managing trades as a group. While Fly #1 overshooting its target, the other two flies in the group stayed within their profit zones, driving outstanding results. Smart adjustments resulted in higher net profit and reduced risk. That's the benefit of trading with layers, adjustments, and a solid game plan.

The Flock O' Flies – Option Expiration of Fly #3

We've already seen the final outcome of Fly #1, including how we managed the trade with adjustments like the "House Money" and "Cocoon the Fly" adjustments. Fly #2 and Fly #3 followed the same playbook of dynamic adjustment. We won't show all the steps again here, but the adjustment logic used for Fly #1 was applied similarly to the other flies.

Now, let's review the final outcome of Fly #3: It expired with a total profit of $1,843 on a $619 entry cost, delivering a +230% return. This trade was managed with layered risk control, and even during drawdowns, our minimum profit since November 7 never fell below $134. This result in the below image demonstrates the effectiveness of strategic adjustments and risk-layered butterfly deployment.

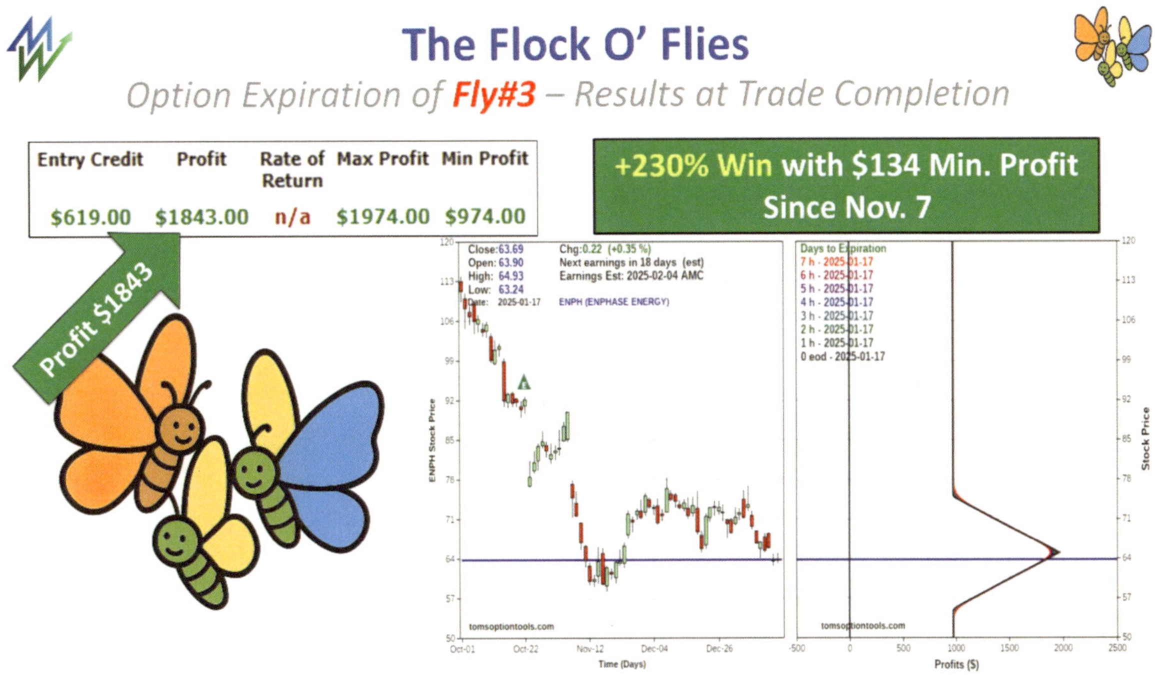

The Flock O' Flies – Guidelines to Consider

Use GTC Orders for "House Money" Adjustments: As soon as a trade is filled, set Good 'Til Canceled (GTC) orders to close half or more of each Fly at a 100% profit. This secures early gains and turns the trade into a "House Money" adjustment, meaning the remaining position has no cost basis.

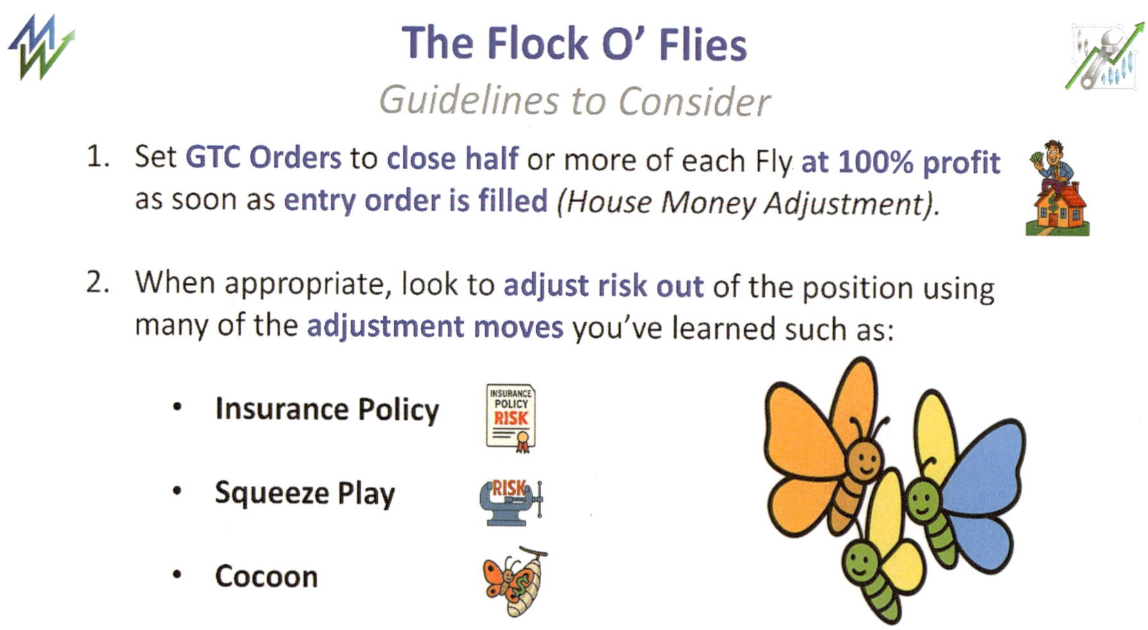

Actively Manage Risk Through Strategic Adjustments: When the timing is right, seek opportunities to reduce risk in the trade using known adjustments, such as:

- **Insurance Policy** – Add protection to guard against adverse moves.
- **Squeeze Play** – Reduce exposure and compress directional risk.
- **Cocoon the Fly** – Lock in profit and eliminate further downside by compressing both wings.

These guidelines help turn trades from high potential into likely winners, aligning with the overall strategy of building low-risk, high-reward trades across multiple targets.

Chapter Summary – The Flock O' Flies Strategy

In this chapter, we examined how to use multiple butterfly spreads—layered across strike prices and expiration dates—to create a flexible, high-reward, low-risk structure called The Flock O' Flies.

You learned how to:

- **Set directional and non-directional traps** using bullish, neutral, and bearish butterflies

- **Layer flies over time** to stay in the game longer while increasing opportunity
- Use the **"House Money"** adjustment by closing half at a 100% gain, locking in a free trade
- Deploy the **"Cocoon the Fly"** adjustment, which combines two "Squeeze Plays" to compress risk out of both wings and guarantee a win

Through the ENPH case study, we observed how:

- One fly overshot the mark, but adjustments turned a loser into a winner
- Layering flies across expirations enabled the other two flies to deliver outsized returns
- The full position, when adjusted properly, outperformed the unadjusted version by both profit and return on risk

Finally, we concluded with clear guidelines to ensure this strategy is repeatable, manageable, and scalable.

The key takeaway? When built and managed correctly, a Flock O' Flies provides you with time, range, and resilience—enabling you to turn a profit in volatile conditions while reducing downside risk.

Now that we're dancing with multiple spread structures, it's time to add another adjustment to your arsenal that will greatly increase your risk management and probability of profit capabilities: **The "Pull a Wing Off" Adjustment**.

CHAPTER 30

THE "PULL A WING OFF" ADJUSTMENT

CHAPTER 30
The "Pull a Wing Off" Adjustment

Sometimes, the smartest adjustment you can make is the simplest one.

When you're trading structures like butterflies, condors, butterfly pairs, or FlyCals, your position is made up of two wings—one on each side. These wings set your risk limits. But guess what?

You don't have to keep both wings.

When directional risk begins to rise—or when your trade leans decisively to one side—you can reduce the risk and pull a wing off.

Just like a butterfly with one wing tucked in and one wing extended, your trade becomes more agile, more adaptive, and often safer.

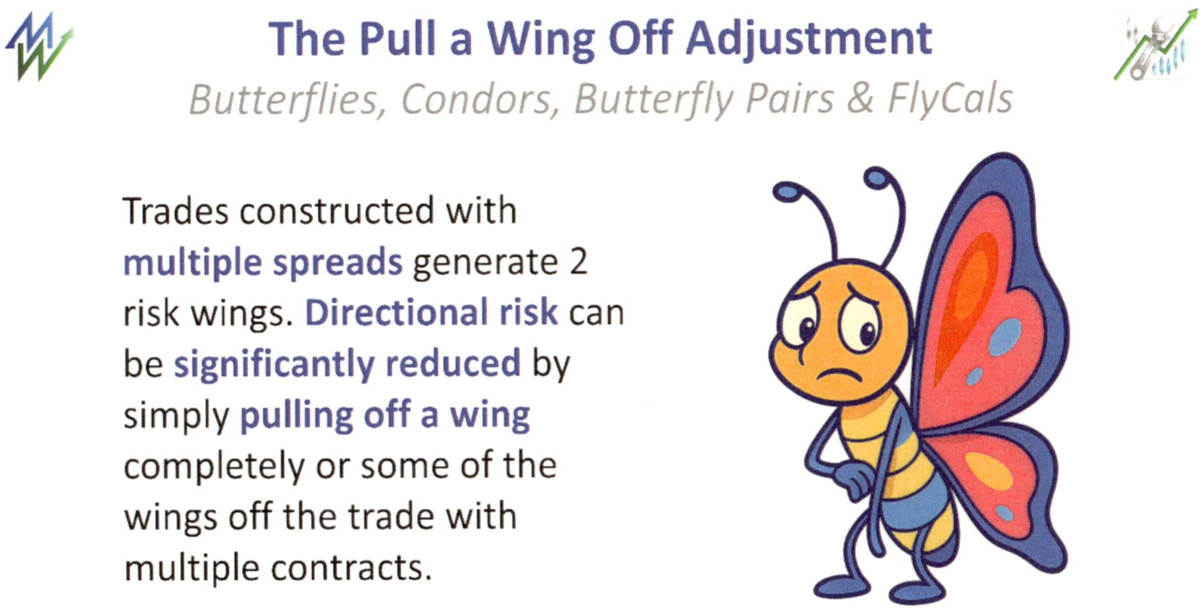

What This Adjustment Does

The "Pull a Wing Off" adjustment allows you to:

- Reduce directional risk when the trade is leaning too hard in one direction
- Remove one side of exposure in multi-leg trades
- Adapt a balanced trade into a skewed but safer structure

By simply selling off one of the wings, or some of the contracts on that side, you shift the risk/reward profile of the position and give yourself more control.

When to Use It

Use this adjustment when:

- You've got multiple spreads creating a multi-winged structure like butterflies, condors, double-wide calendars and FlyCals which will be covered later.
- The trade is shifting toward one side
- You want to stay in the trade, but remove risk from the losing side
- You're working with multiple contracts and can peel off a portion

Gameboard Tip

In the adjustment chess game, this is like sacrificing a pawn on the weak side of the board to strengthen your queen's attack. You're not giving up the whole trade. You're just removing vulnerability and sharpening your edge.

"Pull a Wing Off" – Strategy Profile

Description

The "Pull a Wing Off" adjustment can be applied to any trade involving multiple spreads—most often butterflies, condors, butterfly pairs, or FlyCals. The main purpose of these structures is usually to keep Delta flat while earning positive Theta within a broad profit zone.

This adjustment is simple: You remove one side (a wing) of the trade, either completely or partially, especially when you hold multiple contracts.

Strategies

- Butterflies
- Condors
- Butterfly Pairs

- FlyCals (to be demonstrated in the next chapter)

Outcome

By removing a wing, you:

- Reduce directional risk
- Lower total position risk
- Allow positive Theta to do its job with less interference from unwanted Delta drift

This move is primarily about shifting weight away from the "wrong" side, especially when your trade strongly favors one direction.

Timing

Ideal timing is when:

- Delta and Gamma are increasing, signaling directional exposure
- The market breaks away from one wing and is unlikely to return
- Support/resistance levels or other technical signals suggest the trade won't re-balance naturally

The Pull a Wing Off Adjustment

Description: *The Pull a Wing Off adjustment can be applied to any trade constructed with multiple spreads. Multiple spreads are typically applied to create a wide profit zone in which the trade will profit. The game is usually to keep delta flat while maximizing positive Theta. This adjustment can be applied to the entire wing of the trade or partially for wings with multiple contracts.*

Strategies: *Butterflies, Condors, Butterfly Pairs and FlyCals*

Outcome: *Pulling a wing off a multi-spread trade reduces directional risk, total trade risk and allows positive theta to collect time decay benefits less encumbered by directional risk. Delta risk can be easily reduced with this adjustment.*

Timing: *Apply this adjustment as delta and gamma start to grow (indicating magnified directional risk) and the stock has less likelihood of moving into the losing wing of the trade. Use support and resistance breaks or other technical indicators to trigger this adjustment.*

Summary – Simplify to Regain Control

This adjustment is about **reducing complexity when needed**.

"Pull a Wing Off" shows how to take a multi-leg structure—like a butterfly—and **remove one side to reshape the position**. When the trade is no longer behaving as intended, simplifying and/or reducing the structure can restore flexibility and control.

The key idea:
You don't have to manage complexity—sometimes you remove it.

By pulling a wing, you:

- Reduce structural constraints
- Adapt to directional movement
- Reposition the trade with more flexibility

This move is especially useful when one side of the trade is no longer contributing or is creating unnecessary risk.

The deeper takeaway:
Adjustments aren't just about adding. They're about removing what no longer works.

Now that you can simplify and reshape a position, the final step is climbing to the top of the trading mountain and learning a hybrid structure that combines alternate spread types to elegantly align IV prognosis with Vega: **The "FlyCal"**.

CHAPTER 31

THE FLYCAL

CHAPTER 31
The FlyCal

Let's combine two of our top strategies: The Butterfly and the Calendar Spread.

This strategic combo is known as the FlyCal.

Here's why it's so powerful:

- Butterflies give us defined risk and directional targeting.
- Calendar Spreads bring Vega power and flexibility across time.

When paired, the FlyCal becomes a broad, high-probability net, with Vega tuned to direction and many adjustment options.

It's like setting a wide trap that doesn't just catch the target. It adapts as the target moves.

We will approach this strategy like a chess match: Setup, adaptability, and strategic responses to your opponent's moves.

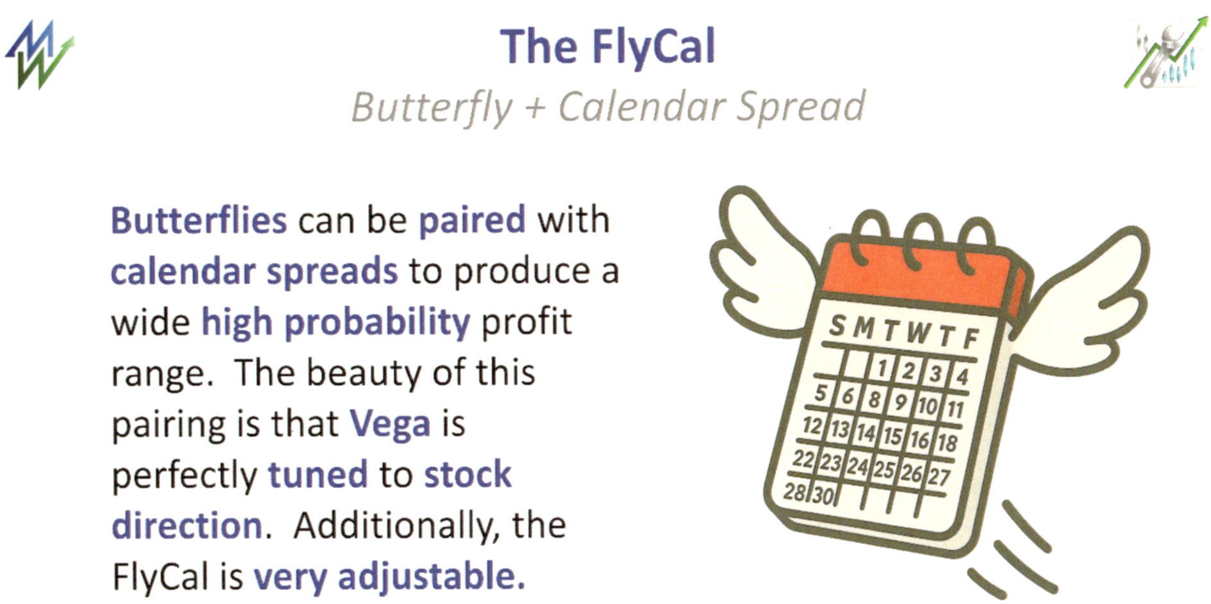

Think of the FlyCal as the top-of-the-mountain strategy. It's sleek. It's refined. And it offers a wide range of adjustment options. If you love to tweak—if that's your thing—then this strategy is going to feel like home. This is the playground for advanced player's, where flexibility and control meet in perfect harmony.

The FlyCal Strategy Overview

The FlyCal is a hybrid options strategy that combines a butterfly spread with a calendar spread to form a wide, high-probability profit zone. Typically, the structure pairs a bullish OTM broken-wing butterfly (BWB) with a bearish OTM calendar spread.

The FlyCal

Description:	*The FlyCal strategy is a combination of a butterfly and a calendar spread. Typically, they are constructed with a bullish OTM broken-wing butterfly (BWB) and a bearish OTM calendar spread.*
Strategies:	*OTM call butterflies, OTM call BWBs and OTM Put Calendar Spreads.*
Outcome:	*Similar to flocks of butterflies, the FlyCal produces a positive theta trade with a wide profit zone producing a high probability of profit. The secret sauce is that the OTM call butterfly offers –Vega and the OTM put calendar spread offers +Vega, tuning Vega to anticipated IV movement, harnessing the power of Vega within the body of the FlyCal.*
Timing:	*Usually, both the butterfly and the calendar are placed on trade inception. However, calendars and butterflies can be added to a trade to form a FlyCal during the life of the trade.*

Strategies Used

- OTM call butterflies
- OTM call BWBs
- OTM put calendar spreads

Outcome

Much like a flock of butterflies, the FlyCal constructs a positive Theta trade with a wide profit range and a high probability of winning. The key is in how Vega is tuned: The OTM call butterfly adds negative Vega, while the OTM put calendar adds positive Vega. This allows traders to precisely tune Vega to match expected changes in implied volatility, concentrating its effect precisely inside the FlyCal structure.

Timing

FlyCals are often built at trade inception, but calendars and butterflies can also be layered later to form a FlyCal mid-trade, offering flexibility and adaptability as market conditions shift.

BWBs: Profiting on Delta, Vega & Theta

Here's where the true power of the bullish broken-wing butterfly (BWB) shines. The chart on the left shows the BWB's risk profile at trade inception—balanced, calculated, and ready.

But look at the right chart, and it's clear: This is not just a one-dimensional play. The BWB is firing on all cylinders—profiting from Delta, Vega, and Theta simultaneously.

- **Delta?** You've got a strong positive push as the stock rises.
- **Theta?** You're collecting time decay like a pro.
- **Vega?** It's negative—and that's exactly what we want. As the stock moves higher, implied volatility usually drops… and -Vega loves that.

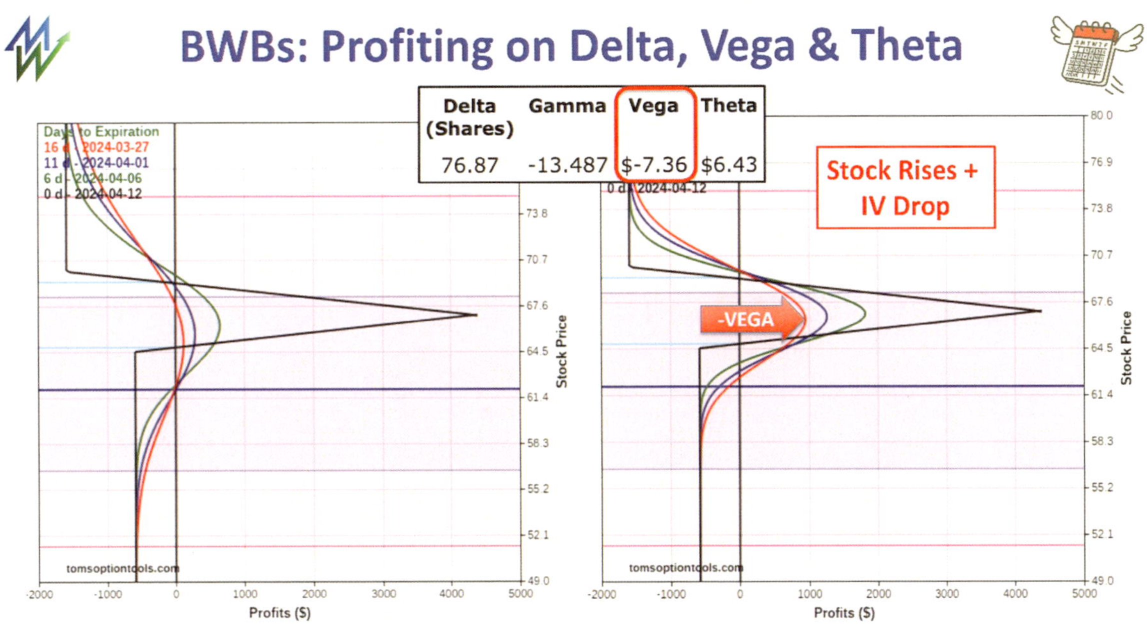

This is a triple-threat strategy—price, time, and implied volatility are all working in your favor. The BWB doesn't just ride the market. It surfs it.

This is your foundational level in FlyCal: A profit engine built on smart design. And when paired with the right calendar wing (as shown in the image below), the symphony becomes even sweeter.

Calendars: Profiting on Delta, Vega & Theta

The chart on the left displays an Out-of-the-Money (OTM) Put Calendar spread at trade inception. Notice the strong positive Vega, which positions this trade to benefit from a rise in implied volatility (IV). Calendars perform well in environments where implied volatility increases and time advances. They're Theta monsters and Vega warriors.

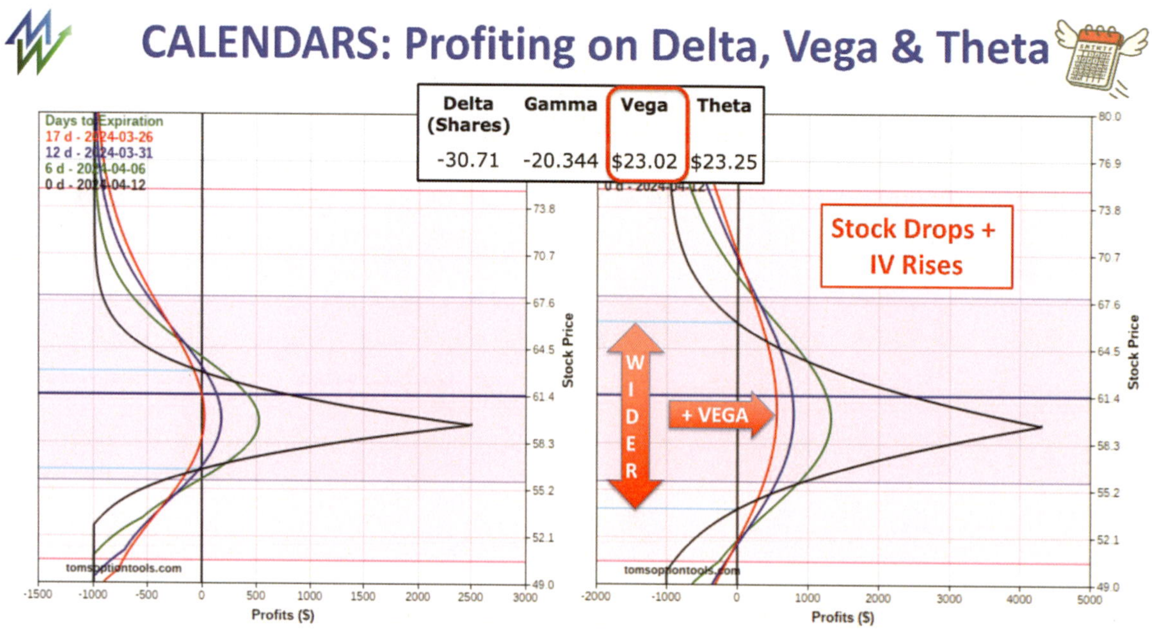

Now, turn your attention to the chart on the right contained in the image shown above. Should the stock drop coupled with the usual IV rush, magic happens. When IV rises, a calendar doesn't just make more money. It spreads its wings. The risk graph actually expands, widening the breakevens and increasing the probability of profit. It's like a parachute that opens wider as the fall gets steeper. Couple that with +Theta and numerous adjustment moves, you're harnessing the Greeks like a pro.

TQQQ FlyCal Construction – A Live Example

This graphic gives us a perfect look under the hood at how a FlyCal is built in real-time.

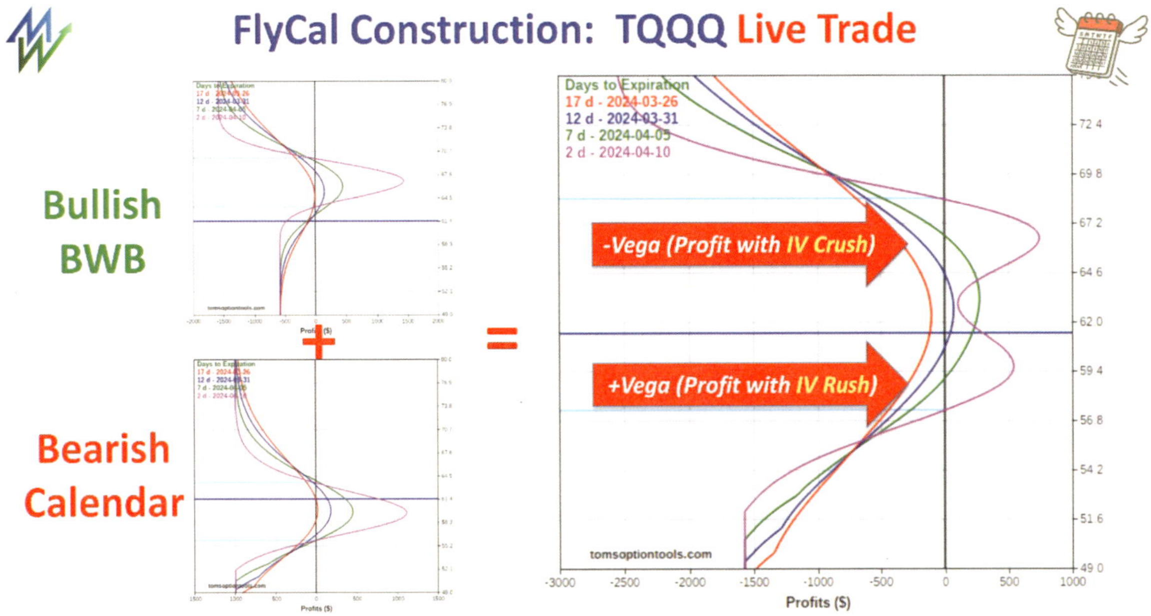

We start with two distinct components:

- A **Bullish Broken-Wing Butterfly (BWB)** positioned above the current price. This setup benefits from positive Delta, positive Theta, and especially when implied volatility (IV) decreases—due to its -Vega component.
- A **Bearish Put Calendar Spread**, positioned further below. This spread is designed to benefit from negative Delta, positive Theta, and positive Vega—making it ideal for rising IV.

Now, here's the key: When we combine the BWB and Calendar into a single position, we get the full FlyCal payoff structure.

- A wide range of profitability
- Theta grinding in our favor
- Vega working both ways:
  - The upper BWB profits from an IV crush
  - The lower calendar profits from an IV rush

That dual-Vega engine provides us with the ideal Vega tuning fork, enabling us to profit no matter what happens with implied volatility—as long as we stay within the game board.

This is the FlyCal strategy in action: Elegant, powerful, and fully customizable.

TQQQ FlyCal – Live Trade Construction

This FlyCal live trade combines a Bullish Broken-Wing Butterfly (BWB) with a Bearish Put Calendar, stacking the Greeks and the probabilities in our favor.

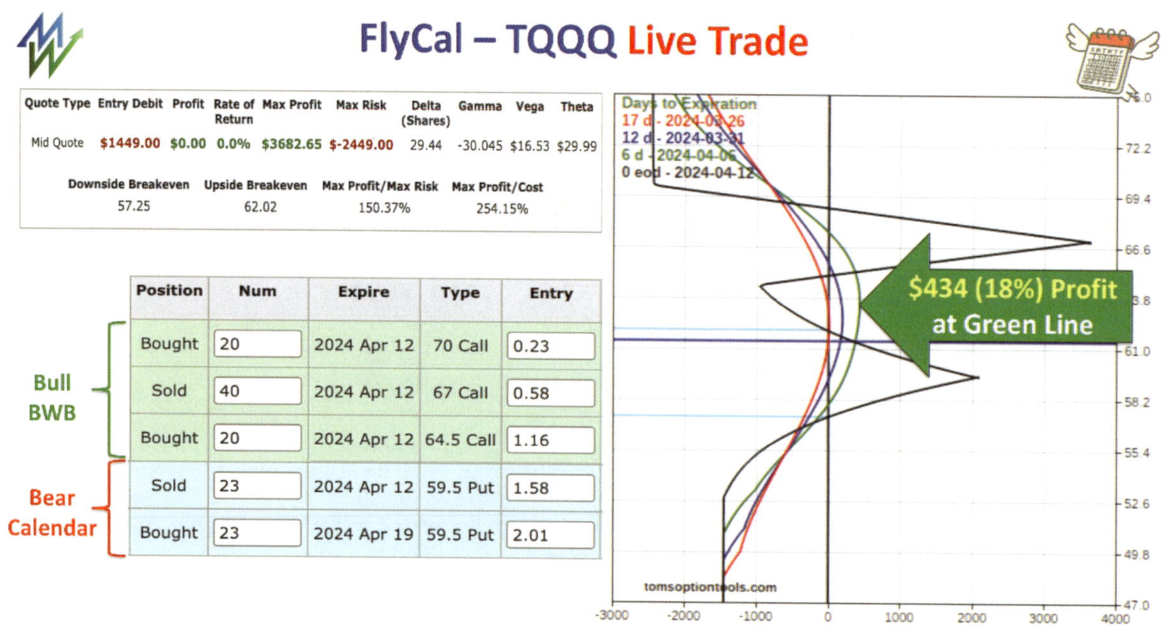

Here's how it's constructed:

Bullish Call BWB (April 12 expiration):

- Buy 20 contracts of the $70 Call at $0.23
- Sell 40 contracts of the $67 Call at $0.58
- Buy 20 contracts of the $64.5 Call at $1.16

Bearish Put Calendar:

- Sell 23 contracts of the April 12 $59.5 Put at $1.58
- Buy 23 contracts of the April 19 $59.5 Put at $2.01

This pairing creates a balanced FlyCal with positive Theta, moderate Delta, and a mixed Vega profile: -Vega from the BWB and +Vega from the calendar, offering flexibility to capture Vega profits from implied volatility changes.

At the green line (which shows the trade's P/L picture with 2/3 of the life of the trade elapsed), the trade displays a $434 profit, representing an 18% return on the $1,449 risked after 11 days into the life of the trade. This strategic setup not only provides directional bias and an edge, but also the ability to adapt and optimize over time.

TQQQ FlyCal Live Trade Getting Hot – Time to Adjust

We're 9 days into the life of our TQQQ FlyCal, and suddenly—April 4 hits with a hard move to the downside. The stock falls nearly 5%, from $62.35 to $57.82, moving right into the danger zone of our lower breakeven.

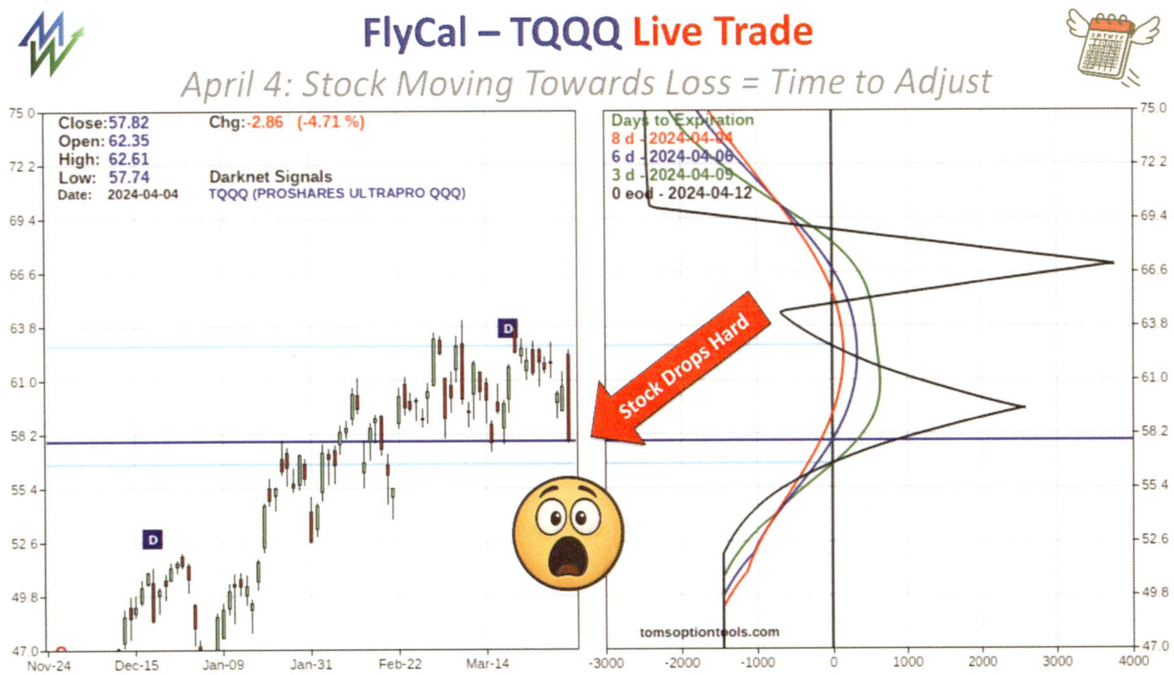

On the risk graph, that move places us squarely inside the bottom wing. And just like in chess, when your opponent suddenly brings out the queen and threatens your king, you don't freeze. You adapt.

Here's where the game gets fun:

- Our FlyCal strategy was designed to dance with Delta, Theta, and Vega.
- But when the board shifts fast, we've got to make a move, not just wait it out.
- This drop is our signal to pivot—before the edge of the profit zone turns into a trap.

Bottom line: This trade isn't over yet—but it's getting hot. It's time to make our move, adjust our pieces, and play defense like a pro.

TQQQ FlyCal Live Trade: Step 1 – Pull off a Wing Adjustment

Step 1: Pull Off the Fly Wing

As the stock dropped sharply and directional risk became too intense to manage, it was time to make the first adjustment: Close the BWB ("Pull a Wing Off" adjustment).

Action Taken:

Sold the BWB for a $120 credit, removing the wing on the call side of the FlyCal.

FlyCal – TQQQ Live Trade

Step 1: Pull Off (Close) the Fly

Sell the Fly

Sold	20	2024 Apr 12	70 Call	0.03
Bought	40	2024 Apr 12	67 Call	0.08
Sold	20	2024 Apr 12	64.5 Call	0.19

$120 Credit

$1,120 Risk Reduction

Remaining Position: Calendar

Entry Debit	Profit	Rate of Return	Max Profit	Max Risk
$1329.00	$-156.00	-11.7%	$2707.41	$-1329.00

Position	Num	Expire	Type	Entry
Sold	23	2024 Apr 12	59.5 Put	1.58
Bought	23	2024 Apr 19	59.5 Put	2.01

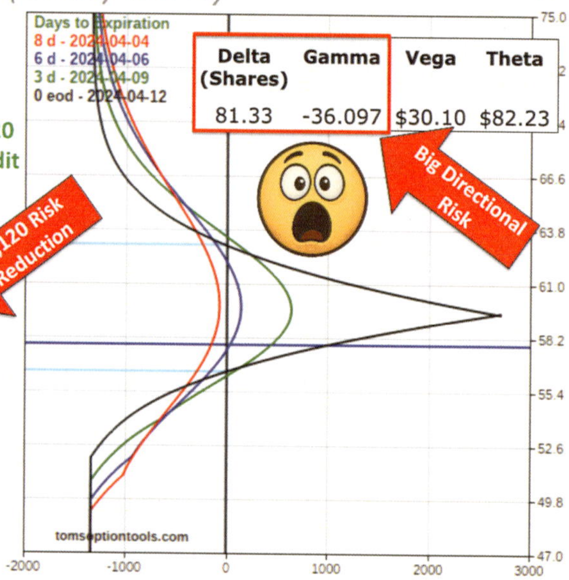

Result:

- Reduced total risk exposure by $1,120.
- Removed the bullish Delta-heavy component, which was stacking up directional risk.
- What remained was the bearish calendar spread, now standing alone.

Remaining Position – Calendar

- **Entry Debit:** $1,329.00
- **Current Profit:** -$156.00
- **Max Profit:** $2,707.41
- **Max Risk:** $1,329.00

Greeks (now calendar only):

- **Delta:** 81.33 (still bullish and needs further adjusting)
- **Gamma:** -36.097
- **Vega:** +$30.10 (IV friendly)
- **Theta:** +$82.23 (time decay working for us)

This step was all about damage control and strategic positioning—removing the first piece from the chessboard to prevent a wipeout and prepare for the next move.

TQQQ FlyCal Live Trade: Step 2 – Move the Catcher's Mitt Adjustment

With the stock falling sharply, it's time for Step 2 of the FlyCal adjustment: We "Move the Catcher's Mitt"—our calendar—from the $59.5 strike to the $58.5 strike.

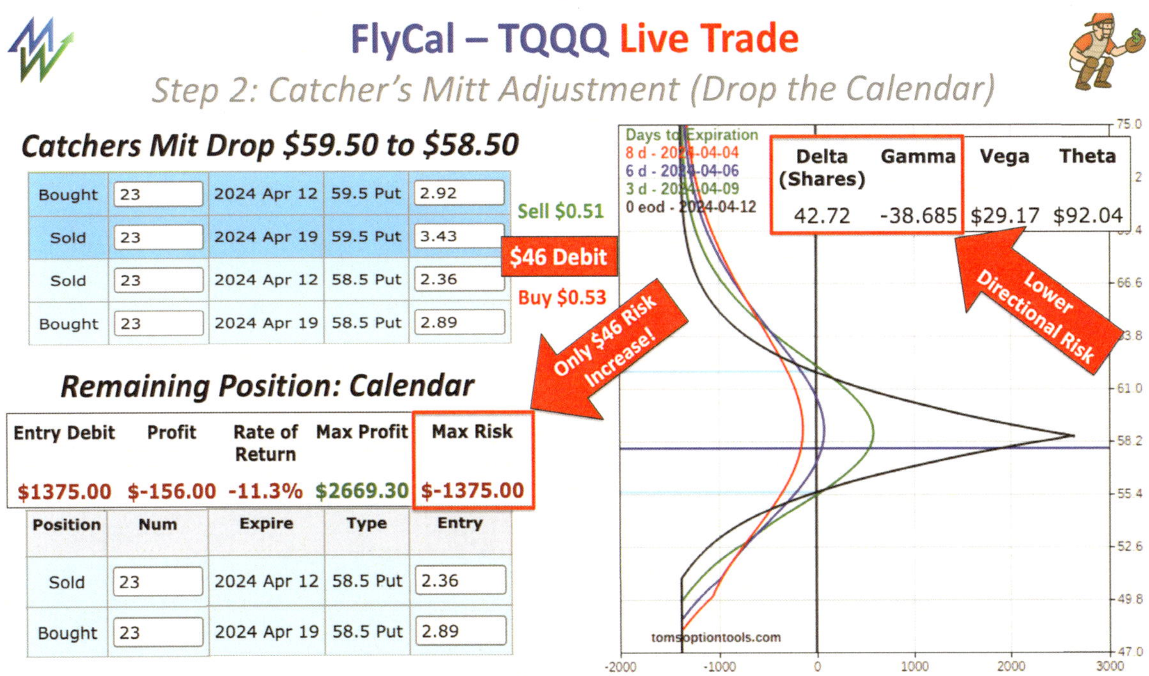

With the stock dropping hard, it's time for Step 2 of the FlyCal adjustment: We shift the catcher's mitt—our calendar—down from the $59.5 strike to the $58.5 strike.

We closed the existing calendar (buying back the Apr 12/Apr 19 $59.5 Put Calendar) for a $0.51 credit and opened a new one at $58.5 for a $0.53 debit, resulting in a total cost of just $46.

Why is this so powerful?

- The move recenters the trade at the new price level, realigning our Greeks for the new reality.
- We retain strong +Vega and +Theta, while reducing Delta from 81.33 to 42.72, cutting down our directional risk substantially.
- All this for a minimal $46 risk increase.

Net result:

We now have a more well-centered, better-protected trade, positioned for sustained profit even in a fluctuating market.

TQQQ FlyCal Live Trade: Big Directional Risk = Time to Adjust

With only 2 days until expiration, the FlyCal trade has an open profit of $465 and showing a juicy Theta of $397.41. This is exactly what we want—a trade that generates solid income as time passes.

However, there's a major concern: Delta = -33.60 and Gamma = -131.836. That indicates we're taking on significant directional risk. A sharp move in the stock—up or down—could cause us to lose that hard-earned Theta.

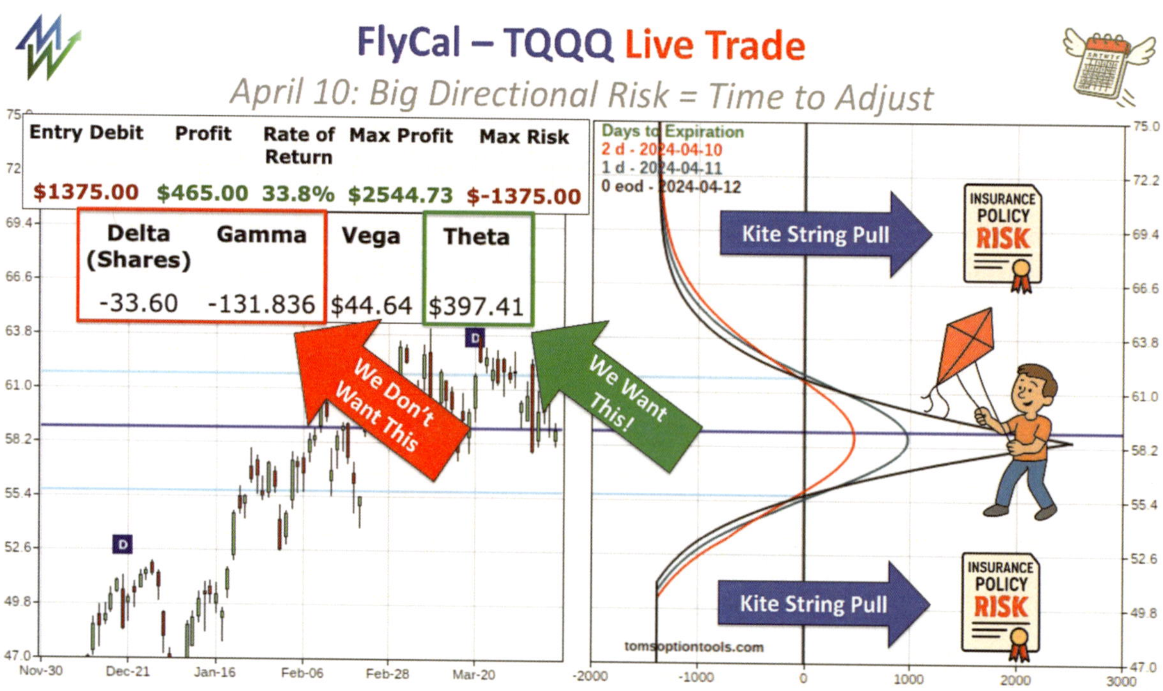

This is the time to act like a seasoned trader. You don't sit on a kite in a windstorm. You pull the kite string and steady the flight. In our FlyCal language, that means it's time for the "Insurance Policy" adjustment.

By adding small protective wings (insurance units) to both sides of the calendar, we're giving ourselves balance. We lock in the Theta and significantly reduce the Delta exposure, while still leaving room for more gains. It's the ideal way to finish a trade strong—with control, confidence, and cash.

Adjustment 3: TQQQ "Kite String Pull" w/ "Insurance Policy" Adjustment

By April 10, only two days before the expiration date, we completed our final strategic step in FlyCal: The "Kite String Pull" utilizing the "Insurance Policy" adjustment. The result? We transformed the trade into a Seagull—an elegant and powerful setup with defined wings and low risk.

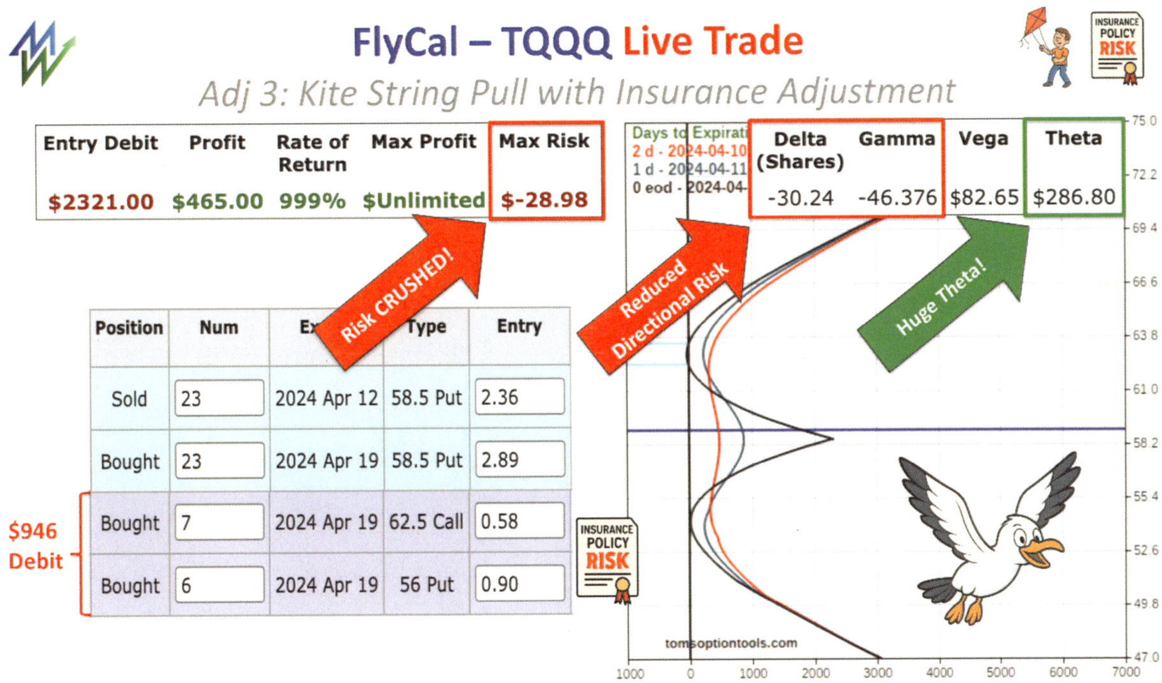

What We Did

- Maintained the central $58.5 Put Calendar.
- Added insurance wings:
  - Bought 7 Apr 19 $62.5 Calls at $0.58.
  - Bought 6 Apr 19 $56 Puts at $0.90.

These additions created a protective range and allowed us to crush risk while maintaining upside and downside potential.

Why It Matters

- **Max risk** dropped from $1,375 to just $28.98—risk crushed.
- **Max profit** is now technically unlimited, thanks to the outer wings.
- **Delta** improved to -30.24, reducing directional exposure.
- **Gamma** softened, helping the trade stay stable as time runs out.
- **Vega** remains powerful at $82.65—ready to benefit from any late IV surge.
- **Theta** continues to shine: $286.80 in daily time decay gives us a beautiful endgame.

Final Form: The Seagull

As we explained earlier, this structure is known as a Seagull—featuring a centered calendar base with wings added above and below. It's perfect for reducing risk late in the trade while maximizing the chance to collect time premium. We've secured the board, eliminated our opponent's checkmate threats, and now we're just gathering pieces one by one until the clock runs out.

This is how pros finish strong—with low risk, high control, and all the edge.

FlyCal Entry Rules

Before deploying a FlyCal, review these six entry criteria to stack the odds in your favor:

1. **Range-Bound Stock**

   Look for stocks trading within a clearly defined horizontal range. This strategy works best when the stock isn't trending aggressively in one direction.

2. **Breakevens at or Beyond Support & Resistance**

   Make sure your profit range extends beyond key support and resistance levels. That provides your FlyCal a "runway" to breathe without needing a miracle.

3. **7–21 Days to Expiration**

   The ideal timeframe. This period offers the perfect balance of Theta decay acceleration without the erratic behavior of options expiring too quickly.

4. **100% Probability Between Expiration Breakevens**

   When the probability of expiring inside your breakevens is 100%—or close—you're holding a strategy built to win.

5. Green Curve ROI ≥ 15%

This is your advantage. You aim to see at least a 15% potential return on investment if the stock falls within your green profit zone.

FlyCal Entry Rules

- **Range-Bound** Stock
- **Breakevens** at or **Beyond Support & Resistance**
- **7-21 Days** to Expiration
- **Probability** Between Expiration Breakevens = **100%**
- Green Curve **ROI >= 15%**

FlyCal Trading and Adjusting Guidelines

1. The game of FlyCals is all about **managing Delta and letting Theta do its thing**. Your job isn't to force profits. It's to shape your trade so that time decay (Theta) becomes your ally while minimizing directional risk.
2. FlyCals are the **"top of the mountain" strategy**. They combine elegance, flexibility, and an expansive adjustment toolkit. If you enjoy being creative and strategic in your trading, you'll love the unlimited adjustment possibilities FlyCals offer.
3. Here are some of the most powerful adjustment techniques you'll use:
   - **Squeeze Play** – Crush and shift butterfly risk when the stock is running.
   - **Stretch Play** – Shift directional risk by widening a butterfly wing.
   - **Cocoon the Fly** – Trap gains and eliminate risk.
   - **Kite String Pull** – Shift directional risk when the stock is running.
   - **Catcher's Mitt** – Reposition your calendar to where the action is.
   - **Insurance Policy** – Slam the brakes on directional risk.
4. To win the game, manage the full process with your 3-part prognosis and the Greeks. Always be aware of your Delta, Vega, and Theta positions.
5. Finally, recognize when to exit. If you've made all your adjustments and the market's not playing along—exit with grace. Sometimes the best choice is to take your gains or protect your capital.

FlyCal Trading and Adjusting Guidelines

1. The game of FlyCals is to **manage Delta** and **allow Theta** to **"Do what Theta Do".**
2. FlyCals are a **"top of the mountain"** option strategy offering **unlimited adjustment possibilities.**
3. Common **adjustment strategies** include:

Squeeze Play

Stretch Play

Cocoon the Fly

Kite String Pull

Catcher's Mit

Insurance Policy

4. **Manage** the entire process with your **3-part prognosis** and the **Greeks.**
5. **Exit** when you **run out of moves.**

FlyCal Chapter Wrap-Up: Master the Mountain

You've just reached the top of the options mountain—welcome to the FlyCal summit.

Throughout this chapter, you learned how the FlyCal combines the strength of the butterfly with the flexibility of the calendar to create a high-probability, highly adjustable strategy. We examined a real FlyCal trade—adjustments included—using live charts and actual moves to show how you can confidently take both offense and defense with confidence.

But here's the thing: What you've seen is only the beginning.

We highlighted just a few of the many adjustments available when trading FlyCals—tools like the "Catcher's Mitt", "Kite String Pull", and "Insurance Policy". There's a whole arsenal of strategic plays still waiting in your toolbox, and the only way to truly master them is to play the game.

FlyCals aren't just trades. They're engaging, dynamic puzzles you get to solve in real time using the adjustments in this guide. Every move is a chess move. Every adjustment is a lever you pull to convert risk into reward, uncertainty into structure.

So, take what you've learned, step into the arena, and start playing the FlyCal game. Because the top of the mountain isn't just for looking. It's for conquering.

Let Theta take the lead. Let Vega align with your forecast. And let you be the master of the most adaptable trade on the board.

See you at the summit.

CHAPTER 32

BOOK SUMMARY

CHAPTER 32
The Options Adjustment Playbook—Book Summary

The Game Is Not the Trade. It's the Adjustment

This playbook teaches a fundamental truth most traders miss:

Trading is not about picking the right trade.
It's about managing the trade after you enter it.

An *adjustment* is any strategic change made to an open position to:

- reduce or eliminate risk
- lock in profits
- improve probability
- stay in the trade longer

The trader who learns to adjust gains control. The trader who doesn't is left hoping.

Take It Further—Join the Club

If you want to accelerate your growth, there's no better way than to **surround yourself with others who are playing the game at a high level.**

Consider joining the **MWTC Trade Club**—a live trading environment where beginners and advanced traders alike are **using these adjustments in real-time**, with guidance from **Mike, Joe, and Gerardo,** three master traders committed to helping you succeed.

Inside the club, you'll find:

- Daily live sessions
- Real trades and real-time coaching
- A thriving community of supportive, serious traders
- Immediate access to new ideas, adjustments, and breakthroughs

We built it to be the **most empowering trading space on the planet**—and it's changing lives.

Learn more and apply at www.mwtradecoach.com.

Play 3 Hands With Mike & Joe

You've read the playbook. Now play it with us.

Mike & Joe invite you to play three live adjustment hands—three real positions taught in our Adjustment Club Online Course, walked through move by move. The pieces in this playbook, in motion.

Scan the QR code below to step onto the board.

Final Word

This book was designed to leave you **touched, moved, and inspired**—not just to trade better, but to trade with joy, clarity, and confidence. I am hopeful that this intention has been fulfilled for you.

Welcome to the game.

Let's play.

GLOSSARY

GLOSSARY

Core Trading Terms & Definitions (A–Z)

Adjustment

A strategic adjustment made to an existing options trade, typically used to **reduce risk**, **lock in profit**, or **extend opportunity**. It's not the start or end of a trade. It's the **mid-game move**, much like a tactical shift in a chess match.

Broken Wing Butterfly (BWB) - Definition

An advanced options strategy that enhances a traditional butterfly spread by **shifting one of the wings** to create an **asymmetrical risk/reward profile** constructed by:

- **Buying 1 lower strike option**
- **Selling 2 middle strike options**
- **Buying 1 higher strike option**—but **at a different distance** than the lower wing

Butterfly

A multi-leg, market-neutral options strategy created by combining a bull spread and a bear spread, typically with **three strikes and equal spacing** (e.g., long 1 lower strike, short 2 middle strikes, long 1 higher strike). Designed to profit in **high volatility environments and price pinning** near the center strike.

Calendar Spread

An options strategy that involves **selling a near-term option** and **buying a longer-term option** at the **same strike price**. Profits come from time decay in the short leg outpacing time decay in the long leg. Can be neutral or directional depending on placement.

Condor

A variation of the butterfly that uses **four strikes**, creating a **wide profit range** with limited risk. Constructed with either all calls, all puts or a combination of both (iron), it is designed to profit in **rangebound markets** and shines in **high implied volatility environments**.

Credit Spread

An options strategy in which the **premium received** from selling one option is greater than the cost of buying another. Common types include bear call spreads and bull put spreads. These strategies **benefit from time decay and a lack of price movement toward the short strike**.

Diagonal Calendar Spread

A hybrid options strategy that combines elements of both **calendar spreads** and **vertical spreads**. It involves:

- **Buying a longer-dated option** (call or put) at one strike
- **Selling a shorter-dated option** at a **different strike** (typically further out of the money)

Greeks

A set of key risk measures that describe how an option or portfolio reacts to changes in market conditions. Traders use them to **adjust, manage, and forecast performance**. Here are the primary Greeks:

- **Delta** – Measures the **sensitivity to price movement**. A Delta of 0.50 means the option gains $0.50 for every $1 the stock moves up. Positive Delta benefits from rising prices; negative Delta benefits from falling prices.

- **Gamma** – Measures the **rate of change of Delta**. High Gamma means Delta is changing quickly. Most relevant near the money and close to expiration.

- **Theta** – Measures the **impact of time decay**. A Theta of –0.10 means the option loses $0.10 per day. Short options gain from Theta; long options lose from it.

- **Vega** – Measures sensitivity to **changes in implied volatility (IV)**. A Vega of 0.20 means the option gains $0.20 for every 1% increase in IV. Long Vega benefits from rising IV; short Vega benefits from falling IV.
- **Rho** – Measures sensitivity to **interest rate changes**. A Rho of 0.05 means the option increases $0.05 for every 1% rise in interest rates. Typically, more relevant for long-dated options.

Implied Volatility (IV)

The market's estimate of **future volatility**, reflected in the price of options. Higher IV means more expensive options; lower IV means cheaper options. IV tends to rise during uncertainty and fall in calm or rising markets.

IV Skew

Describes how **implied volatility varies across strikes or expirations**. For example, IV of a short-term option may be higher than the IV of a longer-term option. An advantage for a calendar spread upon initiation, however should IV rush more in the short option than the long option (e.g. 14-days pre-earnings), IV crush will hurt your calendar.

Long Call

An options position that gives the right to **buy** a stock at a fixed price before expiration. Used when bullish on the stock. Offers **unlimited upside with limited downside** (the premium paid).

Long Put

An options position that gives the right to **sell** a stock at a fixed price before expiration. Used when bearish on the stock. Offers **high upside in a falling market**, with limited risk.

Ratio Calendar Spread

A calendar spread providing a directional bias where you:

- **Buy multiple longer-dated option** (call or put)

- **Sell fewer shorter-dated options** of the same type at the same strike

Risk Graph

A visual representation of how a trade performs across various prices and dates. Helps you compare **unadjusted vs adjusted positions**, evaluate max risk/reward, and visualize how the Greeks behave over time.

Straddle

A neutral, high-volatility strategy involving the **purchase of a call and a put at the same strike and expiration**. Profits from **large moves in either direction** and is highly sensitive to implied volatility changes.

Adjustment Arsenal (A–Z)

1. **Collar**

   Combine a stock position with a long put (for protection) and a short call (for income) to create a risk-defined outcome with capped profit and limited downside.

2. **Collect the Rent**

   Sell calls or puts against existing long positions to generate extra income from stagnant or slowly moving trades.

3. **Cocoon**

   Lock in a guaranteed profit on a profitable butterfly by squeezing both wings inward, often transforming a winning position into a no-risk outcome.

4. **DNA (Delta Neutral Adjustment)**

   Adjust your position to flatten Delta, removing directional exposure when you expect rangebound price action.

5. **Double-Wide**

   Stack multiple calendars at different strikes to create a broader range of profitability and increase your odds of success.

6. **Flock O' Flies**

   Layer multiple low risk butterflies over strike and time to create a high-probability zone of profit.

7. **FlyCal**

   Combine a butterfly and a calendar at different short strikes to provide a wide profit range with layered Vega and Theta advantages.

8. **House Money**

   Sell part of a position after a double or major gain to remove all risk or lock in guaranteed profit.

9. **Insurance Policy**

   Add protective options (like long puts or calls) to limit downside (or upside) risk during uncertain market moves.

10. **Kick the Can Down the Road**

    Roll a credit spread out in time and/or strikes to "sell more time to be right" when your prognosis is still valid.

11. **Kite String Pull**

    Subtly shift a calendar's bias by adjusting short strikes or turning it into a ratio calendar or a diagonalized calendar to guide the position directionally.

12. **Pony Express**

    Reduce risk on a winning long option trade by moving the option further OTM and leave the rest to run for potential additional gains—like sending the profits ahead while keeping the journey going.

13. **Pull a Wing Off**

    Close one side of a butterfly, condor or FlyCal when it's no longer helping, especially when price has moved toward one end.

14. **Seagull**

    A modified calendar structure that neutralizes directional risk and maintains positive Theta. They are typically constructed with ratio or diagonal calendars coupled with insurance (long calls or long puts).

15. **Spread the Spread**

    Add another spread to an existing spread to reduce directional exposure, reduce risk and directional impact (Delta) as price moves.

16. **Stretch Play**

    Widen a wing of a butterfly or condor to reduce exposure on one side while pulling risk out of the weaker side.

17. Squeeze Play

Narrow the width of a butterfly or condor to reduce capital risk or lock in a portion of the profit.

www.ingramcontent.com/pod-product-compliance
Lightning Source LLC
LaVergne TN
LVRC082252220926
848486LV00046B/395